FOREIGN DIRECT INVESTMENT IN TRANSITIONAL ECONOMIES

Foreign Direct Investment in Transitional Economies

A Case Study of China and Poland

Michael Du Pont

First published in Great Britain 2000 by
MACMILLAN PRESS LTD
Houndmills, Basingstoke, Hampshire RG21 6XS and London
Companies and representatives throughout the world

A catalogue record for this book is available from the British
Library.

ISBN 0–333–91790–1

First published in the United States of America 2000 by
ST. MARTIN'S PRESS, LLC.,

Scholarly and Reference Division,
175 Fifth Avenue, New York, N.Y. 10010

ISBN 0–312–23384–1

Library of Congress Cataloging-in-Publication Data

Du Pont, Michael, 1995-
    Foreign direct investment in transitional economies : a case study of
China and Poland / Michael Du Pont.
        p. cm
    Includes bibliograhical references and index.
    ISBN 0–312–23384–1 (cloth)
    1. Investments, Foreign–China–Case studies. 2. Investments,
Foreign–Poland–Case studies.

HG5782.D8 2000
332.67'3'0951–DC21   00-025502

This book is printed on paper suitable for recycling and made from fully
managed and sustained forest sources.

10   9   8   7   6   5   4   3   2   1
09   08   07   06   05   04   03   02   01   00

Printed in Great Britain

To my parents Sophie and Steven, my niece Elizabeth, and in memory of dear aunt Aniela

Contents

List of Tables and Figures

Tables

Figures

Preface

Profound changes are taking place in the nature of international business, both in terms of the drivers of trans-border transactions and the strategic orientation of the firms that engage in these transactions. While the dynamic forces of globalisation and regionalisation, acting in a dialectical manner, form the umbrella under which international business activities take place, it has been the impact of technological change that has enabled firms to act both globally and locally. Companies are searching for partners all over the globe, even to the point of collaborating with current or former competitors. New MNCs from newly-industrialised countries (NIEs) have recently emerged with new forms of investment and motivation, demonstrating that FDI can no longer be analysed in the classical manner as a flow of extra capital into a country where all else is held constant, with the static effects evaluated according to the tenets of orthodox marginal productivity analysis. Nor is it any longer a simple hierarchical process from capital-rich to capital-poor countries. There is growing concern that traditional theories of investment have largely been ineffective in explaining recent trends of flows of FDI, especially in the context of recent changes in the transitional once-socialist economies. There has especially been a need to identify the causes of recent changes in inflow of FDI to post-communist countries.

This book presents a detailed investigation into the recent changes in the patterns and determinants in inflows of FDI to transitional economies in the light of FDI experiences in the economies of China and Poland. China and Poland provide ideal subjects for a case study since both attracted quite sizeable amounts of FDI, once their reform programmes had been introduced, despite both countries adopting quite different approaches on the road of transition to a market economy. It is found that patterns and determinants of FDI in a given country depend crucially on the degree of industrial advancement and the stage of entrepreneurial development of the country, changes in the process of internalisation of production, geography of the country and the nature and timing of policy shifts. There is a significant diversification of FDI in terms of the total number of source countries. In both countries there are differences between developed- and developing-country firms in terms of the size, strategy and form of their investments. The most common form of investment in both countries initially was joint ventures with increasing share-holding by foreign partners, but recently the wholly foreign-owned enterprises are becoming the main driving force of investment. Foreign firms indicate a much higher intensity for exports than local firms. As for the economic effects, FDI in China has so far been heavily concentrated in product lines characterised by high import intensity, limited backward linkages and limited diffusion of technology. In Poland, FDI has been concentrated in mixed product lines characterised by some import intensity and by export orientation, stronger backward linkages and increasing diffusion of technology. These characteristics need not, however, be treated as intrinsic features of FDI in these countries. Rather, they are mostly a reflection of the early stage of FDI participation and the nature of the prevailing investment climate. Moreover, despite the shallowness of new product lines, their development impact in terms of employment generation and knowledge spillover effects appears to be considerable.

MICHAEL DU PONT

Abbreviations and Acronyms

BOC   Bank of China
CCP   Chinese Communist Party
CEE   Central and Eastern Europe
CEFTA   Central European Free Trade Association
CEPR   Centre for Economic Policy Research
CMEA   Council for Mutual Economic Assistance
CPC   Communist Party Committee
CPPCC   Chinese People's Party's Central Committee
DC   developed countries
EBRD   European Bank for Reconstruction and Development
EEA   European Economic Area
EFTA   European Free Trade Association
EU   European Union
EPZ   Export Processing Zone
FDI   foreign direct investment
FSS   Former Soviet States
FTC   foreign trade corporation
GDP   gross domestic product
GSP   generalised system of preferences
ILO   International Labour Organisation
JV   joint venture
IMF   International Monetary Fund
LDC   less-developed countries
MFERT   Ministry of Foreign Economic Relations and Trade
MFN   most favoured nation
MNC   multinational corporations
NIEs   newly-industrialised economies
OECD   Organisation for Economic Cooperation and Development
PAIZ   Polish Agency for Foreign Investment
PRC   People's Republic of China
PBOC   People's Bank of China
PBC   People's Bank of China: the central bank of China
RCA   revealed comparative advantage
RMB   Renminbi (Chinese currency)
SAEC   State Administration of Exchange Control
SAFE   State Administration of Foreign Exchange

SEZ   Special Economic Zones
TVE   township and village enterprise
WFOS   wholly foreign-owned subsidiaries
WTO   World Trade Organisation
UN   United Nations

1 Introduction

Since the late 1970s, foreign direct investment (FDI) in China and in Central and Eastern Europe has attracted considerable attention from both the business and academic worlds. However, very little systematic research has so far been carried out to examine the trends and determinants of FDI in these transitional economies. Most literature published on FDI trends in Eastern Europe and China is of a rather general nature. There is growing concern that the traditional theories of investment have largely been ineffective in explaining recent trends in the flow of FDI, especially with regard to recent changes in these and other transitional economies. No longer can FDI be analysed in the classical manner as a flow of extra capital into a country within which all else is held constant, with the static effects evaluated according to the tenets of orthodox marginal productivity analysis (MacDougall, 1960: 35).

Empirical identification of recent changes in the inflows of FDI to post-communist countries and their changing trends is needed in order to determine what factors influence the inflow of foreign capital into these countries. The present study attempts an investigation into the trends, patterns and determinants of FDI in the light of recent changes in the investment climate of China and Poland. It first develops a framework for analysing the patterns and trends of FDI through a survey of existing literature, and then uses this framework to examine the recent experiences of China and Poland in testing these new forms of FDI, in order to seek out the lessons to be learnt in policy terms from each of these countries. In particular, the aims of the study are four-fold:

1. To examine key aspects of the changes in FDI trends and determinants through a close investigation into the distribution of FDI.
2. To delineate links between these determinants and each country's incentives for investment, as well as each country's progress with economic reform.
3. To identify emerging trends of FDI and their implications for future economic changes.

4.   To discuss policy issues arising from the experience of FDI.

During the past two decades, stimulated by pioneering work by Hymer (1960) and Vernon (1966), and more recently by Dunning (1980), a considerable amount of empirical investigation has been undertaken in this field. The overwhelming majority of these studies has been conducted within Dunning's three-dimensional paradigm framework: ownership advantages, location advantages and internalisation advantages (OLI).

There are several major limitations that should be taken into consideration when using the OLI paradigm as a policy guide. In general, economic theory suggests that MNCs have clear objectives when investing abroad. It lists a considerable number of factors which may influence the decision, but it actually explains only a few of them. It falls short of encompassing all the factors involved. The OLI paradigm, so far the most widely accepted and most comprehensive approach which incorporates several factors, only identifies the conditions which are sufficient or which fail to be sufficient for FDI to be profitable, as well as the conditions under which FDI is superior to other modes of servicing foreign markets. It does not directly refer to the motives for investing abroad. MNCs are global players operating affiliates all over the world. Each one can be considered as a spider spinning a worldwide web. The literature suggests that the value and size of this web may be affected positively by a number of geographically dispersed locations that can be used and served. The rationale for hypothesising such a positive relation is derived from the fact that global players can benefit from lower variable costs due to economies of scale and economies of scope realised in networks. Against this background we can assume that the FDI by MNCs is motivated by a whole host of factors which are closely connected.

The traditional literature claims that only the combined attractiveness of each of the ownership, location and internalisation advantages (OLI paradigm) would provide the conditions required for FDI to occur. More recently it has been demonstrated that FDI may also be undertaken even if the potential host country's locational advantages are large enough to compensate for only small or even negligible firm-specific advantages (Stehn, 1992). This argument has important implications for economic policy towards FDI, as within the OLI paradigm locational attractiveness is the variable which is most perceptible to economic policy. The OLI paradigm postulates only the preconditions to be fulfilled (Agarwal, 1985). These aspects should not be confused. A firm may want to penetrate a foreign market, thus providing the motive for FDI, but it faces a choice. It can serve this market either from its domestic production base or from a foreign base closely located to the market which it wants to penetrate. The OLI paradigm only allows the most effective strategy to be decided once the motivation has been given. On the other hand, Casson (1987: 32–3) has argued that Dunning's ownership (O) advantage is really an internalisation benefit and that ownership advantages are not necessar for FDI. In so doing, he effectively rebutted the validity of the Hymer postulate that FDI is undertaken only by firms that possess some intangible asset in order to exploit the firm-specific ownership advantage in a foreign country. The Hymer postulate is still relevant for some young firms with ownership advantages that allow them to compete in niche markets, but for the well-established MNCs that now dominate international production in well-defined industries and product lines, it is no longer relevant. Furthermore, in view of the differences between countries, motives differ considerably between different markets in which foreign investors are engaged (Agarwal, Gubitz, Nunnenkamp, 1991), thus limiting the validity of the OLI paradigm as the comprehensive approach for foreign firms' investment analyses. These considerations highlight the necessity for undertaking case studies of individual countries in order to build a sound and meaningful empirical foundation for policy discussions on this important issue.

China and Poland provide interesting subjects for a comparative case study of patterns and determinants of FDI in transitional economies on several counts. Both countries offer a particularly illuminating case study for analysing the new FDI structures, given the richness and breadth of the reform experiences. In the framework of the new economic geography, China and Poland also offer ideal sites for new clusters of industrial activity, and consequently for the inflow of FDI: China, as the biggest market in the world with a population of over 1 billion, and an emerging 'Panda' in the fast growing East Asian region, has the potential to shake up existing patterns of investment and trade more than any other recent regional development. Some FDI flows have already shifted from ASEAN countries to China. In a setting of high factor mobility, these shifts may be amplified by investors rushing to join new centres of economic activity (Petri, 1994). Poland, with its strategic location in central Europe acting as a bridge between West and East as well as the gateway to Russia and former Soviet Republics, is also well poised to make an impact. Noteworthy 'too' is the fact that these two countries have chosen completely different approaches in the transition to market economies. China has followed the gradualism approach, while Poland has embraced the 'Big Bang' approach.

Both countries have made concerted efforts to join the world economy in order to gain access to the international flow of trade, capital and technology which is critical to their economic transformation. However, the issues relating to the promotion and monitoring of FDI exemplify the differences between the two countries. These differences and similarities create a lot of argument and policy debate about the structure of FDI in transitional economies. This feature is particularly important because in recent discussions of the role and trends of FDI in transitional countries, the motives of MNCs have become the most controversial issue dealt with (Gatling, 1993; Rojec and Svetlicic, 1994; Jermakowicz, Toft and Bochniarz, 1994; Dunning, 1995a).

The Chinese and Polish transition processes provide excellent examples of the new economic structures implied in the *a priori* theorising on the patterns and determinants of FDI in the context of recent changes in the inflow of FDI. Of course no two countries are alike, and the economic and political context of each policy reform differs. These contrasts make this study even more interesting. The insights gained from an in-depth case study of each country is useful to policy-makers in other transitional countries in identifying critical issues that may come up in the process of transition to a market economy. The relevance of the study, however, extends well beyond its potential use as a policy document. It can be regarded as a model for other countries in transition, especially those which can use the Chinese and Polish findings as a policy-guiding tool in their economic transformation. Therefore, insights gained from this case study would be of value in assessing the relevance and usefulness of these transition models. As Pomfret (1991) has noted, China provides the 'most extensive experience of investing in a communist country'. Furthermore, China's recent experience with FDI may serve as a barometer of likely future FDI patterns and changes in inflows to transitional economies. In spite of the emphasis placed on the issue, no in-depth empirical investigation has so far been undertaken to identify its various dimensions. All of these issues are analysed in the following chapters, together with their policy implications.

METHODOLOGY

The research of the study comprised two key elements: (a) a study of policy reforms in China and Poland since 1979 and 1989, respectively, through a study of policy documents, an academic literature review, World Bank, OECD and IMF reports and other government publications; and (b) a detailed survey of FDI-based firms operating in China and Poland. The firm-level study involved a questionnaire-based interview of management personal from FDI-based firms. A questionnaire was prepared based on research done prior to field work. The questionnaire was translated into Chinese and Polish and the translation was subsequently adjusted to correct unclear statements. The data collected from interviews were supplemented by analysis of firms' annual reports and official governments investment records.

A comprehensive list of foreign firms and their affiliates is available from investment agencies and the Ministry of Foreign Economic Relation and Trade of China (MFERTC), and the Ministry of Foreign Economic Relations of Poland. The list can be easily updated using official records of the Board of Foreign Investment which maintains the records on foreign investment approval (with a clear distinction between approved and implemented projects) with details on key variables such as capital starter, home country, investment size, employment and export value. In analysing the patterns and determinants of FDI, the study covers the period from 1978 to 1996 in China, and from 1986 to 1996 in Poland. The differing starting dates signal the years in which each country embraced the economic reform process and opened their economies to competition with foreign firms

STRUCTURE

The study is organised in nine chapters: Chapter 2 reviews the existing literature on FDI to provide a perspective for the study and methodology adopted. Chapter 3 provides a descriptive picture of the economy of each country during the transition process, with special reference to the efficiency and effectiveness of macroeconomic policies in achieving the goals of utilising FDI in general and promoting manufactured exports in particular. Chapter 4 focuses more particularly on the investment and trade policies pursued by the two countries throughout their differing transitional phases of development towards market-oriented economies. Ensuing incentives and disincentives for FDI, if any, and the regulations of FDI are also discussed, with an emphasis on the national policy of each country.

Chapter 5 analyses general trends and determinants of FDI in each country in order to establish the background required for a comparison by survey. The changing patterns of FDI structures are closely studied with special reference to the source countries of investment and their sectoral distribution. Determinants of FDI inflow into each country are analysed, with particular attention given to import-substitution measures associated with other major factors affecting FDI inflows.

Chapter 6 describes the survey methodology which has been used in the study. Characteristics of the sample are also discussed and the problems with it are analysed. Chapter 7 investigates the trends and determinants of FDI-based firms in the survey data. Locational factors are analysed for each country and comparisons with general trends are discussed. Particular attention is given to any changing patterns and motives affecting FDI inflows to each country.

Chapter 8 examines the performance of foreign investment projects in each country with particular reference to technology, employment and export creation. A comparison between the two countries is also presented. Chapter 9 presents the major conclusions of the study followed by a brief discussion of the policy implications of the findings. Limitations of the study are also addressed and their implications discussed. Throughout the study the structure of each country analysis follows the same pattern to make each case more comparable. In most cases the closest comparative approach is adopted.

2 Trends and Patterns of FDI: Theory and Evidence

INTRODUCTION

The past two decades have witnessed the emergence of a sizeable body of literature dealing with various dimensions of the trends and determinants of FDI flow. The purpose of this chapter is to present the *a priori* view of the issue and to review the related empirical work in order to place the present study in perspective. It is pertinent to mention at the outset that the coverage of the chapter has been deliberately selective, the major criterion being the relevance of the material to the purpose and scope of the present study as outlined in the Introduction. Informal FDI has been omitted due to a lack of data.

In a world of varied market imperfections and constant changes in government policies, advice based on traditional models of pure competition and conventional theories of FDI is not persuasive (Helleiner, 1976, 1978 and 1988). There is, therefore, a need for more analysis of emerging new investment trends in East Asia and other developing countries.

Theories of FDI can be evaluated in terms of several different criteria. One is whether each theory is logically consistent. A second is how well each theory predicts out-of-sample observations and especially how well each theory provides an explanation for the sharp changes in the country patterns of FDI. Most theories of FDI are under-determined and deal only partly with observed trends, which limits the possibility of explaining new trends and limits the tested validity of each hypothesis.

Profound changes are taking place in the nature of international business, both in terms of the drivers of trans-border transactions and the strategic orientation of the firms that engage in these transactions. A number of factors account for the changes taking place in the overall environment for international business, and forces of globalisation and regionalisation have been two of the paramount factors responsible for the transformation taking place in the way firms behave with respect to their foreign operations (Yongwoong and Simon, 1994).

7

While the dynamic forces of globalisation and regionalisation, acting in a dialectical manner, form the umbrella under which international business activities take place, it has been the impact of technological change that has been the enabling factor that has allowed firms to act both 'globally and locally' (Petri, 1994; Yongwoong and Simon, 1994). Technological changes have not simply altered the ways firms conduct their overseas business activities, but they have made possible the creation of a new infrastructure for carrying out and overseeing the diverse set of operations that take place around the globe. For example, the rapid technological advance in electronics seems certain to continue and will shorten even further the life of any new electronic product. Therefore production on a smaller scale will be encouraged, favouring assembly technologies that do not require large fixed investments likely to be found abroad (Flamm and Grunwald, 1985); although still seemingly under the aegis of an individual company, albeit one that is changing its shape, size and organisational design (Yongwoong and Simon, 1994).

THE TRADITIONAL VIEW

There are two major schools of thought concerning FDI. The conventional school, pioneered by Hymer (1960) and Caves (1974), states that FDI is undertaken only by firms that possess some intangible asset. These firms invest in a foreign country in order to exploit the firm-specific ownership advantage embodied in the intangible asset. FDI is, therefore, seen as an aggressive action to extract economic rent from a foreign market (Tain-Jy Chen, Yin-Hwa Ku and Meng-Chun Liu, 1994).

The other school, represented by Vernon and Kojima, portrays FDI as a defensive action undertaken by firms to protect their export market which is either threatened by competitors in the local market (Vernon, 1966) or damaged by unfavourable developments in macroeconomic conditions at home (Kojima, 1973), such as wage increases and/or currency appreciation. 'Defensive' FDI is often made in low-wage countries where cheap labour enables investors to reduce their production costs in order to restore international competitiveness. 'Aggressive' FDI may be made in any countries where local production is seen as the best way to enter the market. If both types of FDI exist in the real world, it is empirically difficult to distinguish one from the other because actual FDI may be undertaken for a mixture of reasons including market exploitation and labour-seeking motives. For example, while Kojima (1973) claims Japanese FDI to be of the 'defensive' type, his example of Japanese FDI in East Asia is criticised for being indistinguishable from the 'aggressive' US investment in Canada or Europe (Mason, 1980). In this regard, China and Poland provide perfect cases for studying the different modes of investment by sector or product.

In these schools of thought there have been several theories developed which we will elaborate separately. In order to present a complete picture of advanced FDI theories in the existing literature, a few differing postulations by other writers will also be reviewed. In order to put the traditional theories into a practical perspective, their application and limitations will also be reviewed.

THEORY

The mainstream history of FDI analysis is now universally regarded as the handiwork of the late Stephen Hymer. Hymer both demolishes the conventional position and lays the basis for a more fruitful approach. As one reads his contentions, it becomes clear that the problem is no longer to explain the movement of funds from one country to another, but rather to understand a qualitatively new form of industrial organisation which coordinates productive activities in many different parts of the globe.

Until his PhD dissertation, it was customary to treat direct, equity investment abroad on a par with 'capital flows' in general: the distinction between portfolio and equity investment, for example, was not important to this way of analytical thinking. Admittedly, this deficiency was one that afflicted orthodox economic thinking of the day: thus, international trade theory focused on interest rate differentials being explanatory of 'capital flows'. Hymer's breakthrough, coming interestingly from the recognition of stylised facts such as the presence of cross-investment and the concentration of foreign equity investment in a few oligopolistic industries which did not rest happily with the interest-rate-differentials theory, was focused on the notion that primary insights into FDI could come only from recognising the oligopolistic industrial structure of the firms making such investments. Moreover, while Hymer's basic notion was that FDI had to be seen in the context of the search for control by oligopolistic enterprises, he indicated the importance of the so-called 'advantages' theory of direct, horizontal investments by multinationals. Thus, Hymer distinctly discussed how a firm would go abroad rather than license or sell its technology, if the special advantages that it possessed (and whose value outweighed the special advantages that local firms would enjoy in their own markets) required its own control. Thus, Hymer was the first to sharply pose the alternatives of licensing technology and of direct investment, and to argue the different reasons why special advantages may not be cashed for the same returns through licensing arrangements and may thus require direct investment abroad, and, interestingly, he also described these as 'horizontal' investments. Hymer's thesis was not only regarded as the first modern industrial-organisational theory of FDI, but also provided the inspiration for other writers like Vernon, Caves and Kindleberger to take this issue much further in the development of FDI theories pertaining to industrial organisation, which in the following sections will be briefly analysed.

Theories of Industrial Organisation

Vernon and Kindleberger argue that for firms to own and control foreign value-adding facilities, they must possess some kind of inventory, cost, financial or marketing advantages, (specific to their ownership), sufficient to outweigh the disadvantages they face in competing with indigenous firms in the country of production (Hymer, 1966). These advantages, which they assume to be exclusive to the firm owning them (hence the expression 'ownership advantages'), imply the existence of some kind of structural market failure.

Another industrial organisation approach to the theory of FDI is based on models of 'oligopolistic competition' and stresses that the advantages that enable a firm to attain a large size in its domestic market facilitate the expansion of its foreign subsidiaries (Caves, 1974). This approach emphasises that once a firm has achieved a superior growth rate, it has a compulsion or incentive to maintain the rapid growth of sales and profits. For an extended period, the growth rate for one or several firms within an industry is higher than that for the industry as a whole – the implication being that some firms with below-average growth rates will leave the industry. As some firms exit, the surviving firms realise a growth rate higher than that of the industry because they take over part or all of the market share of the firms that leave. Eventually the industry becomes oligopolistic, with four to eight firms remaining (Aliber, 1993). At this stage each firm is likely to find it difficult to maintain its growth rate, so it will look to enter foreign markets with new products. FDI occurs because the firm prefers to cross the political boundaries with its traditional product lines. No specific advantage is identified with the source-country firm that would enable it to compensate for the cost of economic distance.

Product Life-Cycle Theory

Vernon and his colleagues at Harvard were the first to acknowledge the relevance of some of the newer trade theories put forward in the 1950s and 1960s to help explain this phenomenon. In a classic article published in 1966, Vernon used a microeconomic concept, 'the product cycle', to help explain a macroeconomic phenomenon, that is the foreign activities of US MNCs in the postwar period.

The product-cycle theory was a response to the observation that US firms were among the first to develop new labour-saving techniques in response to the high cost of skilled labour and a large domestic market (Vernon, 1966). In the early stages of development of a product, firms placed factories close to markets because of the need for frequent feedback from market to plant. Production runs were short because of numerous changes in the future of the model, which meant the demand for skilled labour was large relative to the demand for unskilled labour. To reduce costs, firms revamped the design of their products so that model changes would be less frequent and production runs longer; low-cost unskilled labour could then be substituted for high-cost skilled labour. As the product became increasingly standardised, the need for feedback from market to plant became less frequent, so the distance between the plant and the market could be increased. Unit costs could be reduced further if production was shifted to a foreign country where the wages for unskilled labour was low relative to the wage rate for skilled labour in the source country. The 'implicit assumption' of the product-cycle theory of FDI is that the firms which developed the products in their domestic markets would acquire the manufacturing plants in the countries identified with abundant unskilled labour, rather then sell or license their technology to host-country competitors.

Internalisation Theory

The basic hypothesis of this theory is that multinational hierarchies represent an alternative mechanism for arranging value-added activities across national boundaries to that of the market, and that firms are likely to engage in FDI whenever they perceive that the nett benefits of other joint ownership of domestic and foreign activities, and the transactions arising from them, are likely to exceed those offered by external trading relationships. The core prediction of the internalisation theory is that, given a particular distribution of factor endowments, MNC activity will be positively related to the costs of organising cross-border markets in intermediate products.

The internalisation theory, created by Buckley (1987) and developed by Rugman (1979, 1980), is primarily concerned with identifying the situations in which the markets for intermediate products are likely to be internalised, and hence those in which firms own and control value-adding activities outside their natural boundaries. It seeks to explain the international horizontal and vertical integration of value-added activities in terms of the relative costs and benefits of this form of organisation relative to market transactions.

Macroeconomic Theory of FDI

This theory is essentially an extension of the neoclassical theory of factor endowments to explain trade in intermediate products, notably technology and management skills. A major part of this thesis, set out in Kojima (1973, 1978, 1982, 1990) and in Kojima and Ozawa (1984), shows that whereas Japanese FDI is primarily trade-oriented and responds to the dictates of the principle of comparative advantage, US FDI is mainly conducted within an oligopolistic market structure, is anti-trade-oriented and operates to the long-term disadvantage of both the source and the host countries. Kojima essentially believes that FDI should act as an efficient conduit for trading intermediate products, but that the timing and direction of such investment should be determined by market forces rather than by hierarchical control. His prescription is that outbound FDI should be undertaken by firms that produce intermediate products that require resources and capabilities in which the home country has a comparative advantage, but which generate value-added activities that require resources and capabilities in which that country is comparatively disadvantaged.

By contrast, inbound FDI should import intermediate products that require resources and capabilities in which the host country is disadvantaged, but the use of which require resources and capabilities in which it has a comparative advantage. To the extent that Kojima uses trade models to explain patterns of FDI, he follows in the Vernon tradition. He regards MNCs as creators or sustainers of market imperfections whose impact on resource allocation must be less beneficial than that predicted by perfect competition.

The Eclectic Theory of International Production

The OLI paradigm developed by Dunning (1977) seeks to offer a general framework for determining the pattern and extent of both foreign-owned production undertaken by a country's own enterprises and also that of domestic production owned by foreign enterprises. The 'eclectic theory' of FDI combines the ownership advantage from the industrial organisation approach with the location advantage associated with the product cycle. The OLI paradigm starts with the acceptance of much of the traditional trade theory in explaining the spatial distribution of some kinds of output (which may be termed Heckscher–Ohlin–Samuelson (H–O–S) output). However, it argues that to explain the ownership of that output and the spatial distribution of other kinds of output which require the use of resources that are not equally accessible to all firms, two kinds of market imperfection must be present.

The first is that of structural market failure which discriminates between firms (or owners of corporate assets) in their ability to gain and sustain control over property rights or to govern multiple and geographically dispersed value-added activities. The second is that of the failure of intermediate product markets to transact goods and services at a lower net cost than those which a hierarchy might have to incur. Such variables as the structure of markets, transaction costs and the managerial strategy of a firm's economic activity need to be considered.

The OLI paradigm of international production postulates that the level and structure of a firm's foreign value-added activities will depend on four conditions. These are:

1. The extent to which the firm possesses sustainable ownership-specific (O) advantage *vis-à-vis* firms of other nationalities in the particular markets it serves or is contemplating serving. These O advantages largely take the form of the privileged possession of intangible assets as well as those which arise as a result of the common governance of cross-border value-added activities. These advantages and the use made of them are assumed to increase the

wealth-creating capacity of a firm, and hence the value of its assets (Itaki, 1991).

2. Assuming condition 1 is satisfied, the extent to which the enterprise perceives it to be in its best interest to add value to its O advantages rather than sell them, or the right of use of them, to foreign firms. These advantages are called market internalization (I) advantages. They may reflect either the greater organisational efficiency of hierarchies, or their ability to exercise monopoly power over the assets under their governance.

3. Assuming conditions 1 and 2 are satisfied, the extent to which the global interests of the enterprise are served by creating, or utilising, its O advantages in a foreign location. The distribution of these resources and capabilities is assumed to be uneven and, hence, depending on their distribution, will confer a locational (L) advantage on the countries possessing them over those who do not.

4. Given the configuration of the ownership, location and internalization (OLI) advantages facing a particular firm, the extent to which a firm believes that foreign production is consistent with its long-term management strategy.

The generalised prediction of the eclectic paradigm is straightforward. At any given moment of time, the more a country's enterprises, relative to those of another, possess O advantages, the greater the incentive they have to internalise rather than externalise their use, and the more they find it in their interest to exploit them from a foreign location, then the more they are likely to engage in outbound production. By the same token, a country is likely to attract investment by foreign MNCs when the reverse conditions apply. It also accepts that such advantages are not static and that a firm's strategic response to any particular OLI configuration may affect the nature and pattern of its O and I advantages in a later period of time (Dunning, 1991).

One can suggest that the OLI paradigm offers the basis for a general explanation of international production, a rich conceptual framework for explaining not only the level, form and growth of MNC activity, but also the way in which such activity is organised. Furthermore, the paradigm offers a robust tool for analysing the role of FDI as an engine of growth and development as well as for evaluating the extent to which the policies of source and host governments are likely both to affect and be affected by that activity.

OTHER THEORETICAL CONTRIBUTIONS: A SELECTED VIEW

To complete this short historical review, we briefly consider two other approaches to explaining MNC activity which offer valuable insights into both location and ownership of international economic activity. Both approaches were developed by financial or macro-economists.

The Risk Diversification Hypothesis

This was put forward by Agmon and Lessard (1977), Lessard (1976, 1982) and Rugman (1975, 1979, 1980). Building on some earlier work by Grubel (1974) and Levy and Sarnat (1970), these scholars argued that the MNC offered individual or institutional equity investors a superior vehicle for geographically diversifying their investment portfolios than did the international equity market. This partly reflected the failure of the equity market to efficiently evaluate the risks or the benefits of risk diversification, and partly the fact that, compared with the domestic counterparts, MNCs possessed certain non-financial advantages that enabled them to manage the risks associated with international diversified portfolios more effectively. However, there remains some doubt as to the extent to which the gains of international diversification are reflected in the cost of equity to, or the share prices of, the investing firms (Dunning, 1992).

Macro-Financial and Exchange Rate Theories

Here we consider two forms:

1. *The Aliber model*   Robert Aliber (1970, 1971 and 1993) took as his starting point the failure of financial markets. He argued that a firm headquartered in a country identified with low interest rates will place a higher value on the income associated with particular plants than firms headquartered in countries identified with high interest rates. These national differences in interest rates and in the price of corporate equities means that there are country-specific costs of capital to firms. Thus, firms headquartered in low-interest-rate countries share a locational advantage.
   The key implicit assumption of this theory is that the cost of capital for a multinational firm is not the weighted average of the

costs of the capital for firms headquartered in each of the countries in which this firm has subsidiaries. One implication is that a
firm cannot significantly affect its cost of capital relative to the
costs of capital of foreign firms, because the costs of equity capital
have a large country-specific component. Furthermore, he stated
that the source-country firms take their cost of capital as a given
in their own capital markets; similarly, the host-country firms
take *their* cost of capital as a given. The differences in the cost
of capital to the two groups of firms explain why the minimum
price required by the source-country firms before they will sell
firm-specific knowledge might exceed the maximum price that a
cross-country firm will pay for this knowledge, and why the
market in which firm-specific knowledge is bought and sold is
viewed as imperfect.

2. *Exchange rate model* Frost and Stein (1989) presented a model
in which currency movements affect the geography of MNCs by
altering relative wealth across countries, and demonstrated a significant negative correlation between the value of the US dollar
and the propensity of foreign firms to invest in the USA. However, other writers, like Cushman (1985) and Culem (1988), have
argued that, rather then reflecting relative wealth, exchange rate
movements mirror changes in relative real labour costs, and it is
these that determine FDI. In a test of these alternative proposi-
tions, Klein and Rosengren (1990a) have demonstrated that the
correlation between the exchange rate and US inbound direct
investment during the 1980s supports the former rather than the
latter hypothesis. Klein and Rosengren (1990b) show that relative
wealth is also an important determinant of outward US investment, especially when Japan (where there are significant barriers
to acquisitions and mergers by foreign firms) is excluded as a host
country.

LIMITATIONS OF EXISTING THEORIES

In spite of their successes, however, the traditional theories leave
many recent features of FDI flow unexplained. Recent strategic shifts
in flows of FDI (from developed to developing countries and intra-
Asian FDI flows) and developments in the international division of
labour, influence the location of labour-intensive processes and
component production within vertically integrated international

industries. This indicates further the limited application of these theories in practice.

So far we have discussed various foreign investment and production theories concerning their application to examine MNCs' motives and a country's attractiveness to the inflow of FDI. Although these theories have gained wide coverage in the literature and among policy-makers in developed countries and related international organisations, there are some limitations on their usefulness in the analysis of FDI inflow to transitional economies and developing countries.

Most theories of FDI were developed when firms headquartered in the USA accounted for three-quarters of the total annual flows. The assumption implicit in these theories, or at least in most of them, is that firms that invest abroad need an advantage to compensate for the extraordinary costs of FDI – costs that their host-country competitors do not incur. One test of each theory is whether it is consistent with changes in the geographic pattern of FDI in the last decade, especially with the surge in FDI in the USA by firms from Western Europe, Japan and newly-industrialised countries (NICs) of Asia, as well as the new wave of investment in assembly, processing and manufacture in less-developing countries (LDCs). Thus, the assumption central to each of these theories might be modified so that they are consistent with the changes in the patterns of investment, and then the plausibility of each assumption may be reevaluated; however, they still leave many recent features of FDI unexplained. (Aliber, 1993; Froot, 1993).

Most theories of FDI are associated with the relaxation of one of the assumptions of the competitive model; these theories highlight a particular type of advantage of the source-country firm that enables it to compensate for the cost of economic distance. Some theories highlight firm-specific advantages, which are generally produced within the firm as a way to enhance its competitive position: each firm strives to differentiate its product or processes from those of its competitors. In contrast, other theories of FDI highlight country-specific advantages, which are associated with all the firms headquartered in a particular country. As most theories of FDI are identified with a deviation or departure from the perfect market assumptions, the number of theories is limited by the number of possible imperfections. The large number of theories extant in the literature suggests that many theories are modest variations on the same theme.

The recent FDI surge in US inflows and Japanese outflows illustrates a few examples; Japanese FDI overall, which was historically quite small, exploded across all industries in the last decade, experiencing as an aggregate a seven-fold increase from 1985 to 1989 (Froot, 1993). During this surge, both US inflows and Japanese outflows were particularly large and fast-growing in real estate and financial services. In these industries, however, there was little evidence of meaningful change in competitive advantage. Particularly puzzling is the case of Japanese banks, which during the latest surge went on a much-publicised binge in acquiring foreign affiliates. Many of the banks involved were actually noted for their apparently inefficient operations and low profitability in comparison with US and European companies. These facts suggest that existing theories do not adequately explain either the timing or the magnitude of FDI surges nor their broad cross-industry composition.

Other theories try to explain the timing and economic geography of FDI in a conventional way by looking at perceived location advantages (Dunning, 1980). As expansion through FDI means a higher cost of management, advantageous location is not enough to explain the establishment of foreign subsidiaries in the assembly of components and processing. Unless MNCs possess an advantage over local firms sufficient to offset the cost of international coordination, the benefits of location will be captured instead by indigenous firms (Froot, 1993). The conspicuous case of the auto and electronics industries may not point to a general rule of the old oligopolistic market structures and industry protection as the magnet for inward direct investment (Caves, 1989). Among developing countries, open export-oriented economies such as Hong Kong have been more successful than nations pursuing import-substitution strategies in attracting new investment. The recent phenomenon of a new shift in investment by Korean, Japanese, US and even German car manufactures by moving their assembly and production lines abroad, mostly to cheap labour third world countries, to take advantage of internationalisation of production and division of labour is not fully explained by the traditional theories of foreign investment. New theories have to be developed to explain this new shift in strategies, structure of foreign investment by today's large multi-national car manufacturer.

By contrast, the highly protected apparel and footwear industries in LDCs, according to conventional theory, have attracted relatively little direct investment from abroad. In these low-technology industries, ownership advantages are apparently too small to offset the greater costs incurred by foreign investors (Caves, 1982). The recent new waves of foreign investment by MNCs from Taiwan, Korea, Hong Kong and to some extent Indonesia in Malaysia, Thailand

and China suggest that these theories do not hold strongly in these cases either.

The greatly increased extent of two-way FDI and even of two-way flows within a given industry has blurred the distinction, at least among industry nations, between host and source countries (Dunning, 1985) and creates a gap in the explanation by old theories of the patterns and motivation for FDI by MNCs, thus requiring a fundamental shift in both analytical perspective and policy stance (McCulloch, 1988). Wells (1993) argues that today's 'mobile exporters' are different from earlier waves of investors. The new investments appear to reflect shifts in comparative advantage, as countries like Indonesia become more attractive sites for certain kinds of manufacturing activities. The Indonesian experience shows a growth in investment from other developing countries in recent years. More of that investment comes from Korea and Taiwan than in the past. Moreover, the kinds of investment that dominate have also changed; the new investors are coming for reasons that differ from those that were most common in the past and which had been explained by conventional theories. How well do the old theories (of monopolistic advantage or internalisation) explain the new waves of FDI by mobile exporters in East Asia, the destinations of these flows, the motivations for such investment and its attractiveness to each host country?.

The new wave of investment by Third World multinationals in other developing countries has by now been rather firmly established, documented and described (Wells, 1983; Lall, 1983; Khan, 1987; White, 1987). To a great extent, the investment was associated with small-scale, cost-minimising technologies, with price rather than brand-name competition, but recently they have invested in more advanced technological industries, and the size of investment has increased noticeably compared with the industrialised nations. The average investment in a firm owned by an East Asian developing country was $US15.8 million in 1992, the average for all investors being $US17.5 million (Wells, 1993). These large inflows of FDI in recent years in East Asia clearly indicate that tax incentives are not necessary important for a developing country to attract foreign investment (Guisinger, 1985; Wells, 1986). This new phenomenon creates further problems for conventional foreign investment theories to explain the trends of these 'mobile exports' from Third World countries.

The product-cycle model of international trade and investment offers some understanding of the mobile exporters (Vernon, 1966). Although the theory has become increasingly less useful in explaining trade and investment among the industrialised countries (as their markets have converged and the MNCs have established facilities in a number of countries), it still has some validity in explaining investment flows among countries with quite different income levels. Foreign investment moves, according to the theory, down the ladder of development as products mature. Thus, the movement of investment from the richer developing countries of East Asia into the poorer countries of the region is consistent with the theory to some extent but it has strong limitations when it comes to explaining the likely patterns or industry destinations.

The shift away from traditional majority-owned foreign investment towards 'new forms' of investment in developing countries, notably joint ventures, licensing agreements and more recently co-production and assembly of components, creates an environment for the appearance of smaller internationally-oriented firms with export-oriented manufacturing strategies (Helleiner, 1987) which cannot be explained by the questions relating purely to conventional ownership modalities. Most striking in this is that some firms, notably some Japanese trading companies and recently others based in Hong Kong, already specialise in the assembly of efficient 'packages' of equipment, know-how, management and marketing skills from a variety of sources.

As far as FDI is concerned, Third World multinational corporations (TWMNCs) may play an expanding role in manufacturing for export, not only within the South but also towards the North. Some TWMNCs have developed considerable specialised knowledge of small-scale and labour-intensive production procedures in the manufacturing of standardised products (Helleiner, 1988). Despite this new conventional wisdom, the export-oriented manufacturing TWMNCs and FDI flows deserve more study and encouragement. However, there is still little known about optimal policies relating to them regarding the relative advantages of different forms of investment, different general relationships between host countries and foreign firms in particular industries, either for firms of varying characteristics or for various actors in different kinds of host countries.

EMPIRICAL EVIDENCE

In reviewing the empirical literature, emphasis has been limited to the literature on the causes and consequences of the FDI inflow. It only considers formal FDI flows and the impact of such flows on the export and economic development. Formal FDI includes equity joint ventures, contractual joint ventures, cooperative development and wholly-foreign-owned enterprises, operating within the FDI policy framework.

Beginning with the study by Reuber and associates (1973) into the determinants of FDI flows to developing countries, a large amount of empirical research has been carried out in this field. Both the alleged causes and consequences outlined in the preceding section have been investigated in various ways. A striking feature of this literature is its overwhelming reliance on the OLI-paradigm framework. However, there have been a few sporadic attempts to study the problem from different perspectives.

The existing empirical studies support the view that the traditional classical theories leave many recent features of FDI inflow unexplained. Moreover, the existing studies have focused almost exclusively on the experience of the US, Japanese and European MNCs; the experience of more recent entrants from the developing countries of Asia and Eastern Europe need more attention. Furthermore, recent new clusters of FDI activities in Eastern Europe and export-oriented foreign investment in LDCs require new empirical investigation into the emerging trends and patterns of foreign investment. There is, therefore, a clear clash between the classical approach to FDI and the empirical findings on the level of motivation and inflow of capital. The traditionally accepted explanation of trends and motives of foreign firms to invest abroad have been either disputed or totally refuted when confronted with empirical testing. In general, the conclusions of these empirical studies strongly support the case against the application of the traditional FDI theories. New approaches need now to be sought or developed to help us understand the emerging new waves of FDI flows between countries.

Cross-section Studies

Grunwald and Flamm (1985) suggest that transferring some production processes abroad, with one side primarily furnishing labour services, the other primarily components, is a substitute neither for the traditional exchange of primary goods for manufactured products nor for the 'non traditional' export of products emerging from the NICs or LDCs and their imports of capital of goods and technology. This complementary intra-industry trade is a relatively new addition to the changing international division of labour. The traditional industries have generally been associated with fairly labour-intensive technologies and, due to the persistence of low wage rates in the Third World and the relatively low development costs of establishing a production capability in these older products, these industries have been the leading edge of the burgeoning exports of manufactures produced in developing countries.

The high-tech industries, on the other hand, depend for their success on access to the specialised resources required for research and development and the highly complex production processes. These industries have therefore been located in the developed countries (DCs). As products mature, technology diffuses, high-tech products eventually become traditional products, and production moves to more competitive locations abroad (Bhagwati, 1982).

Volume manufacture in a foreign location for re-export to the home market or other export markets is a qualitatively new feature of foreign manufacturing operations that emerged in the late 1960s. In developing Asia, more than a quarter of the sales made by US affiliates went to the USA in 1977, up from less than 10 per cent in 1966. In electrical machinery, in particular, some 70 per cent of output was shipped back to the USA in 1977. A similar phenomenon appears to have taken place in Japanese multinationals. Japanese data for 1975 show a significant share of sales as exports to Japan from Asian affiliates. Production abroad is even more important in certain high-tech electronics industries, where the products are anything but traditional. Semiconductors alone account for about 40 per cent of the value of US components reimported into that country after overseas assembly, and more than 80 per cent of US semiconductor production is probably assembled abroad. Thailand and Malaysia are also popular locations for labour-intensive industries, but they attract investment into more technology-intensive industries as well, particularly electrical appliances, electronics and metal products. MNCs are underwriting an integrated system of international production, and the world economy is being transformed into a 'global factory'.

Moreover, as Blumberg (1989) has noted, the previous focus on low-cost labour has become subordinated to a new focus on product re-engineering to allow for the use of fewer components and more efficient throughput in manufacturing. Along with competing on the basis of technology, firms are now competing on the basis of time and production efficiency (Yongwoong and Simon, 1994). Within such a system, non-price competitive factors take on greater significance than price-related factors; this is not to say that costs are not important, but that the successful firm must be mindful of the full panoply of competitive factors. As Dunning has indicated, successful MNCs are those which manage a broad range of value-added activities across a diverse set of geographical boundaries, capitalising on the distinctive advantages offered in each of the respective domains.

Helleiner (1973, 1976, 1978 and 1988) in his studies argues that a new orthodoxy has recently emerged to the effect that labour-intensive manufactured exports able to benefit from scale economies derived from sales to world markets, which were underemphasised in the past, must now be encouraged with at least the same vigour with which import-substituting industry was encouraged in the past. Incentives for this purpose are to be offered both by LDCs and by the industrial nations to which they aspire to sell. If the developing countries are now convinced that it is the labour-intensive industrial exports that should be emphasised in the immediate future, and adequate incentives for them are offered, one can be confident that the international business community will be quick to respond. Since the second half of the 1960s, imports into the USA from LDCs under items 806.30 and 807.00 of the US Tariff Schedules, which permit import duties to be levied only upon value-added activities abroad where inputs originated in the USA, rose from $US61 million to $US539 million between 1966 and 1970, or from 4 per cent to over 14 per cent of total US imports of manufactures from LDCs. Imports under these items accounted for approximately 27 per cent of the increase in the total of such US imports in the 1966–69 period, despite their start from a very small base (US Tariff Commission, 1970).

Doner (1991) has further demonstrated the complex forces that drive Japanese automobile firms to extend their local production networks by creating regional production schemes for the supply of auto parts in half-a-dozen nations in East and Southeast Asia, in order to retain and perhaps increase their share of the global automobile market. Due to the new types of re-programmability that have been introduced into the manufacturing process (a process the Japanese have called mechatronics), an entirely new set of economic forces has become predominant, leading to new ideas regarding production volumes, mix and tooling (Yongwoong and Simon, 1994).

Wells (1993) focuses on important recent trends in world FDI transacted by companies he call 'mobile exporters'. Typically these are companies from relatively high-income developing countries seeking low-cost installation to access third-country markets. The rate of growth of mobile-export FDI in some developing countries is quite astonishing. Wells takes Indonesia as his primary example. There the FDI approved during the 1987–90 period was 150 per cent of all the FDI which occurred in that country from 1967 to 1987. The lion's share of this growth was associated with an increase in the role of export-oriented FDI from other developing countries. For instance, from 1977 to 1985 the share of FDI into Indonesia that came from developing countries was only 6 per cent, and during this period Japanese investment dominated. By the first half of 1991, however, other developing countries alone accounted for 56 per cent of projects approved for FDI (in manufacturing alone, the proportion rose to 65 per cent). In sum, this experience shows a growth in investment from other developing Asian countries during the 1990s, both in absolute terms and in the share of total foreign investment. More of that investment comes from Korea and Taiwan than in the past. Moreover, the kind of investment that dominates has also changed: the new investors are coming for different reasons than in the past.

Wells (1993) identifies three major rounds of developing-country to developing-country FDI. The first round was export-oriented, driven by the desire to avoid import quotas in third-country markets (for example in textiles and shoes industries). The second round consisted of trade-substituting FDI-developing-country companies that came to Indonesia fearing that present or future trade barriers would block their access to Indonesia's domestic market. The third round came from companies seeking lower cost export bases for their products. Firms from South Korea, Taiwan, Singapore and Hong Kong have faced currency appreciations, wage increases and labour shortages.

David Yoffie (1993) analyses the evolution of FDI in the semiconductor industry by taking a careful look at industry data. He notes that there is a surprising lack of agglomeration in recent greenfield investment. Secondly, he notes that investments in Southeast Asia have been maintained and expanded, even though the automation of assembly and test processes has diminished the importance of access to low-cost labour. However, over the same period, substantial downstream production (consumer electronics and automobiles) has shifted to this region, and the industrial infrastructure has expanded. Thirdly, he contends that it is surprising to see little FDI into Japan despite the liberalization of FDI regulations and the implementation of the semiconductor trade agreement (SCTA). Furthermore, he argues that the benefit of locating near suppliers has declined. Japanese firms are willing to forego these benefits in order to have production capacity inside actual or potential trade barriers in the USA and Europe.

Lim and Fong (1991) suggest that FDI is no longer a simple hierarchical process from capital-rich to capital-poor countries. Companies are searching for partners all over the globe, even to the point of collaborating with actual or former competitors. The nature of the movements overseas has, in terms of both production, location and research and development (R&D) sites, moved in the direction of what David Teece has termed 'the search for complementary assets' (Yongwoong and Simon, 1994). Firms that engage in overseas operations on either the R&D or production side may, therefore, be less inclined to rely primarily on traditional entry modes such as licensing or equity-based investment and opt for what Charles Oman has termed 'new forms of foreign investment' (Oman, 1984). Large MNCs will move increasingly into the internalisation of their production and marketing, knitting the LDCs into their international activities as suppliers not merely of raw materials but also of particular manufactured products and processes. One can depict this development as the next logical step for international investors following the two previous major stages of resource exploitation and import-substituting manufacturing.

Bhagwati (1985) argues that, where the source of import competition is technical change in progressive, Shumpeterian industries, causing competition among similar products, the response of the producers of import-competing similar products (none dominant) cannot logically be outward FDI since lower factor costs abroad are not what is driving the foreign competition. Rather, it may be the mutual penetration of investment (MPI) response which brings international competitors into cooperation. Further, he stated that MNCs in different countries have R&D-induced advantages in producing different types of sub-products (for example, an MNC in Japan is excellent at producing small cars and an MNC in the USA has an edge in the production of large cars). Instead of competing in each other's home countries or in third markets in both types of sub-products when they only have a competitive edge in one, it would be expected that in this situation it would be most beneficial for MNCs to enter into a mutual equity interpenetration, with production-wise accommodation in sub-product specialisation according to the advantage they possessed. Bhagwati's model predicts that MNCs with R&D-induced specialisation in different types of sub-products within an industry in different countries will interpenetrate each other's investment activities.

Helleiner (1973, 1978 and 1988), Grunwald and Flamm (1985) suggest that manufacturing for export is the 'new frontier' for international business in LDCs, and that processing and component specialisation are likely to become the chief avenues of FDI inflow for LDCs. Incentives are therefore going to be offered in LDCs for the development of industrial exports; one can also expect incentives favouring labour-intensive activities to be increasingly introduced. The multinational manufacturing firm from an LDC is likely to play a major role in the future development of manufactured exports from LDCs. The location in developing countries of relatively labour-intensive processes and component production within vertically-integrated international industries has been an important feature of the international division of labour. MNCs are already lining up their various activities and/or product lines, to the extent that they are separable one from another (where unskilled labour is predominantly used) to discover which are most suitable for relocation to low-wage countries. This development is part of an occurring adjustment process; firms in the DCs adapting to the increasing pressures of domestic real-wage increases and import competition from low-cost sources. The transfer abroad of component assemblies occurs in many industries where the technology of production permits the separation of labour-intensive components from other steps in production. In the next decade or two, processing, assembly and component manufacture for export within vertically-integrated international industries are bound to become an increasingly important element in this development.

Petri (1994) suggests that the variety of activities now being performed for export on this basis in the developing countries is already very large. It may be worth listing some examples in order to show the flavour of these developments: semi-conductors, valves, tuners and other components are manufactured or assembled for a large number of Japanese and US electronic firms in Hong Kong, Singapore, South Korea, Taiwan and Mexico. (The electronics industry is by far the most important industry in this field.) Garments, gloves, leather luggage and baseballs are sewn together in the West Indies, Southeast Asia and Mexico for US and Japanese firms (Helleiner, 1983). Automobile parts are manufactured for British, US and Japanese firms in a wide variety of countries; for example radio antennae in Taiwan, piston rings and cylinder linings in South Korea and Taiwan, automobile lamps in Mexico, braking equipment in India, batteries and springs in Thailand.

The success of any developing country entering this new sphere of international divisions of labour depends crucially on its ability to influence the site-selection decisions of MNCs. It is quite possible for a country, particularly one at a relative disadvantage with respect to labour and transport costs, to build infrastructure and/or offer subsidies to attract this particularly 'footloose' type of manufacturing activity (Helleiner, 1978, 1988).

ANALYTICAL FRAMEWORK

Some of the empirical studies indicate clear changes which are occurring in today's global economy. The focus moves from the decision of whether or not to invest abroad to that of maintaining the competitiveness of an individual MNC (Gray, 1996). Furthermore, FDI by MNCs now plays a major role in linking many national economies, building an integrated international production system, the productive core of the globalising world economy. MNCs deploy their tangible and intangible assets (for example capital, R&D capacity and technology, organisational and managerial practices, trade links) with a view towards increasing their competitiveness and profitability. Another indication of recent changes is that in the early 1990s, most countries or, more particularly, governments of countries, are claiming FDI as 'good news' after a period of being highly critical if not downright hostile to it in the 1970s and early 1980s (Dunning, 1995a). Now one can note increased use of incentives by national and sub-national governments in a competitive environment to attract investors, and the threat of beggar-they-neighbour policies (Dunning, 1995b). Also these incentives differ from country to country, which helps MNCs deploy their assets in cost-effective ways. It is, therefore, not surprising that empirical evidence supports these recent changes in the behaviour and structure of firms' and host-countries' investment environments.

The empirical evidence is not easy to interpret because of differing methodologies, time-scales, investor nationality and type of project (manufacturing, services, R&D, and so on), but to sum up, the major conclusion that can be drawn from a survey of numerous empirical studies is that the recent inflow of FDI to emerging new markets in Central and Eastern Europe (CEE), China and Southeast Asia cannot be analysed by the traditional framework of international production and investment. Generalisations for all post-communist countries are particularly difficult, especially when different policy-reform approaches have been implied and may on many grounds be misleading (Rojec and Svetlicic, 1994; Sachs, 1995; Jermakowicz, 1994). Further research in this field, therefore, needs to focus on studying the problems for each individual country with respect to the uniquely different economic approaches to their common goal of transition to a market economy. In addition, sufficient detailed attention needs to be given to the factors affecting the inflow of capital and its trends.

In analysing the trends and patterns of FDI we adopt and expand on a standard typology developed by a few academics which was presented in the Introduction. In the first category (resource-based manufacturing), the value added in the further processing of local raw materials is frequently not a very high proportion of the value of the material itself. There may, nevertheless, be substantial aggregate value added when realised through this form of manufacturing for export. Some processing activities, however, particularly in the mineral industries, are quite capital-intensive and/or skill-intensive and may not therefore be the most suitable for location in a low-income country. The heavy effective protection offered by the cascaded tariff structure to the processing industries in the developed world is a further significant obstacle to the development of processed manufactured exports of this type (Helleiner, 1973). This is particularly so in those instances when raw material extraction is not under the control of the same firms as the processing. There are, however, new opportunities emerging for growth of trade within the regions themselves (for example the EU–Eastern Europe region and the Southeast Asia region). China, with its rich resource base and as a low-income country has some FDI potential, especially as it is one of Japan's closest neighbours (most Japanese firms undertake foreign investment with a view to securing for the nation a stable and low-cost source of input; UNCTC 1983). In recent years, many NICs have also begun to follow this Japanese investment pattern, and investors from these countries are already involved in resource-based export industries such as petroleum products (Zhu Nai Xiao, 1994; Byrd, 1992).

In the second category (differentiated final goods), foreign firms are more willing to move their production units to overseas locations, especially to developing countries with low labour costs and a familiar host-country environment. These overseas exports of manufactures emerged in industries with relatively high barriers to entry and relatively sophisticated and controlled marketing. They are most likely in those cases where the firm's strategy is built not upon national marketing and product differentiation, but on international production and cross-hauling (Vernon, 1971).

In the evolving context of global competition, a series of new roles have emerged for the developing economies. Among these roles are high value-added manufacturing and small-batch production – for example ASICs (application-specific integrated circuits), specialised engineering for initiating rapid design changes, high-technology production of both software and hardware, and low-cost, high-quality R&D (*Electronic Business Asia*, 1993). By linking up with various economic partners in the NICs and ASEAN, developing countries could stimulate export manufacturing from these countries. Wage increases in Northeast Asian countries indicate recent trends of moving these plants from Japan, Korea, Taiwan and Hong Kong to Thailand, Malaysia and China, and open up the possibility of competitive exports of manufactured goods.

Investment by Japanese firms across the Pacific Rim seems to reflect a fundamental change in focus from 'transaction costs to transaction benefits' (Imai, 1985). Japanese firms now seem much more willing to go outside their traditional subcontracting and sourcing relationships and to plant deeper roots into the local economies of the region (*Economist*, 1993). The Japanese government has inspired all firms to transfer those factories which use more energy and raw materials or large labour forces to developing countries. In 1992, the FDI from Japan to Asia-Pacific developing countries was $US6.187 billion (Yongwoong, 1994).

Standardised labour-intensive consumable (category 3) constitute one of the areas in which developing countries can develop competitive advantages in export-oriented manufacturing. MNCs may choose to locate the production of particular new final products or product lines, presumably those most intensive in the use of unskilled labour or most subject to pollution legislation, in less-developed countries. The role of FDI in this category remains controversial. On the basis of the experience of NICs, it has been argued that FDI involvement is by no means necessary for the successful expansion of these exports as they embody well-diffused technology (Helleiner, 1988; Wells, 1993). The changing role of FDI in the international division of labour, variations in factor endowment and wage growth have opened up the potential for the growth of new trade flows. The potential for trade growth based upon differences in labour costs remains strong, as reflected in the wage variation among Northeast and Southeast Asian countries (Drysdale, 1988). These factors, together with changes in relevant government policies, presents, one can argue, opportunities for developing countries for truly international sub-contracting, which involves indigenous enterprises in those countries rather than mere subsidiaries of foreign firms.

Countries with comparative advantage in labour-intensive goods (category 4), can strongly influence FDI location for labour-intensive processes and component specialisation within vertically-integrated international industries. Since the 1960s adjustment processes have been occurring in DCs, created by the increased pressure of domestic real-wage increases and import competition from low-cost sources (Grunwald and Flamm, 1985). The transfer abroad of component assemblies occurs in many industries where the technology of production permits the separation of labour-intensive components from other steps in production. Assembly operations related to high-tech electronics industries, the production of semiconductor devices in particular, are by far the most important. Other industries with significant assembly operations located in LDCs are electrical appliances, automobile parts, electrical machinery and optical products (Athukorala, 1989). For example, the main parts, assemblies, sub-assemblies and final assembly tasks for the dot-matrix printers of the Japanese company NEC, are provided by eight factories in southern China. The company's personal computers are assembled in Hong Kong using parts and components procured from local suppliers in other parts of Asia (for example Thailand and Malaysia), while the hard-disk drives are produced by a number of coordinated factories in the Philippines (*Business Tokyo*, 1992).

Korean, German, US and Italian car manufacturers are also relocating their assembly operations to countries with low labour costs following the recent shifts in the cost-adjustment processes. Many Japanese computer firms have sought out universities and research institutes in China, for example, as a means to reinforce their manpower ranks with qualified individuals, many of whom are grossly underutilised within the Chinese science and technology establishment. Most importantly, however, these R&D-oriented relationships have started to extend beyond the software engineering area and into new areas such as consumer electronics, semiconductors and air-conditioning. The Japanese identify the main purpose of these new facilities as the performance of design and development (D&D) engineering functions. Toshiba, for example, has moved the design team for VCRs from Japan to Singapore through the establishment of a local subsidiary that now has total design responsibility (*Business Times*, 1994). Matsushita, which is among the leading Japanese manufacturing firms, has probably put together the most well-articulated strategy for the Asia-Pacific region. As of 1992, close to 60 per cent of Matsushita's non-Japanese manufacturing was conducted in the Asia-Pacific region (*Economist*, 1993). This has led to an opening up of many existing 'networks' to a larger and larger number of qualified local firms throughout the Pacific Rim, especially in countries such as Malaysia, Thailand and China (*Asian Business*, 1994).

In some investment decision-making in this sphere, investors attach significant weight to the existence of a large domestic market which can absorb a substantial proportion of output at the initial stage of market entry (Guisinger, 1985). The heavy protection which has been required to enable most import-substituting manufacturing establishments in LDCs to survive today augurs poorly for the possibility of their sustained entry into competitive world markets. It would be, in principle, possible to offer sufficient subsidies, direct or indirect, to encourage export by existing plants at least in those cases where the agreements with foreign investors do not specifically prohibit them.

Helleiner argued that overseas exports of manufactures emerged in industries with relatively high barriers to entry and relatively sophisticated and controlled marketing based on a firm's strategy built on international production and cross-hauling (Vernon, 1971). For example, in Poland Daewoo entered the Polish market and bought a large, antiquated auto company (FSO) on the condition that the Polish government provide it with a 30 per cent tariff protection.

Assembly exports from LDCs have grown much faster than the total number of manufactured exports from these countries. For instance, their share in total US imports of manufactures from LDCs increased from 4 per cent in 1966 to 10 per cent in 1993 (Grunwald and Flamm, 1985). It can be reasonably expected that overseas production arrangements will continue to remain a dynamic growth area in the foreseeable future. For DC firms which operate in industries severely affected by import competition from low-cost sources (such as electronics, electrical goods and automobiles), offshore assembly is crucial for their survival. Governments in these countries also actively encourage such operations through value-added tariff provisions and other measures with a view to cushioning domestic economies against disruptions resulting from rapid import penetration. In these instances, a host government's preference for reducing the role of traditional FDI has been the main influence, but in some cases the initiative has come from the smaller MNCs in NICs and LDCs (Cable and Persaud, 1987).

CONCLUSIONS

The foregoing discussion reveals that empirical work over the past decades has not produced consensus as to the trends and patterns of FDI in transitional economies and developing countries. To comment on the issue of trends and patterns of FDI first, the LDCs exhibit significant differences with regard to (1) source of FDI and newly-emerging patterns in general and at industry level as well, and (2) motivation of foreign firms to move their production lines offshore and the host country's changing investment incentives and attitudes towards FDI. Various analyses of FDI data reveal vast differences in the source and determinants of FDI not only between countries, but also among different industries and manufactured goods (World Bank, 1996; Athukorala and Frank Cong Hiep Huynh 1987; Wells, 1993). A similar conclusion applies to the trends and patterns of FDI in transitional economies (Jermakowicz, 1994; Rojec and Svetlicic, 1994; Lemoine, 1996; Sikora, 1993). In addition, trends of FDI inflow to emerging market economies tend to exhibit different patterns and determinants, thus leading to significant variation in motivational behaviour of foreign firms (Cieslik, 1996; Shultz, 1997; Schmidt, 1994). The preceding observations suggest that new trends are emerging not only among source countries but also among host countries, and they can be associated with globalisation, information technology and the international division of labour.

As to the impact of FDI on the domestic economy, the picture is even more complex. For a given economy, the nature and the degree of this impact is determined by the stage of a country's economic development, economic policy and general business environment. Due to the obvious differences in these features, the impact and benefits of FDI to the domestic economy are likely to vary substantially from country to country.

It is, therefore, not surprising that the empirical evidence as to the role and trends of FDI is rather mixed and, at times, inconclusive. To sum up, the major conclusion that can be drawn from a survey of numerous empirical studies is that with regard to the role, trends and determinants of FDI, generalisations based on traditional theories can be misleading, particularly for newly-emerging transitional economies. Further research in this field, therefore, needs to focus on studying the issues of FDI for transitional countries in detail giving sufficient attention to new emerging patterns and trends of FDI.

3 China and Poland: An Overview

The major conclusion of the previous chapter was that no meaningful analysis of the trends and patterns of FDI can be undertaken without reference to the underlying economic structure and the institutional background of the countries in question. This chapter is therefore intended to provide an overview of the Chinese and Polish economies and to place FDI in the context of these transitional economies in order to lay the foundations for the subsequent analysis. The original reform proposals and the systems in practice will be briefly discussed with regard to various selected functional areas.

CHINA: AN INTRODUCTION

In 1979, China commenced a gradual reform programme to restructure its centralised, communist party-controlled economy. Direct planning controls were relaxed, the decentralisation of centralised decision-making processes was begun, attempts were made to increase reliance on market forces, the development of non-state-owned economic entities was encouraged, and the gradual opening of China's economy to the outside world was introduced. Main economic indicators for the period 1989–96 are shown in Table 3.1

The main changes came in two areas. Agricultural production was predominantly returned to the private sector operating through markets. The government ignored the inflow of informal direct foreign investment by overseas Chinese, predominantly from Hong Kong and Taiwan, in production for export, which enabled export earnings to grow rapidly. In the rest of the economy the Chinese government adopted a cautious and pragmatic approach to economic reforms, proceeding in an incremental fashion. Experimentation with reform started in rural areas. The 'household responsibility system' – that is the return of agricultural production to private farmers, together with increases in the relative prices of agricultural products – brought substantial productivity gains and resulted in a diversification and increase an agricultural production.

34

Table 3.1 *China: main economic indicators*, 1989–96

	1989	1990	1991	1992	1993	1994	1995	1996
Population (mn)	1139.20	1153.30	1170.10	1183.60	1196.40	1209.34	1222.40	1223.90
GDP (current $US bn)	449.10	387.4	406.09	483.00	599.01	522.19	650.12	667.00
GDP (real growth rates)	4.3	3.9	8.0	13.2	13.8	11.9	9.7	9.2
Inflation (% change)	16.32	1.30	5.08	8.85	18.00	24.20	14.80	12.20
Exports	51.86	61.27	70.45	80.52	90.97	119.82	155.77	158.3
Imports (cif)	58.44	52.52	62.57	76.35	103.09	114.56	132.89	138.8
Current account balance	−4.48	11.89	3.02	5.82	−12.40	7.20	14.00	19.5
International reserves	17.02	28.60	42.66	9.44	21.20	51.62	65.00	92.00
Foreign debt	44.79	52.52	60.80	69.30	83.80	90.00	100.00	120.00
Exchange rate vs $US	4.72	5.22	5.43	5.75	5.80	8.45	8.31	8.32

Notes: mn=million, bn=billion, cif=imports on board.
Source: State Bureau of Statistics, *China Country Risk Report*, Political and Economic Risk Consultancy Ltd (PERC), Beijing, 1997, p. 3; State Bureau of Statistics, *China Statistical Yearbook*, Beijing, various years.

Increased opportunities were provided to township and village manufacturing enterprises, which absorbed some of the surplus labour that emerged as agricultural efficiency increased. They began to compete for inputs and to sell to local consumers. They had somewhat less easy access to various subsidies, including cheap credit, and therefore had to be somewhat more efficient than state enterprises. They were consequently more flexible and more responsive to changes in market conditions than state enterprises. An important side-effect was the introduction of market business methods, including payment by results in the enterprises affected and, by example, in other Chinese enterprises. Informal investment in export industries grew rapidly. State enterprises, after a period of improvement in the early 1980s, became less efficient as managers and workers took over control in the late 1980s in their own short-term interest (World Bank, 1990). Productivity of the township and village enterprises was hampered, however, by the low skills of workers and management, shortages of raw materials and uneconomic scales of production. Collective enterprises in urban areas ran into similar problems; although they were often able, nevertheless, to profit by exploiting loopholes in dual pricing.

Before 1979, state-owned enterprises (SOEs), controlled through the central planning system, transferred all their surplus funds to the state, while losses were covered by budget subsidies. Investment funds and some working capital balances were provided to the enterprises through the government budget in the form of grants. The banking system supplied additional working capital at highly subsidised rates. Wages were paid according to a centrally approved scale. The enterprises' responsibility was to fulfil quantitative output targets established by the plan regardless of their financial results. Managers therefore had little incentive to improve efficiency and productivity. The focus of SOE reform was on making the SOEs responsible for their own profits and losses by introducing autonomy of decision-making and incentives for managers.

As in other centrally-planned economies that have not moved to private ownership, the reforms have not been effective. Taxes are decided by bargaining between enterprises and authorities, so that marginal tax rates vary substantially among SOEs (Tam, 1991). A loss-making enterprise is not taxed. This confusion of fiscal and financial measures has made taxation ineffectual. The limited duration of contracts for SOEs created incentives for management to focus on short-term profit maximisation. Costs differed among enterprises because of unequal access to subsidised raw materials and in their ability to sell at market rather than planned prices. These factors, together with price controls and varied access to cheap credit and budgetary subsidies, have continued to distort production and investment decisions.

The government has attempted to reduce the interference of central and local authorities by the introduction of a contract system for some medium and large-scale enterprises as well as leasing arrangements for small enterprises. Mandatory planning has been reduced. The proportion of fixed investment by SOEs financed through the state budget declined, falling from 60 per cent in 1978 to about 14 per cent in 1988. The number of products that were allocated through the central output plan declined from about 250 items in the early 1980s to about 20 items in 1988 (Blejer *et al.*, 1991: 67), but provincial governments have often taken over the planning mechanisms.

Although the reforms contributed to an increase in the growth of output by SOEs, their share in total industrial production fell from 78 per cent in 1978 and 66 per cent in 1985 to 55 per cent in 1990 (Table 3.2). The increasing share of rural and urban collective enterprises and foreign enterprises reflected their greater dynamism compared to state enterprises.

Table 3.2 *China: gross industrial output and shares of industrial enterprises, 1985–90 (Yuan 100 millions, current prices)*

Types	1978	1985	1986	1987	1988	1989	1990
State-owned	3288	6302	6971	8250	10351	12343	13064
	(77.6%)	(65.8%)	(62.3%)	(59.8%)	(56.8%)	(56.1%)	(54.6%)
Collective,	949	3117	3752	4782	6587	7858	8523
	(22.4%)	(32.1%)	(33.5%)	(34.6%)	(36.1%)	(35.7%)	(35.6%)
Township & village							
Individual	n.a.	180	309	502	790	1058	1290
		(1.9%)	(2.8%)	(3.6%)	(4.3%)	(4.8%)	(4.4%)
Foreign	n.a.	117	163	279	495	758	1047
		(1.2%)	(1.4%)	(2.0%)	(2.7%)	(3.4%)	(4.4%)
Total	4237	9716	11195	13813	18223	22017	23924
	(100%)	(100%)	(100%)	(100%)	(100%)	(100%)	(100%)

Note: n.a. = not applicable.
Source: State Bureau of Statistics, *Statistical Yearbook of China*, China Statistical Publishing House, Beijing, 1991.

ECONOMIC STRUCTURE

It has been nearly 19 years since the beginning of China's market-oriented economic reform. During these years of gradual and continuous reform, the structure of the Chinese economy has changed significantly. Today, public ownership develops in conjunction with other forms and, as the strength of the market mechanism continues to grow, the government's method of control over the economy has slowly shifted from direct command to indirect macroeconomic interventions.

According to the objective of the Ninth Five-Year Plan (1996–2000), the aim is to retain the predominance of public ownership – 'SOEs will remain the backbone of the industrial sector but a breakthrough in solving their major and difficult problems has to be made in the years to come' – supplemented by non-state and private ownership, while achieving an effective separation between state-ownership and control of enterprises (IMF Report, 1996: 51). As part of this system, a dual-track ownership structure emerged. The most important component of this dual-track strategy has been the radical restructuring of the ownership pattern by the explosive growth of the non-state sector since 1984. The most prominent type of firm in the 'non-state sector' is the community-owned enterprises in the rural areas known as township and village enterprises (TVEs). In 1988, the Seventh National People's Congress passed a constitutional amendment that endowed the legitimate status of the private economy (Rowley and Lewis (1996)) and (Corne, (1997)) and this sector has grown quickly in the years since then.

At present there are five principal participants in the Chinese economy:

1. state-owned enterprises;
2. collective enterprises – enterprises owned by local groups for which the government is not responsible for wages or similar obligations;
3. private enterprises – businesses operated by private individuals;
4. stock-share enterprises – companies owned partially or wholly by share-holders, including companies partially owned by the state; and
5. foreign-invested enterprises or joint ventures – enterprises owned at least 25% by foreign individuals or companies.

The private enterprises have been growing rapidly in the 1990s. By the end of 1992, approximately 7.7 million (89 per cent) of the retail-sales outlets in China belong to private businesses, and the number of self-employed business people has expanded to more than 15 million in urban areas all over the country. The number of larger private enterprises in the country increased from 91 000 in 1989 to 420 000 in 1994 (*China News Analysis*, October 1996).

The private sector has developed fastest along the south-east coast of China where 70 per cent of the country's private businesses are located. Another 19 per cent are in central China and only 1 per cent are in the western part of the country. But, nevertheless, the role of the private sector in the Chinese national economy today is still small (Table 3.3), and the total number of salaried employees in the private sector is still relatively minor (5.35 million employees; *Economic Information Daily*, May 1995).

Table 3.3 *China: gross output value according to ownership* (%)

	State	Collective	Individual	Other*
1985	64.9	32.1	1.8	1.2
1995	30.9	42.8	13.2	13.1

* mostly private.
Source: State Statistical Bureau of China, *China Foreign Economic Statistical Yearbook*, China Statistical Publishing House, Beijing, 1996, p. 75.

It must be emphasised that the public sector has not been withering away, as suggested in claims that China is 'growing out of the plan' (see, for example, *China News Analysis*, 1 October 1997). The state sector has actually retained its relative standing; SOEs produce approximately one-third of industrial output and provide more than half the total investment in fixed assets. They employ more than 100 million people, representing 18 per cent of the overall number of employed and 70 per cent of the urban employed (staff and workers). There were 35 million more SOE workers in 1994 than in 1978 (Wing Thye Woo, 1995).

SOEs

A key question that has faced economic reformers in China is whether the continuation of public ownership represents as insurmountable barrier to the functioning of markets and efficient resource allocation. In contrast to Poland, China has consistently maintained its preference for public ownership as a means of achieving its vision of a socialist market economy. As envisaged by China's policy-makers, such a system would be characterised by increased competition and the elimination of mandatory planning, but not necessarily by the replacement of SOEs, with private ownership. The most difficult part of the whole economic reform is the restructuring of the SOEs, many of which are loss-making and have become a big burden on the government budget.

The solutions taken into consideration by the government do not emphasise privatisation but rather mergers and takeovers of less-efficient companies by successful ones, and include cooperation with private enterprises. The merging of enterprises, like the splitting up of enterprises into smaller units, has been the aspect of the economic restructuring process aimed at improving economic efficiency. However, certain organisational changes, especially if externally imposed by government authorities rather than determined by internal needs of the organisation, can have a negative impact. To avoid closure of a loss-making enterprise and the associated redundancies, local governments often order another thriving firm to merge with the loss-making one, a practice that, unless carefully organised, could unnecessarily burden a successful firm.

The official line for reform is: 'Seize large enterprises, release small ones'. 'Seize the large' means massive state firms which are likely to lose more money than they earn but which become 'pillars of industry' and count on government support. By letting these firms buy up smaller enterprises and integrate vertically, Beijing wants them eventually to resemble South Korean *chaebols*, dominating the domestic market with the help of government protection before expanding overseas. 'Release the small' means that medium-sized factories are encouraged to explore new management incentives, to auction useless equipment and to merge with other struggling plants – anything to keep production lines running (*Far Eastern Economic Review*, 12 September 1996). The 'large'-category enterprises number approximately 5000, but account for 56 per cent of output value in the state-owned sector. They need to be reformed at all costs. The dead horses among them will be merged with profitable plants.

On the other hand, local governments have been repeatedly told that the time has come to 'release and let live' the approximately 500 000 small SOE enterprises in the country. This 'releasing' does not mean privatisation. The reform of small enterprises, their 'opening and setting free', remains controversial. The 'releasing and let live' policy takes many forms: joint-management by contracting, leasing, trusteeship or commission. Other formulas, however, modify ownership relations (purchase, annexation, share cooperative or sale relationships) and such reforms remain controversial.

Altogether, enterprise reform remains a 'weak link' in the reform of the economic structure. Between 1990 and 1995, the percentage of loss-making enterprises increased from 27.6 to 43 per cent, and losses from yuan 18 to 88.3 billion. The *Economic Information Daily* sums up the situation in a few figures: in 1995, 14 000 large and medium-sized enterprises had losses totalling yuan 35 billion – that is, approximately 34 per cent of the profit made by those performing well. Some 5–7 per cent of SOEs have long stopped production, partly or fully, and these employ 7.5 million people (9.38 per cent of the total workforce). A portion of workers were put on leave and sent home for as long as one year or more. In addition to 'on-leave' surplus labour, many firms had surplus workers in their active workforce as well. According to an International Labour Organisation (ILO) survey, 197 firms (or 66 per cent of those surveyed) reported having surplus labour in their active work force. Overall, for all firms, including those that did not believe they could cut jobs, managers estimated that on average they could reduce employment by 14 per cent without affecting output. In other words, more than 14 per cent of the entire industrial workforce covered in the survey was concealed unemployment or 'in-job' labour surplus (ILO Survey, 1996). A large quantity of the labour force was in a state of idleness, again causing a waste of labour resources.

In 1996, the share of loss-making enterprises was as high as 47 per cent and for the first time total losses of SOEs exceeded total profits; in the first quarter of 1997, losses increased another 11 per cent. Also, total outstanding debt increased by 11 per cent in 1996 and stood at yuan 495.9 billion (7 per cent of GDP) by the end of the year.

The major limits to a thorough reform of the SOE sector are, however, the employment problem, the lack of an adequate social security system, limited management capacities and the existing political power structures. Up to 30 million SOE employees are considered redundant, adding to the 100–130 million rural surplus workers. The employment situation is not truly reflected in the official figures, which report a relatively constant low rate of urban unemployment of 3 per cent, while actual unemployment among industrial workers is estimated by experts of the ILO at more than 21 per cent. Officially, more than 10 million factory workers lost their jobs in 1996, but only 5.3 million were re-employed. Total employment is reported, however, to have increased by 9 million (Podkaminer et al. 1997)

All across China, Beijing is trying to invigorate its lethargic state sector through experiments with management control. The goal is to create a stable of managers with enough entrepreneurial savvy to run the industrial behemoths when they are finally cut loose from state control. Transforming the system more broadly is an uphill challenge, and Beijing recently conceded defeat in its high-profile attempt to make 100 key enterprises responsible to shareholders. Overall, the slide continues. China's state sector is in worse shape now than at any other time in its 19 years of economic reform (*Far Eastern Economic Review*, 12 September 1996). Beijing is in fact investing in declining industries, and when that happens it chokes off growth. Beijing considers that it is stabilising the economy to keep those people employed, but with so many workers coming into the job market it is ultimately investing in instability. Many reformers recommend widespread bankruptcy, but that would tear an ugly gash in China's social fabric (for more details see, *China News Analysis*, 1 September, 1996; Wong, Heady and Woo, 1995). Nonetheless, at the 15th Party Congress in October 1997, the Party leadership decreed that China would bite the bullet and allow more widespread bankruptcies and unemployment.

THE COMMUNIST LEGACY

Before 1978 the Chinese government, through the State Council and its associated commissions, practised comprehensive central economic planning. The State Council was assigned responsibility for guiding economic development by drafting national economic plans and budgets and monitoring their implementation. Government intervention in the economy was pervasive, and central economic planners tried to make most of the decisions concerning consumption, production, employment, income distribution and investment. Production targets were directly assigned to SOEs and indirectly to collective firms and rural production units. Sources of inputs, including raw materials and machinery for both agriculture and industry, were controlled by the central authorities. Prices of goods and services were set by the central and local governments with little reference to their cost of production and relative scarcities.

This Soviet-type central planning by the central government resulted in gross economic inefficiency and slow growth for 30 years. Problems inherent in this economic system were partially recognised but not resolved by two cycles of centralisation and decentralisation of economic control over the period. Occasional moves to decentralisation sought to transfer some control from central to local governments without greater reliance on market forces. Vacillation over planning by the central government resulted in poorly administered economic activities and disorder across the regions.

The economic growth achieved was largely the result of increasing the amounts of labour, capital and land employed, but there was little growth in factor productivity, or in per capita income or living standards. The problems confronting the Chinese economy were similar to the problems encountered by other centrally-planned economies, and these problems were greatly exacerbated by the attempts at self-sufficiency which led to an inward orientation of the economy. Irrational pricing and isolation from foreign competition also aggravated distortions created by the quantitative target planning, increasing overstaffing and inefficiency in production and an emphasis on product quantity and not quality. Biases against individual incentives and labour specialisation bolstered by rigid restrictions on the mobility of labour, the assignment of jobs and the system of lifetime employment led to low labour productivity. Service sectors, following Marxist theory, were neglected. The financial sector was underdeveloped as were transport and trade.

FISCAL MANAGEMENT

Changes in the structure of the Chinese economy and decentralisation of central government power had a great influence on the role of the government budget. In 1978, government budgetary revenues at all levels came to 35.3 per cent of GNP; in 1995 the comparable figure was only around 12 per cent. Government savings were negative. This has been of considerable concern for the Chinese government, especially when the transfer of responsibility of enterprises had been completed by the mid-1980s, but the share of revenue in GNP continued to decline (Table 3–4). Trends in business savings are hard to ascertain due to a lack of data, but it seems that enterprises' capacity to save has increased at a declining rate, as indicated by the trend in enterprise income during 1986–90. This is corroborated by a similar trend in industrial profits. One possible reason for the slowdown is the increase in losses due partly to the distorted price system but mainly to poor management. In addition, enterprises' profits are squeezed from various sources, such as the burden of support for retired and disabled employees.

Table 3.4 *China: central government's budget deficit, 1979–93 (yuan bn)*

Year	Revenue	Expenditure	Deficit	Revenue/ GDP	Expenditure/ GDP
1978	112.1	111.1	1.0	31.2	31.0
1979	110.3	127.4	−17.1	27.7	31.9
1980	108.5	121.2	−12.7	24.3	27.1
1981	108.9	111.5	−2.6	22.8	23.4
1982	112.4	115.3	−2.9	21.6	22.2
1983	124.9	129.2	−4.3	21.5	22.2
1984	150.2	154.6	−4.4	21.6	22.2
1985	186.6	184.5	2.1	21.8	21.6
1986	226.0	233.1	−7.1	23.3	24.0
1987	236.8	244.9	−8.1	21.0	21.7
1988	262.8	270.7	−7.9	18.7	19.3
1989	294.8	304.0	−9.2	18.5	19.1
1990	331.3	345.2	−13.9	18.7	19.5
1991	358.3	381.4	−23.0	18.1	19.3
1992	394.1	414.1	−20.0	15.0	15.7

Sources: State Bureau of Statistics, *Statistical Yearbook of China*, China Statistical Publishing House, Beijing, pp. 31, 209, 1992; Ministry of Finance, *Ministry of Finance Data*, Ministry of Finance, Beijing, 1994.

Scaled to GNP, budgetary revenues have fallen steadily to about one-third of their 1978 level, and under the pressure of this erosion in revenue budgetary expenditures have also been cut back. Overt deficits have been kept to moderate levels: between 2 and 3 per cent of GNP in most years including 1995 (*Beijing Review*, 3–16 April 1996). Deficits of this size are not in themselves enough to destabilise an economy, but they are enough to largely eliminate the ability of policy-makers to use fiscal policy to affect the macroeconomy.

As revenues and expenditure are closely related, the changes in revenues have had a big impact on the reduction in overall budgetary outlays. Reductions in expenditure have been concentrated in investment, defence outlays and subsidies. Budgetary outlays for investment were at their highest in 1978 at 16.2 per cent of GNP and have declined steadily since to only 2.6 per cent of GNP in 1995. Military expenditures peaked in 1979 at 5.6 per cent of GNP and declined to 1.2 per cent of GNP in 1995. Subsidies, including price subsidies and subventions to loss-making SOEs, peaked in 1981 at 8.2 per cent of GNP and declined to 1.4 per cent of GNP by 1995 (*Beijing Review*, 3–16 April 1996). By contrast, government current expenditures have been maintained at almost exactly 10 per cent of GNP throughout the entire reform period. Despite the dramatic decline in revenues, the share of GNP allocated to administration, education and other ordinary government sectors has been maintained, thus the total revenue allocated to these sectors has also dropped dramatically.

The main cause of the decline in budgetary revenues is clearly the result of plummeting remittances from the industrial SOEs. Also part of the problem was the old tax and budgetary system, under which SOE profit remittances funded the bulk of government activities. Since January 1994, a new tax system has been established which creates a nearly uniform value-added tax and profit tax that applies equally to all ownership forms.

A serious problem faced by the Chinese leadership in the process of economic reform was that of inflation. Table 3.5 shows the annual rates of change in retail prices, market prices and the implicit GNP delator in the period 1980–90. None of these indicators accurately measure changes in the general price level, either because of their limited coverage or because of shortcomings in the methods of calculation. Nevertheless, it is clear that inflationary pressures made themselves felt in 1980, 1985 and 1988–89. The situation in 1988–89 was particularly serious; in 1988 market prices surged by more than 30 per cent over the preceding year. Unlike previous increases in 1950 and

Table 3.5 *China: inflation, 1980–90 (% increase over preceding year)*

	Retail prices	Market prices	GNP deflator
1980	6.0	2.0	3.7
1981	2.4	6.6	2.2
1982	1.9	3.5	0
1983	1.5	4.1	1.4
1984	2.8	0.3	4.6
1985	8.8	16.9	9.0
1986	6.0	7.7	4.6
1987	7.3	15.8	5.0
1988	18.5	31.9	11.8
1989	17.8	9.7	9.2
1990	2.1	..	4.1
1991	2.9	..	−1.5

.. = not available.

Source: State Statistical Bureau, *Statistics of China's Commerce and External Economics Relations* (*1952–88*), Almanac of China's Finance and Banking, Beijing, various years.

1960, inflation in the 1980s occurred during a period of rapid economic growth and restructuring, as well as opening up to the outside world. This makes the causes of the inflation unclear, as well as the extent to which it was related to economic reform. The same factors, however, may also exert pressure on the economy in the 1990s.

Inflation is a complex phenomenon, particularly in China where reforms caused political and economic forces to interact generating a mixture of open and repressed inflationary pressures, excess aggregate demand fuelled by monetary expansion, rising wages outstripping productivity increases, persistent structural imbalances and ineffective macroeconomic policies. However, it appears that excess demand rather than cost-push was the principle cause, even though other factors contributed to the problem.

In recent years the government's target of keeping the inflation rate below 10 per cent has been accomplished; the target of a 'soft landing' of the economy was achieved in 1996. The rate of inflation was more than halved, from 14.8 per cent in 1995 to 6.1 per cent if retail prices, the official measure, are considered, and from 17.1 to 8.3 per cent if the consumer price index is taken. However, a substantial increase in stock is reported, which means that the effective rate of growth of the economy is somewhat lower. Exports declining considerably during the first half of the year (−8.2 per cent), slowly started to recover in

1997 (Podkaminer et al. 1997). In 1997 the Chinese economy was expected to grow slightly faster than in 1996.

   The rapid decline of inflation was mainly due to the lower growth in the prices of consumer durables and was helped by a bumper grain harvest for the second consecutive year. In certain categories of consumer durables, for example electric household equipment and electronics, prices fell even in absolute terms due to an oversupply caused by the overinvestment during the boom period 1992–94 and due to sluggish demand. The latter can be explained by the fact that the income of urban households, which is on average more than double that of rural residents, increased at only a moderate rate of 3.4 per cent after allowing for inflation. Given the increased income inequality, this has left many urban families worse off than in 1995. However, rural per capita income increased much faster (8 per cent), and total retail trade was up 13 per cent, even more than in 1995.

FOREIGN TRADE

Before the reforms were begun, China was an insignificant participant in international markets for goods and capital. China's foreign trade system was set up originally as a state monopoly according to the principles set down by Lenin. The foreign trade sector was highly centralised, with all decisions made by the central government's Foreign Trade Ministry, which had branches at provincial and local government levels. In 1977, the sum of imports and exports, or its total trade turnover, was less than $US15 billion and it was only the 30th largest exporting country in the world. As shown in Table 3.7, its share of world trade in that year was only 0.6 per cent, significantly less then in 1927–29 when China's trade attained its peak pre-communist levels, accounting for a little more than 2 per cent of world trade. China's role as a trading nation on the eve of reform was also significantly less than it had been in the 1950s when the Communist party launched its ambitious first five-year plan, which was heavily dependent on the Soviet Union (Lardy, 1994: 3–33).

   Foreign trade has been playing a more and more important role in China's economy; in 1995, exports accounted for 21 per cent of China's GNP. In other words, 21 per cent of China's national production was accomplished through export. China's export composition has also experienced a great change. Before 1980s, China's exports consisted mainly of primary goods, more than one-quarter of which

Table 3.6 *China: merchandise trade (selected years, 1927–93)*

Year	Volume in $US billions	% of world trade
1927	1.33	2.1
1928	1.53	2.3
1929	1.44	2.1
1953	2.37	1.5
1957	3.11	1.4
1959	4.38	1.9
1962	2.66	0.9
1970	4.59	0.7
1975	4.75	0.8
1977	14.80	0.6
1978	20.64	0.9
1980	38.14	0.9
1985	69.60	0.9
1990	115.41	1.6
1992	165.61	2.2
1993	195.72	2.5

Source: State Bureau of Statistics, *Statistical Yearbook of China*, China Statistical Publishing House, Beijing, various years; The Ministry of Foreign Economic Relations and Trade, *Trade Outlook*, Almanac of China's Foreign Economic Relation and Trade, Beijing, various years.

were energy products, especially oil. This situation has, however, changed dramatically. Energy exports dropped from 23.1 per cent in 1980 to 6.7 per cent in 1991, agricultural goods went from 24.7 per cent in 1980 to 15.8 per cent in 1991, and manufactured goods rose from 45.5 per cent in 1979 to 77.5 per cent in 1991 (*China Statistical Yearbook*, 1992), which was much higher than the average (30 per cent) for other low-income countries and comparable to the level of many 'upper-middle-income countries' (World Bank, 1985: 30) reflecting the improvement in China's export composition. During this period, labour-intensive and low-class manufactured goods were the mainstream of China's exports.

In the 1990s, the situation has been further improved. Capital-knowledge-intensive exports have been increasing. In 1995, machinery and electronic products rose to 30 per cent of the total exports from less than 10 per cent in 1988. Another interesting change has been occurring in China's weapons exports; since 1983, China has become the world's fourth largest seller of arms to the Third World. China's weapons sales rose to nearly 5 per cent between 1982 and 1988, from less than 1 per cent in 1978 (Harding, 1992). In 1987 the

Chinese military's chief arms-trading company, Poly Group Corp., sold more than $US500 million in weapons. Some analysts believed that Poly was instrumental in the sale of CSS-2 intermediate-range ballistic missiles to Saudi Arabia in 1987, a deal estimated at more than $US2 billion (*Far Eastern Economic Review*, 12 September 1996).

Capital goods are regarded as the chief goal of China's importing strategy, although in most years since 1979 capital goods comprised only about 40 per cent of total imports, even less than that in 1950. This may reflect the fact that China's dependence on foreign technology has decreased somewhat, and to some degree it is a consequence of the policy to reduce imports of complete sets of equipment. According to official statistics, imports of technology reached $US27 billion in the 1980s and were distributed throughout 75 sectors and all provinces. It is difficult to evaluate exactly how much of a role the imported technology has played in China's economic development due to the absence of enough statistical material. According to official opinion, it has remarkably improved China's technological level and narrowed the existing technological gap between China and developed countries. An estimation made by an official in China's National Planning Committee is that about 60 per cent of added GNP every year was attributed to increased efficiency created by the introduction of technology. It is also said that most of the 329 products that were awarded national prizes in 1989 had some relation to imported technology. Since 1984, each US dollar import of technology created a production value of RMB 3.9, tax income RMB 0.91 and foreign exchange earnings $US0.19 (*People's Daily*, August 1990). The total product value created by the import of technology reached RMB 87.42 billion. The imported technology has built up China's export ability. Now China is exporting such products as televisions, refrigerators and tape-recorders, produced by imported production lines. A survey released in 1990 reports that 13 per cent of the equipment in all Chinese enterprises, and approximately 15 600 types of products, reached world standards due to the introduction of Western technology (*People's Daily*, August 1990). The import of technology, Chinese economists believed, had enabled China to narrow its technological gap with Western countries in many industrial sectors.

Industrial raw materials and semi-finished manufactured goods constitute the largest proportion of total imports; in most years the proportion was 40–60 per cent. This pattern of imports is very similar to that of developed countries and dissimilar to that of developing countries. China has a large territory and is rich in resources, but the endowment per capita is quite limited. This situation has been worsened by the inefficient use of resources and the pattern of industrialisation started in the 1950s, which emphasises resource-hungry industries. Resource use per unit of GNP in China was almost three times as high as in developed countries; as a result the higher the growth rate of the economy, the greater the import of raw materials.

From 1984 to 1988, when the average annual growth rate of its GNP was 11.56 per cent, a vast quantity of rolled steel, totalling 73 million tonnes, was imported (*Statistical Yearbook for Asia and Pacific 1982–89*, 1990). After 1990 a new phenomenon emerged. Most of the foreign direct investment, especially from Hong Kong and Taiwan, was being concentrated on assembly and processing projects, and was therefore heavily dependent on imports of semi-finished products. Thus, the growing number of foreign-funded projects importing raw materials and semi-finished products increased. This trend will probably continue for years. A research report of the Institute of Economic Reform Studies in the State Council says, 'China's rapid economic development was based on its large quantity of imports' (*World Economic Herald*, July 1987).

From the early 1960s to the early 1980s, China purchased large quantities of grain from abroad to supplement inadequate domestic harvests. Alongside this, consumer goods accounted for only 15–25 per cent of total imports before 1983. The rural reform started in the early 1980s enabled China to drastically reduce imports of foodstuffs, which had fallen from approximately 20 per cent of total imports in 1983 to about 3.4 per cent in 1986. After 1987, however, the stagnation in economic reform led China to increase its imports of grain again, so that total imports rose to 4.4 per cent in 1991. It is expected that China will continue to increase its imports of grain until the end of this century. In the mid-1980s, China's imports of durable consumer goods increased noticeably, rising from about 1 per cent of total imports in 1978 to more than 5 per cent in 1984 and 1985 before dropping off slightly in 1986. The imports of automobiles rose to 7.6 per cent in 1985 from less than 1 per cent in 1980 (*China Statistical Yearbook*, 1992).

After 1987, the Chinese government tightened the imports of durable consumer goods again. Moreover, the imported production lines of these goods have been put into production successfully. As a result, the imports of durable consumer goods dropped to 2.59 per cent of total imports and automobiles to 1.9 per cent in 1988. As the increase in imports of durable consumer goods did not completely offset the decline in purchasing of foreign foodstuffs, consumer products as a whole made up a smaller share of China's imports in the mid-1980s than they did between the 1970s and the early 1980s. Since the mid-1960s, Western countries have become China's major trading partners, but between 1987 and 1990 the West's dominant position has decreased marginally. Its contribution to China's imports dropped from 66.9 per cent in 1986 to 49.2 per cent in 1991 because China reduced its imports of durable consumer goods and automobiles, although retaining its imports of grain at a low level. The Western embargo after the Tiananmen Square massacre of 1989 was another factor. The proportion of China's exports to the West also dropped to 34.7 per cent in 1991 from 40.2 per cent in 1986 due to China's increasing export to Southeast Asian countries and the increased protectionism against China's labour-intensive exports (*China Statistical Yearbook*, 1992).

During the period 1979–89, China had a trade deficit with Western countries, while at the same time earning a surplus in trade with developing countries. However, China also began to earn a surplus in trade with most Western countries after 1990. Japan was China's largest trading partner (Table 3.7), with Japan's exports to China mostly consisting of machinery, steel, automobiles and other durable consumer goods. China's purchases from Japan were not fully offset by its exports, a majority of which were textiles, petroleum and coal.

Table 3.7   *China's top trading partners, 1994–96 (total trade in $US bn)*

	1994	1995	1996
Japan	47.9 (20.2%)	57.5 (20.5%)	59.8 (20.9%)
Hong Kong	41.8 (17.7%)	44.6 (15.9%)	46.8 (16.8%)
USA	35.4 (15.0%)	40.8 (14.5%)	44.8 (16.8%)
EU	31.5 (13.3%)	40.3 (14.4%)	43.9 (16.2%)
ASEAN	13.2 (5.6%)	18.4 (6.6%)	21.2 (8.7%)
Taiwan	16.3 (7.0%)	17.9 (6.4%)	18.8 (7.3%)
South Korea	11.7 (5.0%)	17.7 (6.0%)	18.5 (6.9%)
Russia	5.1 (2.2%)	5.5 (1.9%)	5.9 (2.1%)
Others	31.8 (14.0%)	32.3 (13.8%)	33.4 (13.5%)
Total	236.7 (100%)	280.8 (100%)	324.6 (100%)

Source: *The China Business Review, China Data*, Beijing, various issues.

Between 1978 and 1993 China ran huge trade deficits with Japan, except for one year. Although China reduced its imports of automobile, steel and durable consumer goods after 1987, the trade deficit with Japan was still a major issue in China's foreign trade. In 1993 this deficit accounted for 60 per cent of China's total trade deficit (*China Trade Report*, March 1996).

Hong Kong, China's second largest trading partner (between 1989 and 1992 Hong Kong was the largest ahead of Japan), comprised 17 per cent of China's total value of exports and imports in 1993. In 1989 this percentage reached 32.1 per cent. China earns a large trade surplus every year from Hong Kong. Of China's exports to Hong Kong about 40 per cent were consumed in the territory, while the remaining 60 per cent were re-exported to third-party countries like the United States and those countries (or areas) with whom China had no diplomatic or direct relations, such as South Korea (before 1993), Taiwan and Indonesia (before 1992). Similarly, about 75 per cent of China's imports from Hong Kong came from outside the territory (*China Statistical Year Book*, 1992).

The US share of China's trade increased from 6 per cent in 1978 to 14 per cent in 1993 (Table 3.8). From Chinese and UN statistics, China produced a trade deficit for all the years from 1978 to 1991. In 1993 China's trade surplus with the USA was $US22.8 billion. As mentioned above, some of China's exports to the USA were through third-country areas like Hong Kong. Therefore, according to US statistics, the USA had a large trade deficit with China after 1985; in 1993 this deficit was $US22.8 billion. That is

Table 3.8   *China–US trade, 1988–95 ($US bn)*

Year	US exports	US imports	US balance
1988	5.0	8.5	−3.5
1989	5.8	12.0	−6.2
1990	4.8	15.2	−10.4
1991	6.2	19.0	−12.8
1992	7.5	25.7	−18.3
1993	8.8	31.5	−22.8
1994	9.3	38.8	−29.5
1995	11.7	45.6	−33.9
1996	12.6	47.3	−34.7

Source: *The China Business Review, China Data*, Beijing, p. 41, May–June 1996 and 1997.

to say, a large amount of the surplus in trade with Hong Kong in China's statistics is actually China's surplus in trade with the United States (*The Central Daily*, July 1994 and *Newsweek*, May 1991).

Since 1984, China has also rapidly increased its trade with Taiwan and South Korea. In 1994 Taiwan was the fifth and South Korea the sixth largest trading partner of China. China has also expanded its trade with the former Soviet Union, the proportion of which, in China's total foreign trade, rose to 3.8 per cent in 1991 from 1.7 per cent in 1983 (*China Statistical Yearbook*, 1992). Trade with Russia has given China a more diversified set of partners, and China could thus export consumer goods that were unable to find a good market in Western countries. On the other hand, the Russians could sell industrial equipment which, though not the most advanced in the world, would be useful to Chinese enterprises. Rapidly expanding trade reminds the Russians of what can be gained from peaceful behaviour and a full normalisation of relations with China.

A Chinese economist has pointed out to me that given 'China's vast size, huge population, and large economy, it would be unrealistic to attempt to modernise the entire national economy through a growth in exports in the manner of the four little tigers in Asia'. For China, import substitution and export substitution would have to co-exist for a long time. It would appear that China can actually follow a policy of import substitution as a means of developing its capital and consumer goods, and it may also encourage the export of manufactured goods (Kleinberg, 1990). There is, therefore, the potential for the two forms to supplement and permeate each other.

* * *

POLAND: AN INTRODUCTION

In contrast to China's gradual reforms, Poland has embraced the swifter 'Big Bang' approach to economic reform. Profound institutional, economic and technological changes have occurred in the Polish economy since the launching of the radical economic programme in 1990. As a result, Poland has achieved stronger economic growth and has become a much more open economy, more strongly linked to the advanced economies of the OECD countries. Most macroeconomic performance indicators improved markedly during the transitional period (Table 3.9), a trend broadly confirmed so far in 1997. Per capita income in Poland has been rising rapidly over the past few years and present standards are close to one-third of the OECD average (valued at purchasing power parity exchange rates).

In 1991–95, the Polish economy grew more than twice as fast as the OECD average. Growth became increasingly broad-based, even though sharp sectoral contrasts persisted. To a large extent, the strength of the expansion resulted from rapid integration with Western Europe and into the world economy at large, as witnessed by an upsurge in exports and imports (Figure 3.1). Helped by improving profitability and tax inducements, fixed investment boomed, and in 1995 its contribution to the expansion of GDP stood at a par with that of household consumption, boding well for future growth potential.

Table 3.9 *Poland: macroeconomic indicators, 1991–96 (% growth rates)*

	1991	1992	1993	1994	1995	1996
Real GDP	−7.0	2.6	3.8	5.2	7.0	5.5
Consumption	7.5	3.5	4.6	3.0	4.5	4.0
Gross fixed investment	−4.5	2.8	2.9	9.2	19.0	23.1
Government spending	−26.6	10.4	−2.8	3.7	3.6	3.5
Export revenues	−1.7	10.8	1.0	20.5	21.4	25.8
Industrial output	−11.9	2.8	6.4	12.1	9.4	10.6
Agricultural output	−1.6	−12.7	6.8	−9.3	13.0	14.2
Unemployment rate	11.9	13.6	16.4	16.0	14.9	12.7
Budget deficit (% of GDP)	3.8	6.0	2.8	2.7	2.7	2.6
Consumer price index	70.0	43.0	35.3	32.2	27.8	16.8
Gross profit margin (%)	4.6	2.1	2.8	4.1	4.2	4.8
Net profit margin	−1.3	−1.5	−0.5	1.7	2.0	2.6

Source: Warsaw School of Economics, *Poland–International Economic Report*, World Economy Research Institute, Warsaw, 1997, p. 39

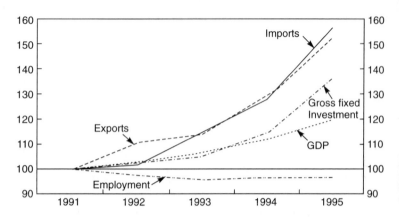

Figure 3.1   Poland: the take-off (index 1991 = 100)

Source: Centre for Eastern Europe, *Poland–OECD Economic Surveys*,
OECD, Paris, 1997, p. 14

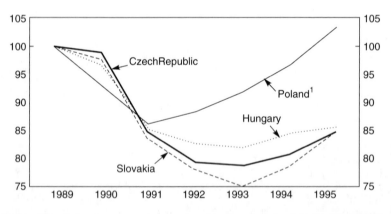

Figure 3.2   Poland: output – international comparison (real GDP, 1989 = 100)

[1]The revised estimate for 1990 is used here (smaller decline)
Source: Central Statistical Office, OECD.

Poland was the first among the countries in Central and Eastern
Europe (CEE) to recover following the initial output collapse associated with transition (Figure 3.2). The pace of real GDP growth rose
continuously from 1992, reaching 5.2 per cent in 1994 and 7 per cent
in 1995. Actual growth thus significantly exceeded the projections for
1994 (4.5 per cent) and 1995 (5.0 per cent) included in the *Strategy for
Poland* (Table 3.10).

Table 3.10 *Strategy for Poland: macroeconomic framework**

	Targets in Strategy for Poland				Outcomes		
	1994	*1995*	*1996*	*1997*	*1994*	*1995*	*1996*
GDP	4.5	5.0	5.2	5.5	5.2	7.0	5.8
Consumption	3.1	3.3	3.6	3.6	3.9	4.1	4.0
Gross fixed investment	6.0	7.0	8.0	8.0	9.2	18.5	18.9
Export volume[1]	6.0	7.0	8.0	9.0	18.3	16.7	17.4
Imports volume[1]	2.5	4.0	5.2	6.0	13.4	20.5	21.6
Foreign trade balance (in % of GDP)[1]	−2.1	−1.7	−1.7	−1.5	−4.7	−5.2	−5.6
CPI (end year)	23.6	16.1	12.0	8.7	29.5	21.6	15.6
Employment	−0.3	0.7	1.3	2.0	1.1	0.3	0.8
Unemployment rate (in % of labour force, end year)[2]	17.2	16.7	15.6	14.0	16.0	14.0	12.4
Labour productivity	4.9	4.3	3.8	3.5	4.1	6.7	8.9
Average wage (gross)	1.5	2.8	3.0	3.1	1.6	4.6	3.4
Average pension (gross)	6.5	1.4	3.1	1.0	4.1	3.2	2.8
State budget revenue	5.3	4.3	4.8	5.5	7.1	4.4	5.3
State budget expenditure	8.0	8.4	1.8	2.1	6.7	4.2	3.8
State budget deficit (in % of GDP)	3.7	3.3	2.8	2.5	2.7	2.6	2.8
Public debt (in % of GDP)	77.7	76.9	74.1	72.4	69.5	56.2	54.3

Notes: [1]Customs-based, excluding unrecorded trade. In 1996, net unrecorded exports may have amounted to close to 5 per cent of GDP. [2] Registered unemployment. Figures are year-average real percentage changes unless noted.
Sources: Centre for Eastern Europe, *Poland – Economic Surveys*, OECD, Paris, 1997, p. 15; Ministry of Finance, *Strategy for Poland*, Warsaw, June 1994; GUS, *Macroeconomic Indicators*, Central Statistical Office, Warsaw, various years.

Growth has become increasingly broad-based as the expansion has unfolded. Whereas in aggregate terms growth was initially confined to private firms, output in state-owned enterprises (SOEs) also bounced back starting around 1994. In industry, the volume of sales by private entities, which had soared by 34 per cent annually in 1991–93, rose further by 26 per cent annually in 1994–95. Sales of industrial state-owned enterprises (SOEs), which had continued to contract through 1993, picked up in 1994, rising by 4 per cent. In 1995 they shrank by 1 per cent. However, the underlying performance of SOEs is understand by these figures which do not take into account privatisation, and those figures of private firms are correspondingly overstated. If changes in name were taken into account, it would probably appear that activity in SOEs continued to expand in 1995, albeit more slowly than in 1994.

Striking contrasts across broad sectors of the economy persisted in 1994 when value-added was rising by 10 per cent in industry, but growth was negative in trade, transportation and construction (Table 3.11). Agricultural value-added collapsed by 15 per cent in 1994, largely because of a severe drought. 1996 growth rates were slightly more uniform, with value-added increasing by 5.9 per cent in trade, 8.6 per cent in construction and 13 per cent in industry. Agricultural output rebounded, with value-added up almost 12 per cent, reflecting a much better harvest (OECD, 1997). Within industry, more

Table 3.11   *Poland: growth of value-added by sector (in %)*[1]

	Share in GDP 1992	1993	1994	1995	1996
Agriculture, forestry, fishing	6.8	5.7	−14.9	11.6	12.3
Industry	34.0	8.8	10.3	9.9	12.8
Construction	7.8	1.1	2.7	7.3	8.6
Trade and repair of consumer goods	13.1	5.8	−1.5	4.4	5.9
Hotels and restaurants	0.4	2.3	7.3	5.9	8.7
Transport, storage and communication	6.2	−5.3	0.5	3.1	5.4
Financial intermediations	0.5	29.1	102.1	19.4	34.6
Public administration and defence	6.1	5.2	7.8	4.1	3.6
Education	3.8	0.1	10.3	1.4	3.2
Health care and social security	4.2	0.5	4.1	2.9	3.4
Other	13.0	−8.4	5.2	3.9	3.4

[1]   preliminary.
Source: Centre for Eastern Europe, *Poland–Economic Surveys*, OECD, Paris, 1997, p. 16; GUS, *Bulletin Statystyczny*, Central Statistical Office, Warsaw, various years.

and more branches participated in the overall expansion: the number of major products for which output was still declining dropped from 36 out of 62 in 1992 to 16 in 1994–95 (see Appendix, Table A3.1(a)). The fastest growth in gross output was recorded in manufacturing, up 13 per cent in 1994 and 12 per cent in 1995 (Figure 3.3). The more dynamic industries included several technology-intensive ones, such as electronics, telecommunications equipment, automative, precision instruments and machinery.

At the regional level as well, an increasing number of *voivodships* (Polish administrative areas) experienced growth, with gross industrial output rising in almost two-thirds of the 49 *voivodships* in 1992, and in all but one by 1994. At the same time, the dispersion of regional growth rates declined, while the proportion of *voivodships* recording double-digit growth rates surged from one-quarter to two-thirds. In 1995, however, as the pace of industrial growth nationwide decreased from 13 to 9 per cent, the dispersion of regional growth rates rose anew. In cumulative terms, the dispersion has been considerable, implying that disparities at the yearly frequency did not mainly reflect a lack of short-run synchronisation across *voivodships*, but that significant and lasting differences in dynamism merged. Indeed, industrial output declined by 10 per cent between 1991 and 1995 in the most depressed area (*Legnickie voivodship*) and surged by 40 per cent in the most dynamic one (*Nowosadeckie voivodship*).

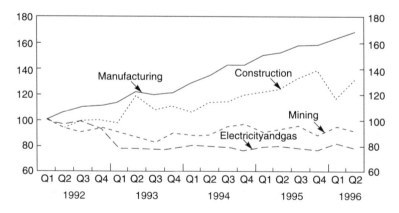

Figure 3.3 Poland: production in the main industrial sectors (1992 Q1=100, seasonally adjusted)

Source: Centre for Eastern Europe, *Poland – Economic Surveys*, OECD, Paris, 1997, p. 17.

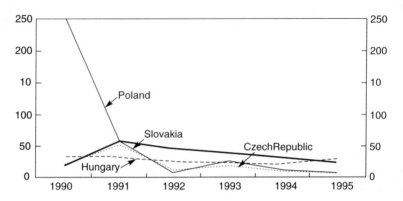

Figure 3.4 Poland: inflation – international comparison (CPI, end-year
percentage change)
Source: Central Statistical Office, OECD.

Since the liberalisation of most prices in 1989–90, inflation has been
steadily declining, and by the end of 1996 the 12-month CPI inflation
rate was down to its lowest point since 1987, reaching 13.8 per cent.
Sporadic short-run deviations from these trends have been observed,
linked to seasonal factors, supply-side shocks or tax measures, but on
the whole inflation has been sustained, if extremely gradual (Figure
3.4). Inflation has, however, been slower than targeted by the government in its budgets: the end-year CPI inflation objectives for 1994–95
were exceeded by large margins, with outcomes of 29.5 per cent in
1994 (against a target of 23 per cent) and 21.6 per cent in 1995 (against
a target of 17 per cent), but in 1996 this fell to 13.8 per cent. Overall,
inflation remained much higher than in the Czech Republic and
Slovakia, but came down below the level recorded in Hungary (Figure
3.4). Relatively tight financial policies, including effective hard budget
constraints, have contributed to maintain the disinflation trend in the
1996–97 period.

ECONOMIC STRUCTURE

Between 1989 and 1996, the nature of the Polish economy changed
radically. The structure of the supply side changed considerably during the first half of the 1990s, largely due to shifts in relative prices. At
the broadest level, the share of services in output soared from 35 per

cent to 53 per cent, while that of industry declined from 44 per cent to 33 per cent (see Table 3.12). The share of agriculture fell from 13 per cent in 1989 to 7 per cent in 1996. By 1995, the share of services was still below the OECD average of approximately 68 per cent. The share of agriculture stood at about the same level as in New Zealand, Ireland and Portugal.

The decline in value-added was relatively larger in industry in 1990–91, and the subsequent recovery swifter. At a more disaggregated level, the relative importance of the various branches within industry underwent durable changes; for example, the share of mining and quarrying plummeted between 1989 and 1995 from 13 to 5 per cent.

Turning to the structure of supply by ownership types, the shares of the private sector doubled over the period under consideration, from 28 per cent in 1989 to 56 per cent in 1996. It had thus regained most of the ground lost under central planning. On the employment side, the share of private activity rose less, from 47 per cent in 1989 to 65 per cent in 1996. Even in traditionally wholly public services such as health care and education, the share of private providers is no longer trivial. The change in the composition of output and the increase in the role of private entities reflected to a large extent the dynamism of

Table 3.12: *Poland: main indicators of economic structure*

Population (millions)	38.6
GDP per head (PPS-1995)	5300
as % of EU-15 average (per cent, 1995)	31
Structure of production: share in total gross value-added (per cent)	
agriculture	7.6
industry	33.3
services	53.1
construction	6.0
Gross foreign debt/GDP (per cent)	32
Exports of goods & services/GDP (per cent)	22
Stock of FDI* (billion)	4.0
per head (ecu)	100

Note: All data for 1996 unless otherwise indicated;* FDI stock converted at end-1996 exchange rate of ecu 1=$US1.25299.
Sources: EU Commission, *Poland–EU Membership*, EU Commission Services, Brussels, July 1997, p. 18; Centre for Poland Transformation, *Poland–Statistical Report*, European Bank for Reconstructing and Development (EBRD), London, 1997.

new private firms, particularly the smaller ones. The number of businesses soared in the early 1990s, helped by relatively liberal rules governing the establishment of new ventures. At the end of 1996, the Polish economy counted over two million enterprises. The greater vitality of smaller and leaner firms has translated into a decline in the relative importance of the larger ones.

The recomposition of output has reflected the change in the nature and content of demand. State orders, rationing through official channels and partly compensatory transactions in shadow markets ceased. Likewise, the rules governing foreign trade were completely overhauled, giving rise to new export and import potential and confronting domestic producers with heightened competitive pressures.

Among domestic components of aggregate demand, a major shift involved the rebalancing of investment and consumption. At current prices, the share of gross fixed capital formation in GDP declined from 22 per cent in the mid-1980s to about 17 per cent in 1995, and that of stockbuilding from 7 per cent to 1 per cent, while the share of total consumption expanded from 70 to 82 per cent. To some extent, the contraction in the share of total investment was the manifestation of a permanent shift from the inefficient regime of over-accumulation of capital and repressed consumption to a less constrained and more balanced one. Consumption patterns also changed considerably, as the choices faced by consumers expanded. Within household consumption, the assortment of foods purchased underwent major changes. At the same time, the share of housing, commuting and health care expenditures increased sharply, reflecting the commercialisation of heretofore heavily subsidised or simple public services.

The share of foreign trade in GDP increased significantly between 1989 and 1996, with exports of goods and services rising from 19 per cent to 26 per cent and imports from 15 per cent to 24 per cent on a national accounts basis. Import penetration in industry doubled, with imports rising from 14.5 per cent of industrial sales in 1989 to 30 per cent in 1996, while the share of exports in industrial sales increased from 14 per cent to 23 per cent in 1996. At the same time, dramatic changes occurred in the direction and content of external trade. Geographically, the lifting of the corset imposed by the former Council for Mutual Economic Assistance (CMEA) and the recessions in the other transitional countries prompted a massive switch from East to West. The share of trade with OECD countries rose from one-half to three-quarters, while that with other countries of Central and Eastern Europe declined sharply.

The composition of trade flows also changed considerably during the first half of the 1990s. Based on a classification of goods according to the 21 lines of the EU combined nomenclature, the share of natural resource-intensive exports declined (to 45 per cent). So did the share of exports embodying a relatively large proportion of skilled labour, capital and technology (to 33 per cent). Correspondingly, the share of exports intensive in low-skill labour rose by 10 percentage points, consistent with the increasing importance of outward processing.

On the import side, the share of natural resource-intensive purchases dropped by 7 percentage points. The share of imports intensive in skilled labour, capital and technology remained stable, at close to one-half. On this very aggregated basis, Poland by 1995 had revealed a comparative advantage in sectors intensive in low-skilled labour and natural resources.

Privatisation and Enterprise Restructuring

Moving to a market economy is clearly intimately linked with the privatisation of state-owned property and the restructuring of production processes. For the economy as a whole, it is estimated that 60 per cent of GDP (EU Report, 1997: 23) is generated in the private sector. The 'small-scale' privatisation of retail, catering and service sectors was more or less completed between 1990 and 1992. The 'Large-scale' privatisation, on the other hand, was slow to take off; up to now, few of the large enterprises have actually completed the privatisation process. The private sector's share in the creation of industrial output reached 52 per cent in 1996. Privatisation is slow in the energy and telecommunication sectors and is strongly resisted in the area of postal and transport services. The process was given some impetus in 1995 with the launch of the mass privatisation programme through the sale of vouchers.

The relatively slow start of large-scale privatisation does not mean that changes in the economy as a whole have not taken place; indeed some large enterprises have succeeded in restructuring to a certain extent while remaining state-owned. However, the extension of the private sector has to large extent come from the birth of new enterprises. This was made possible by the liberal rules on establishing businesses, modest tax incentives, decentralised trade policies and currency convertibility.

The speed of restructuring depends in part on the access to new investment. This can be accumulated through retained earnings, borrowed domestically, acquired through sales of shares or brought in from abroad. Due to the slow privatisation of large enterprises, the borrowing of enterprises has been rather limited, but FDI has recently begun to flow into Poland as opportunities for investment have expanded (for further details about SOEs and privatisation see Dabrowski, 1995; Quaisser, Woodward and Blaszczyk, 1995; Ernst, Alexeev and Marer, 1996).

THE COMMUNIST LEGACY

Before 1989, the Polish economy struggled through a decade of mounting political and economical problems due mainly to the effects of central planning and ideological constraints by the Communist Party. Planning became largely a personalised bargaining process of the 'vanguard party' which degenerated into personality cults and abuses of position by the nomenklatura. The deep inefficiencies of planning became increasingly evident with time. Heavy industries such as machine building and metallurgy were emphasised, while development of consumer goods lagged. SOEs had compulsory targets, administrative allocation of inputs, very limited autonomy, arbitrary shifting of assets and appointment of management by the party bodies (Balcerowicz, 1995).

Decades of bureaucratic allocation created serious distortions, with some sectors (particularly heavy industry) massively overbuilt and others (light industry and services) severely repressed. Relative prices diverged greatly from market patterns, and this meant massive explicit or implicit subsidies among sectors. Energy, housing, public transport and staple foods were extraordinarily cheap, whereas consumer manufactures, if available at all, were often shoddy. Pervasive shortages allowed firms to operate in sellers' markets and reduce incentives to improve quality. With near complete state ownership, enterprises lacked the defined property rights that spur work-effort and profit-making in market economies. Firms had little reason to use inputs efficiently, and strong incentives to hoard both labour and raw materials. Many firms added negative value; at world prices the cost of their inputs would have exceeded the value of their output.

In 1980, food price increases led to a series of strikes inspired by the union-led Solidarity movement. Poland defaulted on its international debt obligations. Unable to service one of the highest foreign debts in the world for over a decade, it could not borrow abroad anymore. The state-controlled part of the economy stagnated completely, and acute shortages occurred, even of basic commodities. The country was heading for hyperinflation and economic collapse. Given this background, the Polish authorities had little choice but to embark on an ambitious stabilisation programme in 1990, designed to arrest the decline in the currency (zloty) and to stabilise overall price levels.

FISCAL MANAGEMENT

Fiscal reform was crucial as the role of the government was redefined and the revenue sources changed. The reform of the tax system was radical and rapid: corporate tax, income tax and VAT were introduced by 1993. Changes in the social security system were also begun, but further reforms were required as the deficit of social security funds continued to increase.

Total expenditure was about 50 per cent of GDP. Subsidies to firms, which in the 1980s formed a high percentage of government expenditure, still constituted 6 per cent of GDP in 1992. Explicit subsidies in the government budget have since been reduced to less then 2 per cent of GDP. Enterprise support has recently reemerged in the context of restructuring programmes, mainly for the coal sector and for toxic waste containment. Implicit subsidies in the form of tax and social security arrears have also not been completely eliminated and new exemptions have been created by the establishment of free economic zones. Since 1993, the cash deficits of the state budget and of the general government (that is including local budgets, social security and other extra-budgetary funds) have remained below 3 per cent of GDP, even excluding privatisation receipts other than leasing revenue (amounting to 0.8 per cent of GDP in 1995) (see Table 3.13 and Appendix, Table A3.1(b) for a more detailed account of Poland's national budget).

Both in 1994 and 1995, higher-than-projected growth and inflation helped contain the deficit of the state budget below target. The growth bonus broadened the real tax base. The net impact of extra inflation was also positive, as in the short run the expenditure side of the budget was less indexed than the revenue side. Fiscal intakes, however, did not rise as much as the size of the unexpected increase in nominal GDP might have suggested, since exports and investments, which are relatively lightly taxed, turned out to contribute more than projected to growth, and also as a result of tariff cuts and falling

Table 3.13 *Poland: general government revenues, expenditures and balance*
(% of GDP)

State budget	1990	1991	1992	1993	1994	1995	1996
Total revenue[1]	34.8	43.9	45.1	47.6	48.3	47.8	48.2
Including transfers	34.8	26.1	27.2	29.5	30.0	29.3	29.3
Excluding transfers	34.8	25.9	27.1	29.4	30.0	29.2	29.3
Local budgets	..	4.6	3.9	4.5	4.5	4.5	4.9
Extra-budgetary funds	11.3	10.4	10.9	10.5	10.8	11.0	11.6
State extra-budgetary units	1.8	1.9	1.6	1.5	1.4	1.4	1.2
Local extra-budgetary units	..	0.9	1.7	1.8	1.6	1.7	1.6
Total expenditure[1]	45.1	45.8	50.0	49.9	50.5	49.7	50.9
Including transfers	34.6	29.9	33.2	32.3	32.7	31.9	31.8
Excluding transfers	26.9	20.5	21.3	20.7	20.6	21.7	21.8
Local budgets	..	4.3	4.2	4.6	5.4	5.4	6.2
Extra-budgetary funds	16.2	17.9	20.8	20.7	20.9	19.2	19.6
State extra-budgetary units	2.0	1.6	1.3	1.4	1.2	1.2	1.1
Local extra-budgetary units	..	1.5	2.4	2.6	f 2.4	2.3	2.2
Total balance[1]	2.8	−2.0	−4.9	−2.3	−2.2	−1.8	−2.8
Including transfers	0.2	−3.8	−6.0	−2.8	−2.7	−2.6	−2.7
Excluding transfers	7.9	5.4	5.8	8.7	9.3	7.6	7.3
Local budgets	..	0.3	−0.3	−1.2	−1.0	−0.9	−1.3
Extra-budgetary funds	−5.0	−7.4	−9.9	−10.2	−10.1	−8.1	−8.1
State extra-budgetary units	−0.2	0.3	0.3	0.1	0.2	0.2	−0.1
Local extra-budgetary units	..	−0.6	−0.7	−0.8	−0.7	−0.6	−0.7
Memorandum items: nominal GDP (in bn zloty)	56.0	80.9	114.9	155.8	210.4	286.0	344.6

Notes: [1] Excluding transfers between the state budget, local budgets, extra-budgetary funds and extra-budgetary units; .. = not available.
Source: Centre for Eastern Europe, *Poland – Economic Surveys*, OECD, Paris, 1997, p. 37.

National Bank of Poland (NBP) profits. In the circumstances, the absence of a tangible improvement in the fiscal deficit in 1995, which would have helped mitigate the inflationary impact of money growth, was somewhat disappointing. The other general government bodies, after transfers from the state budget, displayed a small surplus amounting to 0.5 per cent of GDP in 1994 and 0.8 per cent of GDP in

1995 (OECD Economic Survey, 1997). Developments in this area are dominated by the finances of social security, which account for over two-thirds of the general government expenditures incurred outside the state budget. While contributions were buoyed by the swift growth of the wages bill, outlays also grew rapidly.

Fiscal decentralisation made some headway. A number of expenditures were in the process of being devolved from the central to the local level, with a view to improving efficiency by having decisions taken at administrative levels closer to the final expenditure point. In particular, a November 1995 law transferred a number of tasks (including road maintenance, the running of primary schools, social assistance facilities, local health care services and local cultural institutions) from the centre to 46 large cities (in line with a pilot programme launched in 1994). The law also provided for the transfer of financial resources, *inter alia*, in the form of the allocation to those cities of a share of the personal income tax.

FOREIGN TRADE

The collapse of communism and the demise of 'international' institutions created by the USSR to control its client states, resulted in a breakdown of trade patterns established in the 1949–89 period. Between 1990 and 1995, annual per capita recorded trade in goods and non-factor services (export plus imports) rose from less then $US600 to close to $US1400. At the same time, trade rose from 14 per cent to 23 per cent of GDP measured in purchasing power parity (PPP) terms. By 1996, Poland's share in world trade came close to its share in world population (0.7 per cent). Likewise, the rapid expansion of exports brought Poland close to where its size (population) and income level (PPP per capita GDP) would predict based on cross-country experience (Table 3.14).

Despite a certain increase, Poland's share in the international division of labour is still small, and higher for imports than for exports. The economy's pro-import orientation is additionally reflected by the foreign trade share in Poland's GDP and the value of trade in per capita terms, even though disproportions between imports and exports have slightly narrowed over the last few years.

During the initial two years of the transformation-cum-stabilisation programme, launched by the first non-communist government on 1 January 1990, the reorientation of Polish trade was swift and dramatic. Imports from the Soviet Union and other CMEA (Council for

Table 3.14 *Poland: trade contribution to economic growth, 1990–95*

	1990	1991	1992	1993	1994	1995	1996
Share of global trade (%)							
Imports	0.28	0.38	0.42	0.48	0.49	0.55	0.59
Exports	0.42	0.36	0.36	0.37	0.41	0.47	0.51
Total	0.35	0.37	0.39	0.41	0.45	0.51	0.53
Share in trade in GDP (%)							
Imports	14.9	20.2	19.3	20.9	23.1	25.8	26.4
Exports	16.5	19.2	15.7	13.7	18.5	20.7	21.4
Per capita trade in $US							
Imports	250	406	416	490	559	750	820
Export	376	390	314	368	447	601	745

Source: Warsaw School of Economics, *Poland – International Economic Report*, World Research Institute, Warsaw, 1996, p. 179; Buro do spraw obrotu zagranicznego, *Zestawienie Obrotow Handlu Zagranicznego*, Glowny Urzad Statystyczny (GUS), Warsaw, 1997.

Mutual Economic Assistance) countries fell, and trade with the West expanded spectacularly. The EC (European Community) replaced the CMEA as Poland's major trading partner (see tables 3.15 and 3.16). Fostering the swift expansion of Polish exports and imports, particularly trade with the European Union (EU) (70 per cent of exports and 65 per cent of imports), is the gradual lowering of trade barriers. Another important factor underlying the expansion of trade with EU countries has been the ongoing liberalisation in both directions in line with the provisions of the EU Association Agreement, OECD membership and with GATT (now-WTO) commitments which were signed by Poland in 1994 and 1996 respectively.

Exports are being facilitated by the phasing out of EU tariffs on Polish exports that began in 1992 with the abolishment of duties on almost half of Poland's industrial exports to the EU. By January 1995, approximately 70 per cent of Poland's industrial exports (representing 85 per cent of total recorded exports) benefited from duty-free access to the EU market. Germany remained by far Poland's largest trading partner, absorbing some 38 per cent of exports and accounting for 27 per cent of imports. Trade with others countries in transition started to pick up in 1994, but their share remained small, at 17 per cent of exports and 15 per cent of imports in 1995 (OECD 1997:). The revival of trade with countries of the former Soviet Union, notwithstanding a continuing overall contraction in that region, reflected the

Table 3.15 *Poland: commodity structure of EU imports (%)*

(Commodities excluding fuels)	1988	1992	1993	Changes 1988–93
Agricultural products	18.4	10.8	8.6	−9.7
Food	4.5	3.7	3.0	−1.5
Raw materials	4.7	2.6	3.0	−1.7
Chemicals	7.7	8.8	7.2	−0.5
Leather products	3.7	3.3	2.8	−0.8
Textile products	1.6	1.4	1.2	−0.3
Clothing	10.6	15.5	18.5	7.9
Wood & paper	6.2	7.3	7.4	1.2
Building materials	0.4	0.7	1.0	0.5
Glass	1.2	1.2	0.9	−0.4
Iron and steel	7.8	10.4	8.6	0.9
Non-ferrous metal	9.7	9.6	5.7	−3.9
Engineering products	4.5	5.0	4.7	0.2
Transport equipment	8.4	6.2	11.4	3.0
Electrical machinery	3.3	3.2	4.5	1.2
NEC	6.3	8.6	10.6	4.3
Manufactured products	75.8	85.0	87.5	11.7

Source: Lemoine, *CEEE Export to the EC (1988–93): Country Differentiation and Commodity Diversification*, Centre for Eastern European Countries, Paris, 1994, p. 31.

Table 3.16 *Poland: trade by major country groups in 1995*

	Exports			Imports			Trade balance
	$ mn	Annual growth rate (%)	Share in total exports (%)	$ mn	Annual growth rate (%)	Share in total imports (%)	$ mn
EU	16 357	37.1	70.5	18 791	33.4	64.5	−2 434
Other OECD countries	1 116	14.3	5.0	2 761	32.5	9.5	−1 595
Developing countries	1 735	−3.15	7.5	3 047	32.3	10.5	−1 312
CEFTA	1 239	50.6	5.0	1 622	76.65	5.5	−383
Other EE countries	2 692	60.6	12.0	2 849	32.8	10	−157
Total	23 189	34.5	100	29 070	35.0	100	−5 881

Note: EE=European economies.
Source: Warsaw School of Economics, *Poland – International Economic Report*, World Economy Research Institute, Warsaw, 1996, p. 121.

development of new private-based trade links. Among the most spectacular increases were those of Polish exports of food and machinery
to the Ukraine and Russia.

The merchandise structure of foreign trade changed substantially
during the transition period. Changes included a decrease in the
export share of mineral and agricultural products, raw materials and
chemical products and an increase in the share of manufactured
products, transport equipment, NEC and electrical machinery (see
Table 3.15). The manufacturing industries have been at the centre of
Poland's export drive. Intermediate and investment goods constituted
the bulk of imports, with the share of the former approximately 65–70
per cent, and the share of the latter approximately 13–15 per cent.
Outward processing (the importation of inputs that are processed in
Poland and then re-exported) accounted for an increasing share of
foreign trade. In 1995, this share reached 24 per cent for exports and
12 per cent for imports (in light industry, 82 and 62 per cent respectively). Thus, far from being a symptom of excess demand, import
growth was largely associated with the development of the supply side
of the Polish economy. The changes in the specialisation index of
exports point to the fact that in industrial strategies the inheritance
of the past is still present, but they also show that a rather deep
reorientation is taking place. Poland has kept or developed a strong
specialisation in resource-intensive sectors: for example agriculture,
raw materials, wood and paper, and non-ferrous metallurgy. In the
period 1988–95, it became relatively specialised in labour-intensive
activities such as clothing and furniture, and has managed to maintain
its relative specialisation in transport equipment. Several branches of
machinery have also been among the growing export commodities.

The expansion of foreign trade can partly be linked to the expansion of the private sector, the exports of which reached $US9.6 billion
in 1995. Taken by industry, almost 30 per cent are derived from
electrical engineering, 20 per cent from light industry, 16 per cent
from wood and paper and 12.2 per cent from agro-food. Also, the
private sector dominated exports in certain product ranges such as
agro-food (90 per cent), light industry (80 per cent) and wood and
paper (78 per cent) (World Economy Research Institute, 1996). The
other notable features of private-sector trade included a faster growth
in exports than imports, and a distinct concentration on Central and
Eastern European markets.

In 1995, Poland recorded a deficit with all major groups of trade
partners. The largest part of this deficit was accounted for by the trade

with OECD countries. A comparison of the share of particular country groups in Poland's trade deficit and in trade yields an interesting observation (see Table 3.16): the deficit with the EU and Eastern European countries is smaller compared to their share of Poland's exports and imports. On the other hand, the deficit with other OECD nations and developing countries is significantly higher compared to their share of Poland's trade.

CONCLUSIONS

Since the adaptation of the Open Door policy in 1978, the utilisation of foreign capital has become one of the important dimensions of China's contact with foreign countries in terms of funds, materials, technological exchange and economic cooperation. Effective utilisation of FDI must be accompanied by an appropriate macroeconomic environment. Economic changes that have been discussed in this chapter clearly indicate that China has continued to express a strong desire to stimulate and guide its socioeconomic development through promoting a more liberalised investment framework and through further pursuing economic reform to encourage FDI.

Despite the fact that China has achieved impressive economic growth and increased efficiency and productivity in non-state sectors, the existing economic structure is still inadequate, particularly as it lacks the economic laws that are necessary to strengthen and macro-control the economic order. For example, many SOEs are allowed to operate at a loss, creating strong burdens on the central budget and non-state sector development. Reforms of government organisations should be encouraged, separating government from enterprises and thereby reducing administrative monopolies by promoting competition.

In contrast to China, Poland's initial geopolitical and economic structure created a different approach to economic reform. Poland launched a radical, comprehensive stabilisation–liberalisation programme, freeing 90 per cent of prices, eliminating most trade barriers, abolishing state trading monopolies and making its currency convertible for current transactions. While this 'Big Bang' approach created controversy and negative economic growth during the early stages of transition, Poland now has the potential to build on the substantial achievements of the past economic reforms. There are still structural adjustment problems, including the need to speed up the privatisation programme (especially the privatisation of large industrial SOEs), to control inflation as well as further cuts and a restructuring of the government. However, rapid economic growth and continued economic reforms create new interest and opportunities for foreign investors. There is also a strong influence on the business environment which has led the Polish government to introduce liberal investment policies in accordance with OECD rules. An analysis of investment policies will be discussed in the next chapter.

4 Investment and Trade Policies

In 1978, China began to pursue an 'open-door' policy permitting FDI into the country to modernise the economy. The government introduced new economic legislation, beginning with tentative, experimental draft laws and regulations for trial implementation. By the end of the 1980s in China, a large volume of laws, regulations and other official pronouncements had been enacted at central and local government levels.

The liberalisation reforms in Poland started in 1989 when the first non-communist government began to dismantle the Stalinist model of a centralised planned economy. Unlike China, in Poland most regulations and laws were established in early 1990 at a time when a radical, comprehensive stabilisation–liberalisation programme was being launched. It focused on stabilisation, liberalisation and changes in the tax system and the social security net. A privatisation law was accepted, and many quantitative and other restrictions in foreign trade and investment were lifted in order to introduce competitive pressure on domestic enterprises freed from the command mechanism.

This chapter outlines incentives to, and the regulation of, FDI and related policies in the two countries in a comparative perspective. It focuses principally on policy at the national level, but where appropriate, addresses regional developments. The first section reviews each government's objectives and is followed by an outline of FDI policies.

CHINA: AN INTRODUCTION

Starting in 1979 with the Law of the People's Republic of China on Joint Ventures Using Chinese and Foreign Investment, China developed more than 500 central government and local laws, regulations, orders and other policy pronouncements to govern foreign trade and investment. These indicated that China had the expectation that foreign investors would help to solve major economic problems such as a lack of capital, large pools of unemployment and underemployment, low production efficiency with underutilised machines, and a persistent trade deficit with consequent pressure on foreign exchange resources. It was hoped that FDI would help to expand export capacities to earn the foreign exchange needed to pay for additional imports and to reduce balance of payment constraints. Foreign investment was sought in order to add to capital resources, to obtain modern technology and equipment, improve production capacity and efficiency, increase the quality and variety of products, acquire modern management skills, upgrade the skills of local manpower, and to expand employment and generate public revenues.

The MNCs on their side wanted to enlarge their world market share, to increase profits, and diversify to spread risk. They wanted to capture a share of the domestic market by jumping China's trade barriers. Some also saw opportunities for low-cost manufacturing for exports. China and the MNCs thus had different, but compatible objectives. The reasons why in practice there has been a great deal of conflict lie in the overall economic environment in general and in the FDI policies in particular.

FOREIGN INVESTMENT POLICY

From the very beginning, FDI has been an integral part of China's open-door policy, and as early as 1979 the first law on joint ventures came into force (for more details see Appendix A4.1). The permission to set up joint ventures had not been considered sufficient by the authorities, and was therefore supplemented by a policy promoting the inflow of FDI. The Chinese government under Deng Xiaoping then opted for a location-based policy promoting FDI, with the southern provinces of Guangdong and Fujian expected to become especially attractive for foreign investors. In addition to developing the administrative power of the provincial governments (in the areas of finance and taxation, domestic and foreign trade, planning, pricing, wages and employment), four Special Economic Zones (SEZs) were approved in 1979 and 1980: Shenzhen, Zhuhai, Xiamen and Shantou. Foreign-funded enterprises operating in these zones enjoyed preferential tax treatment, were exempted from import duties on equipment and raw materials used, and exports and imports were not subject to the usual procedures for approval.

Altogether, enterprises in the SEZs were to operate according to the rules of the market. Due to their success, a further opening of new zones followed. All these 'open economic zones' offered special incentives to foreign investors and for promoting foreign trade. In 1992, after Deng's famous 'South China Tour', privileges similar to those of the coastal areas were granted to a number of major cities in inland provinces, particularly in the Yangtze River valley and in border areas, and this heralded a new era in China's FDI policy.

From the very beginning, a certain ambivalence by the authorities arose from the conflicting goals of opening the economy while attempting to ensure an equitable distribution of the benefits of economic growth and of developing an appropriate industrial structure. Obviously, the location-based policy towards FDI was given preference over a sectoral approach as it complied very well with several general principles of economic reform:

1. *Decentralisation*: highly-centralised economic decisions, characteristic of a centrally-planned economy, were considered to have been major obstacles to the development of the Chinese economy in the past; experience with decentralisation could be gained and its effects could be more easily controlled.
2. *Gradualism*: contrary to Poland and other post-communist government policies in CEE countries after 1989, which opted for a quick transformation of their centrally-planned economies into market economies, the Chinese authorities, while preserving the main features of the communist political system, tried to avoid abrupt changes and adopted a gradual strategy: 'Crossing the river stone by stone' as Deng put it. By allowing the market to operate in limited areas, valuable experience was gained before extending the reforms to the whole country.
3. *Principle of greatest efficiency*: Chinese policy was focused on areas in which reforms were expected to succeed with relative ease, and FDI policy followed this principle in various ways. An important determinant for FDI in developing countries is the quality of the existing infrastructure. Under conditions of very limited resources, it is rational for the country to concentrate its efforts on certain promising areas first. Consequently, the first locations chosen to attract FDI were the provinces of Guangdong and Fujian, as well as the first SEZs, situated in the south-east, close to Hong Kong and Taiwan which could be expected to first make use of the new investment opportunities, being familiar both with the language and culture.

In a step away from location-based policy towards FDI, the first guidelines for FDI on a sectoral basis were launched in 1993. They already showed the main characteristics of the 'Interim Provisions on Guiding the Direction of Foreign Investment', which were later put into force on 27 June 1995. According to these provisions, FDI was to be encouraged in agriculture, energy, communications, important raw materials, high technology and the utilisation of resources, especially in the central and western provinces. FDI is still subject, however, to certain restrictions in sectors where China is experimenting with foreign investment or where state monopolies exist in fields in which China can meet local demand through self-financed imports of advanced technology, and in projects for exploiting rare and valuable mineral resources. Prohibited are projects endangering security, or harming the country's social and public interest, and those with adverse effects on the environment or which will damage natural resources. Investments which fit none of these categories are classified as permitted. Together with the Interim Provisions a more detailed catalogue of industries was issued (Guidelines for Foreign Investment Projects), which will be updated from time to time. Xinhua, the official news agency, called the rules 'a manifestation of the Chinese government's intentions to actively, reasonably and effectively utilise foreign funds', and said they embodied a substantial change from the short-term quantitative strategy to a long-term qualitative one in the use of foreign funds. However, there is not much in the Interim Provisions which concerns their implementation, besides guiding the authorities in the approval of FDI projects. Under the emerging new industrial policy it can be expected that preferential treatment will increasingly rely on loans and financial subsidies, and less on profits' tax rates. This leads us to important developments in the second half of 1995.

At the plenum of the CPC (Communist Party of China) Central Committee in September 1995, when the proposals for the Ninth Five-Year Plan (1996–2000) and the long-term perspective until 2010 were discussed, State President Jiang Zemin stressed that the central government's policy towards the five SEZs and New Pudong Area will remain unchanged in principle, but that certain policies will be changed and adjusted according to China's economic development. In a subsequent statement for the press, Prime Minister Li Peng indicated that 'China would ease back on preferential tax and other incentives for investments in its six special economic zones' (*Financial Times*, 5 March 1996).

Concerning the reduction of privileges for foreign-funded enterprises in general, it was clearly stated that such enterprises were
gradually to be treated on an equal footing with national enterprises
especially in regards to taxation. In a first step it was declared in
November 1995 that from 1996 there would be no more tariff exemptions for foreign investors for the import of production equipment. At
the prevailing average tariff rate of 40 per cent this would mean an
average cost increase to foreign investors of 28 per cent as calculated
by the US–China Business Council in Beijing. In addition, a certain
grace period as well as exemptions for special cases were reported, so
the final outcome of the new regulations with respect to foreign
investors cannot yet be assessed.

Summarising China's likely future policies towards FDI, the main
principles seem to be the following:

- promoting FDI according to specific economic sectors;
- decreasing FDI in regions where FDI was strongly promoted in the
  past;
- increasing promotion of FDI in the less-developed regions which
  received little FDI in the past; and
- gradual reduction of privileges for foreign-funded enterprises over
  local entrepreneurs.

However, as indicated by the many differing and ambiguous statements of officials, the implementation of these principles still remains
undecided. This has to be seen in the wider context of an ongoing
struggle between the protagonists of 'quantitative' growth of the Deng
era, and the proponents of a more balanced and 'qualitative' growth
in the group around Jiang Zemin (for further details about China's
specific investment policies see Appendix A4.1).

Tax Policy

The Chinese government recognises that the tax system is the main
criterion for judging whether the investment environment is good, and
that a good tax environment must maintain a stable, reasonable and
equitable tax rate with easy filing procedures and must generally hold
to international practices.

China's tax framework embraces a complex array of income, production and sales taxes, with tax policy being technically formulated
by the Ministry of Finance. Throughout the period since 1980, China

has continuously and selectively, both by region and by FDI perform-ance, used tax incentives as 'economic levers' to guide FDI into its designated regions and sectors. While the economic efficacy of this proliferation remains to be seen, the psychological effect on foreign investors in their response to such spatial and sectoral priorities has been encouraging.

In general, this multi-layered, priority-targeted, and region-exclusive tax incentive structure reflects China's recent efforts in implementing its industrial policies and in accommodating the execu-tion of the uneven development strategy, starting from the coast and moving gradually into its hinterland. Taxation of enterprises with foreign investment provides for reductions in standard rates, exemp-tions and credits, accelerated depreciation and reductions in social security contributions. This is misleadingly labelled as preferential. In practice, many enterprises with foreign investment pay higher taxes than local firms unless local joint ventures can negotiate a good deal.

FDI in different sectors, locations or for different durations in China attract differing tax rates. The tax policy distinguishes four forms of enterprises with foreign investment:

- equity joint ventures;
- contractual joint ventures;
- wholly-owned foreign enterprises; and
- cooperative developments.

Incentives for foreign investors have in theory discriminated against domestic enterprises (but as already mentioned in the previous section most of the privileges for foreign-funded enterprises will be reduced gradually to an equal footing with domestic ones, especially with regard to taxation). The incentives mainly consist of tax concessions including tax holidays, exemption from customs duties, subsidies for infrastructure costs, subsidies to interest rates, and low fees for land use. Some of the incentives have already been withdrawn. Provinces and municipalities give further incentives, which create conflict with national policy. The taxes on enterprises with foreign investment consist of four major types:

- the enterprise income tax;
- the consolidated industrial and commercial tax;
- local taxesl; and

- withholding tax and individual income tax (for details about each tax and incentive see Appendix A4.2).

To avoid losses in its tax revenues, China has successfully nego-tiated the insertion into all its tax treaties, except the one with the USA, of a 'tax-sparing' provision that allows a credit for tax spared by China's tax concessions against the resident state's tax levied on income. In 1980, new tax legislation was passed to deal with joint ventures between Chinese and foreign investment companies. A newly-established joint venture scheduled to operate for a period of ten years or more was to be exempted from enterprise income tax in its first profit-making year, and allowed a 50 per cent reduction in income tax in the second and third years. Joint ventures in farming and forestry and in remote regions were to be allowed a 15–30 per cent reduction in income tax for another 10 years. Further revisions were introduced two years later in 1982 by the State Council so that enterprises with foreign investment in industry, communications, transportation, agriculture, forestry and animal husbandry, scheduled to operate for a period of 10 years or more, would be exempted from income tax in the first and second profit-making years, and would be allowed a 50 per cent reduction in income tax in the third through the fifth years. Only 80 per cent of normal tax rates were levied for 10 years in the following industries: machine building and electronics, metallurgy, chemicals and building materials, light industry, textiles and packaging, medical appliances and pharmaceutical, agriculture, forestry, animal husbandry, agriculture, processing related to these industries and construction. A decision to exempt enterprises with foreign investment but small-scale production (annual income less than one million renminbi yuan) and low profits from local taxes could be made by local authorities.

Provisions in the 22 Articles of the Provisions of the State Council for the Encouragement of Foreign Investment in 1986 exempt export enterprises and advanced technology enterprises from tax. Different status is given to enterprises with foreign investment identified as export enterprises or advanced technology enterprises at different tax rates. Priority is given to export and advanced technology enter-prises through a variety of preferential treatments. They both enjoy rebates of the total income tax paid. Advanced technology enterprises were granted preferential treatment such as eight years of reduced taxation or exemption from normal enterprises income tax. A further three-year extension during which enterprise income tax was paid at half the standard rate could be granted. Larger, technology-intensive, projects of over $US30 million and projects relating to energy, communications or port construction could be levied at the reduced rate of 50 per cent of standard income tax. Preferential treatment was also to be given with regard to royalties for proprietary technology in the form of income tax reductions and exemptions.

Foreign investors in export and technologically advanced enterprises remitting profits abroad were to be exempt from income tax. In effect, these provisions partially repealed Article 4 of the Sino-Foreign Equity Joint Venture Income Tax Law 1980. The State Council provision also exempts export and advanced technology enterprises from paying all subsidy payments for employment to the central government. They must pay labour insurance and welfare expenses, including housing subsidies to local workers through local governments in accordance with local regulations.

Economic Zones

As part of the open-door policy, special economic zones (SEZs) were designed to promote and upgrade the development of Chinese industries in general and attract foreign capital and technology and enhance exports in particular. These provisions are of interest to enterprises established in coastal regions outside the SEZs as well as economic and technology development zones. Tax incentives are now essentially the same in SEZs, economic and technology development zones and most open areas. Foreign-funded enterprises in SEZs have income tax levied on their income at a reduced rate of 15 per cent. The local governments of SEZs determine whether local income tax reduction is granted, and profits remitted abroad are exempt from income tax. Products of exports produced in SEZs are exempt from consolidated industrial and commercial tax, whilst consolidated industrial and commercial tax on products produced and sold within SEZs is levied at half the tax rate.

It is well-established that an efficient, effective and competitive taxation system should be simple and transparent, that is with no greater burdens than in the international arena. It should also be uniformly administered so as to avoid arbitrary measures and discrimination among firms. Chinese taxation of enterprises with foreign participation is not always transparent according to these rules. For example, accelerated depreciation, by reductions in the price of capital, contributes to the trend of substituting capital for labour, which in China often conflicts with national policy. While no research has yet been carried out on its efficiency and effectiveness due to lack of information from the Chinese government, it would be surprising if its effects were different from those in other developing countries.

TRADE POLICY

In China, the trade reforms broke away from the inherited, centralised and inward-looking economic system. Prior to the beginning of the reforms, the organisation of foreign trade in China closely followed the Soviet model, and foreign trade remained completely under central control. On the eve of the reforms in China (1978) foreign economic relations were associated with a strategy of import substitution. The reforms progressively relaxed the monopoly on foreign trade. As Mesnil 1995 put it, 'the dismantling of central planning, the introduction of decentralised incentives . . . uncovered large, previously hidden opportunities for commercial gains, and unleashed previously suppressed entrepreneurial energies' (Mesnil, 1995).

In 1984, the provincial branches of national foreign trade corporations (FTC) became independent financial, operating bodies, and each province was allowed to create its own FTC. As a result the number of FTCs increased from 12 in 1978 to about 1000 in 1986 and to 9000 in 1994. This generated increased competition upstream and downstream: FTCs had to compete for foreign markets, and also had to compete for domestic supply as production units progressively acquired the capacity to choose their FTC (Lardy, 1992; Zweig, 1994). Nevertheless, beyond the joint ventures with foreign capital, a number of production firms, the big exporters, were given the right to carry out foreign trade operations directly. The most dynamic part of foreign trade activity was located outside the state sector, which grew rapidly. Township and villages enterprises (TVEs) became important suppliers of goods for exports. Also, joint ventures with foreign capital increased their share in exports and imports.

In China, attracting FDI has clearly been a priority of trade policy. The first measures of the opening-up policy were to allow FDI and to create special economic zones to attract foreign investors. The policy towards FDI included both strong incentives as well as severe constraints. Joint ventures benefited from tax exemptions and reductions, along with concession import duties (World Bank, 1994). Trade policy has also been used actively to attract foreign capital since measures to protect the domestic market have been taken, frequently under the pressure of foreign investors (EBRD, 1994). China has emphasised the decentralisation of foreign trade decisions and export promotion policies. Not all trade policy measures, however, provided incentives to export. On the import side, liberalisation measures clearly lagged behind the reforms in the export sector. In the early 1990s, the import regime displayed the following characteristics:

- The foreign trade reforms led to a phasing-out of mandatory planning and to a decentralisation of decision-making and responsibilities. The scope of the foreign trade plan was reduced, and in 1992, mandatory planning covered less than 20 per cent of imports. The process of scaling down the plan has been accompanied by the decentralisation of responsibility for implementing the plan and by an increased number of foreign trade companies, mainly at the local level (Lardy, 1992; Fukasaku and Solignac-Lecomte, 1995). The activities of these foreign trade companies remained subject to administrative control (local or central).
- The level of protection remained high. It resulted from the high tariff rate, which stood at 32 per cent (weighted average, see Table 4.1) but also from multiple and overlapping non-tariff barriers, administered by the national or provincial authorities. In 1992, these included:
  - import licensing (covering 25 per cent of total imports in 1992);
  - import rights given to one or a few FTCs for specific products (this channel concerned 32 per cent of imports);
  - direct control on imports of some commodities in the sector of machinery and equipment (this covered approximately 7.7 per cent of imports); and
  - foreign exchange allocations: imports outside the plan were indirectly regulated through the control of enterprise access to foreign currency.

The authorities control approximately 50 per cent of imports in this way.

According to the Memorandum of Understanding on Market Access signed with the USA in October 1992, China has committed itself to dismantling most of these barriers. The measures it has committed itself to take are among those being considered by the members of the World Trade Organisation (WTO), which is examining China's membership. These measures amply show that China's

Table 4.1   *China: tariffs on industrial imports*

	Weighted average
Industrial countries*	5.0
EU	5.7
Japan	1.9
USA	5.4
Czech Republic	4.5
Hungary	13 + 8% surcharge
Poland	9.2 + 6% surcharge
Bulgaria	16.0
Romania	7.0
Brazil	15.0
India	54.0
China	35.0

*   Pre-Uruguay Round.
Source: Lemoine, *Trade policy and Trade Patterns During Transition: A Comparison between China and the CEECs*, Centre for Eastern European Countries (CEP II), Paris, 1996, p. 15.

trade regime is still very far from liberal. They include: publishing trade laws and regulations, restrictions on internal directives, identifying agencies involved in the import-approval process, lower tariffs, and the elimination of all import licensing requirements, quotas and controls by 1997.

- As the implementation of trade policies has become decentralised, assessing the precise degree of liberalisation is complicated. The whole system of tariffs and non-tariff barriers is characterised by a low degree of transparency and a lack of neutrality (IMF, 1994). The tariffs are set at a high level, but there are many tariff exemptions that benefit exporters: the materials and components imported for export processing, as well as equipment and machinery imported by joint ventures and by export processing enterprises are exempt from customs duties. As a result of these concessions, which encompass half of all imports, the tariff revenue actually collected as the percentage of total imports declined steeply during the transition, and the ratio stands much below that of the Poland or other CEE countries (see Table 4.2).

China's trade policy is moving along the track of the fast growing Asian countries, where import liberalisation has been slow and trade

Table 4.2   *Revenues collected from customs duties*

| | Tariffs and imports % | | | |
	1991	*1992*	*1993*	*1994*
Hungary	na	10.7	10.7	9.7
Poland	10.4	12.2	12.9	10.0
	1978	*1983*	*1988*	*1993*
China	15.3	12.8	7.5	4.3

Sources: As for Table 4.1.

regimes could be defined as 'mixed' (Helliwel, 1995; World Bank, 1996). China's present trade regime looks to be very different from that of the CEE countries, and close to that implemented by the newly-industrialising economies (NIEs). The bias in favour of exports in China's trade regime reinforces these characteristics.

On the export side, export promotion was at the core of the Chinese strategy of opening up, and has been aimed at developing a modern export sector. This strategy was supported by the existence of a strong comparative advantage in labour-intensive industries. As Audretsh (1995) points out, such traditional industrial policies, with selected targets (firms or industries), prove to serve well in a situation of industrial catching-up, where comparative advantages are relatively evident.

The export-oriented strategy relied on a broad set of devices: export plans were progressively phased out and were abolished at the beginning of the 1990s, but they were replaced by different instruments that combined to form a vigorous policy of export promotion. Contracts were signed by the FTCs with the Ministry of Foreign Trade and Economic Relations (MFTEC) in regard to foreign exchange earnings. As an incentive for implementing these foreign exchange targets, exporters were allowed to retain a fraction of their foreign currency earnings. The retention schemes were highly differentiated according to geographic locations and industrial sectors. The reform of foreign exchange since January 1994 has abolished the retention scheme, and all exporters are required to exchange all their foreign currency earnings. In return, buying foreign currency for import purposes was to be made easier. Under the new foreign exchange guidelines the RMB (renminbi) is 'conditionally' convertible for certain trade transactions. This means that Chinese importers with a valid import contract and required licences or quota permits can, in principle, purchase foreign exchange without receiving prior authorisation from the State Administration Exchange Control.

Another incentive scheme relied, as mentioned above, on tariff exemptions and concessions that were implemented to stimulate export-oriented activities. Furthermore, in the second half of the 1980s, the authorities created 'production networks for exports' in order to stimulate high-performing enterprises in selected industrial sectors, using investment financing and the guaranteed supplies of inputs. Finally, the policy of attracting FDI has also aimed at expanding export capacities as joint ventures are required to balance their foreign exchange imports and exports.

Up to the mid-1990s, China followed diverging trade policies. In November 1995, major trade reforms were announced which included substantial tariff cuts that would reduce its average tariffs to 24–25 per cent, as well as eliminate quotas, licences and other import controls on over 30 per cent of the commodities subject to such restrictions. These measures, together with the new policy towards FDI (that intends to remove the preferences enjoyed by the coastal provinces and export-processing operations), would mean a substantial change in China's trade policy. They would reduce the bias in favour of exporting activities and lead to a readjustment of imports in favour of domestic demand.

FOREIGN EXCHANGE CONTROL SYSTEM

Foreign exchange activities had been handled by the People's Bank of China (PBOC) before March 1951, when the Bank of China (BOC) was re-established to handle foreign exchange business and assumed most of the control over foreign exchange. However, until March 1979, the BOC was only a PBOC agent. Decisions on foreign exchange control were made by the State Planning Commission, the Ministry of Finance, the Ministry of Foreign Economic Relations and Trade and the PBOC. Also, the BOC had been the sole source for handling foreign exchange business, including import and export banking, before the establishment of the China International Trust and Investment Corporation (CITIC) in October 1979. Later, designated foreign exchange banks were allowed to engage in foreign currency operations. On 27 April 1994, the China Import and Export Bank was established.

In March 1979, Beijing established the State Administration of Exchange Control (SAEC) and also its local branches directly under the State Council to assume the PBOC's functions as the administrator of overseas business. Between January and August 1982, the SAEC and the BOC were both put under the control of the Import and Export Administrative Commission of the Ministry of Foreign Economic Relations and Trade. Subsequently, the SAEC took over the BOC's responsibilities in the enforcement of foreign exchange laws and regulations, the promulgation of exchange rates, unified administration of foreign exchange, the planned management of foreign exchange revenue and expenditure, and the supervision of international payments. The BOC was still in control of foreign currency deposits and loans, import and export banking, international settlements, international remittances, overseas Chinese remittances, and foreign exchange transactions. The BOC would also undertake SAEC's tasks where no SAEC branches existed (Chen Bo-chih, 1995).

Beijing has also endeavoured to enact laws and regulations on the management of foreign exchange, foreign funds and foreign-funded banks. According to the Provisional Regulations on Foreign Exchange Control enacted in December 1980, planned management of foreign exchange revenue and expenditure is imposed on enterprises, organisations and groups; and centralised management of foreign loans is also practised. In March 1981, Beijing enacted the Tentative Measures on Loan Extension to Joint Ventures. The Regulations on Extending the Business Scope of Existing Overseas Chinese and Foreign Banks in Shanghai enacted in October 1984 allowed these banks to engage in six kinds of foreign exchange business including foreign exchange loans, discounts, remittances and documentary bills, and so on. However, up to March 1995, foreign banks were still banned from taking RMB deposits or extending RMB loans.

The PBOC decided the official exchange rates until the SAEC was established in March 1979. The SAEC then decided the official exchange rates according to the situation of mainland China's international payments and the exchange rates of its trading partners, though changes in the official exchange rates remained relatively rare. Since 9 April 1991, the SAEC has flexibly readjusted the official exchange rates according to long-term developments in international payments, the exchange rates of trade partners, and the daily exchange rate fluctuations of major international currencies. Since then, the official exchange rate of RMB against the US dollar has changed several times (*Access China*, 1997).

On 29 December 1993, the PBOC issued a notice on further reforms of the exchange control system, which took effect on 1 January 1994. The main reform measures included the abolition of foreign exchange certificates, the establishment of a unified, managed floating exchange rate system, the establishment of an interbank foreign exchange transaction market, and the replacement of the foreign exchange quota-retaining system of Chinese enterprises by a bank-based system of foreign exchange transactions. Specifically, the last measure features implementation of a settlement system for foreign exchange revenue and allows for conditional convertibility of RMB in connection with current account items (Wang Ya-ke, 1994). The PBOC enacted the Regulations on the Administration of Foreign-Funded Financial Institutions on 25 February 1994 and the Tentative Regulations on the Administration of the Settlement, Sale and Payment of Foreign Exchanges and the Tentative Regulations on the Administration of Foreign Currency Accounts on 1 April 1994. These three regulations all took effect on 1 April 1994.

FOREIGN EXCHANGE POLICY

Before 1979, China operated a highly concentrated foreign exchange management policy, unifying both foreign exchange revenue and expenditure and defined expenditure of revenue: all foreign revenue had to be sold to the state, and when foreign exchange was needed it was allocated by the state. The rate of foreign exchange was set by the state, and foreign exchange capital and foreign exchange business were managed and handled by the Bank of China. In 1979, China began restructuring its foreign exchange system, gradually taking the path of the market.

There were two main kinds of exchange rates in China before 1 January 1994; the adjusted exchange rate (EXADJ), and the official exchange rate (EXOFF). The former was influenced more by the demand and supply of foreign exchange markets. As the inflation rate started to climb and the real interest rate gap between China and the USA started to widen after May 1991, the adjusted exchange rate of the RMB against the US dollar devalued from 5.58 in January 1991 to 10.05 in June 1993, while the official rate remained stable at about 5.32 to 5.72 between 1991 and 1993. Enterprises with foreign investment were concerned with foreign exchange risk and the effects of a devalued Chinese currency over a period of years. The devaluation of the renminbi exchange rate has resulted in the appreciation of foreign capital in which equity is denominated. Overseas borrowing in foreign currency seems cheaper relative to local borrowing in Chinese currency. The devaluation of Chinese currency would apparently make domestic market-oriented production less profitable than export-oriented production in terms of repatriation of profits in foreign currency. Repatriation of profits in foreign currency is thus related to the market orientation of major products of foreign-funded enterprises. However, the continuing devaluation of the Chinese currency in the long term would undermine the value of foreign capital denominated in Chinese currency (*Access China*, 1997).

To promote a more stable investment environment, at the beginning of 1994 the government made major changes in the system of foreign exchange by removing the double-track system, settling foreign exchange by banks, and making the renminbi convertible under the current account. In June 1996, the People's Bank of China: the Central Bank of China (PBC) published Regulations on the Management of Foreign Exchange of the People's Republic of China (PRC), which went into effect on 1 April 1996. In June 1996, the PBC published Regulations on the Settlement, Sales and Payments of Foreign Exchange and decided to incorporate the sales and purchase of foreign exchanges of foreign-funded enterprises into bank settlements from 1 July of the same year. Since 1 December 1996, China has effected the convertibility of the renminbi under the current account, defining the framework of a new foreign exchange system. The foreign exchange rates would mainly be decided by the overall monetary situation. The basic money supply, the loan scale and interest rates would also have a direct and sensitive impact on the changes in foreign exchange rates.

Until 1988 there were some restrictions in remitting profits and dividends and repatriating capital. Net profits after paying taxes could be remitted abroad from the foreign exchange deposit account of joint ventures upon application to the Bank of China. For the transfer of capital in foreign exchange, investors had to apply to the State Administration of Foreign Exchange (SAFE) or its branch offices. Foreign staff could only remit or take abroad an amount in foreign exchange not exceeding 50 per cent of their legitimate net salary earnings. If the remitted amount was more than 50 per cent of their income, investors had to apply to the SAFE or its branch offices. These restrictions created negative business perceptions, and were relaxed in 1988. In practice such regulations were, in any case, not adhered to. Since foreign enterprises and joint ventures import inputs into production and export some outputs, they can remit profits by other than arm's-length pricing.

LABOUR MARKET POLICY

In accordance with the Law of the PRC on Joint Ventures Using Chinese and Foreign Investment, the employment and dismissal of staff and workers of a joint venture should be provided for in accordance with the law in the agreement and contract of the parties to the venture. Labour policy for foreign-funded enterprises was mainly concerned with four aspects:

- recruitment and dismissal in labour contracts;
- training;
- labour payments; and
- insurance and welfare benefits.

In earlier years, the employment of staff and workers in a joint venture was recommended by the local department in charge of the venture or the local labour office. Dismissal had to be approved by the department in charge of the venture and the labour management department. Informal investors would face little problem with this situation. Autonomous rights of employment for joint ventures were extended in 1986; with the assistance of the local labour office, a joint venture, with the agreement of the Chinese authorities, could employ and dismiss workers.

Enterprises with foreign participation were obliged by contract to train Chinese workers but had no control over selecting candidates for training. Staffing difficulties had their roots in controls over domiciles and cumbersome recruiting systems. In a centrally-planned economy, firing a person was more difficult than hiring one, and this resulted in enterprises with foreign participation being overstaffed with non-productive or unqualified workers, adding substantially to the cost of operations. These situation created conflicts and dissatisfaction among foreign investors. By 18 May 1988, the State Council approved new legislation which gave power to enterprises with foreign invest-ment to conduct employment matters independently, in accordance with current international practices. But these rules did not work in practice; dismissal of workers was limited only to cases where criminal offences had been committed.

Labour policy requires that workers in enterprises with foreign participation receive more than workers in similar SOEs. The figures of nominal wages are misleading because enterprises with foreign participation have to pay high 'on costs'. All enterprises with foreign participation usually pay the workers at least 120 per cent of their normal entitlement in similar SOEs (Table 4.3). They must also make payments to a retirement and pension fund and an unemployment insurance fund for Chinese employees. Foreign investment firms must also make payments to subsidised housing; that is, the cost of the building and/or purchase of housing for local staff and workers, as well as the cost of living subsidies. Much of the payment is not made directly to workers but to local governments and their firms which contract the workers. This is not mandatory, however, for foreign investors outside the major cities. From 1987, export-oriented and advanced technology enterprises have paid relatively smaller subsidies, known as the commodity price adjustment subsidy, to the local finance departments. A comparison of manufacturing wages with other developing countries in shown in Table 4.4.

Table 4.3   *China: wages and benefits to workers in firms with foreign participation*

Guandong and three special economic zones
  Total labour charges which are made up of
    70% wages paid directly to workers
    5% welfare expenses
    25% labour insurance and subsidies
Annual permissible labour charge increase: 5–15 %

Shanghai
  Wage (which includes basic wages, allowance, bonuses)
    not less than 120% of wages in similar SOEs
Pension insurance
  equivalent to 30% of total wage bill, paid monthly to the Shanghai People's
    Insurance Corp.
Food and fuel subsidies
  30 renminbi yuan per person, paid to the Shanghai Finance Bureau
Housing subsidy
  30 renminbi yuan per person, paid to the Shanghai Finance Bureau

---

Source: Business International, *Joint Ventures in PRC: A Corporate Guide*, Hong Kong, 1985.

Table 4.4 *Manufacturing wages (US cents per hour, 1984 average)*

China	16.6 to 41.5
Philippines	24.7
Indonesia	30.2
India	32.1
Thailand	41.1
Malaysia	103.5
Hong Kong	144.1
Singapore	153.8
Taiwan	179.4
Poland	120.0

Source: Business International, *Joint Ventures in the PRC: A Corporate Guide*, Hong Kong, 1985, p. 144.

The training of workers and staff in joint ventures has been regulated to a much lesser degree than the payments of employees. It is in the interest of enterprises with foreign participation to train labour to improve efficiency and productivity. Where labour is constantly being turned over, however, the incentives for training are reduced. The overpricing of labour and underpricing of capital encourages the use of machinery instead of labour, further limiting training responsibility.

PRIVATISATION POLICY

A key question that has faced economic reformers in China, as elsewhere, is whether the continuation of public ownership represents an insurmountable barrier to the functioning of markets and efficient resource allocation. In contrast to Poland, China has consistently maintained its preference for public ownership as a means of achieving its vision of a socialist market economy. As envisaged by China's policy-makers, such a system would be characterised by increased competition and the elimination of mandatory planning, but not necessarily by the replacement of SOEs with private ownership as in a capitalist system. The objective is to retain the predominance of public ownership (as mentioned in the Ninth Five-Year Plan (1996–2000) such that SOEs will remain the backbone of the industrial sector, but a breakthrough in solving their major and difficult problems has to be made in the years to come), supplemented by non-state and private ownership, while achieving an effective separation between state ownership and control of enterprises (IMF 1996: 30).

As the Chinese government has pointed out that SOEs are still the backbone of industry, the solutions taken into consideration do not emphasise privatisation but rather merger and takeovers of less-efficient companies by successful ones, and include cooperation only with private enterprises. From this ideological standpoint many critics object that selling means that 'the state economy abandons its own enterprises, and thus is unable to play its leading role and stabilise the market'. In other words, a state enterprise is more than the value of its assets. Selling may allow better use of state funds, but at the price of losing one state enterprise. These doubts, however, do not reflect the facts. In practice, these sales do not represent a selling-out or privatisation, because the buyers are the staff members and workers of the enterprise. All these processes were major topics for discussion at the National Party Conference and the Chinese People's Party's Central Committee (CPPCC) in March 1996.

So far, several 'experiments' have been launched with the aim of concentrating, restructuring and increasing the cooperation of SOEs with other enterprises, either privately or collectively owned. To try to revive at least one sector, the government has tried to transform some of its lumbering, loss-making military enterprises into civilian manufacturing firms, but only a limited number have started to generate profits. China has also tried to reduce the production capacity of its ailing textile industry, with many such plants setting up stores and restaurants to create jobs for surplus workers (*China Daily*, 5 April 1996). Until now, Beijing policy was, 'let state enterprises lumber along, merge some, fiddle with new management incentives, foist their pension obligations onto local government, and wait' (*China News Analysis*, 1 September 1996). This is surely not the sort of reform most Western analysts have in mind. The new policy discourages bankruptcies. Laid-off workers have to be re-employed by local governments. The most desperate companies can expect bailouts. It's not a plan so much as acknowledgment of the lack of one.

The recent 15th Party Congress identified the reform of ownership as a major weapon in the struggle to reform the state sector. The CPC announced a strategy which would manage the privatisation process at its own pace and follow its own way to avoid conflict between powerful actors in the state sector in accordance with their political agendas. There are three distinct types of reform which relate to three different levels in the organisation of the state sector:

- the changes in the bureaucracy running the enterprises;

- the development of companies to manage state assets at the local level; and
- the conversion of the enterprises into shareholding companies.

In the meantime, if these reforms are to succeed the state must send out clear signals to its enterprises by developing further strategies to carry through the ownership reforms. Among these, the most crucial for the future of the restructuring process will be a sound competition policy, the reform of the banking sector, and a speeding up of reform of the social security system. Also, China will have to improve the legal framework for the privatisation process, protecting shareholders' rights, controlling the actions of the public assets management companies and allowing the creation of investment funds independent of the government. External investors (foreign nationals, banks, investment funds) will have to feel that their rights as investors are sufficiently protected to allow them to inject capital into the state enterprises, bringing along with them an expertise and an intention to carry out restructuring.

*   *   *

POLAND: AN INTRODUCTION

There are high expectations of FDI in the transition process in Poland, a country with a very limited capacity to generate capital and to change its structure due to a long history of central planning and mismanagement. Poland expects FDI to play a major role in three areas: first and foremost, it expects FDI will stimulate the privatisation process of its economy, thereby not only converting the structure of the Polish economy into an efficient one, but also playing a major role in integrating the economy into the international system; secondly, FDI is expected to be a strong contributor of foreign capital which Poland needs due to its currency shortages; and finally, Poles expect that a further benefit of FDI will not only be the introduction of modern technology know-how, but also managerial skills. The major argument is that foreign investment, through its introduction of modern technology and international connections, will change Poland's export structure to high-value-added products (Jermakowicz and Bochniarz, 1991).

The objectives of MNCs have not always been compatible with national policies, especially in times of globalisation, technological change, spatial organisation of economic activity and increasing competition for market share. The reasons why in practice there has been a great deal of conflict, lie in the overall economic environment in general and in the FDI policies in particular, as mentioned earlier. Poland aimed to attract FDI with a variety of policy instruments and changes to its legal system. It also offered a wide rage of incentives, including tax holidays and subsidised credits to foreign investors. These major policies which affected the entry and operations of FDI will be discussed in detail in the following section.

FOREIGN INVESTMENT POLICY

The first Polish foreign investment regulations were in force by the end of the 1970s when the communist government created limited business opportunities for Polish émigrés looking to invest from abroad. A major liberalisation came in 1986, from which date foreign investment legislation became progressively more liberal, opening more sectors of the economy to foreign investors, allowing the full transfer of profits abroad and, finally, giving investors more control over their ventures. This meant a basic departure from the enclave-model approach to foreign investment. Since the departure from the enclave model in the late 1980s, and the gradual shift toward the national treatment approach (Kubielas,1996: 20–35) finally adopted in the 1991 FDI law, we can now distinguish many changing periods in FDI policy.

Before 1989, foreign capital participation was allowed only in the form of foreign partnerships limited to small-scale production and joint ventures with minority foreign interests. The establishments thus formed were subject to a complicated procedure of authorisation which excluded entry into sectors deemed important for social or state interests. They were also subject to severe restrictions on the repatriation of profits and capital invested, which were made dependent on the result of their hard currency balance of payments, with the remainder of their hard currency proceeds being compulsorily resold to the central bank under strict exchange controls. All tax allowances were strictly related to the company's export performance. With limited access to the state-regulated distribution of material supplies, and effective prohibition on the acquisition of real estate,

these partnerships and joint ventures were essentially treated as for-
eign-financed vehicles/enclaves earning hard currency for the
central bank of Poland. Without compensation guarantees in the
event of expropriation, with licences usually issued for only ten
years and restricted transferability of ownership interest even
within Poland, it is not surprising that these partnerships and joint
ventures usually adopted a 'quick buck' strategy, turning in extremely
effective export performances in market niches with unusually high
profitability.

However, the average capital investment per firm was always as low
as possible (tending to the minimum foreign capital requirement of
$US50 000). The investors were usually people of Polish origin (Polo-
nia-Poles living abroad) living in neighbouring countries, content to
spend their profits on living expenditures in Poland (Jermakowicz,
Bochniarz and Toft 1994:18).

The first big wave of new FDI establishments came after the joint
venture law was fundamentally amended in 1988, and reached its peak
in 1990. The law was further modified in December 1989 in connection with the liberalisation of the foreign exchange law, and again in
July 1990 in connection with the law on privatisation. The whole
package was a major step towards a national treatment of companies
with foreign participation. Joint ventures gained free access to all
material supplies and the right to acquire real estate under a permit
of the Ministry of the Interior. The restrictions on majority holdings
were abandoned, though the transfer of shares and the initial setting-
up of operations still required a permit from the Foreign Investment
Agency.

The regulations on the expatriation of profits were much relaxed,
though the connection with a company's hard currency balance of
payments was maintained, while the proceeds from the sale of shares
on the dissolution of the company could not be transferred until 10
years had elapsed, unless the proceeds were in hard currency or the
company was liquidated pursuant to a judicial execution (for example
expropriation). This was still enclave treatment in comparison with
what home enterprises enjoyed, but continued drawbacks were significantly counterbalanced by privileged tax status, as joint ventures
gained a general three-year income tax holiday combined with three-
year concessions on import duty of production inputs. It turned out to
be a genuinely attractive legal arrangement for foreign investors,
provoking a massive explosion in new registrations with relatively
small amounts of capital invested. These investors followed what

might be called a foothold strategy, marked by presence rather than extended economic operation.

The final step towards the national treatment of FDI was made with the enactment, in July 1991, of the Law on Economic Activity with the Participation of Foreign Parties. Under this law, practically all restrictions on the transfer of profits or equity capital were abandoned. The requirement that the setting-up of such activities be authorised by a state body was also abandoned, except for a few special areas (defence, sea and airports, legal practice and real estate services) where permits would still be required, as they would also need to be where privatisation of state enterprises was involved. At the same time, however, the automatic three-year corporate tax exemptions were also discontinued except for investments above ECU 2 million, or if joint ventures were located in a depressed area with high structural unemployment, or brought with it new technology, or exported more than 29 per cent of its output.* At the same time, a total guarantee of payment of equivalent compensation for losses in the event of expropriation was now offered by the Ministry of the Treasury. These new regulations may be regarded as the most important factors in the second wave of FDI inflow, in 1992, which was comparable to the first one in terms of the number of establishments, but far more impressive in terms of capital invested with the annual inflow reaching nearly $US1 billion for the first time, and all this despite sharply declining profit margins on sales and returns on equity. At the same time, foreign investors significantly increased their stake in established joint ventures as measured by the percentage of foreign capital participation or average capital invested per firm. This may have signalled a change in investment strategy in favour of more long-term involvement, less affected by the short-term prospect of a temporary tax holiday. This process of the liberalisation of FDI legislation culminated in the Law on Companies with Foreign Participation of 14 June 1991.

This Law was amended in March 1996, abolishing special administrative requirements for setting up and operating a company with foreign capital so that the conditions offered to foreign investors were equal to those enjoyed by local businesses. A permit would be required when a legal entity transferred state-owned assets to a joint venture. Poland also signed bilateral agreements on the protection and promotion of foreign investment with several countries. In July 1996, Poland became a member of the OECD, which, along with the liberalisation of capital flows, included changes making it easier for foreign companies to set up in Poland. More generally, all new laws are now screened for compatibility with EU legislation, while existing ones are to be gradually reviewed and amended in the same direction. ·

The following legal forms are available to a foreign investor who wishes to establish a business entity in Poland (for details see Appendix A4.3):

- a limited-liability company (Sp.z.o.o.), in which shares are issued in exchange for contributed capital;
- a joint-stock company (S.A.), which differs from a limited liability company (apart from the required minimum of equity capital) in that there is a possibility of issuing bearer shares; companies listed on the Warsaw Stock Exchange must have a joint-stock form; or
- a representative or branch office.

A foreign investor may enter Poland in order to:

- establish a limited-liability company, in which the foreign investor may join other foreign or Polish investors or be the sole owner;
- establish a joint-stock company with other foreign or Polish shareholders (but not alone). The establishment of a joint-stock company generally requires at least three founders;
- establish a joint-stock company with other foreign or Polish shareholders with equity raised through a public subscription of shares (a separate permit issued by the Securities Commission is required for a public offering); or
- acquire an interest in an existing Polish limited-liability or joint-stock company.

Tax Policy

Poland moved quickly, early in the 1990s, to established a modern tax structure. In doing so, it closely followed the Western European pattern combining personal and corporate income tax with a value added tax (VAT) and several excise taxes. After six years, the legislative work was largely done. New, Western-style taxes have performed very well but with less net effects on public finances and private enterprise operations than the raw data suggest (World Bank Country Study, 1994). New challenges are now emerging for further liberalisation and changes in tax regulation in accordance with the country's transition to a market economy and its accession to the EU. The major changes in tax regulations should concern new tax rates, capital group taxation, and the issue of transfer pricing (for details about taxes see Appendix A4.4).

Tax Incentives

The Council of Ministers' regulation concerning new investment tax reliefs was published in *Dziennik Ustaw* (*Journal of Laws*) nos. 18/94 and 68/94. It introduces investment tax relief for limited-liability companies, joint-stock companies, state-owned enterprises, cooperatives and other business entities. Foreign investors enjoy equal treatment with Polish investors. The law granting the possibility of deductions specifies six situations in which persons can take advantage of reliefs:

- Parties that invest at least ECU 2 million: parties that have invested no less than ECU 2 million before starting operations may deduct this sum from their revenue in a given year and over the next three years (up to 25 per cent per year).
- Exporters: if a company's export-derived profit constitutes more than 50 per cent of the export revenue derived from export in a given year and exceeds ECU 8 million, taxpayers may deduct their investment expenses from their revenue. A possibility thus exists for a revenue deduction of up to 50 per cent.
- Licences, patents, results of domestic R&D projects: taxpayers who incur investment expenditures upon the purchase and installation of machines or devices, or connected with the implementation of licences, patents and results of domestic development projects can deduct the investment sum from taxable revenue. A possibility exists for a revenue deduction of up to 50 per cent.
- Sale of sea products and processed fish outside Poland (SSW 234): taxpayers who derive profits outside Poland from the sale of sea products and processed fish to foreign parties, and who have invested in machines and devices, have the right to deduct expenses worth up to 50 per cent.
- Profit margin: a company's profit must constitute at least 4 per cent of revenue in the sectors of food processing or construction services, or 8 per cent of revenue in other cases. All taxpayers who have met this condition may deduct the whole or part of their investment expenses from their taxable revenue. The maximum deduction from revenue cannot exceed 25 per cent per year.

- Medicines, medical equipment and ISO 9000-quality systems: tax-payers purchasing machinery or equipment or constructing buildings to set up a high-quality security system for production, or implement a certified ISO 9000-quality system are allowed to deduct expenses for the above equalling up to 50 per cent of taxable revenue.

Reliefs defined in the Council of Ministers' regulation do not apply to taxpayers who have already taken advantage of any other reliefs or deductions (including tax reliefs defined in the Law on Companies with Foreign participation of 14 June 1991). In the case of concurrence of deduction rights, the taxpayer may take advantage of only one of the rights. Also, Poland has signed withholding tax rates for double tax treaty relief with many countries (for details see Appendix A4.5) (PAIZ, 1997; Dutkiewicz, and Sowinska 1996)

Economic Zones

To boost the economies of poor Polish regions, the government has launched a series of Special Economic Zones centred on aging heavy industries. The first zone 'Euro-Park' (designated SSE in Polish) opened in 1995 in the southern town of Mielec, where aircraft manufacture had been located. Four SSEs were created near Czestochowa, Katowice, Lodz and Suwalki in 1996; another four were due to be established in 1997. Also, the Council of Ministers proposed the establishment of so-called separate investment-project concentration areas in late spring 1996. The separate project concentration areas were to be set up in areas vacated by state farms and in communes with only one major workplace. Provincial governors and provincial tax offices would draw up area maps.

The main idea behind these special areas is to give investors tax breaks, although they are smaller breaks than SSEs can offer. To encourage investment in regions with high unemployment, the Industry Ministry is considering social-security breaks, making investors exempt from ZUS social insurance premiums, which currently boost employers' labour costs by approximately 48 per cent (Dutkiewicz and Sowinska 1996). The Polish government has also established four duty-free zones in major big cities.

TRADE POLICY

The reform process began in 1990 when Poland abolished the state monopoly and administrative management of foreign trade; the trade system was largely liberalised and made transparent, with customs duties becoming the main trade policy instrument. Foreign trade corporations were dismantled and all firms and individuals could take part in export and import operations. The number of firms engaged in foreign trade increased, and private enterprises grew rapidly, especially in import activities. The most dynamic part of the foreign trade activity was located outside the state sector, and this non-state sector accounted for an increased share of trade flows (see Table 4.5)

The increased share of private firms in foreign trade resulted from the creation of new private firms and from the privatisation process itself. Joint ventures with foreign capital also gained increased importance both in exports and imports (Lemoine, 1996). Despite these changes, SOEs still retained an important position in export supplies, thus confirming the fact that in the area of foreign trade the SOEs were able to adjust their behaviour to the new incentives (Naughton, 1995). Initially, Poland used trade policy as an instrument to combat near hyperinflation in 1990–91. Thus, most non-tariff restrictions were eliminated (January 1990) and customs duties were suspended on 4500 import items (June 1990), with the average applied tariff being only 5.5 per cent, so as to use import prices as transmitters of world market prices. Thereafter, to support the budget and the balance of payments, the tariff suspension was withdrawn (August 1991) and the average unweighted most-favoured-nation (MFN) tariff rose to 18.4 per cent. This was followed by the implementation of an across-the-board 6 per cent import surcharge (which was due to abolished in 1997), from which only alcoholic beverages, tobacco products, fuels and automobiles were exempted (World Bank 1994: 63–70).

Table 4.5   *Poland: The private (non-state) firms in foreign trade*

Activity	1993	1994	1995	1996
In exports (%)	44.0	46.4	48.6	52.7
In imports (%)	59.8	60.2	61.7	64.5

Source: Warsaw School of Economics, *Poland – International Economic Report*, World Economic Research Institute, Warsaw, 1996, pp. 61–78

To assist the transformation process, the EU improved access to its markets, initially through a bilateral trade and cooperation agreement (September 1989) that provided for the phasing out of selective quantitative restrictions (QRs) over a ten-year period and granted MFN status, including the more favourable generalised system of preferences (GSP) treatment for some goods (January 1990). In December 1991, the EU further opened its market for Poland, when the Association Agreement with Poland, Hungary and Czechoslovakia was signed. This agreement fostered further expansion of trade with the EU, the share of EU partners in Poland's external trade having already become more important than for several EU countries themselves, underlining Poland's continued integration with Western Europe.

Exports are being facilitated by the phasing out of EU tariffs on Polish exports that began in 1992 with the abolishment of duties on almost half of Poland's industrial exports. By January 1995, around 70 per cent of Poland's industrial exports (representing 85 per cent of total (recorded) exports) benefited from duty-free access to the EU market. This privilege was extended to steel products in January 1996, and encompass textiles and clothing as well from January 1997 and voluntary export restraints were lifted in this sector by March 1998. Among the remaining barriers to exports to the EU are antidumping actions, mainly affecting the metallurgical and chemical sectors (Foreign Trade Research Institute, 1995). In 1998 most of the barriers to export to the EU were removed in the spirit of closer economic integration of Poland with the EU on the way to full membership by year 2003 or 2004. In addition, there are some self-imposed export quotas, such as for raw skins and metal scrap (however, Poland agreed in early 1996 to relax some of those export restrictions), as well as some export licensing requirements (for petroleum products, dairy items and textiles).

On the import side, the Uruguay Round led Poland to liberalise 96 per cent of its tariffs on industrial goods (exceptions included motor vehicles, automotive components, oil and some textile products), and later included all tariffs on agricultural products. The phasing out of tariffs stipulated in the European Agreement started on the Polish side with the abolishment in 1992 of customs duties on one-quarter of its industrial imports (especially capital goods and raw materials), followed by a series of cuts in the remainder spread out over the second half of the 1990s. From 1999, most imports of industrial goods from the EU should enter Poland duty free. Tariffs on imports from other countries of the Central European Free Trade Association (CEFTA) are also subject to accelerated cuts. As a result, the trade-weighted average tariff for industrial goods declined to 9.5 per cent in January 1995 and 6.75 per cent in January 1996 (see Table 4.6).

In the case of agricultural products, the average import tariffs remain much higher, partly due to the conversion of non-tariffs into tariffs. Under the Uruguay Round Agreement, agricultural tariff ceilings were to be reduced by 36 per cent in six annual instalments from 1995, but given that the ceilings are not binding on most items, actual tariff rates may not fall that much (OECD, 1997: 19). To further diversify its geographical expansion of trade, Poland signed similar agreements with the European Free Trade Association (EFTA). The agreement with EFTA parallels in many ways the EU Association Agreement, but could be considered more liberal overall. Tariffs and QRs are eliminated for all industrial goods (except textiles and metallurgical products, mainly steel); there is a completely free trade in fish products; and processed agricultural products receive the same treatment granted to EU goods before the introduction of the European Economic Area (EEA). Furthermore, foreign payments and pricing mechanisms within the former Council for Mutual Economic Assistance have been transformed into a standard system of payments for transactions valued at world prices, and most of these transactions are now settled in convertible currencies. Internal subsidies have been reduced or in some cases completely eliminated. Producer subsidies were of two types – direct trade subsidies and production subsidies. Direct trade subsidies have mostly been eliminated, while production subsidies have been reduced by varying degrees. External subsidies, which allowed intra-CMEA prices to deviate substantially from world prices, have been eliminated (Drabek and Smith, 1995).

Table 4.6   *Poland: import tariffs (%)*

	1994	1995	1996	1997	1998	1999	2000
Agricultural products	2.04	19.52	20.17	19.77	19.37	18.98	18.60
Industrial products	18.38	14.49	9.78	4.92	3.58	2.50	2.15
Combined	19.48	16.30	11.03	6.70	5.47	4.48	4.12
Imports surcharge	6	5	3	0	0	0	0

Note: The rates overstate actual tariffs in so far as they abstract from tariff suspensions, which as of January 1996 were equivalent to about one percentage point.
Source: Centre for Eastern Europe, *Poland – Economic Surveys*, OECD, Paris, 1997, p. 125.

In 1994, the government implemented an export promotion programme, including tax and financial incentives as well as the provision
of guarantees and insurance. Tax incentives consist of VAT refunds
for export products, income tax relief for investors involved in export
promotion, and property tax relief for companies investing in exports.
Financial relief will be provided by the National Bank of Poland
(NBP) through attractive refinance credits to institutions financing
exports. Finally, the Export Credit Insurance corporation (KUKE)
will be recapitalised ($15 million) and an additional fund will be
established for the provision of export insurance against non-commer-
cial risk.

FOREIGN EXCHANGE CONTROL SYSTEM

Legislation governing foreign exchange transactions is aimed at
defending the domestic convertibility of the zloty. Polish currency as
well as securities expressed in Polish currency may be transferred
abroad and from abroad without any limitations. The limitations
relate to foreign exchange values which principally means foreign
exchange currency and international money Special Depos-
itory Rights. Clear distinction is made between 'foreign' and 'domestic
entities' which have different rights and responsibilities. 'Domestic entities' relates to companies set up under Polish law including
also those companies with foreign capital. The representative offices
of foreign-based campanies are also classified as 'domestic entities'
'Foreign entities' relates to companies based outside Poland, branch
offices and representations abroad of banks and insurance companies
with their seat on the territory of Poland as well as natural persons
with their residence outside Poland PAIZ, 1996; KPMG–Polska 1995.
There are a number of general regulations relating to foreign exchange
transactions:

- all domestic settlements, with few exceptions, are made in zloty.
  Use of foreign currencies for this purpose is prohibited;
- all receivables of foreign origin, denominated in foreign currencies,
  must be immediately transferred into Poland (for instance current
  payments to Polish companies from foreign importers may not
  exceed a three-month period).

It is however permissible to:

- credit foreign or Polish importers subject to informing the NBP about the transaction, and within generally accepted terms of such credits on world markets;
- offset mutual, current receivables and liabilities with a given client up to $US50 000;
- collect receivables of up to $US10 000 in any form.

Companies treated as 'domestic entities' may hold a foreign currency account in Poland or abroad only in exceptional cases, with the permission of the NBP. Moreover, they may buy foreign currencies in order to settle foreign exchange liabilities subject to the following general rules:

- payments for goods and services must be properly documented by invoices;
- payments of dividends abroad may only take place after an audit of the company's financial statements.

Foreigners working in companies and representative offices are not subject to the above restrictions. They are allowed to transfer foreign currencies to Poland, to keep foreign currency accounts in foreign exchange banks and to buy Polish zloty, depending on their needs. The transfer of foreign currencies abroad nonetheless requires that their origin be documented.

FOREIGN EXCHANGE POLICY

During the 1980s, the value of the Polish zloty was determined in terms of a basket of currencies and adjusted periodically with a view to securing the profitability of Polish exports. In addition to the official market, there was an unofficial market for foreign exchange where the value of the zloty was determined by market forces. As inflation accelerated, the size and frequency of adjustments in the official exchange rate increased.

The liberalisation of the foreign exchange system has been an important component of trade policy. In Poland, as in most CEE countries, the initial devaluations were followed by the reappreciation of the currencies (IMF, 1994). At the beginning of 1990, internal convertibility of the zloty was introduced and the foreign exchange market for current transactions was unified at a rate of Zl 9500 per

US dollar, which involved a 31.6 per cent devaluation of the official rate (Table 4.7). Alongside the official fixed exchange rate, the parallel market rate continued to be determined freely by market forces in a market where a large number of small foreign-exchange dealers (*kantors*) have participated.

The purpose behind fixing the exchange rate was to break Poland's emerging hyperinflation – in the latter half of 1989, the monthly rate

Table 4.7 *Poland: exchange rate policy*

Period	Exchange rate policy	Action	Comments
Before 1990	Multiple exchange rates, adjustable peg to a basket of currencies	Frequent and substantial devaluation	
1 January 1990	Fixed exchange rate system	Unification of official and black market rates; devaluation (31.6%)	Exchange rate: Zl 9 500 per $US
17 May 1991	Fixed exchange rate system	Devaluation (16.8% against the dollar, 14.4 against the basket); shift from a dollar peg to a basket peg	Exchange rate: Zl 11 100 per $US Basket includes: 45%, deutsche mark 35%, pound sterling 10%, French franc 5%, Swiss franc
15 October 1991	Pre-announced crawling peg	Rate of crawl announced: 1.8% per month (Zl 9 per day)	Basket unchanged
25 February 1992	Pre-announced crawling peg	Devaluation (10.7% against the basket); rate of crawl: 1.8% per month (Zl 11 per day)	Exchange rate: Zl 13 360 per $US Basket unchanged
10 July 1992	Pre-announced crawling peg	Rate of crawl: 1.8% per month (Zl 12 per day)	Basket unchanged Technical adjustment made
27 August 1993	Pre-announced crawling peg	Devaluation (7.4% against the basket); rate of crawl reduced: 1.6% per month (Zl 15 per day)	Basket unchanged
10 February 1995	Pre-announced crawling peg	Devaluation (6.7% against the basket); rate of crawl reduced: 1.2% per month (Zl 9 per day)	Exchange rate: Zl 9800 per $US Basket unchanged
20 January 1996	Pre-announced crawling peg	Rate of crawl reduced: 1.0% per month	Basket unchanged Technical adjustment made

Sources: Ministry of Finance, *Poland – Exchange Rate*, Ministry of Finance, Warsaw, 1997; IMF, *Poland – The Path to a Market Economy*, Occasional Paper no. 113, IMF, Washington DC, 1994, p. 46.

of inflation averaged 30 per cent (IMF, 1994: 45–54). In May 1991, in order to reverse the outflow of foreign currency reserves and the loss of international competitiveness, the exchange rate arrangement was shifted from the dollar peg to a peg based on a basket, given an increased concentration of trade with Western Europe, and the zloty was devalued by 14.4 per cent against this basket. The latter was composed of five main convertible currencies, roughly in proportion to the currency composition of the Polish trade turnover. Furthermore, to reduce the loss of competitiveness while at the same time maintaining the role of the exchange rate as a nominal anchor, a pre-announced crawling-peg system was introduced on 15 October 1991. This active crawling-peg policy was accordingly set below the projected inflation differential with trading partners.

The rate of crawl has also been lowered once, which is consistent with the authority's determination to reduce inflation. Under the new system, the official exchange rate against the same basket would depreciate daily, so as to achieve a depreciation of 1.8 per cent per month (approximately 24 per cent on an annual basis); the daily correction was intended to lower the trade risk associated with sharp and unpredictable exchange rate adjustments.

In 1995 the NBP continued with the exchange rate policy initiated in 1991. Its aim was to limit the impact of devaluation on inflation, ensure a safe level of foreign exchange reserves and protect the competitiveness of Polish exports. The main change which took place in 1995 was the introduction of a floating exchange rate mechanism on 16 May. The following considerations argued for letting market instruments play a greater role in the determination of the exchange rate:

- sustained economic growth;
- a surplus in the supply of foreign exchange reserves; and
- liberalisation of foreign exchange regulations.

The move to a more flexible exchange rate mechanism was made with a view to reducing the influence of foreign exchange reserves on money creation. The exchange rate of the zloty against convertible currencies on the interbank market is allowed to float but with fluctuations confined within a 7 per cent band of the central bank rate. The new arrangement aimed at increasing the bank's freedom of action in disposing of foreign exchange reserves and in their exchange rate policies towards customers. The object of this liberalisation measure was to stimulate competition on the interbank market and to lower the costs of servicing customers (OECD 1997). The objectives of the exchange rate policy have been preserved thanks to the following elements of the new system:

- retention of the principle of monthly devaluation of the zloty;
- the possibility of influencing the market exchange rate through NBP intervention.

The rules of the new exchange rate system provide for three kinds of rates:

- the central (par) rate;
- the fixing rate; and
- the exchange office rate.

The central rate is fixed by the NBP every morning as a par rate on the basis of information from the Frankfurt market. It is subject to a monthly devaluation of 1.2 per cent against a basket of currencies. The fixing rate is the closing price on the interbank market expressed in terms of two currencies: the US dollar and the deutsche mark. The margin of permitted fluctuation around the par values is 7 per cent. It is used as the official rate for statistical purposes. The exchange office rate is freely determined on the currency market by each office.

LABOUR MARKET POLICY

The major framework for labour policies is provided by the Law on Employment and Unemployment of December 1989. This law was changed so many times during 1990 and 1991 that a replacement was needed (a new law was drafted in 1996 and some adjustment was made in 1998). Other supplementary legal Acts have been issued to establish the legal background for specific labour market policies; the Ministers of Labour and Social Policy share responsibility for the implementation of these policies. Labour market policies are financed by the 'Labour Fund', whose revenues come from compulsory contributions paid by employees (in 1993, 3 per cent of an employee's gross wage) and state budget transfers. Total revenues of the fund increased from 4600 to 24 000 billion zlotys between 1990 and 1992, that is from 0.6 to 2 per cent of GDP (Gora, 1994; PAIZ, 1995–97).

Similar to other CEE countries, until 1993 the Labour Fund was primarily utilised for paying unemployment benefits; roughly 86 per cent of the fund was spent on this sector. The share of unemployed persons receiving benefits among all unemployed has substantially decreased over time, from 70 to 40 per cent between 1990 and 1993 (Gora, 1994), although the number of recipients has tripled. The decline of the coverage stems from the aforementioned change to the regulations.

Companies with foreign participation can employ any number of personnel. There are no limitations either to the number of employees or to their remuneration. Recruitment and dismissal in labour contracts is free and based on international practice. Joint ventures can freely chose their own hiring and firing strategies as necessary. Companies with foreign participation can also determine their own organisational structures and personnel policies. Enterprises with foreign investment are obliged by contract to train Polish workers, but local labour offices do not interfere in the selection process for training. An employment contract may be concluded for an unspecified period, for a specified period or for the period required to carry out a specified piece of work. Such contracts may be preceded by a contract for a trial period which shall not exceed two weeks. In the case of a managerial or other independent post, or post carrying significant personal liability for property entrusted to the employee, the trial period can be up to three months.

Labour policy regarding wages in enterprises with foreign participation is on an equal footing with normal entitlements in similar local enterprises. Insurance contributions to the social security scheme (ZUS) are 48.5 per cent of gross salary comprising 45 per cent for social security, 3 per cent for the Unemployment Fund, and 0.5 per cent for the Employee's Benefit Guaranteed Fund, for both Polish and foreign citizens. These are paid entirely by the employer, who must register with the ZUS department responsible for the region in which the employer is located within 10 days after the first employee has started work. In addition, employers of companies that are not covered by collective labour arrangements are required to establish social benefit funds. The mandatory annual contribution to the fund is 37.5 per cent of the average monthly salary in the national economy multiplied by the number of employees. Table 4.8 shows a comparison of monthly wages for countries in transition.

Table 4.8   *Poland: monthly wages in the economies in transition*

Country	Wages in $US/month
Bulgaria	114
Croatia	250
Czech Republic	221
Estonia	85
Hungary	317
Latvia	98
Lithuania	65
Poland	194
Romania	82
Slovenia	421
Slovak Republic	201
Russia	99

Sources: Centre for Eastern Europe, *Poland – Economic Surveys*, OECD, Paris, 1997, p. 180; EU Commission, *Poland Membership to EU*, Commission of the EU, Brussels, July 1997, p. 119.

Products and services produced or provided improperly by the employee due to his own fault can be penalised by the withholding of some or all of his remuneration; on the other hand, the employee is entitled to remuneration for interruptions in employment which are not his fault. Finally, if some problems arise with reference to an employment contract or other related matters, the case can be brought before the employment courts by either the employer or the employee.

PRIVATISATION POLICY

Policies to deal with state enterprises had to take into account the influential position of Polish workers, both within the enterprises and in the legislature. In 1989 the Solidarity movement struggled with a fundamental debate over the role of workers in management. Many members of Solidarity, although supporting the freeing of markets, wanted a system of workers' management. The liberal intellectuals, however, argued that such a system would create too much rigidity, pointing to the unsuccessful Yugoslav policies to support their position, and were strongly supported by Western advisers, the IMF and the World Bank. The Polish government has tried hard to control the privatisation process, and there was a political consensus when the Mazowiecki government came to power to prevent at all costs the continuing 'nomenklatura' privatisation. The cost of doing so was to recentralise the process in the new Ministry of Ownership Transformation; however, government privatisation programmes proved very difficult to implement, and the most effective forms of privatisation were those that depended the most on initiatives from below and required the least government control and decisions, such as the very successful privatisation of small shops and firms in 1990.

There have also been debates over another important question: what should be done to promote good management in enterprises that may not be privatised, at least in the relatively short term, because of their functions (for example public utilities), the absence of buyers or the strong preference of their workers? Programmes were introduced in some industries to deal with such enterprises, and legal forms for independent state firms do exist, but a general policy covering the remaining state sector is still in the process of being developed. Policies governing the remaining state enterprises are assessed in the following section.

Methods of Privatisation

Privatisation has been proceeding along three main routes. The first, under the heading of direct privatisation or liquidation, covers small and medium-sized enterprises. The second route, usually referred to as indirect or capital privatisation, concerns larger firms and involves open sales of shares and the search for strategic outside investors. The third route, mass privatisation, is meant to distribute ownership rights to all citizens. This only started in 1996 and on a fairly limited scale but increased its scale during 1997/98. In addition, a number of SOEs have been commercialised – that is, transformed into wholly-state-owned joint-stock companies (for details about each privatisation see Appendix A4.6).

By the end of 1995, privatisation or commercialisation had been initiated in less than half of the SOEs that existed in 1990 when the process began, and privatisation had been completed in less than 20 per cent of cases (Table 4.9). Even in the latter, the state has sometimes retained a substantial proportion of shares, remaining the controlling shareholder. Direct privatisation has followed two tracks. A substantial portion of enterprises were subject to Article 37 of the 1990 Privatisation Law, the assets and liabilities often being leased to insiders as the first step towards an eventual purchase; this method strengthens the control of the enterprise by workers and management.

Table 4.9   *Poland: progress of ownership transfer*

	1990	1991	1992	1993	1994	1995	1996
Total number of SOEs	8453	8228	7245	5924	4955	4357	3987
Bankruptcy (article 19 of SOE Law):							
Started	18	540	857	1082	1245	1358	1780
completed	0	19	86	186	303	396	590
Direct privatisation (article 37 of the							
Privatisation Law):							
started	31	449	719	917	1042	1149	1540
completed	0	182	475	707	945	1054	1280
Converted into JSC*	38	260	480	527	723	958	1240
NIE-programme	0	0	0	0	0	321	589
Capital privatisation	6	27	51	96	147	219	280
Public offerings	5	11	12	15	19	22	25
Trade sales	1	16	39	81	110	132	156
Mixed methods	0	0	0	0	3	5	7
Tenders	0	0	0	0	0	0	3
Debt–Equity swaps	0	0	0	0	15	60	80
Total:							
started	87	1249	2056	2526	3010	3465	3850
completed	6	228	612	989	1395	1669	1790
Income privatisation (flows in mn zloty):							
total		170.9	484.4	780.4	1594.8	2641.7	
leasing/sales of liquidated assets	n.a.	46.4	171.8	287.0	322.9	406.2	186.6
capital privatisation	n.a.	124.5	308.7	439.4	846.7	1714.2	1100.9
bank privatisation	n.a.	0.0	3.9	54.0	425.2	521.3	150.6

Notes: * joint-stock companies; n.a. = not applicable.
Sources: Centre for Eastern Europe, *Poland – Economic Surveys*, OECD,
Paris, 1997, p. 67; Ministry of Privatisation, *Privatisation in Poland*, Ministry
of Privatisation and Central Statistical Office, Warsaw, 1997.

A large number of enterprises in poor financial condition were liquidated in accordance with the provisions of Article 19 of the 1981 Law
on SOEs, the assets being mainly sold to private entrepreneurs; this
has proved an efficient way to put idle productive capacity back into
use. The sale of immobile and social assets, however, has been more
difficult and, as is evident from Table 4.9, this type of liquidation
procedure usually takes several years to be completed. Capital privatisation has been the main source of revenue for the budget even
though it concerned a much smaller number of firms. In 1994–95,
the scope of capital privatisation increased, extending notably to the
tobacco industry. Many deals involved foreign buyers, who in 1995
accounted for two-thirds of the revenue from capital privatisation. In
a number of cases the foreign investor had to offer employment or
wage guarantees to the incumbent workforce. Finally, a growing share

of income from ownership transfer is coming from bank privatisation (OECD Report, 1997; Staar, 1993).

Assessing the merits of alternative privatisation methods with respect to corporate governance is complicated by potential selection biases: it cannot be ruled out that post-privatisation performance was superior under one scheme or other because the pool of the firms covered by the latter was better to begin with. Nevertheless, a conclusion reached in many surveys is that the most impressive improvements in enterprise performance were obtained through capital privatisation especially when it involved foreign investment. Two advantages of this mode of ownership transfer are that it brings in an outsider motivated by the firm's future results rather than by the protection of insider rents, and that it is often accompanied by a significant injection of fresh human, physical and financial capital. It should also be noted that several new private firms started operations with assets that formerly belonged to SOEs and that they have prospered.

In September 1996, after three years of tempestuous discussions and negotiations, a Law on the Commercialisation and Privatisation of SOEs was enacted. The Law does not alter the basic principles of multi-track privatisation but does include several new rules. The Law continues to provide for the commercialisation of large SOEs slated for subsequent privatisation, but the consent of enterprise insiders is not required any more. Such commercialisation involves the abolition of the workers' council as a management body, depriving it of the ability to block privatisation. A new option is commercialisation without subsequent privatisation, applicable in particular to enterprises requiring restructuring. In this case, commercialisation is to be decided by the government as a collective entity rather than by the Ministry of Privatisation (Dabrowski, 1995).

Ownership transfers in 1996 were expected to involve the initiation of the direct privatisation of 150–200 enterprises and the acceleration of capital privatisation, which would embrace approximately 90 firms, including a number of very large ones such as Polish Airlines (LOT), the Katowice Steel Mill and, the copper producer Polska Miedz (the latter will constitute one of the biggest privatisation deals in the CEE), and most of the large enterprises was finaly privatise in 1998/9 up to 20–25 per cent of shares of the company went to foreign firms. Capital privatisation in 1996 was also scheduled to encompass firms in the chemical, pharmaceutical, food, machinery, building materials and trade sectors. In 1999 direct privatisation accelerated specially capital privatisation which embraces new sectors of the economy such as telecommunication, mining, and transport. New coalition government especially it's Minister of Finance, Mr Balcerowicz is determined to close down inefficient enterprises and finalise the privatisation of the rest left behind.

CONCLUSIONS

Foreign investment policies have been shaped by general economic policies which in turn create the investment environment. China's import-substitution policy push for advanced rather than appropriate technology, and policy-induced price distortions, negative real rates of interest, high wages for unskilled labour and undervalued foreign exchange rates have been pervasive. The effect of policy distortions often led local governments to intervene, either by directly imposing decisions on recruitment and local market access or else by offering enough cheap credit or subsidised inputs to make the desired decisions profitable from an enterprise's perspective. The interest rate on bank loans was kept far below the market-clearing level, but some unfavoured firms cannot obtain enough of the credit they need. Not only was the interest rate low, but both interest and principal payments were normally tax deductible. The Chinese economic system favoured highly capital-intensive industries and technologies, resulting in the allocation of resources in very different directions from those seen in developing market-oriented economies. This kind of policy environment serves as an impediment to the export performance of enterprises with foreign investment in manufacturing, in turn limiting the contribution of FDI to economic development in China.

In contrast to China, Poland up to mid-1994 accepted a mixed policy of import substitution and export promotion dictated by a different economic environment. Prices for goods and interest rates were liberalised and set by the market, and exchange rates were determined in terms of a basket of currencies to secure the profitability of Polish exports. Convertibility of the Polish zloty was introduced; the foreign exchange market for current transactions was unified; and the zloty was devalued to create a more competitive edge for Polish exports. Interest rates were reduced and the producer-price-based real effective exchange rate appreciated. The exchange rate of the zloty against convertible currencies on the interbank market was allowed to float but with fluctuations confined within a 7 per cent band of the central bank rate. The new arrangement was aimed at increasing the banks' freedom of action in the disposal of foreign exchange reserves and in their exchange policies towards customers. The objective of these liberalisation measures was to stimulate competition on the interbank market and to lower the cost of servicing customers. In addition to these exchange and interest rate policy actions, import tariffs and import surcharges were cut several times. The surrender requirement for export proceeds was abolished, which also reduced conversion costs borne by the enterprises. These kinds of policy measures serve as a stimulation for export performance for enterprises with foreign investment, and as a significant contribution to the expanding role of FDI in the economic development of Poland.

5 Trends and Patterns of FDI: An Overview

This chapter examines the patterns and trends of FDI inflow into China between 1979–96 and Poland between 1989–96, with particular attention to FDI in manufacturing. At the beginning of the chapter, a survey of global trends is undertaken in order to place the experiences of China and Poland into perspective. Based on published official data it discusses the trends, investment sources, ownership, regional distribution and sectoral characteristics of FDI.

GLOBAL TRENDS AND PATTERNS

After a brief decline during the early 1980s, global FDI flows have increased dramatically. During 1986–95, the amount of global FDI grew at an annual rate of 30 per cent, rising from $US78 to $US315 billion (United Nations, 1996: 5–28). In 1995, the developed countries received 64 per cent of this amount, with Western Europe (40 per cent) and North America (24 per cent) absorbing the largest shares (the amount of FDI received by Japan was relatively small, constituting only about 2 per cent of the global total). These figures point to the dense networks of cross-holdings of production and financial assets among the industrialised countries of the world.

[The developing countries have received increasing amounts of total global FDI inflows.] In 1996 they received record inflows of $US100 billion (32 per cent) of the total FDI. This amount, was concentrated among a few host countries, so that 32 per cent of the global total (or about 74 per cent of the amount received by the developing world) went to the top ten countries. These are newly-industrialising countries (NICs) that command large domestic markets and/or serve as dynamic export platforms (Singapore, China, Malaysia, Mexico, Thailand, Brazil, Argentina, Taiwan, Indonesia and Egypt).

The sectoral destination as well as the country origination of FDI have undergone some changes over time. The relative share of FDI in the primary sector has fallen, whereas those in the secondary and tertiary sectors have risen. Among the major investor nations, FDI in the primary sector exceeded 14 per cent of the total FDI portfolio only in the case of the Netherlands and the UK (United Nations, 1996). The bulk of investment has gone to the manufacturing and service sectors in particular. Consequently, the traditional form of Western investment in the developing world's mineral and cash crops has declined in importance.

Most of the FDI still originates from developed countries. In 1995, five countries, (Japan, the USA, France, Germany and the UK) were responsible for 75.7 per cent of the value of the global FDI outflow (UN, 1996). However, motivated by concerns with rising labour wages, pollution cost and foreign protectionism, several NICs have also begun to invest more FDI. For instance, Taiwan invested $US24 billion in FDI in 1989–95 and the amount for Korea was $US11 billion in these six years. They have become net capital exporters, whereas the reverse has been true for the USA (whose FDI inflow has been several times larger than its FDI outflow in the recent past). Among the major home countries for FDI, Japan and the UK led the USA in the value of net FDI outflow during recent years.

The emerging patterns reflect recent and ongoing trends. Firstly, rising FDI emphasises the growing importance of intra-firm trade; that is, transactions among the subsidiaries of the same multinational corporations (MNCs). It has tended to displace arms-length transactions, and thus to create comparative advantages due to domestic sourcing, economies of scale, transfer pricing and captive markets. Disparities in such advantages can in turn alter international trade balances and national industrial competitiveness. These considerations augment the traditional incentives for FDI that stem from the desire to prolong product cycles and to protect market share (Knickerbocker, 1973; Vernon, 1977).

Secondly, the ongoing process of globalisation as well as the regionalisation of national economies tend to spur FDI. The diffusion of production techniques, the standardisation of product design, the easing of transport and communication barriers and the conventions of subcontracting and local sourcing have facilitated this investment, especially of the export-oriented kind.

Thirdly, the diminishing amount of official development aid, the debt crises of the early 1980s and the examples of Asia's export-oriented economies have increased the relative acceptance of FDI in many developing countries. At the same time, a process of privatisation has been evident in a number of capitalist economies, developed or developing, whereby governments deregulate industries and abandon the less-efficient public enterprises. These trends as well as a general turn away from the import-substitution approach to industrialisation have opened up more opportunities for FDI.

Fourthly, the developments just noted have been most dramatic in the economic reforms of the former socialist economies. In an ironic reversal of the dependency theory, officials in Eastern and Central Europe, China and Vietnam have eagerly sought FDI in their attempts at market liberalisation and export expansion. Although starting from rather low levels, FDI inflow has expanded rapidly for some. For example, from 1986 to 1996 its value rose from $US 0 to 420 million for Vietnam, from $US16 million to $US12 billion for Poland, and from $US1.8 to $US170 billion for China (World Investment Report, 1996). The incorporation of those countries into the capitalist world economy appears to augur more competitive bidding for FDI.

CHINA: TRENDS IN FDI INFLOW

The growth of FDI in China is one of the most dramatic consequences of China's change in economic policy from a planned economy towards a market economy. Since the beginning of the open-door policy in 1979, China estimates 260 109 foreign investment projects to have been contracted worth $US440.7 billion. However, it is also true that almost 90 per cent of the total number of contracts were undertaken in the five-year period 1991–95, with 80 per cent of the total value accounted for in that same period. The total utilised amount of FDI rose from the initial $US110 million in 1979 to 140 billion in 1995 with over 260 000 projects approved by the end of 1995, at an annual growth rate of 57.12 per cent. Since 1993, China has become the second largest FDI recipient in the world (following the USA) and the single largest host country among developing countries (UNCTC) 1994 and 1995: 53). As Table 5.1 reveals, there was a slow inflow of FDI in the early 1980s (even a decline in 1985), with considerable fluctuations from year to year until the early 1990s. Up to 1986, foreign investors found it extremely difficult to undertake commercial transactions in China because of the lack of a legal framework and little attention being directed towards attracting foreign investment.

Table 5.1　*China: development of FDI, 1979–95*

Year	No. of projects	Contracted* ($US billion)	Implemented* ($US billion)
1979–82	922	6.01	1.17
1983	470	1.73	0.64
1984	1 856	2.65	1.26
1985	3 073	5.93	1.66
1986	1 498	2.83	1.87
1987	2 233	3.71	2.31
1988	5 945	5.30	3.19
1989	5 779	5.60	3.39
1990	7 273	6.60	3.49
1991	12 978	11.98	4.37
1992	48 764	58.12	11.0
1993	83 000	111.0	27.5
1994	47 490	81.4	33.8
1995	37 126	90.3	37.7
1996 (forecast)	14 061	45.6	19.8
Total	260 109	440.7	151.6

Note: *　contracted-FDI based on signed contracts, but not always actual inflow; implemented-FDI which actually was officially invested in host country.
Source: MOFTEC, '*Zhongguo Duiwai Jingi Maoyi Nianjian*', *South China Morning Post*, 13 February 1996.

In 1986 and 1987, more serious attention was given to the foreign investment environment: investment incentives were provided and the legal environment for FDI was better defined. Due to these changes there has been an increase of FDI inflow into China which has been growing continuously ever since (Table 5.1). There was, however, a halt in 1989 after the Tiananmen incident as China was sanctioned by a number of Western countries. In addition, an economic retrenchment programme, initiated in 1988 to curb high inflation rates, had an adverse effect on FDI in 1989. According to the data published by MOFTEC, the pledged FDI projects declined from 5945 in 1988 to 5779 in 1989, representing a negative growth rate of −2.8 per cent. In the second half of 1990, FDI in China began to recover as Western countries gradually normalised their relations with China and accepted China's tough stance on the pro-democracy movement.

Before analysing the data it is important to mention the reliability of the Chinese statistics and the vast differences between signed and implemented projects. As source materials the data should be interpreted with care because the various calculation methods, the lack of an agreed nomenclature for different categories, the absence of certain statistics and indeed the use sometimes of statistics in support of propaganda, often make it necessary to stand back a little from official figures and make some adjustment to the interpretation. The vast differences between signed and realised projects presented in the right-hand columns of Table 5.1 is related to the foreign investment environment, particularly to the government regulations and laws. Long delays in the approval procedure, heavy government regulations, rigid laws and red tape force many firms to abandon many signed projects. Further obstacles encountered by foreign firms will be described in detail in Chapter 7.

Analysing Table 5.1 reveals the first big jump in FDI in 1992 when foreign companies established more projects (116 per cent), worth more in pledged investment (111 per cent) than in the complete period 1979–91. Although there were increased commitments to larger projects in China, the average external investment contract continued to be relatively small at about $US2.5 million in 1995 (*South China Morning Post*, 13 February 1996). This big increase in 1992 happened after the FDI environment was spurred along by Deng Xiaoping's visit to Southern China in January 1992, when he argued for a more rapid development of the open-door policy. It was also helped by the adaptation of the 'socialist market economy' doctrine at the 14th CCP (The Chinese Communist Partys) congress held in October 1992. The high growth rates in 1992 and 1993 were partially related to the huge investments in real estate from overseas.

Despite its steady long-term uptrend, FDI in China has experienced short-term fluctuations that tie in closely with the stop–go economic policy cycle of the Chinese economy. For instance, in terms of contracted value, FDI registered substantial increases of 124 per cent and 43 per cent in 1985 and 1988 respectively, when the Chinese economy was growing rapidly. However, it dropped to 52 per cent in 1986 and recorded a marginal growth in 1990 as a result of economic retrenchment. Moreover, the utilisation ratio (utilised amount/contracted amount) dropped steadily from 60 per cent in 1989 to 23 per cent in 1993, implying that the economic projects generated from FDI had slowed down. In other words, although the Chinese economy has maintained a double-digit growth over the last three years, the anti-inflationary measures have slowed down the process of economic projects, leading to an uneven distribution of resources and uneven economic development across the country.

There are several other indications of slow-down in inflows of FDI to China. This is due partly to investment policy changes in relation to the cancellation of many investment incentives and partly to the emergence of investment alternatives in East Asia, CEECs and the former Soviet Commonwealth Independent States. External investment decreased in 1995 to $US90.9 billion, down 3 per cent on 1994's $US93.7 billion and 26.2 per cent lower than the record $US123.2 billion in 1993 (*South China Morning Post*, 13 February 1996). The number of contracts signed also fell to 37 126, down 22 per cent on the 47 490 in 1994 and less than half the record 83 000 contracted projects in 1993. This trend can also partially be explained by the changing government regulations regarding the FDI environment, where the government has slowly withdrawn preferential tax treatments and other incentives in accordance with the 'national treatment' strategy announced in the Ninth Five-Year Plan (1996–2000), where foreign funded enterprises would be treated on an equal footage with domestic ones. It is also partly due to increased government experience in the selection of projects, becoming more targeted to the needs of the country's economic development and its economic development policy.

OWNERSHIP STRUCTURE

Chinese statistical authorities categorise FDI projects into five different groups: equity joint ventures, contractual joint ventures or co-operative joint ventures, joint development, wholly foreign-owned enterprises and other foreign investment (including imported inputs for processing and assembly). Table 5.2 indicates that equity joint ventures have been the most popular form since the mid-1980s, constituting about half of the foreign capital directly invested, but the growth of wholly foreign-owned enterprises has been the most rapid form in recent years. Contractual joint ventures have started to decline in recent years. Joint development ventures pertain mainly to offshore petroleum exploration, a form of FDI that was extremely popular in the early 1980s but which has been declining in recent years.

Equity joint ventures (EJVs) have become increasingly important since 1985. By the end of 1995, 161 361 equity joint ventures had been approved with an intended investment of $US185.5 billion, of which $US15.2 billion had been invested by the end of 1990. They therefore

Table 5.2 *China: FDI by institutional form ($US bn)*

Year	Contracted			Utilised			No. of projects approved		
	CJVs	EJVs	WFOE	CJVs	EJVs	WFOEs	CJVs	EJVs	WFOE
1979	–	0.01	–	–	–	–	–	6	–
1980	0.5	0.06	0.01	–	–	–	321	20	4
1981	0.13	0.03	0.26	–	–	–	70	28	14
1982	0.93	0.03	0.05	0.53	0.10	0.04	402	29	12
1983	0.50	0.19	0.04	0.23	0.07	0.04	330	107	18
1984	1.48	1.06	0.08	0.46	0.26	0.02	1,089	741	26
1985	3.50	2.03	0.03	0.58	0.58	0.01	1,500	1,412	46
1986	1.36	1.38	0.02	0.79	0.80	0.02	582	892	18
1987	1.29	1.92	0.47	0.62	1.48	0.03	786	1,399	45
1988	1.62	3.13	0.48	0.78	1.98	0.23	1,621	3,909	410
1989	1.08	2.66	1.65	0.75	2.04	0.37	1,179	3,659	931
1990	1.25	2.70	2.44	0.67	1.89	0.68	1,317	4,091	1,860
1991	2.14	6.08	3.64	0.76	2.30	1.14	1,778	8,395	2,795
1992	13.25	29.13	15.70	2.12	6.12	2.52	5,711	34,354	8,692
1993	2.55	55.17	30.46	5.24	15.35	6.51	10,445	54,003	18,975
1994	20.30	40.19	21.95	7.12	17.93	8.04	6,634	27,890	13,007
1995	17.83	39.74	33.66	7.54	19.08	10.32	4,787	20,455	11,761

Notes: CJVs = contractual joint ventures; EJV = equity joint ventures; WFOE = wholly foreign-owned enterprises.
Source: Chyungly Lee, 'FDI in China: Do State Policies Matter?', *Issues and Studies*, Taipei, no. 7, July 1997, p. 61.

played a central part in the government's strategy to attract foreign investment. Indeed, they were the government's preferred mechanism for introducing FDI into China during the 1980s, mainly because they allowed the Chinese government to retain influence through its ownership position, through which the Chinese state could arguably exert the greatest degree of control. These ventures were also relatively well-established compared to other investment forms, which made it much easier to obtain comprehensive information about them. They are limited-liability companies established by two or more partners that pool assets to create a separate legal entity for the purpose of undertaking a specific business (such as producing cars). The objective is usually to extend or complement the business of the investors. The size of most EJVs is relatively small, particularly those from Hong Kong and Taiwan. Equity joint ventures can now be found in every province of China, and about 68 per cent of all joint ventures are found in manufacturing (Pearson, 1997; Li Kui-Wei, 1997).

In the first few years of opening up to the outside world, FDI in China mainly took the form of contractual joint ventures (CJVs) as well as joint development ventures and 'compensation trade and export processing ventures'. Together, these accounted for 82 per cent of foreign investment during the period 1979–84. CJVs in particular were generally smaller in scale and were found in low-skill, labour-intensive industries which were located mainly in the four SEZs and Guangdong Province. A majority of the investors took advantage of the low wages and cheap land prices in China. In addition, the forms of CJVs were quite flexible and usually required no cash outlay by Chinese partners. As Table 5.2 indicates, the number of projects and intended value of contractual joint ventures plunged from 1500 projects with an intended value of $US3.50 billion in 1985 to 582 projects with an intended value $US1.36 billion in 1986, slowly recovering in 1988 after the first legislation for CJVs was enacted. It then started to decline again in 1993 from 10 445 projects to 4787 in 1995 (Chyungly Lee, 1997).

As shown in Table 5.2, EJVs have become increasingly important since 1985. The number of wholly foreign-owned enterprises (WFOEs) also surged after 1987 whereas CJVs and 'other investment ventures' declined. In 1987, WFOEs accounted for only 1.7 per cent of actual FDI; in 1995 there was sharp rise to $US10.32 billion. These enterprises accounted for 24.6 per cent of actual FDI that occurred after China passed the Law of the PRC on Wholly Foreign-Owned

Enterprises in April 1986. The increase of WFOEs was due mainly to three factors. Firstly, there was a huge surge of FDI from Taiwan in the late 1980s, and Taiwanese investors are usually inclined to control their own companies rather than to cooperate with partners. Secondly, considerable cost and time problems involved in the coordination of technology and management deemed essential in EJVs and CJVs were avoided by establishing WFOEs. Thirdly, there was greater acceptance by the Chinese government of WFOEs which are export-oriented and bring into China much needed foreign-exchange earnings. Up to now, WFOEs have been small in size and mostly established in SEZs and coastal areas (Chyungly Lee, 1997). As sole owner, the foreign investors bear all the risks and formally have rights to management and all (after tax) profits.

During the 1980s and in the early 1990s, the average size of contracts in EJVs and CJVs fell (Table 5.3). This may be because China is not as attractive to MNCs as initially thought, and there are more regulations of informal Overseas Chinese investments. The duration of contracts has been quite flexible, foreign investors theoretically being permitted to extend the duration at will without any restrictions in most sectors. In January 1986, the Joint Venture Law was amended so that the duration of joint ventures could be extended from 30 to 50 years or even more. It is interesting to note the sharp increase in average size of WFOEs. This development underlines the increasing confidence felt by foreigners seeking to make long-term commitments in the wake of improvements in China's legal framework and investment environment.

Table 5.3 *China: average size of foreign firms, 1979–95 ($US mn per agreement)*

Type	1986	1987	1988	1989	1990	1991	1992	1993	1994	1995
EJVs	1.5	1.4	0.8	0.7	0.7	0.6	0.6	0.5	0.4	0.3
CJVs	2.3	1.6	1.0	0.9	1.0	0.8	1.1	0.9	0.7	0.5
JDVs	13.5	1.6	11.7	20.4	38.9	26.7	21.6	18.9	16.7	10.3
WFOEs	1.1	10.2	1.2	1.8	1.3	1.6	1.9	2.3	2.6	2.9

Note: JDVs = joint development ventures.
Sources: Data for 1986–91 are calculated from the Statistical Bureau, China Statistical Information and Consultancy Service Centre, Beijing, 1992, pp. 353–55; data for 1992–95 are calculated from the State statistical Bureau, China Statistical Publishing House, Beijing, 1996, p. 286.

SECTORAL COMPOSITION

The objective of China's economic policies in the early stages of transition was to attract import-substituting industries to the country; China tried to promote its development through highly protected import substitution. Thus, it attracted a significant amount of FDI in the industrial sector during the initial years (Table 5.4). On the other hand, it is clear that foreign investment has been skewed towards the tourism and hotel industry, whereas agriculture has received a minimal share of FDI. During 1983–84, the tourism and hotel industry accounted for 37.4 per cent of total FDI with a value of $US103 440 million. By 1986 the amount of FDI in this sector reached nearly 60 per cent of all foreign investment. Foreign investors concentrated on the service sector during those early years because the investment climate in industry was less than satisfactory. At the same time, the payback period for investment in hotels was shorter than in industry, which was attractive to many investors.

Table 5.4　*China: value of FDI by sector, 1983–95 (%)*

Sector	1983	1984	1985	1986	1987	1988
Tourism, real estate and services	4.7	32.7	35.9	57.1	39.7	10.0
Agriculture, forestry and fishing	2.0	2.7	2.0	2.2	3.4	3.9
Light and heavy industry	13.7	21.5	37.6	27.7	47.9	75.9
Communications, post and telecommunications	3.2	2.9	1.7	1.2	0.4	1.7
Commerce and catering	2.1	3.8	8.3	3.5	0.8	1.2
Finance and insurance	18.9	33.1	5.8	4.5	5.7	3.8

	1979–89	1990	1991	1992	1993	1994	1995
Tourism, real estate and services	25.2	6.8	12.6	31.1	39.3	29.4	26.4
Agriculture, forestry and fishing	3.1	1.8	1.8	1.2	1.1	1.2	1.6
Light and heavy industry	52.9	84.4	80.3	56.9	45.9	47.4	54.6
Communication, post and telecommunications	1.3	0.6	0.8	2.7	1.3	1.8	2.1
Commerce and catering	4.7	1.7	1.4	2.5	4.1	5.3	5.8
Finance and insurance	10.5	0.8	0.8	2.2	3.4	3.8	3.9

Source:　State Statistical Bureau, *Foreign Investment in China*, China Statistical Information and Consultancy Service Centre, Beijing, pp. 315–18.

With the promulgation in 1986 of the Provisions of the State Council for the Encouragement of Foreign Investment (the so-called Twenty-Two Article Provisions), the industrial climate improved. Also, the Regulations on Guiding Foreign Investment Operations, approved by the State Planning Commission in 1987, played a role in attracting investors to ventures in the industrial sector. Consequently, there has been a larger share of FDI to the industry sector ($US17.76 million or 47.9 per cent in 1987, see Table 5.4) but FDI in the real estate and hotel sector was still substantial ($US14.71 million or 39.7 per cent) in 1987. Due to the surplus of hotel rooms from earlier investments, China temporarily halted further investment in hotels in 1988. Thus, FDI in industry continued to increase significantly in terms of both relative share (over 80 per cent in 1990 and 1991) and absolute value (from $US7.8 million in 1987 to $US512.54 million in 1993) when it reached its peak (see Table 5.5). After 1993, however, we can see a slowly declining trend.

By the end of 1987 the inflow investment into infrastructure, power generation and distribution had remained very low. These areas require relatively large amounts of investment and are heavily regulated. Investors in these areas face difficulties in repatriating foreign exchange profits abroad. FDI in other sectors, such as commercial and financial service industries, was negligible. The official view is,

Table 5.5   *China: contracted FDI by sector ($US million)*

Sector	1986	1987	1988	1989	1990	1991	1992	1993	1994
Agriculture	0.62	1.25	2.09	1.21	1.22	2.20	6.78	11.91	9.72
Industry	7.85	17.76	40.21	46.64	55.69	96.23	326.67	512.54	439.53
Construction	0.53	0.55	1.19	0.67	1.81	1.34	18.39	38.78	23.94
Transportation and tele-communication services	0.33	0.16	0.91	0.52	0.36	0.95	15.43	14.90	20.30
Commerce, food service and Material supply	1.00	0.29	0.64	0.67	1.07	1.74	14.44	46.06	39.22
Real estate, public residential and tourism	16.17	14.71	5.30	5.24	4.52	15.04	180.8	437.71	238.62
Health care, sports and social welfare	0.16	0.11	0.05	0.36	0.38	0.64	3.95	4.77	19.79
Education, culture and arts	0.41	0.14	0.44	0.07	0.05	0.56	0.97	4.52	6.08
Scientific research	0.00	0.01	0.07	0.04	0.32	0.19	0.62	5.88	2.74
Others	1.26	2.11	2.04	0.58	0.53	0.89	13.17	37.82	26.87

Source: Data for 1986–90 are calculated from the State Statistical Bureau, Almanac of China's Foreign Trade and Economic Cooperation 1990–1994, *China Foreign Economic Statistics 1979–1994*, Beijing, published by China Statistical Information & Consultancy Service Centre, 1995, pp. 320–50.

however, that the sectoral balance of FDI since 1984 has improved toward more investment in manufacturing (Table 5.5).

The Tiananmen Incident in 1989 dealt a serious blow to tourism, and FDI in hotels shrank even further, but as people's memories faded, tourism fully returned to normal in 1992. Notwithstanding the marked shift in favour of manufacturing, the service sector continued to be a substantial recipient of foreign capital at the beginning of the 1990s (Table 5.5).

Most of the FDI projects in China are in export-oriented manufacturing industries. During the period 1979–93, the percentage share of the manufacturing industry by the number of projects and contract value was the largest at 74.1 per cent and 52.8 per cent, respectively. However, with the structural changes in the Chinese economy, the pattern of investment began to change also. In 1989, for example, 83.3 per cent of FDI was in manufacturing and mainly concentrated in the export sectors. However, by 1993 its share had dropped to 45.9 per cent while the relative share of real estate and public utilities had shot up to 39.3 per cent from 9.4 per cent in the same period. Although the manufacturing industry continues to capture a large amount of FDI, it is increasingly being targeted at the domestic market. FDI has begun to concentrate more on infrastructural developments so as to maintain a longer economic life. This can also be confirmed by looking at the share of investment in different sectors in the last 14 years (Table 5.4). The gap in the share between those two sectors has been narrowed, suggesting that the development of infrastructure has become the major task. FDI in manufacturing was concentrated in low-end, labour-intensive industries rather than capital or skill-intensive enterprises. This was generally demonstrated by the small size of projects. In 1995, the average size of an industrial project was $US1.12 million. Larger-scale projects were normally found in the real estate, public utilities and services subgroup, which includes hotel development.

There are indications that China has been able to attract more capital-intensive projects in recent years. According to Chinese officials, 'productive' (non-service-related) projects accounted for 90 per cent of total projects approved (Li Ku-Wei 1997). Also, the Chinese government put forward the policy of exchanging market share for technology. Foreign-funded enterprises (FFEs) could sell their products made by advanced technology and could also sell the products as substitutions for imports. This created many opportunity spaces for the FFEs and the hope that the Chinese government would shift FDI to more capital- and skill-intensive industries. The most recent five-year plan (1996–2000) gives priority to FDI for agriculture, energy, communications, imported raw materials, high technology and utilisation of resources, especially in the central and western provinces. Moreover, the manufacturing industry was to increase productivity and efficiency by better management techniques but also by a higher growth of engineering and high-tech industries like machinery, electronics and biotechnology. Export-oriented, high-tech FDI and import-substitution investments will have special preference, especially if they are shifted from coastal areas to the western and central regions, regions relatively neglected so far.

SOURCE-COUNTRY COMPOSITION

Since 1979 more than 40 countries or areas have invested in China (see Table 5.6). On the one hand, FDI in China by country of origin shows a significant concentration in terms of the total number of investing countries. On the other hand, it also reveals a greater concentration in terms of the amounts invested by the source countries and the changes in the shares of investment stock made by various source countries between 1979–1994. As shown in Table 5.4 from the period 1979 to 1994, Newly Industrialising Economies (NIEs) Hong Kong, Taiwan, Singapore and South Korea have been the major investors, accounting for 73.9 per cent of the total accumulated FDI inflows into China. Among NIEs, Hong Kong and Macau have been the largest investor areas taking up to 62.2 per cent of total FDI inflows, followed by Taiwan (8.02 per cent), Macau (1.56 per cent), Singapore (1.45 per cent) and South Korea (0.82 per cent) (Chen Chunlai, 1996; Chyungly Lee, 1997).

It should be stressed that published FDI figures for Hong Kong are overstated; in fact part of the investment flow from Hong Kong originated in Southeast Asia. Some overseas Chinese and Taiwanese investors invested in the mainland through subsidiaries registered in Hong Kong to avoid scrutiny from their home countries. Investing in China by wealthy overseas Chinese businessmen was politically sensitive in some Southeast Asian countries such as Indonesia, and in Taiwan investors were legally prohibited from investing in China prior to 1990, although Taiwanese businessmen found ways to circumvent government restraints by registering ventures through Hong Kong. The rule was relaxed in 1990 to allow Taiwanese firms to invest

Table 5.6 *China: FDI inflows by source country, 1979–94 ($US millions at current prices)*

Source country	1979–86	1986–89	1989–94
Hong Kong	876	5 693	48 764
Taiwan	–	–	8 269
USA	256	783	5 844
Japan	247	1 091	5 145
Singapore	7	134	1 900
Macau	–	78	1 381
South Korea	–	–	1 216
UK	54	67	996
Germany	19	99	629
France	33	44	409
Developing countries	950	6 466	65 279
Developed countries	684	2 435	14 863

Note: For further details about source countries and regions see Appendix A5.1.

Source: Calculated from the various issues of the China Statistical Yearbook, *Almanac of China's Foreign Economic Relations and Trade*, Beijing (Zhongguo Duiwai jingji Maoyi Chubanshe), MOFERT, various issues, Beijing.

in the mainland through proper registration with the Taiwanese government. Consequently, future accounting for FDI through Hong Kong will be more accurate, but data on investment flows for previous years coming from Hong Kong include Taiwan and other Southeast Asian interests. Moreover, there are some China-funded firms in Hong Kong and Macau that have established joint ventures with other domestic Chinese firms. These so-called 'bogus blue-eyed' joint ventures were established to take advantage of the preferential treatment given to joint ventures. Clearly, the existence of this 'reverse investment', as it often called by the Chinese, overstates the flow of foreign investment funds from Hong Kong (Chyungly Lee, 1997; *The Economist*, 1996).

After Hong Kong, the second largest foreign investor in terms of contractual FDI value for the period 1979–91 was the USA (see Table 5.6) at over 9.6 per cent, followed by Japan (7.5 per cent), Germany (2.1 per cent) and Singapore (1.7 per cent). The USA and Japan have been by far the largest foreign investors among developed source countries investing in China. No other single developed country has invested more than 1 per cent in China, including the Western European countries even though they are main source countries in international FDI. Developing countries' investment in China is very small, 0.31 per cent for other Asian countries and 0.17 per cent for Eastern European countries.

In the two periods 1979–91 and 1992–95, the share of investment in China from various source countries changed greatly. The share from the NIEs increased substantially from 61.7 per cent to 77.8 per cent, mainly the result of investment from Taiwan and South Korea. In the period 1992–95, the share of Taiwan's investment stock in mainland China exceeded that of the USA and of Japan. It rose from $US3.12 million to $US9.21 million in 1995. Taiwan is now the second most important investor in China. Investment flows from South Korea have also become increasingly important: in 1992–95, South Korea's investment position climbed from obscurity to fifth place, its accumulated FDI in China reached $US1.28 million, close to the total FDI inflows from the UK to China and larger than those from any other Western European country.

Another significant increase in the share of accumulated FDI in China was made by the ASEAN countries. Their combined share increased from 0.52 per cent in 1979–91 to 1.88 per cent in 1992–95. Among ASEAN countries, Thailand has been taking the leading position to invest in China, followed by Malaysia, Indonesia and the Philippines. By contrast, the share of accumulated FDI in China for all developed source countries has declined. From the period 1979–92 to 1992–95, Japan's share declined from 14.11 per cent to 5.45 per cent, the US's share from 11.71 per cent to 6.87 per cent, and Western European countries' share also declined from 6.74 per cent to 3.56 per cent.

Since the NIEs' investments, particularly those of Hong Kong, have been the largest part of the story of FDI in China, it is worth looking at them in a little more detail. The remarkable intensity of the NIEs' investments in China is explained both by factors which led to the rapid emergence of NIEs as source countries of FDI, and by specific developments in China. Two factors are important: firstly, rapidly rising real wages in the NIEs rendered many labour-intensive industries uncompetitive, and FDI was seen as a means of utilising accumulated managerial and technical expertise in those industries; and secondly, the NIEs are upgrading their technology and restructuring their economies as they accumulate human and physical capital relatively rapidly compared with other countries. FDI is an efficient means to transfer their labour-intensive industries abroad to earn a return on their accumulated assets in these activities. Perhaps even more important in explaining the upsurge was the remarkable coincidence in timing of China's economic reform and the NIEs' economic restructuring. A gold-rush mentality developed among NIE investors towards China's reforms, precisely at the time that NIE firms were eagerly seeking out overseas investment opportunities.

The rapid increase in FDI in China from ASEAN countries (Thailand, the Philippines, Malaysia and Indonesia) in the late 1980s and early 1990s resembled the early pattern of investment from the NIEs in most respects. In general, the changing domestic economic structures and extensive overseas Chinese business networks have led to and facilitated companies of ASEAN countries to venture into China. Investments from developed countries are somewhat different from those of NIEs and other developing countries. This is due firstly to the fact that the technological gap between the developed countries and China is relatively large, and the transfer of technology is hampered to a certain extent by the appropriateness of technology. Secondly, the firms of developed countries usually possess more advanced technology and production techniques (Table 5.7).

The differences between developed countries and NIEs as well as between developed and developing countries has been demonstrated very strongly in investment patterns of various source countries. Table 5.8 clearly indicates the differences in evolution of the economic and technological levels of various source countries, the relative sector investment intensity changes from labour-intensive industry to capital-intensive and to human-capital-intensive industry, indicating the investment sequences as countries change their proportion of factor endowments and their economic and technological structures.

Table 5.7   *Relative sector investment intensity in China by source countries (%)*

Sector	ASEAN	NIEs	Western European	Japan	USA
Labour-intensive	142	109	95	76	81
Capital-intensive	44	112	77	67	75
Human-capital-intensive	72	88	127	161	148

Note: Table presents the relative sector investment intensity of source countries in the three manufacturing sectors. These indicators show the share of that sector in the total inflows from this source, compared with that sector's share in total inflows from all sources.
Sources: MOFERT, *Almanac of China's Foreign Economic Relations and Trade*, China Statistical Publishing House, Beijing, various issues; State Bureau of Statistics, *China Statistical Yearbook*, 1995–97.

Table 5.8   *China: the average size of FDI projects, 1979–95 ($US mn)*

Countries	1979–91	1992	1993	1994	1995
Hong Kong/Macau	1.03	1.30	1.51	1.52	1.54
Taiwan*	0.90	0.86	0.91	0.92	0.89
USA	2.51	0.96	1.01	1.04	1.08
Japan	2.07	1.20	0.85	0.89	0.90
Germany	9.81	1.00	0.78	0.85	0.91
Singapore	1.63	1.34	1.69	1.70	1.74
UK	5.53	2.27	5.71	5.68	3.80
Australia	1.88	0.77	0.83	0.80	0.85
Canada	1.71	0.80	1.23	0.90	0.97

Note: *Taiwan's data for 1983–91.
Sources: State Statistical Bureau, *Zhongguo Duiwai Jingji Tongji Daquan*, China Statistical Information and Consultancy Service Centre, Beijing, various years; *Editorial Board, Almanac of China's Foreign Economic Relations and Trade*, Beijing, various years.

As illustrated in Table 5.8, investment projects made by Taiwan and Hong Kong are small in scale, with an average value of $US0.90 million and $US1.03 million respectively. The average project size for Hong Kong investors increased in 1994 and 1995. The average size of FDI from Germany is the largest at $US9.81 million, followed by the UK at $US5.53 million and the USA at $US2.51 million during 1979–91. The average Japanese FDI project is quite small, but the Japanese FDI in China accounts for only 1.3 per cent of Japan's total overseas investment and 6.5 per cent of its total investment in Asia. In view of Japan's huge economic power, its proximity to China, and its traditional cultural ties with China, the relatively small total FDI has been disappointing. This can be explained partially by the relative difficulty in transferring Japanese technological know-how to China, and partially by the huge bilateral trade surplus in Japan's favour. China has been critical of Japan's reluctance to invest more, particularly when the good performance of Japanese FDI is taken into consideration.

REGIONAL DISTRIBUTION

China's foreign investment policy has had an important geographical dimension: the reformers targeted China's coastal areas as the leading regions for the country's economic development and as the places from which the development process could spread to the rest of China. The Chinese government originally emphasised that FDI should flow primarily only into specially designated areas, hoping that by isolating foreign investment it could observe its activities and guard against any negative effects that might appear. This uneven development created huge conflicts between coastal and inland provinces, it also put pressure on the central government in terms of the huge influx of unskilled labour mainly from western rural provinces to urban areas of the east coast of China in terms of social accommodation in the cities. The close geographical proximity and tight cultural and linguistic links between southern China and the overseas Chinese communities in Taiwan, Hong Kong and Macau have also directly contributed to the observed geographical pattern of China's FDI.

Thus, locational benefits appear to be a prime consideration for investors contemplating participation in any FDI venture in China. In the fierce scramble to secure foreign capital, many municipalities have sought to bypass central regulations by offering potential overseas investors additional benefits such as concessions on land rentals, labour charges and other local levies, both legal and illegal. Such preferential treatment often outweighs the advantage which the status of being an SEZ confers over other areas designated for foreign investment, creating conflicts of interest with the central government's development policies.

China's coastal areas were the first regions targeted for the country's economic development (Tables 5.9 and 5.10); up to 1992 they absorbed more than 80 per cent of the total capital. However, the inflow of FDI has taken place in three distinctive investment areas. The first areas were the five Special Economic Zones (SEZs) which were created in early 1979 in Shenzhen, Zhuhai and Shantou in Guangdong Province, Xiamen in Fujian Province and Hainan Province, all of them on the south-east coast. They accounted for over 20 per cent of total FDI during the period 1979–89. In the SEZs, foreign investors could expect preferential treatment with respect to tax incentives, flexible arrangements for land use with reductions in charges, reduced welfare contributions, flexible arrangements for employing labour and the possibility of preferential prices for raw materials and equipment. However, the unique role of SEZs as attractions for foreign investment declined after the first phase of the investment policy.

In 1984, the Chinese government designated 14 major coastal cities as 'open cities' and granted them many of the privileges it had earlier

Table 5.9 *China: actual utilised FDI, by province and area ($US mn)*

	1979–86	1986–89	1989–95
Coastal regions			
Beijing	1.40	9.16	39.91
Shanghai	1.48	8.69	93.26
Jiangsu	0.18	2.44	135.94
Fujian	0.61	5.1	127.9
Shandong	0.19	1.98	82.86
Guangdong	7.23	27.17	339.1
Central regions			
Shanxi	–	0.18	2.43
Hubei	0.12	0.57	20.43
Hunan	0.09	0.15	14.09
Jilin	0.01	0.09	9.81
Heilongjiang	0.17	0.73	11.28
Henan	0.06	1.12	12.65
Western regions			
Sichuan	0.15	0.53	21.3
Gansu	–	0.03	1.66
Ningxia	–	–	0.27
Guizhou	0.02	0.11	3.44
Yunnan	0.04	0.15	2.89
Qinghai	–	0.03	0.08

Note: Selected regions are included which have had some foreign capital inflow.
Source: State Statistical Bureau, *China Foreign Economic Statistical Yearbook*, China Statistical Publishing House, Beijing, various years.

Table 5.10 *China: regional share of actual utilised FDI ($US bn/%)*

Regions	1986–91		1992–95	
	Amount	*%*	*Amount*	*%*
Coastal region	14.51	91.93	95.04	88.14
Central region	0.67	4.25	9.03	8.38
Western region	0.60	3.82	3.76	3.48

Source: Chyungly Lee, *FDI in China: Do State Policies Matter*, Issues and Studies, Beijing, no. 7, July 1997, p. 46.

reserved for SEZs. These 'open cities' were given greater autonomy in policy-making, were allowed to offer special incentives (such as tax holidays) to encourage FDI, and were authorised to set up special districts, so-called 'Economic and Technological and Development Zones'. In 1992, these 'open areas' received some 82.3 per cent of all contracted foreign investment. Guangdong province attracted the largest amount of total investment, while Jiangsu, Fujian and Shandong provinces had increased their relative shares during 1989–95 (see Table 5.9).

The next areas opened to foreign investment were the remaining inland provinces, which are backward in terms of both their economy and their infrastructure. In terms of the growth trend of FDI inflows during the period 1986–95 as shown in Table 5.10, the three provincial groups have experienced different patterns. As FDI surged during the period 1991–94, there were some shifts in geographical distribution. The five SEZs remained important, but their share of FDI had declined relative to that of the coastal provinces in 1992 and 1993. Of the 'open coastal cities', Dalin and Shanghai recorded the largest increase in terms of percentage share. Although Guangzhou's FDI increased in absolute terms throughout the period, its relative share remained rather stable at about 5.5 per cent. Open coastal areas continue to absorbed the lion's share of FDI with larger percentage shares during 1992–95 (see Table 5.10) as compared to the period 1986–91. On the other hand, Beijing's FDI declined in relative terms over the period 1990–94. Another notable recent development is that inland areas have attracted more FDI, although their relative values are not very significant. Within the eastern region, there is a shift of FDI inflows from the south-eastern towards the north-eastern provinces. Guangdong's share in FDI inflows has declined steadily as FDI inflows into Jiangsu, Zhejiang, Shandong and Hebei provinces have increased. The proportion of investment to China's hinterland increased by 60.9 per cent to an overall contracted inward investment share of 17.7 per cent. Traditionally, businessmen from Hong Kong and Taiwan have concentrated their investments in the Pearl River delta and Fujian province; there is a notable trend that more investors from Hong Kong and Taiwan are seeking investment in the Yangtze River delta and some inland areas.

FDI AND TRADE ORIENTATION

Since China started its open-door policy, the country's exports have expanded at an average annual rate of 16 per cent, enabling its export position to improve from 32nd in 1978 to 10th in 1995. In 1993, the year when China achieved a trade surplus with the USA of $US23 billion, foreign-funded firms accounted for 27.5 per cent of China's exports and for all of the growth in its exports over 1992 (*The Economist*, 18 March 1995).

The domestic market-orientation of FDI was more strictly controlled to ensure that the SEZs no longer served as off-shore centres for illegal transactions in foreign exchange and trade for the interior. It was evident in 1986 that the Chinese government wanted to discourage foreign investment in tourism and real estate and encourage it in export-oriented and technologically advanced industries. They emphasised the SEZs and 14 coastal cities, and in those areas the volume of exports by enterprises with foreign investment increased after 1986 and their share in total exports became significant (Table 5.11), but the percentage of the foreign-enterprise output which was exported in 1990 was still low at less than 5 per cent, lower than the national average of 9.7 per cent. This suggests that about 90 per cent of foreign enterprises' output in the SEZs and the 14 coastal cities was directed to domestic markets, and that most enterprises with foreign investment were domestic market-oriented in those areas (except in Fuzhou and Yantai).

Table 5.11   *China: exports by foreign-invested enterprises (FIEs) and total merchandise exports, 1985–95 ($US bn)*

Year	Total exports	Annual export growth of FIEs (%)	Exports of FIEs as % of total exports
1984	26.14	–	–
1985	27.35	0.4	1.5
1986	30.94	0.8	2.6
1987	39.44	1.2	3.0
1988	47.52	2.4	5.1
1989	52.54	3.6	6.9
1990	61.98	6.0	9.7
1991	71.84	9.2	12.7
1992	85.00	12.3	18.9
1993	91.80	17.2	21.5
1994	121.00	27.3	21.6
1995	148.80	35.2	39.5

Sources: State Bureau of Statistics, *International Financial Statistics Yearbook of PRC*, Beijing, various years; State Statistical Bureau, Zhongguo Tongji Nianjian, *Statistical Yearbook of China 1991–95*; *China's Foreign Trade 1991–1995, China Foreign Economic Statistical Yearbook*, China Statistical Publishing House, Beijing, various years.

Since 1987, the share and amount of FDI in export manufacturing has gradually increased. By 1990, with the emergence of new forms of joint ventures (including some of the Chinese companies from Hong Kong, which were exporters before entering into joint ventures), exports by foreign-funded enterprises increased rapidly from a negligible base by an average annual growth rate of 73 per cent. The share of enterprises with foreign investment in China's total exports increased from 1.5 per cent in 1985 to 39.5 per cent in 1995 (Table 5.11). In addition, the exports of enterprises with foreign investment soared by 45 per cent while the exports of processing-assembling operations grew by only 4 per cent (*China Business Review*, May–June 1995). In recent years, foreign-invested ventures have been allowed to sell a substantial portion of their input on the internal market and many processing-assembling operations have thus been converted into foreign-invested enterprises.

Since 1990 foreign-invested enterprises have played a more and more important role in China's export (see Table 5.11). Jia Wei and Chen Wenhoug, (1993) and others have even said that these enterprises have become the major driving force of the fast growth in China's exports. The important role played by foreign-invested enterprises in this transformation of the export structure is clearly brought out by the data reported in the table; the share of foreign firms in total exports increased from 1.5 per cent in 1985 to 39.5 per cent in 1995. The contribution of foreign firms so far has been emphasised in relation to total gross export earnings and its influence on the balance of payments position. However, there are other factors which have to be taken into account. In this context it has been argued that the presence of foreign firms has positive effects on the performance of local firms, and there are reasons to argue that the presence of foreign firms seems to have generated favourable spillover effects on the export performance of local firms (and thus on the overall export level) in two ways. Firstly, following the entry of foreign firms into food-processing and other industries in China, many international buyers which had long-established market links with these firms also set up buying offices in the country. These buying groups have subsequently begun to play a crucial role in linking local firms with international markets. Secondly, many local firms make use of joint venture operations with foreign investors as a means of acquiring production and international marketing skills required for the successful operation of their own independent units. All the above facts suggest that the spillover effects of the presence of foreign firms have, to a significant extent, contributed to the export success of local firms.

However, negative effects cannot be ignored. Most of the foreign-invested enterprises are assembly and processing factories set up by Hong Kong and Taiwanese investors. Through these projects, Hong Kong and Taiwan have readjusted their industrial structures, transferring labour-intensive and export-oriented production to China, thus promoting China's labour-intensive exports. In 1995, the export of processing trade run by foreign-invested enterprises was valued at $US10.09 billion (up 29.7 per cent from the previous year), and accounted for over 40 per cent of the total number of foreign-invested enterprises' exports. The total value of exports in 1995 by these enterprises stood at $US46.9 billion, and the value of imports at $US62.9 billion. There has been a low involvement of capital-and technology-intensive products in exports by foreign firms.

*   *   *

POLAND: TRENDS IN FDI INFLOW

Up to 1989, foreign investment in Poland was negligible, whether measured in terms of the number of projects or dollar value. Most projects established were foreign partnerships set up in the 1980s (688 entities), and there were also some 1986–law-based joint ventures (53). In 1989 a number of new joint ventures were registered (867) of which only a minority (241) actually became operational (Table 5.12). In 1990 a wave of newly registered joint ventures hit the Polish economy, raising the total number of these entities to almost 3000 (with the number of foreign partnerships marking time).

This new wave of foreign-based projects came after the joint venture law was fundamentally amended in 1988 and reached its peak in 1990. The law was further modified in 1989 in connection with the liberalisation of the foreign exchange law, and in July 1990 in connection with the law of privatisation. The second big wave of joint ventures came in 1992, resulting in more than 10 000 entities registered (the number of partnerships had fallen back by this time). The total number of FDI-based establishments had reached nearly 16 000 by the end of 1993, and 20 000 by December 1994. This mushrooming of projects formally registered (especially in 1991–92) must be attributed

Table 5.12 *Poland: number of establishments with foreign participation, 1989–94*

No. of establishments	1989	1990	1991	1992	1993	1994
Joint ventures registered	867	2 799	4 796	10 131	15 393	19 312
JV operational	241	1 119	2 207	5 740	7 935	n.a.
Foreign partnership	705	730	442	440	425	425
Total entities operational	946	1 849	2 659	6 180	8 360	n.a.
JV operating, % of registered	27.8	40.0	46.0	56.7	51.6	n.a.
JV registered, % change	–	322.8	171.3	211.2	151.9	125.5
JV operational, % change	–	464.3	197.2	260.1	138.2	n.a.
Total entities operational, % change	–	195.5	143.3	233.3	n.a.	n.a.

Note: n.a. = not applicable; – = zero.
Source: PAIZ, *List of Major Foreign Investors*, PAIZ and Ministry of Privatisation, Warsaw, various years.

to foreign activities in trade and other services. In these sectors foreigners mostly invested just the minimum deposit demanded by law, and investment was mostly factor-price-driven in labour-intensive industries like leather, clothing and shoes. This trend closely followed the patterns of foreign trade with the EU, especially Germany (Lemoine, 1994). Such industries became the major engine of growing exports, especially in subcontracting activities. The average capital investment per firm was as low as they could get away with (tending to the minimum foreign capital requirement of $US50 000). These investors followed what might be called a foothold strategy, marked by presence rather than expected economic operations. Large-scale investments have usually been made only in the raw material and the manufacturing sectors and they are relatively small in number. In 1996 the number reached 29 000, one-third of these established projects being wholly-owned by foreign investors (PAIZ, 1997).

After 1993 there emerged a new shift in the pattern of FDI. The FDI stock showed strong increases by one year, and, also strong increases occurred in the capitalisation of firms as well as increase in the inflow of foreign capital by the largest firms (Table 5.13). The largest 20 foreign investors in Poland accounted for 55.8 per cent of all investment and 55 per cent of all investment commitments: a high capital concentration of FDI in Poland (Jermakowicz, 1994: 18–24).

The most striking feature of this development was a steady rise of the equity share of foreign investors, from 24 per cent in 1989 to 8

Table 5.13 *Poland: flows and stock of FDI, 1990–96 ($US)*

Year	Value of capital	Stock of FDI
1990	89	–
1991	291	380
1992	924	1,304
1993	1 600	2 900
1994	1 300	4 200
1995	2 500	6 700
1996	3 455	10 155

Source: As for Table 5.14.

per cent in 1995. This observed trend signifies that foreign investors were changing their investment strategy and beginning to take higher shares. Investment became more factor-endowments-driven in skill-intensive industries. Their typical investment option shifted from joint venture with foreign capital minority participation, towards the wholly-owned subsidiary (WOS) with a majority holding by a foreign partner. At the same time, the average FDI per firm rose from $US50 000 in 1989 to $US820 000 in 1996 (Table 5.14). This may have signalled a change in investment strategy in favour of a more long-term involvement, less affected by the short-term prospects of a temporary tax holiday.

According to the data of the Polish Agency for Foreign Investment (PAIZ), the level of FDI in Poland at the end of December 1996 was $US12 027 million (including equity and loans). Over two-thirds of that total investment came from the largest foreign investors. By the end of 1995 there were 362 investors who had invested over $US1 million, whilst at the end of July 1996 the number had risen to 492.

Table 5.14 *Poland: structure of FDI-based firms, 1989–96*

	1989	1990	1991	1992	1993	1994	1995	1996
Foreign participation (%)	24.3	40.7	36.6	57.7	72.8	78.4	80.3	82.6
Average FDI per firm ($US 000s)	50	94	146	245	387	420	586	820

Sources: EU, *Foreign Investment in Poland*, Foreign Trade Research Institute, Warsaw, various years; Glowny Urzad Statystyczny, *Analiza Wynikow Ekonomicznych z Investycjami Zagranicznymi*, GUS, Warsaw, 1997.

e additional 130 companies appearing on PAIZ's list were new investors, or shareholders of companies already involved in investment (PAIZ, 1997).

OWNERSHIP STRUCTURE

Formal investment flows into Poland can be divided into three categories:

- greenfield (new investment started by foreign firms);
- indirect acquisition through establishment of a joint venture; and
- direct acquisition, through which a foreign investor buys a share (partially or entirely) in a local company.

The last form is closely related to the privatisation process. Table 5.15 illustrates the dramatic change in the structure of the investment modes between 1990–95. Although the value of two modes of investment has increased, the proportion of greenfield investments has changed significantly over the five years.

First of all, an impressive increase in the role of greenfield investment is observable. In 1989 only $26 million were investments in new companies, but by the end of 1995 these investments were six times higher and constituted more than half of all FDI inflows (58.4 per cent). This increase is the best indicator of the increase in the trust in the Polish market and the growing willingness of firms to start new ventures.

A second clearly observable phenomenon is an increase in the receipts from direct acquisition. Between 1990 and 1993, FDI inflows into Poland were mainly privatisation-driven. In 1989 only $US15.5 million was received from privatised firms, which constituted 19.7 per cent of all inward investment, whilst in 1994 the receipts for privatisation were more than 15 times higher ($US678.9 million) and constituted 49.3 per cent of all inflows. There was, however, a decline in 1994 and 1995 due to a lack of government commitment and the strong resistance of labour unions towards the privatisation of SOEs; there was no clear government policy regarding privatisation.

A third phenomenon is a decline in the share of FDI in joint-venture establishments. In 1989 joint ventures were the only attractive method to improve the financial situation of SOEs, but by 1995 they

Table 5.15 *Poland: forms of investment between 1990–95*

Year	Greenfield		Indirect acquisition		Direct acquisition		Total	
	$	%	$	%	$	%	$	%
1989	26 514	27.5	54 399	56.4	15 500	16.1	96 413	100
1990	72 992	35.7	91 266	44.6	40 200	19.7	204 458	100
1991	180 666	42.5	126 796	31.4	105 300	26.1	403 646	100
1992	320 272	47.1	9 712	1.4	35 000	51.5	679 984	100
1993	692 092	50.3	4 934	0.4	678 903	49.3	1 377 929	100
1994	923 034	56.4	1 860	0.1	430 450	43.5	1 355 349	100
1995	1 280 500	59.4	720	0.1	380 452	40.5	1 661 672	100
Total	3 496 070	54.6	590 076	8.3	2 000 805	37.1	5 496 875	100

Sources: Calculated from data provided by the Ministry of Privatization and GUS, various years; CASE, *Foreign Privatisation in Poland*, Warsaw, 1994, p. 20.

played only a very marginal role (0.1 per cent). Greenfield investments and privatisation had become more attractive paths.

A fourth phenomenon is the relatively faster growth of greenfield investment than direct acquisition (privatisation) investment. Privatisation was a hit in 1992 when it constituted 51 per cent, but in 1994 it seems to have grown more slowly than new establishments, partly due of course to the slowing down of the privatisation process by government and partly due to the election in 1993.

The growth of greenfield investment is also impressive in terms of the number of enterprises. In 1993 there were 26 greenfield investment projects, which constituted 26.7 per cent of all FDI, as opposed to 9 indirect acquisitions which comprised 7.5 per cent of foreign investors' projects and 15 direct acquisitions which constituted 12.5 per cent of all cases (Jermakowicz, 1994: 20). An analysis of the capital invested by both groups, however, shows that indirect and direct acquisition have contributed relatively less capital than greenfield investments in both aggregate and average investment per enterprise. This suggests that more and more foreign investors are thinking of a long commitment to the Polish market and believe in the success of the economic reform process.

Between 1990–93, FDI was mainly driven by privatisation. Investors acquiring Polish firms directly within the framework of the privatisation process contributed over $US2 billion or 43 per cent of the total FDI capital contribution in the years 1990–95. The average foreign share in capitalisation per firm, however, shows enormous differences. Greenfield investment amounted to only $US129 000 per firm in 1993, whereas the average share in capitalisation per joint venture was US$360 500 (nearly three times more), and per direct acquisition US$18 020000 (149 times more) (Jermakowicz, Bochniarz, and Toft 1994: 20–5). In 1996, greenfield investment amounts increased to over US$4 million per firm, indicating a strong increase and changing patterns of investment, from small shops stablished by small investors, mostly from Germany (around 27 per cent), to quite substantial investment by large investors such as Fiat, Daewoo, Ford and Pilkington (PAIZ, 1997). In privatisation through direct acquisition, mostly large firms are involved (Fiat in car manufacturing or IPC in the paper and cement sector). This suggests that the type of foreign investment targeted was more scale-intensive, in line with the country's adjustment process from resource and cost-efficiency-driven to more domestic-market and export-oriented-investment-driven establishments.

SECTORAL COMPOSITION OF FDI PROJECTS

In the early 1990s, Poland did not have clear priority areas for FDI, which was mostly attracting industries which could bring high and quick returns on investment. In the latter half of 1994, the government announced an industrial policy priority for FDI and adjusted its investment policy in line with this new direction. It was expected that FDI would flow to those areas where Poland had a strong comparative advantage. From Table 5.16 we can see that the majority of capital (around 62 per cent) invested went to industry, and its total value at the end of December 1996 was $US7482.9 million (while official commitments were $US6816.9 million). The value of investment in the remaining sectors of the Polish economy was more than $US4.5 billion, but in this case also investment in one sector dominated the remaining sectors – of this $US4.5 billion, $US2522.9 million went to the finance sector. The lowest amount of investment was attracted by agriculture ($US15 million) and the municipal economy ($US24.8 million) (PAIZ, 1997).

The data in Table 5.17 show changing trends in the sectoral distribution of the stock of FDI in manufacturing industries between 1989 and 1996. It is clear that the food industry has attracted the largest share of foreign investment of all the manufacturing sectors, rising from 9.4 per cent of total investment in 1989 to 21.0 per cent in 1996. Second position in 1996 was taken by the electro-machinery

Table 5.16   *Poland: FDI by sectors, 1995–96 ($US mn)*

Sector	1995	1996	
	Equity & loans	*Equity & loans*	*Commitments*
Industry	4 325.6	7 482.9	6 816.9
Construction	496.2	607.2	251.1
Agriculture	9.0	15.0	–
Transportation	29.9	48.0	4.5
Telecommunications	289.7	587.6	380.7
Trade	364.3	709.6	297.8
Municipal economy	22.8	24.8	6.7
Finance	1 278.6	2 522.9	273.4
Insurance	16.0	29.7	2.2
Total	6 832.2	12 027.7	7 933.3

Source: PAIZ, *List of Major Foreign Investors*, PAIZ, Warsaw, various years.

Table 5.17   *Poland: sectoral pattern of FDI in manufacturing,*
1989 and 1996

Sector	1989 (%)	1996 (%)	1996 $US mn
Food	9.4	21.0	2535.3
Textile & apparel	5.9	2.5	301.2
Wood & paper	7.2	5.0	608.4
Chemicals & plastic	8.4	5.1	624.4
Metals	4.8	1.2	108.3
Electro-machinery	6.8	17.0	2039.6
Precision instruments	0.8	2.6	316.9
Motor & transport equipment	4.0	6.9	826.8

Sources: EU, *Foreign Investment in Poland*, Foreign Trade
Research Institute, Warsaw, various years; PAIZ, *List of Major
Foreign Investors in Poland*, Warsaw, various years.

sector, which rose from 5.8 per cent in 1989 to 17.0 per cent in 1996.
The next sector was motor and transport equipment which increased
from 4 per cent in 1989 to 6.9 per cent in 1996. The shares of these
three sectors taken together in the total stock of FDI amounted to
about 50 per cent of all the capital invested in the secondary sector
(PAIZ, 1993–96; Foreign Trade Research Institute, 1991–95). There
was a marked decline from 7.2 per cent to 5.0 per cent in the
wood and paper industry as well as a decline in the chemicals and
plastics industry from 8.4 per cent to 5.1 per cent. A stronger decline
occurred in the textile and apparel industry, which supports the evidence of a changing strategy towards foreign investment from short to
long-term commitments. Small portions of FDI went to lower or
medium-technology industries with relatively high capital intensity,
most probably seeking to taking advantage of natural-resource
endowments rather than cheap and well-educated labour (Kubielas,
1996).

It is evident from Table 5.17 that the two highest ranked (in
technological terms) sectors in machinery – electric and electronics –
exhibit an increasing comparative advantage and receive higher and
increased shares of FDI. Foreign investors have been attracted by
locational advantage (Dunning, 1995(b)) and have contributed to
technological improvements in these industries. It is interesting to
note that it was precisely the electronics and office-equipment industries which provided the main vehicle for the impressive technological
catch-up by the Asian (tigers).

FDI in traditional sectors (clothing, apparel and so on) shows a clear sign of decline, cheap labour not providing a strong enough advantage for foreign investors. FDI was attracted by locational advantages but was not the most important mode of technology transfer into those sectors, with structural adjustment in these traditional industries occurring in a Ricardian way (investment was mostly resource- and cost-driven in the form of joint ventures and subcontracting), without major capital and technology flows. These sectors constitute the largest and most rapidly growing category of Polish subcontracting exports to Germany. Outward processing was, therefore, the main factor in this pattern of Ricardian adjustment in traditional sectors, based on technology-transfer modes like licensing and subcontracting.

The motor vehicle industry showed an increasing share of total Polish FDI over the period, starting from small amounts of capital inflows but by the end exceeding the share of the traditional sectors. One may infer that this was due to a high initial revealed comparative advantage and high labour intensity, complemented by capital inflow to create the required factor conditions. Finally, the food-processing industry absorbed a large and stable share of FDI inflow despite its relative unattractiveness in terms of revealed comparative advantage at the starting point.

The data point towards industries identified as scale-, capital- or human-capital-intensive being the leading targets for FDI in Poland, rather then the traditional labour-intensive sectors. This suggests that Polish unqualified labour is rather expensive in relation to other possible host countries, as measured by its relative productivity, and that by contrast, skilled labour reveals some comparative advantage as expressed in terms of its relative cost. Factor price conditions of this kind may prove to be a key link in moving from factor-price-driven adjustment to the use of high-skill human capital.

SOURCE-COUNTRY COMPOSITION

The majority of investors come from the EU or from those countries which have historically been Poland's trading partners. The role of immigration (Polonia) also plays an important part in the source of FDI inflow (Rojec and Svetlicic 1994; Jermakowicz, 1994). According to the volume of invested capital, the USA is in first position among all investing countries: at the end of 1996 the value of US investment was $US2965.6 million which constituted 24.7 per cent of the total value of investments (see Table 5.18). Next was German investment with a value of $US1524.4 million (16.7 per cent), followed by international companies such as Swedish-Swiss ABB in third position with $US1493.0 million at the end of 1996. The following positions were Italy at $US1223.8 million (around 10.2 per cent), the Netherlands at $US951.7 million (7.9 per cent), and France at $US 899.9 million (7.5 per cent) (PAIZ, 1997). The data from PAIZ confirm the concentration of capital: among 93 countries whose capital is represented in Poland, five of them (USA, Germany, Netherlands, France and Italy) accounted for 75 per cent of total foreign capital invested (PAIZ, 1997).

In terms of the number of FDI projects, Germany occupies first position with 113 projects, followed by the USA with 77, France 42, the Netherlands 32 and Austria and Sweden 30 projects each (Table 5.18). In terms of capitalisation per project, however, Italy occupies first position, having invested 35.4 per cent of Poland's foreign capital. The average size of Italy's firms amounts to US$925.8 million, the result of the large capital investments made by Fiat, Luccini Groupe and Frotrade Financing. Germany in turn has a large number of firms with very small average capital amounting to US$87 800 per firm, and according to average investment Germany is ranked 18th amongst all countries.

Table 5.18   *Poland: FDI by country of origin, December 1996*

Country	Equity & loans $US mn	Commitments $US mn	No. of companies
USA	2965.6	2669.9	77
Germany	1524.4	756.4	113
International corps	1493.0	188.4	15
Italy	1223.8	1199.8	29
Holland	951.7	309.1	32
France	899.9	537.3	42
UK	509.0	363.9	21
Sweden	361.3	82.6	30
Switzerland	357.7	13.6	8
Australia	328.1	67.0	3

Note: For more details about source countries see Appendix A5.1.
Source: PAIZ, *List of Major Foreign Investors in Poland*, PAIZ, Warsaw, 1997.

From the investment-strategy perspective, Italy accounts for 50 per cent of foreign acquisitions while its share in greenfield investments has been relatively low at 3.5 per cent. On the other hand, the USA, Germany, Sweden and the Netherlands account for 64.6 per cent of the FDI projects, and their combined share of greenfield investments is over 61 per cent (Jermakowicz, 1994; Ministry of Foreign Economic Relation of Poland, 1996). While examining this pattern, it is interesting to note the historical relationships which are mirrored in today's investment patterns. Those past relationships have created a tradition of familiarity with the region and, today, firms from those countries are less wary of Poland and tend to invest greater amounts. The EU accounts for 64.5 per cent of the capital invested, and 62.3 per cent of FDI projects, and holds the majority stake followed by the USA, Canada and Australia. It is interesting to note the increase in share from several Asian countries: Korea and Japan (0.8 per cent) capital and (0.4 per cent) projects (PAIZ, 1996/7 and GUS, 1996). There is little investment from CEECs although there is some investment from Russia in the construction of a gas pipeline from Siberia to Western Europe.

FDI AND TRADE ORIENTATION

Since 1990, the development of exports has been accompanied by substantial changes in their commodity composition. These structural changes in Polish exports were related to the readjustment towards the EU markets after the collapse of the CMEA and the loss of traditional industrial goods markets. The changes confirm that the export drive had been led, up to 1993, by labour-intensive industries (such as clothing, leather or furniture), but that new trends are also emerging indicating that several branches of the manufacturing industries such as cars, electrical appliances, engineering and NEC are among the fastest growing export sectors. (See Tables 5.19 and 5.20)

The manufacturing industries have stood at the centre of the export drive while the share of raw materials, energy, agriculture and food products has declined. This indicates that export performance was achieved in industries with different factor intensities: labour-intensive industries such as textiles, as well the growing number of 'modern' industries incorporating different proportions of skilled labour, capital and technology (for example mechanical industries and transport equipment). These trends point to newly-emerging competitive

Table 5.19 *Poland: exports to OECD countries, average annual change (%)*

Exports	11989–94	1995	1996
Total	13.0	16.7	19.8
Manufacturing industry	20.1	24.5	28.6

Sources: Lemoine, *Trade policy and Trade Patterns During Transition: A Comparison between China and the CEECs*, Centre for Eastern European Studies, Paris, 1996, p. 22; Ministry of Foreign Trade, *Poland Trade Report*, Ministry of Foreign Trade, Warsaw, 1997.

Table 5.20 *Poland: index of structural changes in exports to the OECD(%)*

	1988	1993	1996
Total exports	42	49	60
Manufactured exports	34	43	54

Source: As for Table 5.19.

industries, a breakaway from past inertia, and the emergence of new specialisations which may change the patterns of comparative advantage from the past.

FDI-based firms have undoubtedly been the engine of manufactured export growth over the period (Table 5.21), and there is a close correlation between the growth of manufactured exports and the share of foreign firms in them. The share of foreign firms in the total export of manufactures increased from 3.2 per cent in 1989 to over 62 per cent in 1995. Also possessing ownership advantages over home enterprises in terms of technology (Dunning, 1985), they have been the engine of change in the sectoral and commodity structure of exports to Western markets.

Table 5.21 *Poland: exports of FDI-based firms in manufactured exports*

Exports	1989	1990	1991	1992	1993	1994	1995
Exports ($US mn)	105.7	866.4	745.8	1356.8	2245.9	3450.6	5456.0
Exports as % of total manufactures	3.2	28.7	26.3	32.3	48.4	54.7	62.8

Sources: EU, *Poland – Foreign Trade*, Foreign Trade Research Institute, Warsaw, various years; Department of Statistics *Foreign Trade Report*, Ministry of Foreign Trade, Warsaw, 1996.

CHINA AND POLAND: COMPARATIVE ANALYSIS

Ownership Structure

In China more than half of the FDI is in the form of joint ventures. Since 1987 the number of wholly foreign-owned enterprises has shown an increasing trend, but still remains low in comparison with other forms such as equity joint ventures. The size of most joint ventures is relatively small, particularly those from Hong Kong, South Korea and Taiwan, with low levels of capitalisation per project and little technology transfer. The equity share of foreign investors in joint ventures usually accounts for 50 per cent. By contrast, in Poland the investment option has shifted from joint ventures towards the wholly foreign-owned subsidiary, and such enterprises have become the major form of investment. In terms of percentage shareholding, foreign investors are the main shareholders with over 50 per cent of control; the majority of them are large MNCs which invest in large development projects and transfer updated technology. The size of the projects and capitalisation per project were much larger than in China. Projects in Poland show high capital intensity and a high investment value.

Sectoral Composition

FDI in China has been mostly concentrated in tourism, real estate and service sectors, although manufacturing industries show increasing trends and continue to capture increasing amounts of FDI in terms of percentage and value. However, FDI in manufacturing was concentrated in low-end, labour-intensive industries rather than capital or human-capital-intensive sectors of industry. This was demonstrated generally by the small size of industrial projects. Large-scale projects were normally found in the real estate, hotel and service sectors. The payback periods for investment in hotel or real estate are shorter than in industry, which has been attractive to many investors and has in some cases attracted speculative investors. In Poland, the majority of foreign capital invested (over 60 per cent) went to industry and the rest to the telecommunications, trade and finance sectors. FDI in manufacturing sectors with high intensity of capital or human-capital shows high and increasing shares of inflows. Industrial projects have been mostly large projects with large amounts of capital invested and technology involved.

Source Country

In China there is a clear pattern of concentration of FDI inflow. Over 70 per cent of it comes to China from NIEs, especially from Hong Kong and Taiwan. Investment from developed countries such as the USA, Japan, the UK and Germany shows a slower pace in terms of projects and value. Investment from Hong Kong or Taiwan is mainly in labour-intensive projects, small in scale, with a low level of capitalisation and little technology transfer, what little there is mostly being old and not very efficient. Investment from developed countries is mostly capital or human-capital-intensive, but with low levels of capitalisation per project and secondhand technology transfer; state of the art technology transfers are rare. By contrast, source-country composition in Poland is more diversified. The majority of investors come from developed countries of the EU, North America and Australia with high capitalisation ratios per projects. Investment from these countries is mainly in capital and human-capital-intensive projects with a high level of technology transfer, often advanced or state-of-the-art.

Regional Distribution

China's selective economic policy creates uneven regional economic development, which strongly affects the inflow and location of FDI. The majority (over 80 per cent) of foreign investment is concentrated in coastal areas, while inland provinces remain backward and undeveloped. The inflow of FDI into these provinces continues slowly and remains at a very low pace. Provinces which have benefited most have been those with a close geographical proximity to Hong Kong or Taiwan, and this unequal distribution creates conflict between the provinces and also between the provinces and the central government. In comparison, the distribution of FDI in Poland has been more evenly spread, but there are still large differences between north and south voivodship and the less-developed and more agriculturally oriented voivodships of north-east and south-east Poland. Less attractive regions have been given top priority in government economic policies in terms of economic development and the creation of attractive environments for foreign investors.

FDI and Trade Orientation

Most foreign firms in China are oriented towards the domestic market. Export-oriented firms show an increasing trend but still account for only a small percentage of total exports. Most foreign-invested enterprises are for assembly and processing, set-up by Hong Kong and Taiwanese investors. The majority of them are promoting China's labour-intensive export goods with low value-added, instead of technology-intensive or human-capital-intensive goods. By contrast, foreign-based firms in Poland are a mixed bag, some domestic-market-oriented and some export-oriented. FDI-based firms have undoubtedly been the engine of manufactured export growth, they accounting for over 60 per cent of manufactured exports. They are promoting Poland's new competitive industries with different factor intensities, incorporating different proportions of skilled labour, capital and technology.

CONCLUSIONS

Since 1979, foreign investors have been keen to enter the potentially large markets in China, and this was encouraged by the establishment of the four Special Economic Zones at the beginning of the 1980s as part of the initial stage of China's 'open policy'. The trends and fluctuations of FDI inflow into China reflect major changes in Chinese policies. The value of FDI has been increasing from a negligible base, but by 1990 the value of annual FDI inflow into China was higher than for most other East Asian developing countries. Also, by the end of the 1980s the inflow of FDI had started to enter inland and western regions of China. FDI has not always been used efficiently in accordance with China's comparative advantage due to import-substitution policies.

In 1990, after the introduction of a bold liberalisation programme, foreign investors slowly started to enter the Polish market. This was further encouraged by the government's announcement of the mass privatisation of state owned enterprises, but still the mass privatisation was not fulfilled. The trends and intensity of FDI inflows into Poland were strongly influenced by economic reforms and the government's commitments to further liberalisation of the Polish economy. The strong progress of economic reform and its large domestic market have helped Poland to become a major attraction for foreign investors, especially for the large MNCs. By 1996, the value of annual FDI inflow into Poland was higher than for most other countries of Central and Eastern Europe, as well as the former Soviet independent states.

6 A Survey of FDI Firms in China and Poland: Methodology and Characteristics of the Sample

In order to help understand the findings of the survey, this chapter describes the methodology by which the research was conducted. It identifies the sources of evidence and any problems envisaged and how they were overcome. The limitations of the study are addressed in Chapter 9.

METHODOLOGY

The research strategy of the study comprised two key components: (a) a study of policy reforms in Poland and China since 1989 and 1979 respectively through library research; (b) interviews with specialists in Beijing, Hong Kong and Warsaw; and (c) a detailed survey of FDI-based firms operating in China and Poland. This latter firm-level study involved a questionnaire-based interview of management personnel from FDI-based firms (for a sample of the questionnaire see Appendix A6.1). The firm-level study also involved compilation and analysis of information from official records of the World Bank, OECD, IMF and other investment and government agencies of China and Poland as well as records from government departments.

In the first stage of the investigation a select set of parameters were established and utilised to define a *population stratum* drawn from the main population, according to the three main parameters:

1. The amount of FDI had to be > $US1 million.
2. A major Western firm had to be involved.
3. Timing of investment between 1979–96 for China, and between 1989–96 for Poland.

The four industries: agriculture, food-processing, car manufacture, and paper and cement were chosen because they offered a diverse set of characteristics from the point of view of technology, scale requirements and raw materials dependency. In the survey, the paper and cement industries were treated as one because the sample data supplied by Chinese officials conflated them as one sector. On the basis of the preceding chapters, I designed, tested and utilised a questionnaire in a survey-based interview of a selected sample of firms. These comprised approximately 320 local firms in China and 320 in Poland with foreign participation that had been established via an act of FDI. From this overall group of around 640 firms, a sample totalling 430 individual firms was selected for use in the study. The questionnaire itself was targeted at the respective senior executives of these local firms with foreign participation operating within China or Poland via FDI.

THE SURVEY DESCRIPTION

The survey was conducted between late April and the latter half of October 1996, and again between April and June 1997. The interviews were usually preceded by a letter of intent, sent by mail to the total of 430 firms with foreign participation operating in China and Poland. A second letter enclosed a copy of the questionnaire, whose structure varied very slightly between those used in Poland and those for China.

The questionnaire was used to structure the interviews for both countries, although some adjustments were made when the special circumstances of a firm, or the interview, indicated that this was desirable. For Poland, interviews were conducted with the chief executive or managers selected from the list supplied by government investment agencies; in some cases lower-level managers were interviewed. In most cases, the letter of intent was personally addressed by name to the local chief executive of the firm, and, furthermore, the contact details of each of the firms were verified using all available resources. It should also be noted that every effort was made to increase the actual response rate as well as the completeness of questionnaires based on the interviews. In many cases, for example, personal phone calls were made following the interviews. Finally, all participants in the survey were given a personal written guarantee of complete confidentiality of their responses. In two cases it was impossible to interview a firm contacted for inclusion in the survey; in a few others, not enough information was received for incorporation in the analysis.

A different procedure was adopted with respect to interviews in China. The first three weeks were spent in discussions with government officials and industry organisations, to become conversant with the institutional structure of the selected industry and to create relationships with the officials involved. This relationship was important for the arrangement of interviews with representatives of selected firms. In both countries, a large number of firms had to be interviewed to obtain a satisfactory coverage of FDI patterns and determinants. Thus, over 25 firms were interviewed in each of the industries. In all cases, valuable data was also received from company annual reports, which was especially important for the final analysis. Notes of the interviews were taken on the questionnaire forms.

Altogether, interviews were conducted with executives who handled the FDI of each firm and who played the most important role in effective FDI decisions. In some firms, more than one person was interviewed. There were several firms where the respondent did not answer the questions completely, stating confidentiality, company policy and competition as the reason. Interviews commonly lasted between one and two hours – a considerable expense for the businessmen. In the majority of the firms, an interview with the managing director, or equivalent, was generally requested. Some questions, especially those of a historical nature, were beyond the first-hand experience of the interviewees from some firms, and in these cases current firm members were asked to answer to the best of their knowledge.

The cooperation and support extended to the survey was a continual inspiration, but there were some difficulties. In some cases time was limited, and it was necessary to confine the interview to what appeared to be the most important questions. In these cases the open questions on FDI strategy and motivation were given greatest prominence. Language difficulty was not a problem in Poland as I speak Polish fluently. In other cases, where non-Poles served as managers, the use of English among persons involved in FDI was quite high. Language difficulties were more prominent in China, where most officials had a very limited command of English. In most cases the interviews were conducted by surrogates, and in some cases problems with the exact translation from the native language to English were encountered. Logistical problems of other types were also more common in China, where bad infrastructure slowed the pace of the survey to about half that in Poland.

CHARACTERISTICS OF THE SURVEY RESPONDENTS

In the majority of cases a letter of intent was personally addressed to a named individual who was usually a top senior executive of the local firm within the population sampled (see Appendix A6.2). Besides being asked to state both their name and position within the firm, information was also requested on the respondent's nationality.

From the data available on this question three trends seem to emerge. Firstly in terms of the survey as a whole, just under half of the respondents, or 39 per cent, stated that they were host-country nationals. Secondly, only six of the respondents claimed dual nationality which somehow clarifies the issue of foreign firms employing expatriate executives to run their foreign operations. A third trend that emerges from the data is that British firms tend to place British nationals in the top positions of their local firms, as do US firms to some extent. However, this situation cannot be generalised for all local firms with British or US-based foreign participation given the limited number of cases available. Overall, with the exception of the British cases cited, there appears to be very little correlation between the nationality of a top executive and the nationality of their respective firms.

CHINA: THE SURVEY

From 315 FDI-based firms, a total of 215 were identified of which 100 responded to the letter of intent and were willing to participate in the survey, the other 115 refusing to participate in interviews (details from the survey are addressed in the next chapter). The response rate was approximately 48 per cent. The survey was based on four industries: agriculture, food- processing, paper and cement, and car manufacture. In terms of distribution of FDI-based firms, approximately 64 per cent of the entire survey sample was concentrated in six provinces (see Table 6.1). Five of the provinces surveyed are located along the coastline of the country. The survey revealed some general characteristics as well as those peculiar to FDI among these four sectors.

Table 6.1   *China: sample distribution*

Region	Total identified	Surveyed	Refused to participate
Beijing	21	18	3
Tianjin	10	2	8
Shanghai	20	7	13
Shangdong	16	6	10
Jiangsu	25	15	10
Zhejiang	10	4	6
Guangdong	25	12	13
Fujian	15	6	9
Liaoning	8	2	6
Jilin	10	4	6
Heilongjiang	6	4	2
Anhui	8	3	5
Shanxi	1	1	n.a.
Shaanxi	4	1	3
Hebei	10	4	6
Hubei	8	4	4
Hunan	5	2	3
Guizhou	3	1	2
Sichuan	5	2	3
Guangxi	3	1	2
Henan	2	1	1
Total	215	100	115

Source: Author's survey data.

Table 6.2   *China: legal status of the FDI-based firms*

Legal form	No. of firms	%
Solely-owned proprietors	19	19
Joint ventures	63	63
Other	18	18
Total	100	100

Source: Author's survey data.

A Profile of the Local Firms with Foreign Participation

In terms of the legal status of the local firms with foreign participation (see Table 6.2), the sample is strongly dominated by joint ventures, with 65 firms (65 per cent) in this category, followed by 19 solely-owned firms (19 per cent).

Table 6.3   *China: start of operations pre-1989–96 (%)*

Year	%
Before 1989	3.5
1989	.2
1990	7.3
1991	18.4
1992	31.5
1993	22.2
1994	2.3
1995	2.0
1996	3.1
Total	100

Source: Author's survey data.

Within the limits of FDI laws and regulations, full ownership control by the foreign partner's foreign wholly-owned firms are still not a very common form of investment; most foreign investors take joint ventures as the safest and most secure option for operations in China. According to the survey sample, over 70 per cent of the firms started operations between 1991 and 1993 (Table 6.3), with only a small percentage of operations being set up in other periods.

POLAND: THE SURVEY

From the 215 firms originally contacted, a total of 100 responded to the survey, of which 89 returned the letter of intent and indicated their willingness to participate in interviews. Another 11 firms replied, but participated only in selected areas of the questionnaire (for details about the survey see Appendix A6.1). The sample was fairly well-balanced across each of the chosen industries (agriculture, food-processing, paper and cement, and car manufacture) with a high response rate. Over three-quarters of the firms surveyed were concentrated in six voivodships, and all had invested more than $US1 million, with sales over $US5 million (see Table 6.4).

Table 6.4 *Poland: survey response rate*

Category	Agriculture		Food-processing		Car manufacture & Assembly		Paper & Cement	
	No.	%	No.	%	No.	%	No.	%
Completed interview	23	11	29	14	21	10	27	13
Replied unable/ unwilling to participate in the study because of:	15	7	18	8	14	7	17	8
Returned incomplete	2	1	3	1	4	2	2	1
No-response	9	4	12	5	8	4	11	5
Total	49	23	62	28	47	23	57	27
Total number of completed respondents				100	48%			
Total number of letters of interest mailed				215	100%			

Survey by voivodship[*]

1. Warsaw	17
2. Katowice	13
3. Szczecin	12
4. Gdansk	11
5. Lodz	10
6. Krakow	10
7. Poznan	6
8. Bydgoszcz	5
9. Bielsko-Biala	4
10. Wroclaw	4
11. Lublin	3
12. Rzeszow	2
13. Elblag	1
14. Zielona Gora	1
15. Lomza	1
Total	100

Note: [*]This administration division of Poland by 32 voivodships soon ceased to exist; a new division of Poland body into 12 voivodships will be implemented in accordance with Poland's historical division.
Source: Author's survey data.

A Profile of Polish Local Firms with Foreign Participation

In terms of the legal status of the local firms surveyed (see Table 6.5), the sample is strongly dominated by limited liability companies with 45 firms (51 per cent), followed by companies limited by shares with 31 firms (34 per cent).

According to the survey sample, most firms with foreign participation started their activities (Table 6.6) in 1992 (32% of firms), followed by 22 per cent of firms deciding to invest in 1993. It is clear indicated that after the launch of the bold reforms in 1990 by the Balcerowicz programme, foreign investors took a slow 'wait and see' approach before making a strong commitment and accepting the reform process as successful.

Table 6.5 *Poland: legal status of local firms*

Legal form	No.	%
Company limited by shares (firm SA)	31	34
Limited liability company (Sp.z.o.o)	45	51
Other	14	15
Total	89	100

Source: Author's survey data.

Table 6.6 *Poland: start of operations,*
(1989–96)

Year	% of firms
1989	4.2
1990	7.3
1991	26.4
1992	32.5
1993	22.2
1994	2.3
1995	2.0
1996	3.1
Total	100

Source: Author's survey data.

7 Determinants of FDI: Survey Findings

This chapter has two main parts. First I provide an overview of the industries covered in order to place the ensuing discussion in context, followed by a presentation and discussion of the findings of the survey. The major economic factors which have determined formal FDI inflows into China between 1979 and 1996 and into Poland between 1989 and 1996 are analysed, with particular attention given to the effects of the host country's business and investment environments as important factors influencing foreign firms' investment decisions. In the final section a comparison between the two countries is made.

AN OVERVIEW OF THE INDUSTRIES

Trends and patterns of FDI are studied relating to four industries: car manufacturing, food-processing, paper and cement, and agriculture. Before we discuss the results of the survey, it is important to put these findings in perspective by identifying the characteristics of these industries and the market forces that affect their structure and competition.

CHINA

Motor Vehicles

The worldwide automobile industry is characterised by a relatively small number of large producers. Compared with many other industries, car manufacture is technologically footloose: the raw materials, infrastructure and factors needed for production are found in many countries. Automobile plants are usually located near rail and port facilities, and they need a reasonably large labour pool in the immediate area to draw upon because the average size of an automobile facility is relatively large. Differences in labour costs do not play an important part in manufacturers' calculations of the relative advantages of alternative sites.

China, with a population of more than one billion, is by far the largest potential market for motor vehicles in the world (Table 7.1). By the end of 1993 there were only 8 176 000 vehicles in China, just seven vehicles for every 1000 people, the lowest figure for per capita vehicle ownership in the world, along with India (Institute of Developing Economies, 1995: 1). But one has to remember that the purchasing power of the local population is still relatively small (GDP per capita of about $US400); most people cannot afford a car, and currently only 15 per cent of all cars sold are purchased by individuals (Langlois 1997).

The domestic car industry is currently engaged in large-scale reorganisation and reconstruction. Misguided central policies and scattered investments have left the industry highly fragmented, redundant and inefficient. To restructure the industry the government unveiled its Automotive Industrial Policy in July 1994, aimed at shaping car manufacturing into a 'pillar industry' and reshuffling China's top 20 manufactures into three or four conglomerates (policies of Big Three and Little Three), each with a production capacity of 300 000–500 000 cars per year. The government also has plans to trim the number of top manufacturers to seven or eight. In addition to 122 car makers, China has about 600 auto-refitting factories and more than 3000 spare-parts factories (Langlois 1997). Most of the factories operate on a small scale, with some having annual outputs of less than 100 units. Also, China has strong regulations in relation to local-content requirements as part of its automotive policies to promote China as a world-class manufacturer. At a project's initial launch, 40 per cent of the vehicle's value must come from parts produced in China. That percentage should rise to 60 per cent in the fifth year of operations, and 80 per cent in the seventh. To encourage foreign firms to increase local content, the government has increased tariffs on imported parts,

Table 7.1   *China: passenger car demand, 1995–97*

	Units (10 000s)				Percentage			
	Private	*Taxi*	*Public*	*Total*	*Private*	*Taxi*	*Public*	*Total*
1995	5	7	21	33	15.2	24.2	63.2	100
1996	7	9	22	38	18.4	23.7	60.5	100
1997*	9.5	10	25.5	45	21.1	22.2	56.7	100

*   Estimate
Source: Aude Langlois, *Car Trouble?*, China Trade Report, May 1997, p. 7.

and banned the import of completely knocked-down kits for local assembly (CKD kits) (*Journal of Asian Business*, 1996: 71).

Under the Ninth Five-Year Plan (1996–2000), China plans to invest renminbi 46.7 billion ($US17.7 billion) to develop its eight main car and mini-car manufacturers, including its three major sedan producers – Shanghai Volkswagen, First Automotive Works-Volkswagen and Tianjin Automotive Industry Group Corp. In July 1994, the government had set annual production targets at 3 million by the turn of the century, but under the Ninth Five-Year Plan this was lowered to 2.7 million units. But some analysts estimate that a more realistic target is 2.25 million units. In 1996 China produced 1.54 million units according to the Ministry of Machine Building, up from 1.45 million in 1995, a 7.3 per cent year-on-year increase. Shanghai Volkswagen remained the dominant market leader, over 200 000 units produced backed by a 52 per cent rise in unit sales. The next was the China First Automobile Group joint venture with Audi/Volkswagen (approximately 190 000 units), Tianjin Automotive Industrial Group joint venture with Daihatsu (approximately 150 000 units), Dongfeng Motor Group joint venture with Citroen (148 000 units), and Beijing Automotive Industry Group joint venture with Peugeot (146 000 units) (Langlois 1997).

The trouble is that demand is not keeping pace with production capacity (Table 7.2). Of the 1.54 million units produced in 1996, just 1.32 million were sold according to the 1996 *China Automotive Industry Yearbook*. One reason for sagging demand over the last four years has been the government's strict control of car purchases by state

Table 7.2   *China: output and sales of passenger cars by model, 1996*

Model	Production	Sales	Sales/output ratio (%)	Market share (%)
Santana	183 886	183 221	99.93	52.24
Jetta/Golf	25 653	23 457	91.44	6.69
Audi	7 837	7 773	98.67	2.20
Small Red-Flag	8 920	7 976	89.42	2.27
Fookang	7 714	5 782	74.95	1.65
Cherokee	26 050	24 654	94.64	7.03
Peugeot	2 300	2 540	108.58	0.69
Charade	82 393	79 448	96.43	22.65
Alto	14 287	15 262	106.82	4.35
Skylark	505	810	106.40	0.23

Source: Aude Langlois, *Car Trouble?*, China Trade Report, May 1997, p. 9.

enterprises and government departments. To put these restrictions into perspective, 86 per cent of all cars sold in China in 1995 were sold to government agencies or SOEs.

Demand by product in 1997 (Table 7.3) shows that approximately 45 per cent were heavy commercial vehicles, 28 per cent were passenger cars and 27 per cent were light commercial vehicles.

Despite all the challenges, foreign car makers began turning their attention to the Chinese market in the early 1980s. Between 1979–96, a total number of 384 projects were set up between foreign and Chinese partners, with a total of $US1.32 billion of FDI. Out of this foreign capital inflow, $US1.180 billion was invested between 1990–96, representing 89.6 per cent of the total gross investment. Germany remains the biggest foreign investor, with $US367 million which represents 27.9 per cent of the overall FDI in the Chinese auto industry. The USA is ranked second with $US213 million (16.5 per cent), followed by Hong Kong with $US162 million (12.2 per cent), Japan $US160 million (12.1 per cent), Italy $US151 million (11.5 per cent) and France $US82 million (6.2 per cent). As these figures indicate, over 51 per cent of total FDI in car industry comes from European major car makers such as Volkswagen, Mercedes-Benz, Fiat, and the Citroen–Peugeot group.

The majority of the plants are located in inland provinces such as Sichuan, Shaanxi, Hubei and Jinling where SOEs have established production bases. These large SOEs team up with foreign car makers, mostly in joint ventures or cooperative ventures, in order to gain capital, technology and manufacturing know-how. Wholly foreign-owned projects are not permitted in the auto industry, which the government regards as an important strategic sector of the national

Table 7.3 *China: demand by product, 1997 (%)*

Sedan	28.13
Light truck	19.88
Light bus	14.12
Medium truck	13.00
Mini bus	11.38
Mini truck	9.25
Heavy truck	2.25
Medium bus	1.68
Large bus	0.32

Source: As for Table 7.2.

economy; to lose of control of ownership of the industry to foreigners would be seen as reducing government policy influence. Further more, the government will have to approve all changes in a manufacturer's planned capacity. Foreigners can own up to 50 per cent of vehicle manufactures, and 100 per cent in component-systems production, but they are prohibited from holding stakes in parts-makers.

Over 95 per cent of foreign-funded joint ventures are domestic-market oriented; only a negligible part of components and parts production is exported (Langlois 1997). Most of these large car makers take advantage of their brand name, marketing skills, and know-how in competition with local firms. Most projects are medium sized, between $US1–10 million, accounting for 70 per cent; only 4 per cent of the projects represented $US10 million investment per project. Also interesting to note is that the FDI utilisation rate for the car industry recorded an average of 38 per cent.

Food Processing

The food-processing industry differs from the other three in a number of important respects: food production is, for the most part, a technologically mature industry, and companies are distinguished less by their possession of proprietary technology than by brand names and managerial styles. Production is seldom integrated worldwide, but rather takes the form of relatively small-scale, import-substituting investments in host countries, often making extensive use of local raw materials. In developing countries, governments make special efforts, including controls and subsidies, to ensure that food prices are kept low. Because food manufacturing is technologically relatively unsophisticated and food pricing is politically sensitive, governments have ambiguous, fluctuating and even sometimes contradictory policies toward multinational food producers.

The Chinese Ninth Five-Year Plan outlined the guidelines for the food industry for the near future. The development of the food industry is of very great importance in promoting the development of the rural commodity economy, entailing the coordination and development of related industries such as fodder, packaging, chemical industry, and improvement of people's living standards by supplying more nutritious produce. Since the 1980s, China's food-processing industry has undergone considerable development and has formed a production system with more varieties, progress in technology, increasingly abundant products, and improved networks of transport and sales.

The sector has tremendous long-term potential for expansion. The total value of China's food-processing industry hit renminbi 425 billion in 1996, up roughly 18 per cent from the previous year. It is China's third-largest industry, following textiles and electronics. Families' spending on food grew 152 per cent between 1985–95, a higher rate than spending on clothing (145 per cent), rent (121 per cent) and household articles (125 per cent) *(China Trade Report,* January 1996). Moreover, food-processing hasn't kept up with food output; its value is just one-third that of China's agricultural output, whereas in developed countries the value of processed foods is typically 100–200 per cent of the agricultural output value *(China Trade Report,* March 1996). This means that a large proportion of food entering people's homes in China is in crude form. The greatest areas of opportunity are in the processing of convenience foods, production of foods aimed at groups with special needs such as infants and elderly people, and raw-materials processing.

Since the 1980s, foreign food companies arrived in force with technology and capital, investing heavily in the sector. In 1984 the industry for the first time recorded an initial overseas investment of $US2.07 million, and since then FDI in the industry has accelerated, reaching $US254 million in 1996 – 24.2 times higher than in the first year. Moreover, most of these gains were realised during the 1990s, accounting for 95.7 per cent of the total accumulated investment. The majority of the investments were in the form of joint ventures, but there are also majority foreign-owned enterprises.

The ventures run the gamut from modest strawberry and broccoli farms to ambitious big-budget operations such as those run by Thailand's Charoen Popkhand Group, and by Western food giants such as Swiss Nestlé, Danish Globe AS and American Kraft. Food concerns from Taiwan have been especially aggressive, betting on foods designed for a Chinese palate. Hong Kong ranked first in FDI with $US110 million or 43.47 per cent; second ranked is Switzerland with $US38.15 million (15 per cent), the third is the USA with $US35.47 million (14 per cent); next is Australia with $US31 million (12 per cent), Japan with $US17 million (7 per cent), Italy with $US13 million (5 per cent) and Taiwan $US12 million (statistics for 1997).

But the investment climate is in flux. New policies that threaten to increase the tax burden have made some types of food-processing less attractive, especially for medium-sized firms of over RMB 50 million, which are the majority in the food-processing sector. Rising land and labour costs have further chipped away at margins. The picture is brighter for a few big food-processing firms with over RMB 100 million investment per project. These large firms can cope more effectively with the cost problems by using their brand names to advantage, and their managerial know-how, technology and marketing skills are powerful tools in negotiations with the government. The majority of these large projects are wholly foreign-owned firms, largely food giants located in big cities along the coastline where demand for grain, cereal flake, seaweed fried foods and meat-processing products is high. Other foreign investors are interested in regions with abundant farm resources, such as Liaoning and Jilin provinces. Most of the enterprises aim to see a large portion of their production distributed in the local market, and some firms' sales are over 80 per cent in the domestic market, showing that the Chinese government has slowly abandoned its policy of forced exports by foreign firms. Many small or medium-sized firms from Asian countries such as Hong Kong, Taiwan and Thailand export over 40 per cent of their output. In regard to inputs, only a few firms import more then 30 per cent of their total inputs from overseas.

Agro-Business

China, as a major agricultural country, has always faced fundamental issues in relation to agriculture, the countryside and the farmers. China's rural areas have carried out successful reforms since 1978, which have facilitated rural economic development, but agriculture's share of national income has fallen from around 30 per cent to 20 per cent since 1978. For many years, China's agricultural sector has been taxed in order to support industrialisation (Lardy, 1983; Lin, 1994).

Prior to economic reform, farm products were classified into three categories, according to how they were sold by farmers. The first category was comprised of unified procurement commodities which included grain, cotton, edible oil and oil bearing crops. The second category, dual-track commodities, included meat and aquatic products, tobacco, tea, silk and sugar. Third, there were zero-quota commodities, consisting primarily of fruits and vegetables. The growth of China's agricultural sector since 1978 was reflected in the impact of agricultural policy reforms across all three categories of farm products. The major policy changes were: privatisation of farming through the household responsibility system (HRS); the support of rural industrial development, that is township and village-owned enterprises (TVEs), to enhance the overall rural economy; and the reform of mandatory procurement quotas and prices for agricultural commodities.

After the first wave of reform, China's agricultural production growth was abnormally high for a few years due to one-time productivity gains from improved incentives (Table 7.4). However, subsequent agricultural development during the 1980s and early 1990s reforms have not been without policy problems (Carter and Fang Cai, 1996). China's policy-makers are obsessed with domestic grain output, and it is an understatement to say that the domestic balance of long-term supply and demand for grains is a politically sensitive issue in China. On the demand estimates, it has been estimated that China may need to import about 216 million metric tons of grain by the year 2020 (Brown, 1995, p. 19), which is an amount greater than the total world trade in grains today. In China, grain production is relatively land-intensive (Table 7.5) compared to many other agricultural products (for example cotton, sugar, fruits and vegetables), which are more labour-intensive. Hence, the comparative advantage of grain production in China is questionable. In the long run, China will most likely develop an increasing grain deficit due to the combined factors of rising domestic incomes, a growing population, and a declining sown acreage. China's arable land per capita is already on the low side, and decades of communist party depredation have made matters even worse. Also a major concern that immediately emerged following the establishment of the HRS was the fragmentation of farms. According to Lin (1995), economies of scale were sacrificed in the household-based system, but the gains from the superior incentive structure of that system more than compensated for losses of economies of scale from the elimination of the previous

Table 7.4 *Average growth rates of gross value of agricultural output,*
1979–96 (%)

	GVAO	Cropping	Forestry	Animal husbandry	Sideline production	Fisheries
1979–93	6.1	4.3	5.1	9.2	13.1	11.7
1979–84	7.7	6.9	7.7	9.7	15.5	7.9
1985–93	5.0	2.7	3.3	8.9	11.2	14.2
1990–96	4.3	2.9	3.0	6.7	9.4	10.4

Sources: State Bureau of Statistics, *Statistical Yearbook of China*, Beijing, (SSB, 1993, 1994 and 1997); Carter and Feng Cai (1996), The 1990 Institute, San Francisco, 1996, p. 12

Table 7.5 *China: grain production, 1978–96*

	Grain output (mmt)	Grain sown area (mn ha)	Grain yield (kg/ha)
1978	304.8	120.6	2596.0
1979	332.1	119.3	2784.8
1980	320.6	117.2	2734.5
1981	325.0	115.0	2827.5
1982	354.5	113.5	3124.4
1983	387.3	114.0	3396.0
1984	407.3	112.9	3608.3
1985	379.1	108.8	3483.2
1986	391.5	110.9	3529.3
1987	403.0	111.3	3622.0
1988	394.1	110.1	3578.6
1989	407.6	112.2	3632.4
1990	446.2	113.5	3933.0
1991	435.3	112.3	3875.8
1992	442.7	110.6	4003.8
1993	456.5	110.5	4130.8
1994	444.5	109.3	4066.8
1995	434.5	108.6	3980.4
1996	439.4	107.9	3897.6
Average growth rate (%)			
1978–84	4.8	−1.1	5.5
1985–96	1.7	0.04	1.6

Note: mmt = million metric tonnes, ha = hectare.
Sources: State Statistical Bureau, *Statistical Yearbook of China*, Beijing, (SSB, 1997), Carter and Zhong, *China Ongoing Agricultural Reform*, San Francisco, 1996, p. 13

team system. Farms were further fragmented into four or five tiny sections, scattered in different locations, and a strategy of land reconsolidation was introduced which aimed to reduce the number of plots farmed by one household, but did not enlarge the size of farms as a whole.

In summary, the major issues facing further development of China's agricultural sector include the following:

- the apparent slowdown of agricultural productivity growth;
- the lack of properly functioning markets for farm products and farm inputs;
- excess labour in agriculture and the rising gap between rural and urban incomes;

- the slowdown of rural light industries' (i.e. TVEs) absorption of labour;
- capital outflows from agriculture to rural light industry and urban industry; and
- property rights and land-tenure issues.

Despite all these problems, the agricultural sector has witnessed an increased interest from foreign investors. Although some subsectors receive government aid, this does not imply that all subsectors are necessarily weak. Agriculture is now the largest sector in the country that has seen the least exploitation as an investment recipient. The Chinese government has given top priority and firm support to the sector for the development of foreign investment.

The opening of Chinese agriculture took place in a gradual fashion, in line with the general pace of the country's economic reform programme. The industry attracted an accumulated amount of $US2.6 billion in FDI between 1979 and 1996, of which 88.6 per cent was realised during the 1990s. It represented roughly 1.5 per cent of the total amount of FDI nationwide over the same period. The major investor is Hong Kong, which took the lion's share of total FDI in the agricultural sector with $US1.2 billion, accounting for 46.9 per cent. FDI from the USA, Singapore and South Korea stood at $US258 million, $US219 million and $US197 million, respectively, representing 9.9 per cent, 8.4 per cent and 7.6 per cent of the total. Investment from Thailand, Japan and Canada stood at $US160 million, $US159 million and $US85 million. Other major investors come from France, Sweden, the UK and Taiwan.

The utilisation of foreign capital has boosted the development of Chinese farming and the rural economy. It has offset Chinese shortages of financial inputs in agriculture, introduced advanced technologies, brought in improved varieties and fine breeds, and helped raise the productivity of local farming and animal husbandry. The majority of the projects are medium-sized investments between RMB 10–100 million per project, with a strong orientation towards the domestic market. But there are some exemptions where a few firms, located in Guandong province, sell over 50 per cent of their production abroad. Notably, there are also projects with net assets above RMB 100 million funded by large MNCs from Western countries which have a strong comparative advantage in the agricultural sector in relation to technology, know-how and marketing skills, such as FDI projects from the USA, Switzerland, Holland and Denmark, and these projects are mostly capital-intensive. A clear majority of invest-ment in agriculture is in the form of joint ventures with majority foreign shareholding; only a few are wholly foreign-owned, by medium-sized firms from Thailand and Denmark.

In conclusion, FDI in agriculture is focused primarily on China's farm product-processing projects, and inflows of capital that go to crop farming remain at a relatively low level. This is partly due to the country's relatively backward development of agricultural production and partly because crop farming returns in china are kept low by government policy. Currently, foreign-funded farming enterprises account for less then 1 per cent of the production of China's state and collective-owned farms combined (these are largely plantations that have sought foreign partners).The number of employees in these enterprises represents less than 0.01 per cent of the country's total, and under these circumstances it would appear that FDI in Chinese agriculture is still only in an embryonic phase.

Cement

Under the Five-Year Plan from 1996–2000, China set up the guidelines and objectives for the cement industries. The major objectives of the plan are to improve the quality and varieties of products. Currently, more than 80 per cent of the cement produced in China is of low and medium grade. With the help of the World Bank's private-sector finan-cing arm and the International Finance Corporation (IFC), the Chinese government planned to start 10 cement production projects which will help to bring technology and expertise in the Chinese cement industry up to world standards as well as promoting environmental protection standards set by the World Bank (*The China Daily*, 5 April 1997). Many of the existing cement projects in China damage the environment.

Demand for cement is strong in view of the boom in the real estate and tourism sectors, although the government made some restrictions for this sector. Large infrastructure projects financed by the government have also increased demand for cement, especially for motorways and dams. Since the reform, demand in the housing sector increased, espe-cially after the government launched its '2000 Comfortable Housing Programme', a nationwide project in 1994 to improve housing quality with the application of advanced technology and products. The Minis-try of Construction has approved the establishment of 63 pilot housing projects across the country; the homes are being sold mainly to families with middle and high incomes (*The Hong Kong Times*, 17 March 1997).

Overseas investment has been growing rapidly in the construction industry since the implementation of the open-door policy. In the cement industry, foreign investment grew from less than $US700 000 in the late 1970s to about $US86 million in 1996. In total, the industry has attracted $US441 million between 1979–96, with a $US392 million inflow during the 1990s, representing 88.9 per cent of the industry's total inflow. The major investor is Hong Kong with $US217 million or 49 per cent of FDI utilised by the industry. Second is Australia with $US82 million (19 per cent), third Japan with $US48 million (11 per cent) and fourth the USA with $US32 million (10 per cent), then France, Bermuda and Macau. With those foreign funds, a large number of big and medium-sized cement plants were built in Jiangsu, Shandong, Fujian and other regions, which has led to a steady growth of the industry's output. The gross value of production rose to 490 million tons in 1996, up by nearly six times over the early phase of the reform (*The China Daily*, 17 March 1997).

Most projects are joint ventures with an equity capitalisation ratio between RMB 10–100 million per project, and are usually run by medium-sized firms with a strong domestic market-orientation. But there are also many large projects of over RMB 100 million run by well-known multinational cement producers such as the French company Lafarge SA, Hong Kong Tysan Holdings, the Japanese cement maker Nihon Cement Co. Ltd and Yantai Mitsubishi Cement Co. Ltd, which is the biggest cement exporter in China. These companies have a very strong influence on the structure, competition and intensity of the Chinese cement industry. They not only bring advanced technology or managerial techniques, but also supply high-quality products and varieties; the companies' products no. 525 and no. 625 cement are the first-choice materials of many Southeast Asian construction teams. The companies are mostly export-market oriented, often selling over 60 per cent of production abroad. Yantai Mitsubishi Co. exports around 80 per cent of its production of 3000 tons of cement daily. This is exported to South Korea, Singapore, Malaysia, Hong Kong and Taiwan. Most of these projects are capital-intensive with majority shareholdings by foreign investors. Of course, one has to take into consideration the recent financial crises in most East Asian countries, which will have a strong influence on the demand for Chinese cement in the near future. The large cement producers which export the majority of their production to those countries will have to readjust their market strategies and production to local needs.

Paper

In the paper industry the Chinese government has put strong emphasis on the development of a modern industry based on new technology and production techniques, especially in bleaching paper to reach environmental standards. Under the new policy, some restrictions were put on the duty-free import of paper raw materials which must first be exported as finished products, and then re-imported by end-users to box their products. Until now most factories have shipped their products duty-free directly to other foreign-owned plants within China that use them to package toys, garments, electronics or other goods for export. The Chinese government wanted to prevent the leakage of goods into the domestic market.

In the paper industry, the average annual amount of FDI inflow stood at only $US11 600, but increased to $US151 million in 1996. The industry accumulated $US434 million of foreign capital between 1979–96, of which 97 per cent was brought in during the 1990s. Again, Hong Kong was the major foreign investor, with $US266 million, representing 61 per cent of the industry total. Next was Indonesia with $US50 million of investment (12 per cent); Macau $US45 million (10 per cent); Thailand $US38 million (8 per cent); and the USA with $US21 million (5 per cent).

At present, there are over 100 joint and contractual joint ventures that make paper products scattered across the country. Foreign capital has to a great extent helped to improve product quality and technological processes, as well as industrial output. In 1996, the industry produced 29.24 million tons of machine-made paper and paper boards, an increase of over five times compared with the late 1970s and early 1980s. Most of the projects are small ($US50 000) and medium-sized plants between RMB 10–30 million with a strong domestic-market orientation. Most of them are labour-intensive, with less-advanced technologies which often cause environmental damage.

POLAND

Motor Vehicles

The Polish car industry had been dominated by a few large SOEs which have a monopoly in the domestic market. In line with the economic transformation programme of shock therapy of 1990, these enterprises were specially targeted for industrial restructuring to increase efficiency and competition. In conjunction, subsidies were to be withdrawn, whilst incentives were provided to stimulate foreign investment. The objective of the government was to subject the car industry to market forces as the sole instrument for restructuring, hoping that loss-making, insolvent enterprises would collapse and that their assets – which in any case are highly specific – would be taken over by other healthier ones or, preferably, by MNCs. The government did not have a clear policy for industrial restructuring, especially in relation to the car industry, and in the 1990s the industry experienced severe problems under the new economic regime.

The government began to recognise that the car industry needed intervention in order to smooth the privatisation process and its economic and political consequences. Interventions have been *ad hoc*, and a quasi-industrial policy was adopted to coordinate investment and production strategies for the industry as a whole. The bulk of the car industry in Poland is now under foreign ownership, and it appears that two foreign firms, Fiat and Daewoo, are likely to dominate Polish car production by the end of the decade (Table 7.6). But this domination will, to a certain extent, be challenged by the two largest motor manufacturers in the world, Ford and General Motors. They have recently committed themselves to invest in greenfield plants in Poland: Ford in Plonsk for the assembly of 30 000 Escort cars and Transit vans, and GM in Gliwice for 100 000 cars in an integrated car plant with press shop, body plant, paintshop and final assembly facilities (*Financial Times*, 5 March 1996).

Fiat has remained the dominant market leader, with a 26 per cent market share (over 150 000 units produced). The next is the Daewoo Group, with a 24 per cent market share (approximately 140 000 units produced), then Volkswagen, Ford and Mercedes Benz with up to 5 per cent each of market share. Despite the fact that many Poles own cars, production is not keeping pace with market demand. In 1996 over 375 900 cars were sold on the Polish market, including 57 100 imported (in this imported pool of cars many thousands of cars are brought to Poland mainly from Germany illegally, trying to avoid taxes and duties), and also Poland exported over 165 000 units, while production capacity reached only 380 000 units (PAIZ, 1997).

As Table 7.6 shows, the car industry in Poland is characterised by low capacity utilisation, and there is a huge potential for production expansion and employment. As the table indicates, employment has

Table 7.6   *Poland: employment, output and capacity utilisation for the car industry, a comparison between 1989–96*

	1989			1996		
	Employment	Output (000s)	Capacity utilisation (%)	Employment	Employment reduction (%)	Output (000s)	Capacity utilisation (%)
FSM, Bielsko-Biala (owned by Fiat)	27 587	206	98	13 000	32	280	89
FSO, Warsaw (owned by Daewoo)	24 302	99	83	19 400	19	92	75
FSC, Lublin (owned by Daewoo)	8 361	12.7	58	6 000	26	9	40
JZS, Jelcz (owned by Mercedes Benz) represented by SZL	8 630	7.4	90	3 050	64	1.6	45
FSC, Starachowice (owned by Mercedes Benz) represented in Poland by Sobieslaw Zasada Ltd (SZL)	13 832	9.5	79	2 500	82	3.5	80
Autosan, Sanok (owned by Daewoo and Mercedes Benz)	6 189	3.2	100	2 100	63	1.8	38
FSR, Poznan (owned by Volkswagen)	2 678	4.5	82	1 780	45	2.8	49

Sources: 1989 output figures from *The East European Motor Industry*, Economist Intelligence Unit, Special Report no. 1167, London, tables 33 and 35; 1989 employment figures from *Lista 500, Zarzadzanie*, 6 July 1990, Warsaw, pp. 46–63; 1996 figures from *Auto Technika Motoryzacyjna*, April 1997, Warsaw.

been slightly reduced, because the government used its policy of full employment to insist in negotiations with car makers that contracts should guarantee to keep the whole labour force at least up to 2–3 years. For example, GM as well as Daewoo guarantee that they will not shed workers until the year 2000. The potential for import is large, but the government strictly controls the pool of imported cars, and has used its import quotas as incentives for major car makers to enter the Polish market.

Competition in the Polish car industry is severe, and many well-known car makers have problems in entering the market or guaranteeing future contracts. An example is the French car maker Citroen-Renault which lost its contract bid for FSO to the US car-maker giant GM. Many foreign investors see the big Polish market as having a potential for development and expansion, taking into consideration the saturated market for cars in the West.

Between 1989–96, a total of 38 projects were set up between Polish and foreign partners, with a total of $US1.12 billion of FDI. Italy remained the biggest investor with $US888 million, which represents 43 per cent of the industry total. South Korea ranked second with $US170 million (23 per cent), third was the USA with $US72 million (6.3 per cent), followed by Germany's $US47 million, Sweden's $US31 million and Japan's $US12 million.

Most of the projects are located in central and southern Poland where big Polish state-owned car factories had been established. Foreign investors own over 50 per cent or even 80 per cent of the shares and have majority control. Most of the investment has been in the form of joint ventures, dominated by large car makers with high capitalisation ratios per project, between $US5–20 million. Over 90 per cent of foreign-funded enterprises are domestic market-oriented, but still foreign firms exported over 165 000 units in 1996. The leader in the Polish car industry was Italian Fiat which exported approximately 150 000 Fiat Cinquecianto model '900' to France, the UK, Italy, Spain and Benelux in 1997. Also, some units had been exported to China under barter trade agreements between Poland and China. The South Korean car maker Daewoo is slowly expanding exports from Poland (especially the Lanos model) to countries such as Cyprus and other Asian and South American countries using its international marketing network (Makowski, 1997).

Food Processing

Food-processing has been one of the most consistently expanding sectors of the Polish manufacturing industry during the period of transition, mainly due to the relative stability of the domestic market in 1990–91 as well as the sector's good export performance. In 1996 exports of food-processing products amounted to 20 per cent of total Polish exports (around $US2.5 billion) (Smolarek, 1996), and covered 48 per cent of all supplies of consumer goods for the domestic market. Food-processing provided approximately 7.5 per cent of GDP in 1996 and 25 per cent of global industrial output in that year (PAIZ *Data Sheet Series* 1997). By 1997, production in this sector was 35 per cent higher than in 1992. Despite the fact that the food-processing industry was one of the branches of the Polish economy in which improvement of product quality and variety was most visible, further changes are needed in this sector to modernise the assortment of goods and increase their attractiveness.

According to government policy, development should take place first in the following areas: beer and malt production, rape seed processing and vegetable oil production, potato processing, vegetables processing, meat production and highly processed food (fast food, food concentrates, confectionery). The basic aims of Poland's policy in food-processing are to achieve greater export orientation, to implement modern technology and achieve a better and stable level of quality. These activities are to be implemented mostly by large and medium-sized factories (70 per cent of Poland's production potential).

The food-processing industry in Poland is undergoing a process of changing ownership. The share of the private sector amounted to approximately 62 per cent in 1996, and about 32 per cent of the SOEs in this sector have been privatised. In addition, by 1997 173 SOEs had been transformed into State Treasury companies for further privatisation. In 1996 the food-processing sector employed 460 000 workers (3.1 per cent of the total Polish workforce) in 2022 enterprises. Among 1300 larger enterprises employing over 50 workers there were 428 SOEs and 872 private enterprises. Several thousands of small private enterprises of the handicraft type also operate (Smolarek 1996). The most important branches in terms of output share and profitability, as of 1996, are summarised in Table 7.7:

Table 7.7   *Food processing in Poland: production, structure and profitability*

	Production (% of total)	Profit (% of net income)
Meat processing	13.7	1.2
Spirits industry	13.4	11.6
Diary processing	9.8	2.3
Ale production	5.8	1.8
Sugar processing	4.9	2.3
Confectionery	4.8	6.9
Fruit and vegetables	3.8	−4.7
Milling and pasta	3.5	−1.1
Oils and fats	2.9	5.2
Eggs and poultry	2.5	−0.10
Fish processing	2.0	1.0
Food concentrates	1.8	5.9

Source: PAIZ, *PAIZ Data Sheet Series*, Warsaw, August 1995.

The financial situation of the particular branches within this sector is diverse, and assessment of the financial state of the main processing trends shows that the most profitable areas are in secondary processing (sugar, food concentrates production) and the production of stimulants (apart from the wine-making industry). These branches have a high capability for internal capital accumulation (over 6 per cent of sales), a high investment rate and low long-term indebtedness (Pilarczyk, 1996).

The food-processing sector is one of the most interesting agreas of the Polish economy for foreign capital. Many foreign firms have already established joint ventures with Polish enterprises or greenfield investments in food and drink production. Most of the major world companies in food-processing such as Coca-Cola, Pepsico, Nestlé, R.J. Reynolds, MacDonald's, Gerber, Schoeller and many others have already started production in Poland. It is clear that food-processing has been the most attractive industrial sector for FDI, attracting $US2.54 billion of FDI between 1989–96 and representing over 21 per cent of total Polish foreign investment, with over $US1.2 billion committed in the future. The major investor has been the USA with $US509 million, which represents 20 per cent of total FDI; second was Switzerland with $US254 million (10 per cent), third Germany with $US199 million (8 per cent), then Holland with $US166 million (6.5 per cent), followed by Denmark with $US87 million, and the UK with $US70 million.

The majority of the investment projects are owned by the food-processing giants with capitalisation ratios between $US5–25 million per project; they are mostly wholly foreign-owned or with majority shareholdings by foreign investors. Most of them produce for the domestic market but also successfully export over 30–40 per cent of their production to Western markets, where Polish food-processing products have a good market reputation in terms of taste, quality and assortment. These well-known firms have had positive effects on the food-processing industry structure through intensive modernisation. Through new investments and the modernisation of plants, there is now a greater share of processing high value-added products, especially in sectors having higher growth dynamics.

Agro-Business

The agricultural sector in Poland suffers from several major underlying problems. There is low productivity because of the fragmentation and small size of private firms; the basic infrastructure is poor; and the ability of farmers to meet the challenges of a market economy and the associated objectives of economic policy are limited. Polish agriculture is in a different situation *vis-à-vis* other branches of the national economy. The utilised agricultural area (UAA) is 18.8 million hectares, representing 60 per cent of the total land area. The land/population ratio in agriculture of about 0.5 hectares per person is relatively high, but the quality of land is rather poor and is associated with a low level of precipitation, especially in the central plains. The share of good quality soils is only 11 per cent of the utilised agricultural area, medium and low quality soils representing respectively 54 per cent and 35 per cent of the UAA (OECD, 1995, *Review of Agricultural Policies: Poland*).

Unlike other former socialist countries, most farmland in Poland has always been in the private sector. However, a socialised sector also existed, with state and cooperative farms. In 1995, the relative sizes of the private and socialised sectors were as shown in Table 7.8. Family farms occupied 14.2 million hectares, which represented 76.2 per cent of all agricultural land in the country. These farms were characterised by dispersed structural farming, with a resulting high level of employment as well as an excessive amount of fixed property. Most of them managed to create only subsistence increments to family consumption (Miller, 1997). The average area of the farms amounted to 6.3 hectares, and their total number was 2.1 million. The level of employment measured by the number of fully-employed persons was 24.9 people per hectares of agricultural land (Pyrgies, 1995).

Table 7.8   *Poland: agro-business, 1995*

	Private farms (share in total, %)	Socialised farms (share in total, %)
Land	76	24
Labour	80	20
Total production	77	23
Market production	73	27
Fertiliser purchases	64	36
Tractors	86	14

Source: Centre for Co-operation with the Economies in Transition, *Poland Agriculture*, OECD, 1996, p. 42.

The second group of farms were state-owned agricultural enterprises (PPGR), which occupied about 20 per cent of the total agricultural land in the country, with an average area for each enterprise of 2800 hectares. Most of these PPGRs are concentrated in the northern and western parts of Poland. Their share of land does not reflect their significance in the use of land resources, due to the fact that strong regional differentiations have not been taken into account. In the northern and western voivodships, the share of the PPGR in utilising land was significant and amounted to 30–40 per cent, but in 17 voivodships, mainly central and southern ones, the share did not exceed 5 per cent. The share of the public sector in employment was somewhat smaller than in the use of agricultural land and amounted to 10.4 per cent. Overall, about 470 000 people were employed in the PPGR, which means 13.4 people per 100 hectares of agricultural land. Together with the families of workers, the number of people related to the public sector in agriculture reached 2 million (OECD, 1995, Review of Agricultural Policies: Poland; and Pyrgies, 1995).

The third group of farms were cooperative farms. These agricultural-production cooperatives occupied 3.6 per cent of agricultural land, with an average area of 300 hectares. Due to their forms of organisation, management systems, as well as their financial and economic systems, these were more similar to the state farms than to the family farms.

From the data, it is apparent that two sectors dominated Polish agriculture, with significant differences in their scales of production, levels of technology, as well as the forms of ownership. Each of these sectors is characterised by specific weaknesses, the overcoming of which is a condition for their further development. In relation to individual farming the weakness is, above all, the dispersed structure of the farms. The major weaknesses of the state sector are excessive employment, over-investment in buildings, the overburdening of social functions, as well as over-extended and unmanageable organisational structures.

Despite the downward output trend, agriculture's contribution to GDP in 1996 still represented 6.8 per cent of total GDP at current prices in Poland. In the same year the agricultural labour force represented about 23 per cent of the total working population (OECD Report, 1997). The marked difference between the agricultural contribution to GDP and the share of the total labour in agriculture indicates a relatively low agricultural labour productivity. In recent years, increasing unemployment in non-agricultural activities has diminished the possibility of finding employment outside agriculture.

Since 1989, with the transition from a centrally-planned economy to a competitive market economy, the main objectives of agricultural policy have been the modernisation of agriculture and its adjustment to market mechanisms in order to improve the productivity and efficiency of the agricultural sector and to increase standards of living in rural areas. There are two main groups of instruments specific to the agricultural sector. One consists of measures to support market prices, regulating domestic prices in conjunction with import barriers; and social measures aimed directly at raising farm income. With the reform of social security in 1990 and the extension of the entitlements and benefits of the retirement-pension scheme to private farmers, government spending on social measures for farmers increased dramatically to more than two-thirds of total budgetary expenditures on the agro-food constituencies in 1991–93 (Portugal, 1995).

The other group of instruments involves the reduction of the cost of inputs to farmers through subsidies and cheap credit, and state-funded general services intended to improve the productivity base of agriculture. These instruments will in future have to be in line with EU membership and will have to conform with the Common Agricultural Policy (CAP). Agriculture could become one of the major obstacles to Poland's admission to the EU, and further reform both of the CAP and of Polish agricultural policies will be necessary.

In regard to structural adjustments in farming, the government needs to develop a medium-term structural policy, to develop a market for private land transactions and leasing, and to privatise state farms, so as to create a structure of farms that will be able to compete on the international market. To these ends, the government has begun to divest itself of state land, but the results of this process have been slow. The main reasons are a lack of capital and the location of state land resources, which are for the most part too far away from the private farms to allow them to expand. The lack of a legal framework for the privatisation process has also led to a cautious application of the privatisation programme and has impeded the divestiture of state farms.

Agriculture is the sector of the national economy which attracts the lowest amount of foreign investment. Between 1989–96 the investment amounted only to about $US15 million, less than 0.5 per cent of Poland's total investment. Part of this investment comes from the Swiss government – $US7 million to develop an agro-food auction in Poznan. The main investment comes from Holland, about $US8 million, which was invested by Nutricia in dairy farms and by Agro East Europe BV in potato farms to produce chips, crisps and similar products. The next investor was Denmark with $US3.5 million invested in pig breeding in Koczala (Slupsk voivodship) as a joint venture with Polen Invest A/S; the third was Belgium's $US3 million investment by Dossche in a meat farm near Sandomierz. Also, McDonald's and Pizza Hut have invested in corn and grain farming near Warsaw, to secure fresh and regular supplies for their restaurants in Warsaw where there is a huge demand.

Cement

The construction industry plays a vital role in the development of the Polish economy. After Poland started its transition to a market economy and liberalised its domestic market, new opportunities emerged for the construction industry as well as for the closely related cement sector. There is expected to be an increasing demand for development of infrastructure such as toll motorways and a roads network, the Odra River transport, lower Vistula cascade, water treatment plants for over 300 cities, construction of hotels and other facilities for tourism, industrial park development and housing.

Housing is a particularly important sector for the government, but the housing situation in Poland is very difficult. According to conservative estimates, 1 500 000 dwellings are needed in the period 1995–2000, not including repairs and renovations (including thermo-insulation) of existing buildings, especially the older types. This task will require high-quality building materials including cement. The total construction market value is estimated to be around $US10 billion (Gnat 1996).

The market potential for the cement industry is high, and demand is expected to grow at 10–13 per cent annually. The value of sold cement in 1996 was around $US490 million, with production of over 12 million tons. Most of the firms operating in the cement industry are large enterprises employing over 50 persons per firm, as well as a few medium-sized firms (PAIZ and Ministry of Physical Planning and Construction 1997). To increase competition and modernisation of the industry the government issues many incentives and regulations in line with its policy objectives. The main aim of government policies are the introduction of advanced and clean technology for the production of cement, to increase the quality and varieties of products, to create conditions favouring further economic growth, and to encourage FDI in the cement industry. So far the industry has attracted over $US270 million between 1989–96, which represents 0.8 per cent of total national accumulated investment. The major investment comes from Germany, at $US108 million, which represents 40 per cent of the industry's total, second was France with $US66 million (24 per cent), third was the International Corporation (Belgian–German) with $US54 million (20 per cent), followed by Ireland's $US22 million (8 per cent) and Turkey's $US20 million.

The cement industry is mostly wholly foreign-owned by large cement producers such as Germany's Dyckerhoff, Miebach, the French Lafarge, Cementeries CBR (Belgian–German owned), and the Turkish Rumeli Group. Most of these projects have high capital to labour ratios, at between $US5–10 million per project, and a strong domestic-market orientation. They play an important role in the cement industry's restructuring and the modernisation of its internal structure through increased efficiency and competition. Most of the inputs come from the domestic market and are characterised by good quality and varieties of raw materials.

Paper

The paper industry compared with other domestic industries has a comparative advantage in terms of a lower cost level and also a considerably higher profitability rate on its net and gross turnover. During 1993–96, the consumption of paper in Poland increased annually by about 10–12 per cent; almost 1.5 million tonnes of paper were produced, with per capita consumption increasing to 41 kg. In order to sustain this growth, however, the paper industry requires further investment as well as progress on the privatisation front (Dabrowski and Stanislawczyk, 1997). The main objectives of government policies in regard to the paper industry are to make improvements in operating practices and product quality, to reduce imports and to increase foreign investment by creating a more friendly business environment. Many government regulations have been scaled down and special incentives introduced to create more competition and to stimulate local firms.

In 1996 the sales of paper reached almost 2 per cent of total domestic sales, while pulp and paper exports constituted 2.25 per cent ($US515 million) of total domestic consumption. Increasing demand is evident from the fact that Poland imported an estimated

$US1.09 billion worth of paper products, nearly twice as much as it exports. Although total imports into Poland were only 5.5 per cent higher than exports, the consumption of paper was proportionately greater than other industrial products. By the end of 1996, it was estimated that the consumption of pulpwood would have increased to 4445 million m³ for the production of 981 000 tonnes of pulp. Due to modernisation and investment, domestic pulp production capacity reached almost 1 million tonnes by 1996. Nevertheless, the construction of a new pulp mill is needed (Dabrowski and Stanislawczyk, 1997). Increasing wastepaper consumption provides some compensation for domestic pulp shortages, and in 1996 650 000 tonnes of wastepaper were used in the production of paper and board, including 60 000 tonnes of imported wastepaper. Exports of a mere 6000 tonnes of wastepaper, however, were of little significance (PAIZ, 1997).[b]

Traditionally, the greater part of paper production in Poland has been for packaging purposes. In 1996, corrugated materials, together with sack paper and wrapping paper, amounted to 780 000 tonnes, that is 54.7 per cent of total paper production. The slow growth in exports, due to increased consumption of packaging in Poland, was marked by a slight increase from 295 000 tonnes in 1994 to 370 000 tonnes in 1996. The amount imported was more noticeable, from 333 000 tonnes in 1994 to 425 000 tonnes in 1996. Over 60 per cent of the imports came from Germany, Finland, Austria and Sweden.

The larger mills are located in northern Poland. The market leader is IP-Kwidzyn (majority owned by IPC US) with 464 000 tonnes of paper production. It exports over 36 per cent of its production and recently strengthened its position by acquisition of the greater part of the Klucze mill's shares. The Klucze mill manufactured almost 20 000 tonnes of tissue 1996. The second largest is Celuloza Swiecie (owned by Intercellulosa AB Sweden) with production of 423 000 tonnes of paper. Intercell SA Ostroleka (owned by Inter Paper Holding AG of Liechtenstein), with 240 000 tonnes of paper production, is the third biggest producer in Poland, and also converts paper into corrugated board and boxes, sacks and packaging.

The leading mills achieve the highest productivity, almost 135 tonnes of paper for each employee, compared with Western standards of 140 tonnes. Further improvements in the operation of mills and product quality are being implemented by these larger mills. The traditionally strong areas of the Polish paper industry (corrugated board, paper sacks and packaging) are promoted as the most profitable in terms of investment. An example is the success of

Celuloza Swiecie and the impressive development of Intercell SA Ostroleka, which after acquiring the conversion plant at Lodz (now Intercell-Scanbox) in 1994 started production as the Nordic Box paper-converting plant two years later with great success (PAIZ, 1997).[a]

The pollution level of Polish mills is nearing the standards set in Western Europe, and improved pollution control is also noted in smaller mills. This is the result of cooperation with Western companies involved in the abatement of water and air pollution, and the assistance provided by the Pulp and Paper Research Institute at Lodz. Progress in the reduction of freshwater consumption within a closed production system, however, has caused an increase in the consumption of chemical additives used by such modern technology.

The favourable conditions for the growth of the paper industry in Poland are connected to the availability of raw materials, as well as an increasing demand for paper products by a large domestic market. The industry attracted around $US497 million of FDI between 1989–96, which represented 4.3 per cent of Poland's total national investment. The USA is the dominant investor with $US370 million, representing 74 per cent of the total FDI investment. Second is Sweden with $US69 million (13.9 per cent), and third was Switzerland with $US33 million (6.6 per cent), followed by the UK's $US12 million, Liechtenstein's $US7.5 million, Austria's $US3 million and France's $US2 million. The majority of the projects are large mills in the form of majority shareholding joint ventures with capitalisation ratios between $US4–10 million and employing more than 50 persons. Most of the firms are domestic-market oriented, but some of the large firms such as IP Kiwidzin, Celuloza Swiecie or Intercell SA Ostroleka export over 30 per cent of their production to Western markets.

COMPARISON BETWEEN CHINA AND POLAND

Motor Vehicles

The car industry in China is more fragmented than in Poland, but in both countries car manufacturing has been inefficient. The main difference between Chinese and Polish car manufacturers lies in their ownership structures. In China, in line with Party policy, wholly foreign-owned enterprises have not been allowed, and the majority of shares are controlled by state enterprises. In Poland, the main car manufacturers are foreign-owned with the majority of shareholding in joint ventures. The major players in the car industry are a few large car makers which control most of the Polish market.

In China, in contrast there are many car makers representing major car producing countries, still engaged in low-production units, and some of these car makers produce far below their production capacities. In both countries utilisation ratios are very low and there is a large potential for improvement. Most of the plants employ quite a large number of people, especially in China. It is interesting to note that major Japanese car makers still show a low profile in both countries. In regards to capitalisation ratios per project there is quite a significant difference between China and Poland, with projects in Poland exhibiting higher capital/labour ratios than in China.

Food Processing

The food-processing sector in China is more labour-intensive than in Poland and is occupied by medium-sized firms with low capitalisation ratios. Most of the firms are domestic-market oriented with low export intensities. Productivity is still low and technology transfer is not always up-to-date. Awareness or popularity of Chinese food-processing products by brand or variety amongst domestic and foreign consumers is much lower than among Polish counterparts; most Polish food products have a high reputation among Western customers. The major differences between the Chinese and Polish food-processing industries are in their ownership structures and production orientations.

In Poland, most of the major food-processing plants are wholly foreign-owned with high investment per project and a strong export orientation. These plants are mostly owned by big food-processing giants using highly-updated technology. Compared with China, the Polish food-processing sector is one of the most profitable export-oriented area, of the economy. It possesses a strong comparative advantage compared with other sectors in terms of productivity, quality and efficiency. In contrast, Chinese food-processing is more labour-intensive and not yet well-developed; processed foods still lack high quality, and production takes the form of relatively small-scale import-substitution. A large proportion of the food entering people's homes in China is still in unprocessed form.

Agro-Business

Agriculture in both countries has been a low-priority sector under government policy, characterised by low productivity, inefficiency, excess labour and out-of-date technology. But there are also many major differences between the two countries. These difference again pertain to the ownership structures, as well as the control of farm inputs. In China most farming was previously owned and managed by village cooperatives and by the state or provincial government, and there was strict control of agriculture products which had to be supplied to the state. The quota and prices of farm products were fixed by the state and any market for farm products and farm inputs was lacking. The majority of the labour force was employed in farming, creating an excess of labour, inefficiency and low productivity which resulted in a widening gap between rural and urban incomes. Foreign investment in both countries has been at a low level, and in China is focused primarily on processing; and inflows of capital that go to crop farming remain at a relatively low level. In Poland the majority of agricultural land was and is owned by private family farms, and the state control of farms is at low level. There is much less labour employed in agriculture and the markets for farm products and farm inputs are better developed. Family farms now have better incentives for increased productivity, quality and varieties thanks to a strong local-market demand, competition and export incentives.

Cement

The cement industry in China is more labour-intensive than its counterpart in Poland. The capitalisation ratios are still low and most of the firms are medium-sized plants almost entirely domestic-market oriented. The industry is still heavily regulated, and control by the state often influences competition and prices for cement products. The majority of the investors come from Asian countries with low investment per project. These operations are more labour-intensive and mostly transfer second-hand technology.

Competition is often hampered by government regulations and policies. The quality of the products is still low, with limited varieties. Most of the projects are in the form of joint ventures and often controlled by inefficient state enterprises. The cement industry in Poland is mostly controlled by foreign-owned large firms with high capitalisation ratios and advanced technology. These large enterprises have a very strong influence on the structure, competition and intensity of the Polish cement industry. In contrast to China, the cement industry in Poland requires high start-up capital for the cement plants and their operation.

Paper

The paper industry in Poland compared with its counterpart in China has a comparative advantage in terms of cost, and a higher profitability rate on its net and gross turnover. It is also less regulated than in China and has more freedom in terms of imports of materials. In China the paper industry is dominated by small and medium-sized enterprises with a strong domestic market-orientation, whilst in Poland it is mainly dominated by large mills with advanced technology and high capitalisation ratios. Again, in terms of ownership structure there are major differences: in China most of the projects are joint ventures with almost equal control by the state and foreign partner. In Poland the majority shareholders are foreign firms with majority control over the paper plants. In fact, most of the large mills are wholly foreign-owned by big paper companies.

DETERMINANTS OF FDI

As discussed in Chapter 2, the existence of ownership, location and internalisation advantages (the OLI paradigm) is a necessary condition for FDI to occur (Dunning, 1985), but more recently it has been argued that location advantages of a potential host country could be both a necessary and sufficient condition for FDI (Stehn, 1992). FDI may be undertaken even without firm-specific advantages on the part of the foreign investor if the potential host country's location advantages are large enough to compensate for minimal or even negligible firm-specific advantages. This argument has important implications for economic policy towards FDI, as within the OLI paradigm locational attractiveness is the variable which is most perceptible for economic policy.

A set of eight factors was used in the survey to group either responses or to create statements regarding both locational and motivational issues pertaining to the investigation. These eight categories were labelled as market, resource, labour, cost efficiency, strategic position, know-how, geographic location and investment climate factors. These eight factors affecting FDI were primarily based upon an existing taxonomy created by others: the first six factors were generally an expansion of Dunning's (1993) terminology, while the remaining two factors, geographic location and investment climate, were developed from a variety of sources related to previous studies on the subject of MNC activity and FDI.

CHINA: DOMESTIC MARKET SIZE

As Table 7.9 shows, market considerations stand out as the most important factor emphasised by the firms surveyed (53 per cent), despite some restrictions imposed by the government on domestic sales. Taking into consideration the huge potential market of over 1 billion people, the robust economic growth in recent years and the increasing purchasing power of the Chinese people, particularly those of the coastal provinces, investors are beginning to consider China as a viable market for their products, with an enormous potential for development.

Table 7.9   *China: determinants of FDI*

No.	Category	Importance of factor				
		Very	*Fairly*	*Little*	*Irrelev.*	*Total*
1.	Market potential: • to access/supply the local market • growth potential • development of local market	53	18.5	9.5	19	100
2.	Low labour cost	18	25.3	15.6	41.1	100
3.	Rich resources	14.0	32.5	17.4	46.1	100
4.	Investment climate: • government policies • investment incentives • import substitution • political stability	6.5	34.6	18.6	40.3	100
5.	Others: • transportation cost • follow the competitor • technology transfer • weak industry	20.8	32.3	20.4	26.5	100

Source: Author's survey data.

The next most important motives indicated by the firms surveyed were labour costs (cited by 18 per cent of the firms), government incentives and stable policies (16 per cent) and supply of raw materials (14 per cent). It is interesting to note the high score of 'others' (20 per cent), which included many factors apart from market or labour considerations. The low share of labour as a motivating factor in the four industries surveyed can be explained partly by the low labour-intensive nature of the industries, and partly by the divisibility of the industries' production processes. For example, the modern food-processing industry, which is increasingly automated, is capital-intensive and technology-intensive. A share of the domestic market, more than cheap labour, is a crucial factor for investors to invest in China.

Some industries like agriculture and cement are more labour-intensive and show higher labour motivation rates (8 per cent) than the survey average. These industries also show a higher percentage of 'other' factors (20 per cent and 36 per cent respectively). Advanced technology, weak industry competition, government regulations and industry potential were amongst the other factors stated by the firms surveyed as motivational factors. As Table 7.9 shows, the investment climate (16 per cent) also proved an important factor for foreign investors; local authorities do not interfere in the running of factories and are less stringent about health, safety and environmental limits to corporate growth.

It is interesting to note the different patterns emerging amongst foreign investors. Investors from Japan, the USA, Sweden and Germany were motivated by demand-side factors such as China's domestic market size and market potential (80 per cent), whereas the supply of cheap labour and materials was relatively less important. Firms from these countries were domestic-market-oriented in contrast to firms from Taiwan, Hong Kong, South Korea and Singapore, which were export-oriented. These latter firms were motivated by production-related considerations such as reducing production costs and the supply of cheap labour (78 per cent) rather than market factors. It is apparent that investors from Japan, the USA and Germany chose market-seeking strategies with a strong emphasis on the shape of the local market. FDI from all sources was not export-oriented in the Kojima sense. Under inward-looking or import-substitution policies, tariff-jumping FDI is common in developing countries.

FDI is thought to be motivated by the degree of foreign market share which may have been previously served through exports (Hughes and You, 1969), because the introduction of projectionist measures and trade barriers affects the cost of exporting to the host country if import-substitution industrialisation has been pursued. China's inward-looking strategies create an environment which discriminates between import-substitution and exports and attracts FDI to less-export-oriented industries. It therefore attracts FDI which is less aligned with the country's comparative advantage and efficient use of resources and factor endowments.

Investors from Hong Kong, Taiwan or South Korea were mostly motivated by production costs and chose cost-seeking strategies with a strong emphasis on the cost of labour as the main reason for investment. Labour shortages and rising wages in those countries are making assembly processes less and less viable at home so that labour-intensive production of low-end products is largely subcontracted to China, resulting in the establishment of small to medium-sized factories as was indicated in Chapter 5.

COST OF LABOUR

One of the major advantages claimed for investment in China is the abundance of cheap labour. In this survey, labour costs refer to the total payment to workers, and include basic wages, bonuses, rewards and other subsidies or fringe benefits. The monthly payment to an unskilled or semi-skilled worker in the four industries ranged from RMB590–680. For skilled workers, technicians and supervisors, the payment varied from RMB1500–1600 per month. In other industries, the wage levels for both types of workers were roughly the same.

Firms generally indicated that labour was cheap compared with other developing and developed countries, but that it was unskilled, not well-trained and not very efficient. Among the 100 respondents who revealed their motives for investment in China, only eight firms (8 per cent) indicated that labour costs were a major factor in their investment decisions; for the others it was not particularly significant. As a percentage of the total production costs, labour accounted for only 19.7 per cent (exceptions were the motor car and cement industries, at 29.8 per cent and 27.8 per cent respectively). Thus, overall, the low cost of labour in China is not an important advantage except for those few firms which saw a comparative advantage when compared with the high wages of equivalent workers in newly-industrialising economies (NIEs).

An overwhelming majority of the responding firms (85 per cent) expected labour costs in China to rise in the next three to five years from 1996. Only a very small minority (5 per cent) expected it to decrease. Apart from money wages, it should be noted that a lot of firms in China provide workers with subsidised meals, living quarters and allowances for other basic necessities, and the cost of all these items will rise over time. In addition, a new law effective from 1 January 1995 introduced an upper limit on working hours and over-time. It also specifies minimum wages, welfare, retirement protection and conditions for layoff due to redundancy.

The quality of labour was also an important consideration for the sample firms. Views ranged from high efficiency to lower quality. In comparison with the investor's home country or other developing or developed countries, thirty-three (38 per cent) of the firms put quality on a par with other countries (Table 7.10). Thirty-one firms (36 per cent) indicated the quality to be good or better than other developing countries. Twelve firms (14 per cent) put the quality of skilled labour lower than equivalent workers in other developing countries. The main weaknesses of Chinese workers are said to be low skills, a poor work attitude, lack of discipline, lack of innovation and high absenteeism. Most complaints came from Japanese, South Korean and US investors (56.4 per cent), less from Hong Kong, Taiwanese, German and Singaporean investors (21 per cent). A number of firms considered these limitations, which contribute to low labour produc-tivity, as being largely influenced by the legacy of the state policy of life employment and the 'iron rice-bowl' strategy employed during earlier decades.

Table 7.10 *China: comparison of quality of skilled labour with other countries*

Comparison	No. of firms	%
Lower	12	14
Same	33	38
Good	15	17
Better	16	19
Other*	10	12
Total	86	100

* = Better than developing countries.
Source: Author's survey data.

Table 7.11 *China: measures to improve productivity*

Improvement measures	No. of firms	Percentage of total
Education/training	21	23
High wages	24	26
Bonuses/incentives	23	25
Advanced/strict management	10	11
Discipline/penalties	4	4
Qualified workers	2	2
Pay by contract work	3	3
Upgrade equipment	3	3
Improve conditions	2	2
Other	1	1
Total	93	100

Note: Other includes self-control.
Source: Author's survey data.

However, a culture of productivity is emerging in the private sector, as foreign firms have started to change the attitudes of workers by education, training and the employment of strict management measures. As Table 7.11 indicates, over 21 firms (23 per cent) use education and training as one of the measures to improve labour productivity, and another 23 (25 per cent) use bonus-structure incentives to encourage labour efficiency and productivity. Only four firms used disciplinary measures against workers to enforce work discipline and efficiency; two of those were Korean and two came from Taiwan. It was found that most firms (85.6 per cent) expected the level of professional and technical skills of China's labour force to improve in the near future. According to the State Statistical Bureau, the industrial production of China maintained a high level of growth of 18 per cent in 1995; and incremental output value reached RMB1.83 trillion (Investment in China, Federation of Hong Kong Industries, 1995). These official statistics seem to corroborate investors' expectations that labour productivity will improve in China.

SUPPLY OF RAW MATERIALS

Most firms expected access to cheap and good quality raw materials to be one of the advantages offered by the host countries. With its rich resource base, China can offer a diversified range of inputs for foreign firms. As Table 7.12 shows, over 32 firms (33 per cent) out of ninety-eight respondents import less than 5 per cent of their inputs from overseas. Twenty-six firms (27 per cent) import one-fifth of their inputs. Only 6 firms import more than 70 per cent of their inputs from overseas.

Firms are therefore concerned with the cost and reliability of the local supplies. There were criticisms that the quality of major inputs is generally inferior and that the government had put some restrictions on the import of other important inputs. In line with its import-substitution policy, China has continued to protect import-substitution industries by quantitative import restrictions and prohibitions, tariffs, quotas and other subsidies for import-substituting enterprises. In fact China has tried to promote its development through highly protected import substitution and subsidised export promotion. These measures have led to the overvaluation of foreign exchange, a bias against exports and hence a balance of payments problem. This kind of strategy imposed by the Chinese government creates many problems for foreign investors, especially those who import more than half of their raw materials for production.

As Table 7.13 shows, over 39 firms (41 per cent) of the 95 respondents reported some difficulties with the import of their inputs. The most common complaint related to the approval procedure (expressed by 13 firms), and high tariffs (indicated by twelve firms). Many firms from the USA, Japan, Sweden and Germany producing for the local market raised few problems about cost and unreliability of other inputs like water and electricity supplies.

Table 7.12 *China: Percentage of inputs from overseas markets*

Percentage	No. of firms	Percentage of total
less than 5	32	33
5–10	30	31
10–20	26	27
20–40	10	11
40–50	8	9
50–70	6	6
70–90	2	2
90–100	4	4
Total	98	100

Source: Author's survey data.

Table 7.13　*China: import restrictions for inputs*

Restrictions	No. of firms	Percentage of total
No imports	5	5
No restrictions	51	54
Approval procedure	13	14
High tariff	12	13
Quota problems	5	5
High price	3	3
Import licence problems	2	2
Quarantine	1	1
Information	1	1
Customs office difficulties	1	1
Policy restrictions	1	1
Total	95	100

Source:　Author's survey data.

Forty-five firms which sourced their raw materials locally, and therefore more cheaply, considered their costs of production to be considerably lower than those of their counterparts in Singapore, Thailand, the USA and Japan. Costs of production in China could be reduced further and become more internationally competitive with higher work standards. Many firms, in general, expected the prices of raw materials to rise alongside other factors of production; in this survey, 75 firms (78.5 per cent) shared this expectation. Their negative view of the prices of materials was in line with their view on China's inflation problem. Besides, the strong growth of industrial production in China is likely to increase the demand for raw materials and push up prices. The gradual relaxation of price controls on essential industrial materials would have the same effect.

THE BUSINESS ENVIRONMENT

Since 1979, China's investment environment has undergone dramatic changes, and given the present trend of economic growth such rapid changes are likely to continue in the foreseeable future. As China's business environment is an important factor affecting a firm's profitability and future planning, it is important to know how businesses perceive the future. In this survey, all of the 100 investors in China were requested to express their views on 10 key issues concerning China's business environment, broadly categorised into four groups:

(1) government regulations; (2) taxation; (3) capital markets; and (4) political and macroeconomic factors. For each issue, investors were asked whether they believed it would improve, worsen or remain unchanged for the next three to five years. Results of this survey are analysed in the following sections.

Regulations

One of China's major internal policy aims is to be accepted as a full member of the World Trade Organisation (WTO), formerly GATT, and to this end China has been progressively liberalising its trade system and opening up more of its domestic market. Part of this liberalisation process involves changes in its FDI laws in line with international standards, and improvments to the investment environment by giving more freedom in operation and ownership to foreign investors.

Investment licensing has been a serious constraint on foreign firms in setting up operations in China. There were major complaints from the firms surveyed about long delays in application procedures and bureaucratic red tape, in addition to the fact that the functions and responsibilities of different government departments are not well-defined or publicised. The problem of corruption was also raised as one of the major issues. Twenty-five firms indicated constraining effects in approval procedures due to administrative inefficiency and to the government departments' final clearance. In addition to administrative inefficiency, firms also indicated that corruption and different local government regulations had been stumbling blocks in application registrations and approvals. The relative assessment by firms of the constraining effects of various aspects of the regulatory system is summarised in Table 7.14.

Import regulations were also considered a serious constraint on foreign firms, with 16 firms reporting them to be a strong constraint, and 52 considering them to be a moderate to strong constraint. Firms in car manufacturing especially expressed strong concerns over tariff rates and other trade barriers; specifically recommending that there should be better immigration and import/export procedures, standardisation of trade documents, reduction of import taxes and relaxation of foreign exchange control. It was also reported that existing import clearance practices are particularly cumbersome when it comes to the computation of duty and documentation.

Constraining effects of labour regulations were considered to be moderate to strong, with 29 firms (29 per cent) reporting them to be a

Table 7.14 *China: overview of constraints – regulations*

	Respondents' responses to constraints 1–5* (%)					
	1–2		3–4		5	No response	Total
	No. of firms	%	No. of firms	%	No. of firms		
Investment licensing	21	12	41	9	16	0	100
Export regulations	36	15	31	5	12	1	100
Import regulations	19	12	45	7	16	0	100
Tax regulations	3	3	56	13	25	2	100
Government labour regulations	10	4	41	15	29	0	100
Land regulations	6	3	32	19	39	2	100
Environmental regulations	5	3	40	14	37	0	100
Anti-trust regulations	75	6	12	1	6	2	100

* Constraining effects were given a scale of between 0 and 5 according to intensity, where 1 indicates no constraint, 3 medium constraint and 5 strong constraint.
Source: Author's survey data.

strong constraint. There are no official labour unions and the government labour offices usually take responsibility for labour relations. In practice, in-house workers' associations do operate, and most firms have no problems with these unofficial unions. Only two firms reported some problems with unions, the major problems coming from party officials who acted at the same time as labour representatives (Table 7.15).

The state control of labour unions often insulates foreign investors from labour problems. Especially firms from car manufacturing and the paper and cement sectors reported serious problems with local government labour offices. In the car industry, large car makers have

Table 7.15 *China: role of labour unions*

Role of union	No. of firms	Percentage of total
No unions	11	11
Negative	2	2
Small role	6	6
Neutral	1	1
Positive	78	80
Total	98	100

Source: Author's survey data.

problems with the hiring and firing of their workers; although a law exists which provides for the termination or recruitment of employment, it remains virtually unused because of the power of the local labour offices. These offices often interfere in the management of human resources by issuing controversial labour regulations which decrease the power of a firm's management. Also, local or provincial governments introduce extra tariffs or provisions on firms relating to social benefits. In addition, safety and health procedures have often been used as bargaining powers by local authorities, so that in practice compromises are difficult to reach and disputes affect day-to-day operations.

Suggestions were offered by some firms for improvements in the resolution of disputes; one, for example, was to establish an arbitration system that is quick and transparent in operation. In some cases, third parties or countries were suggested as a better option than the government courts. A second suggestion was to give more freedom to firms in their everyday management of labour relations and to reduce political interference by party officials in dispute settlements. Another suggestion was to establish more education and training programmes for government labour officials in accordance with internation labour organisation standards and regulations.

Problems with environmental regulations were reported to be moderate to strong, with 37 firms (37 per cent) reporting strong constraints, and 54 firms moderate to strong constraints (Table 7.14). These problems have mainly been encountered in the paper and cement and car manufacturing sectors. Many government regulations imposed on the paper and cement firms were purely finance-driven and have increased costs of production. The cost of cleaning up water or land which has been polluted in the past by local or provincial governments has often been forced onto foreign firms, and disputes arise over who should pay for such cleaning-up operations. Four firms complained about the inadequate disposal system and supply of clean water, and 12 firms from the paper sector indicated problems with the disposal of waste chemicals. The plants were located near rivers to ensure easy access to water for the production process, but this location posed severe problems for local agriculture and pasture. Such chemicals are dangerous and take a long time to break down for safe disposal in compliance with environmental regulations. This disposal problem significantly increases the cost of production in China. In other countries most plants are located in urban areas which enable them to use the city disposal system. Ten firms (42 per cent) from the car manufacturing sector expressed serious concerns about the absence of transparent and clear environmental regulations relating to car pollution and safety standards procedures.

Taxation

China's tax system has been criticised as too complex and clumsy. A plethora of tax items such as product tax, value-added tax and business tax are listed in official documents, and there have been complaints about their clarity. Besides, enforcement may not be standardised in different regions. Fifteen firms reported that taxation was a strong constraint on the expansion of operations; these firms complained about high tax rates and asked for more tax incentives (Table 7.16). Eight firms (32 per cent) from the paper and cement sector expressed particular concern about this issue. Apart from tax, it was also suggested that various surcharges and fees should be minimised and standardised, and four firms (17 per cent) expressed strong concern about this matter. Company taxes, at 40 per cent, are not regarded as too high, but the extra fees, surcharges and local government taxes were regarded as strong constraints on overall operational costs.

Most firms also expressed some concern about the transparency and consistency of taxation laws as well as red tape and inefficient tax departments. Firms from the car industry indicated clearly that quotas and import-duty concessions are big incentives to expand operations. Most car makers import many parts for assembly from their home markets, and high import duties represent substantial tax and cost constraints on investors. Quotas become a big problem for car makers as the government's strict enforcement of its import-substitution

Table 7.16 *China: overview of constraints – incentives*

	Percentage of Respondents					
	1–2		*3–4*		*5*	*No response*	*Total*
	No. of firms	%	No. of firms	%	No. of firms		
Level of taxation	5	7	55	18	15	0	100
Import duties/quotas	10	18	51	11	10	1	100

* Constraining effects were given a scale of between 0 and 5 according to intensity
Source: Author's survey data

policy forces many foreign firms to source locally. Local inputs often do not meet the desired quality standards of international practice, reducing the value and attractiveness of final products. Six firms (25 per cent) from the car sector, which had a high percentage of inputs from overseas, rated import duties and quotas as a strong constraint on expansion of their operations.

A common concern expressed by many foreign firms was that the incentives structure was highly unfavourable to production geared to the domestic market, compared to export-oriented production. Firms which produced for the local market had a problem obtaining approval for imported inputs and experienced long delays in the process of registration, whereas firms which were export-oriented had no problems or delays obtaining such approval. Many of the firms indicated that they had to use political connections or other means of persuasion (financial donations, presents or gifts) to obtain quick approval for imported inputs. There are also restrictions on overseas borrowing for these firms, so that they are exposed to high local interest rates (28 per cent) and some periodic credit restrictions imposed by state banks. Part of this restriction reflects the government's determination to reduce negative effects on the balance of payments and overvaluation of foreign exchange. In addition, taxes enforced by the state and local governments are increasing and apply at many points in the market chain.

Capital Markets

Regarding China's capital market, views were much more diversified. Access to short-term domestic borrowing was not considered by foreign firms to be a serious constraint, but money market instability, in particular rising inflation problems due primarily to an overheated economy, were causing problems for foreign firms as the price of wages, land, raw materials and credits increased (Table 7.17). In response to inflation, the Chinese government has adopted macroeconomic control measures by tightening credit expansion and discouraging borrowing activities. Long-term domestic finance is available to all firms operating in the private sector, including foreign-owned enterprises, from the People's Bank of China and its branches. However, there are some limits on borrowing, depending on the type of investment project and its structure. Only three firms reported that access to domestic finance was considered to be a strong constraint on the expansion of operations, but 75 firms reported moderate to strong constraints on domestic borrowing.

Table 7.17   *China: overview of constraints – capital market*

	Percentage of Respondents						
	1–2		*3–4*		*5*	*No Response*	*Total*
	No. of firms	*%*	*No. of firms*	*%*	*No. of firms*		
Access to domestic sources	10	14	58	15	3	1	100
Access to overseas sources	37	20	25	16	1	0	100
Cost of finance	–	4	52	21	22	2	100
Access to foreign exchange	8	13	56	17	6	0	100

* Constraining effects were given a scale of between 0 and 5 according to intensity.
Source: Author's survey data.

Access to overseas borrowing was not considered by foreign firms to be a constraint (Table 7.17), but there were some serious complaints about administration and approval procedures, documentation required and red tape. Apart from the Bank of China, there are many specialised banks such as the China Investment Bank, ICBC, BOC and CITIC Industrial Bank, which lend intentionally for joint-venture investment within the private sector. Most of these banks have no limits on their borrowing capacity, but again the availability of any loan will be dependent upon many factors.

In general there were not many complaints about access to finance, but the cost of finance attracted many criticisms and complaints. Increasing inflation and interest rates on credit created unfavourable conditions for borrowing. In addition, the high bad-debt ratios of banks, due primarily to the growing accumulation of bad debts from SOEs, has put pressure on the cost of borrowing. Cost of finance was reported to be a strong constraint on expansion of their operations by 22 firms, and a moderate to strong constraint by 21 firms. There are clear indications for government fiscal and monetary policy to be adjusted and the enforcement of strict rules in regard to lending by banks to SOEs. This kind of situation, where credit is available but expensive, only acts as a disincentive for foreign investors to expand their operations.

Policy Uncertainty and Macroeconomic Instability

Since the adoption of the open-door policy and market-oriented economic reforms in 1978, internal and external policies have undergone changes to create a favourable investment environment. Due to the determination of policy-makers to follow the present path of development, it is generally expected that China's robust economic growth can be sustained in the foreseeable future. A stable and healthy policy is regarded as an important factor to attract investors.

As indicated in Table 7.18, uncertainty about the future directions of government policy was considered by foreign firms to be a constraint. Although only 6 firms reported it to be a strong constraint out of ninety-nine firms surveyed, it was considered to be a moderate to strong constraint by 58 firms. Broadly speaking, there is a perception that the government has shown its strong commitment to economic reform and the directions and objectives of China's future economic reforms clearly laid down by the Party in 1997. So far the government has shown strong leadership in the development of correct policies towards the encouragement of foreign investment and in the further expansion of its open-door policy.

Operations are difficult where there is uncertainty about prices of inputs and tariffs and other levies on imported inputs. Uncertainty about prices policy was reported to be a strong constraint on operations by 8 firms, but a moderate to strong constraint by 67 firms. One criticism was that prices of raw materials were too high and have increased production costs. Uncertainty about the future exchange rate also has this effect, and makes it difficult to price a product. This was a key issue for four firms from the car manufacturing sector, which imports car parts for assembly. Two firms expressed concerns about government policy regarding land prices, especially a recently introduced value-added tax on land which might lead to further increases in land costs.

Table 7.18   *China: overview of constraints: macroeconomic 'political' social*

	Respondents' responses to constraints 1–5* (%)									
	1–2		*3–4*		*5*		*No Response*		*Total*	
	No. of firms	*%*	*No. of firms*	*%*	*No. of firms*	*%*	*No. of firms*		*No. of firms*	*%*
Labour relations	23	23	60	61	9	9	0		99	100
Policy uncertainty	29	29	58	59	6	6	3		99	100
Law and order	23	23	68	69	4	4	4		99	100
Price uncertainty	17	17	67	68	8	8	7		99	100

*   Constraining effects were given a scale of between 0 and 5 according to intensity.
Source: Author's survey data.

Low political risk is regarded by foreign investors as an important factor in the general investment climates, and the social-political stability of the host country has a strong influence on a foreign firm's strategy and future investment decisions. It determines whether the foreign investor takes a long or a short investment commitment (Dunning, 1995(b); Gray, 1996). Uncertainty about law and order was not considered to be a constraint, although two Japanese firms expressed concern about China's future stability and the ability of the government to maintain social harmony amongst the different ethnic groups as well as the present political status quo.

CHINA AS AN ALTERNATIVE INVESTMENT LOCATION

In the early 1990s, most countries were acclaiming FDI as 'a good thing' and modifying their attitudes towards it, for example in East Asia and Eastern and Central Europe (Dunning, 1994). These countries are now approaching the 'take-off' stage in their economic development, and at the same time the competition for the world's scarce resources of capital, technology and organisational skills is becoming increasingly intensive. Each country is trying to create the most attractive investment environment in order to score well in the eyes of foreign investors as a preferred location site.

Foreign investors with a strong involvement in other Asian countries were asked to compare China's business environment with those other Asian host countries. In general, the majority of investors indicated China to be a low-risk country, and many believed that the Chinese government would maintain political and social stability in the coming years. According to the criteria of investment licensing, import regulations, tax, labour inputs, service inputs, infrastructure and cultural environment, China as a developing country was ranked very high (Table 7.19), except for service, infrastructure and telecommunication facilities. The highest marks that China received came from Singaporean, Thai, French, Hong Kong and Canadian investors. The most dissatisfied with China's business environment were investors from Japan, South Korea, the USA, Taiwan, Sweden, Holland and Switzerland. In terms of the progress of economic reform, China was ranked much higher than Vietnam, Burma, Laos or India. Still, in general, China ranked second after Singapore but ahead of Vietnam as the most attractive country for investment. (The survey preceded the collapse of these countries' currencies.) To some extent,

Table 7.19 *Countries'
attractiveness to investors*

Rank	Country	%
1	Singapore	69.8
2	China	69.7
3	Vietnam	59.8
4	Malaysia	58.7
5	Indonesia	52.6
6	Thailand	49.3
7	India	45.2
8	Philippines	34.1
9	Pakistan	28.6
10	Sri Lanka	20.7
11	Bangladesh	14.5
12	Cambodia	9.8

Note: 100%= highly attractive;
0% = completely unattractive.
Source: Author's survey data.

China's huge potential market and rich resource base creates some bias against other countries.

It is interesting to note that China compares quite favourably with Singapore except for port facilities, telecommunications, service inputs and labour quality, but it is much more advanced than India and is regarded as a more attractive place to invest. India's huge market cannot compensate for slow economic reforms and political risk. Compared with another transitional country, Vietnam, China has been regarded as more advanced and easier to deal with; labour productivity, service and infrastructure are considered to be superior to those in Vietnam. China compares favourably with Malaysia and Indonesia for all criteria except labour productivity and service inputs. The comparison with Thailand was similar to that of Indonesia and Malaysia except in the case of infrastructure. The analysis suggests that foreign investors ranked very highly in their assessment a country's economic and political environment. The countries which scored the lowest percentage in the their eyes were considered politically unstable and risky for investment operations. High political risk acts as a deterrent to any potential foreign investors. In general, many foreign investors have an optimistic view about China's business environment, even though at present there are many threats and problems.

*   *   *

POLAND: DETERMINANTS OF FDI

An investigation of the motivational factors affecting the foreign investor's decision to invest within a specific host country was undertaken using both open and closed questions. From the sample, clear sequences of FDI determinants emerge. In the process of Poland's transition to a market economy the sample group (see Table 7.20) indicated that cost factors were the key motive associated with investment (63 per cent), followed by market factors (56.7 per cent), then labour factors (48.9 per cent) and investment-climate factors (39.5 per cent). This supports the suggestion that Poland has developed a strong specialisation in the resource-intensive group (according to manufacture for export taxonomy) and capital–skill–labour-intensive sectors (group three) (Helleiner, 1973; Lall, 1983; Lall and Siddharthau (1982); Wells, 1986; Grunwald and Flamm, 1985; and Athukorala and Menon, 1995)

DOMESTIC MARKET SIZE

The motives mostly emphasised were future economic growth, to access/supply the local market, and exploitation of the market. It should also be noted that export-oriented market factors like expansion to Eastern Europe and the former Soviet Union were indicated to be of strong importance. The reason is simple: firms want to grow. Given the constraints of a saturated and only slowly growing domestic market in Western Europe, firms are driven to sell their products abroad. Research on FDI, therefore, has stressed the size and growth of foreign markets as the most important variables for explaining the geographical pattern of FDI (Kravis and Lipsey, 1982; Culem, 1988; Wheeler and Mody, 1992). Although for the time being the Polish market is relatively small, its potential and future growth offer foreign firms great opportunities.

A firm which enters a market can quickly get a pioneer bonus. For example, in the car sector, Fiat the Italian car maker established joint ventures with a Polish SOE, FSO Zeran in 1989, with the objective of production and trading activities in the partner's home market. That objective was in perfect harmony with the company's philosophy of acquiring the highest possible market share in the fields belonging to its special line by purchasing the local production capacity as a capacity suitable for development. Fiat wants to succeed in meeting

Table 7.20 *Poland: location-specific advantages*

Factors	Importance of factors (%)				
	Very import-ant	Fairly import-ant	Little import-ant	Irrelev-ant	Total
1. Cost efficiency factors: • cost of labour • cost of materials • opportunity to reduce operating cost • to increase profit levels • avoidance of tariff and non-tariff barriers	63.5	19.8	8.8	17.9	100
2. Market factors: • to access/supply the local market • growth potential of the local market • to developed the local market • export base for countries within EE and former SU	56.7	24.4	12.3	18.6	100
3. Employment factors: • supply of skilled labour	48.9	25.4	13.9	26.8	100
4. Investment-climate factors: • ownership guarantee • reliable legal system • availability of land • reliable transport	39.5	25.8	15.6	31.1	100
5. Resource factors: • access to supplies of raw materials • to secure needed inputs	30.4	15.3	17.8	49.5	100

Source: Author's survey data.

one of its most important strategic objectives – increasing its share of the Polish market. Currently the company owns 16 per cent of the Polish motor car industry, a share that makes it a market leader (Porter, 1990).

However, it should be noted that export-oriented market factors fared well, too. In fact, market factors focusing on export activities with the future expansion to the Eastern and FSU markets were mostly mentioned by investors from the USA, Germany, the Netherlands and Switzerland (around 60 per cent importance). For example, in the paper and cement sector, Henkel Bautechnik, a German producer, has established a joint venture with a Polish partner, Starporkow, for producing building materials. Initially, Henkel was only interested in a bridgehead for organising sales: its strategy was that market penetration by exports should come first, and the establishment of a production base should come later. This fits the usual pattern of sequencing and timing of FDI. Obviously, establishing a production base in Poland is often just the first step to further engagements in other Eastern markets on an experimental basis. The strategic objective of Henkel in Poland has been the expansion of its activities to the Baltic states, the Ukraine and Russia. Poland is a convenient place to test and check how well a product can be sold and produced under the conditions of a post-communist economy.

Investigation into country motivational factors for investment shows different patterns emerging among different source countries. An average of 50 per cent of respondents indicated the importance of factors such as economic growth. Investors from Sweden (63 per cent), Switzerland (60 per cent) and France (56 per cent) indicated higher-than-average importance of these factors, while investors from Italy (43 per cent), Holland (46 per cent) and Austria (48 per cent) showed a lower emphasis on these factors. There were also notable differences in the importance of the market size. The average for the survey was 47 per cent, with investors from Italy (60 per cent), Holland (59 per cent) and Sweden (56 per cent) indicating a higher importance, while investors from Germany (41 per cent), Austria (42 per cent) and Belgium (40 per cent) showing a lower importance of market factors.

The above analysis shows that different strategies have been used by different foreign investors. Investors from Italy, France, Holland and Switzerland chose market-seeking strategies with a strong emphasis on supplying the local market and the cost of labour. One can conclude that FDI was attracted by location advantages and the supply of cheap labour – this can be called import-substitution FDI (Dunning, 1993). Investors from the USA, Germany, Canada and the UK, on the other hand, were mostly motivated by strategic reasons and chose strategic asset-seeking FDI (Markusen, 1995), and exploitation of cheap labour was not the main reason for investment – the emphasis was more on export-oriented FDI.

Rojec and Svetlicic (1994) and Jermakowicz (1994) suggest that foreign investors entering the CEE markets follow two different generic investment strategies: Type I import-substitution FDI and Type II export-oriented FDI. Type I or import-substitution investments are focused on local markets and allow production to being for local markets of simple products and commodities with uncomplicated technology to avoid import barriers. Strong evidence of this can be detected in the Polish car industry. Peugot, Volkswagen, Opel and Volvo have pursued pure market-seeking strategies, and their investments have been import-substitution-driven to gain access to the local market. Type II investments, or export-oriented FDI, are made to develop a firm's specialisation in the production of products for the world market on an integrated basis. These types of investment are made to achieve a competitive advantage through low taxes, a favourable geographical location, access to resources and/or low labour costs.

Type I investments are typically smaller than type II, because they involve simple processes or the final assembly phase of processes. Import-substitution strategies currently dominate in the paper and cement, car assembly and, to some extent, in the food-processing sectors. However, based on the survey of four industries in Poland, a clear trend has emerged indicating a mix of type I and type II investment strategies. In food-processing and agriculture, as well as in the paper sector, clear evidence emerged of type II strategies (14 firms exported more than 56 per cent of their production), while in the cement sector over 78 per cent of its production was sold on the local market. Poland seems to represent an even mix of type I and type II investment strategies; it has managed to attract some large investments in car manufacturing and the paper sector (for example, Fiat, International Paper, Volkswagen, General Motors), but the majority of firms in the car industry and paper and cement sectors still created type I investments with production or service for local markets.

LABOUR SUPPLY

The supply and quality of labour were also important considerations for the firms surveyed. Table 7.21 shows that responses ranged from high professional skills to a lower quality of organisational skills, with the majority of the sample stating that Polish labour was 'as efficient as foreign competitors'. The main weaknesses of Polish workers were lack of organisational skills, innovation and to some extent a lower labour productivity. Labour productivity per firm was much higher in firms with foreign participation (around 78 per cen) than in local ones, and higher than the average national level of 60 per cent (ILO, 1997). A number of firms indicated that a different culture of productivity is emerging in the private sector, but on the other hand unions are still strong and often create a lot of constraints for company policies aimed at increasing productivity. Following the changes in the 1995 labour accord, the government has been trying to encourage a more cooperative approach between unions and the management of foreign firms.

Table 7.21 *Poland: assessment of work force (%)*

Assessment variables	Low	Medium	High
Work discipline	4.2	46.8	48.6
Productivity of labour	5.6	47.0	40.3
Quality	4.2	45.6	49.5
Innovation	19.3	52.3	26.1
Professional skills	2.8	43.5	53.0
Organisation skills	19.8	55.6	20.5

Source: Author's survey data.

The highest assessments of the Polish workforce were for its quality of work and discipline (around 50 per cent of respondents); lowest marks were awarded for innovation and organisational skills. It is not surprising when we take into consideration over 50 years of central planning and the fulfilment of quotes as the required targets of state-owned enterprises under command economies. Innovation was never encouraged, nor was an environment created for its growth. The evidence suggests that innovation and management skills were never part of SOE labour policy; fulfilment of the Plan was the main target, not the quality or attractiveness of the product.

At the industry level, the lowest innovation was shown in the paper and cement sector (22.5 per cent) and the food-processing sector (18.6 per cent). Regarding work discipline, investors from Switzerland indicated the highest mark (68.0 per cent), while investors from Holland gave the lowest (39.3 per cent). In the eyes of British investors the Polish workforce scored highest in productivity (60.9 per cent), but lowest by French investors (36.7 per cent).

Taking into consideration the quality of work, we can again note large differences among foreign investors. The highest mark the Polish workforce received came from German investors (55.1 per cent) and the lowest from the British (41.9 per cent); but at the same time British investors assessed the highest level of innovation (38.7 per cent) of Polish labour. By contrast, Italian investors indicated a lower level of innovation (17.4 per cent), but they gave a high mark for professional skills (65.2 per cent) compared to Dutch investors (42.9 per cent). Organisational skills had mostly been noted by British investors (32.3 per cent), as opposed to the French (10.0 per cent). The survey indicated strong variations in Polish labour assessment at both industry and employment levels.

COST OF LABOUR

One of the advantages claimed for investment in Poland is the availability of cheap, skilled labour compared with other Western countries. When asked about the relative attractiveness of Polish wages compared to other transitional countries, a fairly typical response was that Polish wage levels were about on a par with those of competing post-communist countries such as Hungary, the Czech Republic, Romania and Bulgaria, as indicated in Chapter 4. In the early stages of investment, labour cost becomes one of the less important factors, even though some firms saw a comparative advantage when compared with the high wage levels of workers in developed countries.

The survey shows that motivational factors like the cost of labour provoked differential responses among foreign investors. With a survey average of 60 per cent, the cost of labour was a very important factor among investors from Sweden (65 per cent) and Italy (62 per cent) compared with investors from the USA (35 per cent), Germany (40 per cent) and Canada (41 per cent). At the industry level, the cost of labour was an important factor for investors in the paper and cement sector (70 per cent), though less important for the food-processing sector (50 per cent). Overall, the trends seem to dispel the myth that foreign firms are simply exploiting the East as a low-cost production base for export to the West. From the above analysis, clear patterns emerge indicating that investors from Switzerland, Holland, Italy and France chose cost-efficiency-seeking strategies with a strong emphasis on the quite cheap cost of skilled labour as opposed to investors from the USA or Canada.

The traditional sector 2 according to the Helleiner taxonomy (clothing, furniture, and so on) attracted quite large amounts of FDI, but relatively less as the 1990s progressed, although it still represented the largest and highest growth category of Polish subcontracting exports to Germany. One can conclude that here FDI was attracted by location advantages as well as the supply of cheap labour. German investors in the early 1990s took advantage of the wage differential between the two countries; most German investment was small (for example sweetshops) and profit-maximisation driven.

The car industry increased its share of total Polish FDI most strikingly over the period studied, starting from small amounts of capital inflow in 1990; by the end of 1995 it exceeding the share of the textile and footwear sector, which was the traditional sector of unskilled labour-intensive Polish export products, mainly to Germany. One may infer that this was due to a high initial revealed comparative advantage (RCA) and high initial labour intensity – to be complemented by capital inflow to create the required factor conditions. However, if we look at trends and determinants in Table 7.20 over the period 1989–93, we find that it was probably not the factor conditions that mattered so much as the quest for a share in the domestic market. Thus foreign investment into these scale-based industries was attracted less by cost-efficiency considerations than by technological ownership leads over indigenous firms (Markusen, 1995; Dunning, 1985), and ease of domestic market penetration on account of lagged demand for these standardised mass consumption products (Buckley and Casson, 1985). This would explain the dramatic decline of Revealed Comparative Advantage (RCA) for this sector; FDI inflow was here driven mainly by market-seeking strategies.

A first glance at the sectoral distribution of FDI in Poland suggests an interpretation not altogether consistent with the prevailing opinions on cheap and unskilled labour in Poland. The data point towards industries identified as scale- or capital- and human-capital intensive being the leading targets for FDI in Poland, rather than the traditional labour-intensive sectors. This suggests that Polish unskilled labour is rather expensive in relation to other possible host countries as measured by its relative productivity, and that, by contrast, skilled labour reveals some comparative advantage in terms of its relative cost.

BUSINESS ENVIRONMENT

Regulations

One of Poland's top foreign policy aims is a gradual integration with the European Union and Western economic structures, and so far, great strides have been made in achieving that goal. In mid-1996 Poland became a member of the OECD. In anticipation of accession, Poland adjusted its laws to liberalise the flow of goods and services, including changes to make it easier for foreign companies to set up operations in Poland. In May 1994, Poland signed the European Association Agreement which set deadlines for the adjustment to and implementation of EU regulations.

Table 7.22 *Poland: review of constraints – regulations*

	Respondents' responses to constraints 1–5 (%)*					
	1–2		*3–4*		*5*	*No*	*Total*
						Response	
	No. of firms	*%*	*No. of firms*	*%*	*No. of firms*		
Investment licensing	26	34	28	5	–	7	100
Export regulation	19	24	31	17	6	3	100
Import regulation	32	22	24	9	13	0	100
Tax regulation	27	19	34	11	9	0	100
Labour legislation	12	16	21	26	21	4	100
Land regulations	35	22	21	10	7	5	100
Environmental regulations	11	24	38	18	6	3	100
Anti-trust regulations	54	21	19	6	0	0	100

* Constraining effects were given a scale of between 0 and 5 according to intensity
Source: Author's survey data.

Investment licensing and export and import regulations have not been a serious constraint on foreign firms setting up operations in Poland (Table 7.22). Import regulations are quite favourable and have been slowly adjusted to comply with EU agreements. Furthermore, many trade regulations have been liberalised in the spirit of OECD accession. However, there are some complaints about the administration of customs, especially in the car manufacturing and food-processing sectors. The constraining effects of import regulations were considered to be moderate to strong, with six (22 per cent) firms reporting strong constraints. Some firms indicated serious problems relating to incoming inputs for food-processing and car parts caused by the lack of transparent and firm rules. The existing import clearance practices usually involve large and cumbersome documentation and duty calculations.

There are some indications of the constraining effects of labour regulations, which were considered to be moderate to strong, with 41 per cent of firms reporting strong constraints. Under a new accord between the government, labour unions and companies signed in 1995, more emphasis has been placed on cooperation rather than confrontation such as strikes and other means. Labour unions are very strong in Poland and often create many problems for the operations of foreign firms. One such problem is the constant demand for financial benefits under the threat of strikes, and in 1995 there were over 215 strikes and labour disputes. The government has tried to resolve these disputes through better cooperation between unions and management, often acting as negotiator. Over 27 firms indicated that they had been involved in labour disputes for not more than 1–2 months, the problem usually being resolved in a short time.

There was also some concern regarding environmental regulations. Several firms reported the lack of an adequate waste disposal and supply system in the food-processing sector, a problem which significantly increases foreign firms' costs of production. Stiglitz (1989) and Wallis and North (1986) have indicated that the organisational and transaction costs of economic activity have become relatively important, and there is some evidence that these costs are also positively related to the complexity of a nation's industrial structure. Countries which can offer business environments that are conducive to minimising these costs are, *ceteris paribus*, likely to gain an increasing share of inbound investment.

Taxation

As Dunning (1993) points out, only governments which are successful in reducing or helping to reduce the transaction and coordinating costs of economic activity, and which best enable their firms to surmount the obstacles to structural change, are likely to be the most successful, not only in attracting the right kind of FDI but to do so at the least real costs. Part of these transaction and coordinating costs lie in the financial system.

Taxation levels were not considered to be a serious constraint on the expansion of operations. Company taxes, at 40 per cent, are not regarded as a problem, but the tax system is still not transparent. In particular, the institutional framework of the taxation system has to be reformed to satisfy the changing investment environment. All foreign firms enjoy tax holidays ranging from three to five years, but over 36 firms' complained that bad administration of the tax system created many delays in foreign firms' operations. A common concern was that the rigid and inflexible bureaucrats of tax offices at the regional level, together with a cascade of taxes, had become major obstacles to smooth operations.

The government has taken some action by employing specialists from the World Bank to develop a more transparent tax system. In 1992 it replaced the turnover tax with VAT (the so-called common tax on products and services). Foreign companies, joint ventures and foreign individuals in principle pay the same taxes as Polish legal and natural persons unless agreements on the avoidance of double taxation state

Table 7.23   *Poland: assessment of financial system*

Category	Positive		Negative	
	No. of firms	*%*	*No. of firms*	*%*
Tax system	59	62	36	38
Banking system	55	58	40	42
Export insurance	52	55	43	45
Credit insurance	50	53	45	47
Cost of local credits	44	46	51	54

Note: The figures are drawn from a sample of 95 firms.
Source: Author's survey data.

otherwise. The government has also tried to establish more efficient and unified tax offices across the country. Table 7.23 shows that the incentive structure was not so favourable regarding export insurance. Over 40 firms expressed some concern in relation to well-developed and easy access to export insurance; this poses a great threat to foreign firms which produce for export. Also, 51 firms indicated that they cannot always borrow overseas, so they are directly exposed to high local credit costs and periodic credit restrictions imposed by banks. This is a clear indication that on the macro level Poland has made some progress in the transition to a market economy, but on the micro level it still lags far behind and requires a very strong commitment by the government to reform its financial system, especially the credit system.

Capital Market

Over 20 per cent of the sample gave a negative response concerning the operation of the capital market, especially in terms of the cost and supply of credit for local firms. This clearly undermines not only the running of an operation but also its further expansion, as operating costs are increased. Increased competition and the creation of new local banks with specific roles to play in the supply of credits for the private sector could be the answer.

Access to short-term borrowing was not considered to be a big constraint by firms with foreign participation (see Table 7.24). Money market instability, in particular unpredictable borrowing rates due primarily to high inflation and government borrowing, were causes of financial management problems for private sector firms. Firms in the food-processing and car manufacturing sectors

Table 7.24 *Poland: overview of constraints – capital market*

	Respondents' responses to constraints 1–5* (%)						
	1–2		3–4		5	No Response	Total
	No. of firms	%	No. of firms	%	No. of firms		
Access to domestic sources	30	32	21	9	7	1	100
Access to overseas sources	27	39	25	2	7	0	100
Cost of finance	19	35	15	22	8	1	100
Access to foreign exchange	31	32	18	14	5	0	100

* Constraining effects were given a scale of between 0 and 5 according to intensity.
Source: Author's survey data.

especially complained about the high interest rates for local borrowing. It is not surprising that many firms looking for finance through foreign banks did not always find this to be cost-effective either. Long-term domestic finance is available from the Polish Commerce and Trade Bank to all foreign firms, but this is not always adapted to the private-sector demand structure. The Polish Commerce and Trade Bank has no limit on borrowing internationally for joint-venture investment with the private sector. On the other hand, the survey suggests that some recent improvements have been made by the government in relation to the access and cost of credits for foreign firms. Also, the government offers special cheap credits to firms which target areas of economic activity of particular concern to the government, such as employment or infrastructure.

During 1996 and 1997, foreign investors have borrowed more than before, suggesting that improvements in the capital market system have been made. In 1996, 58.4 per cent of foreign firms used domestic borrowing, compared with 25.7 per cent in 1993; an increase was also noted in terms of the value of the credit. Major suppliers of credit were the Polish banks (77.6 per cent) compared to foreign financial institutions (28.7 per cent). Inflation has been curtailed, and interest rates on credit have been decreasing, creating favourable conditions for lending. Also, institutional reforms of the Polish banking system with the help of the IMF and Dutch, Austrian and French banks have created an environment where investors feel much safer in Poland than before.

At the industry level, most credit was taken by investors in food-processing and agriculture (over 50 per cent of respondents). Over 73 per cent of firms did not have any problems with the payments, and if some problems did occur they were mostly related to factors beyond the firm's control such as:

- demands for too early repayment by banks (15.6 per cent);
- high interest (13 per cent); or
- changes of bank arrangements (6.7 per cent).

Policy Uncertainty and Macroeconomic Instability

It is interesting to note that after six years of transformation to democratic institutions there are still some concerns about the political situation expressed by foreign investors, who often state that the political situation in Poland is not very stable for foreign investment (Table 7.25). In 1993, Poland witnessed many strikes and unrest, which created a risky investment environment, and uncertainty about the political and social situation in Poland was reported to be a strong constraint to expansion of operations by nine firms. Investors from Switzerland (three firms) and Austria (two firms) rated Poland as a high political-risk country, in contrast to the USA, France and Sweden who assessed the political situation to be favourable for foreign investment activities. A few investors reported that constantly changing governments and fragmented opposition parties, together with the Solidarity Union, created an impression of instability and risk. This kind of situation results in the delay of many projects and prevents foreign investors from taking decisive strategic actions.

Uncertainty about the future directions of government policy was reported to be a strong constraint to expansion of operation by 10 firms, and a moderate to strong constraint by 29 firms. One of the major criticisms was a lack of commitment by the government to the privatisation process; there was a high expectation of the government's role in the process, but an awareness of splits in the coalition government.

Broadly speaking, there is a perception of a lack of policy direction in the government and a lack of strong leadership, even though the government has expressed a strong commitment to the privatisation process in its 'Strategy for Poland-2000'. Many conflicting views and disputes have arisen in the government regarding the method of privatisation, strong concerns have also been expressed by investors over the progress of the privatisation reforms. This can be interpreted partly as a result of a split between the coalition parties in power, which prevents any elected party from taking decisive action, but there is also

Table 7.25   *Poland: overview of constraints – macroeconomic, political, social*

| | Respondents' responses to constraints 1–5* (%) | | | | | | | |
| | 1–2 | | 3–4 | | 5 | | No Response | Total |
	No. of firms	%	No. of firms	%	No. of firms	%	No. of firms	No. of firms
Labour relations	31	39	40	50	9	11	0	80
Policy uncertainty	25	31	29	36	10	12	6	80
Law & order	43	54	30	38	7	9	0	80
Increased taxes	23	29	37	46	16	20	4	80
Price uncertainty	40	50	37	46	0	0	3	80

* Constraining effects were given a scale of between 0 and 5 according to intensity
Source: Author's survey data.

concern over the strong influence of the Solidarity Union block on government policy decisions and its implications for the future direction of government policy towards the encouragement of foreign investment.

Foreign investors suggested that operations are also difficult where there is uncertainty about tax, inflation and duty levies. Five firms indicated strong concern about constantly changing regulations relating to duty levies and exchange rates, which make it difficult for them to import inputs at stable prices. This was a key issue for firms which imported car parts and agricultural products as their major inputs. Uncertainty about the future inflation rate also raised concern, especially in regard to the cost of local raw materials and inputs. Six firms also indicated strong concern over the probability of increased taxes. There was an indication of concern relating to the prudence of the Polish Central Bank in regard to its relationship with government economic policies and, as a result, issues such as the exchange rate, interest rates and the budget deficit.

POLAND AS AN ALTERNATIVE INVESTMENT LOCATION

Foreign investors in Poland with business operations in other Eastern European and former Soviet Union countries were asked to compare Poland's business environment; 88 firms responded. Firms with wide Eastern European and former Soviet Union (FSU) country involvement ranked their investment in Poland as being low-risk, owing to the advanced progress of economic, political and social reforms and the commitments of the newly-elected liberal government. They were confident that in the long run business would grow much faster than before. Over 60 firms ranked Poland as the most attractive country for investment according to the general business environment, a very high ranking in this context. Firms also ranked Poland as the number one location preference, and only Hungary and the Czech Republic were even in the race in the general overview.

According to the criteria of labour productivity, quality of services, service inputs, infrastructure, quality of telecommunications and reliability of water and electricity supplies, only Hungary was ranked with Poland, the other countries being regarded as less attractive and more risky. In terms of reform progress and development of a market economy, Poland was ranked much higher then all CEE and FSU countries (see Table 7.26). The highest mark Poland received came mainly from investors from the USA, Germany, Holland, Italy, France, Sweden, Korea, Japan and the UK. According to this comparison, Poland compares very favourably on almost all counts with the two large competing regions of Central and Eastern Europe.

Poland, as a transitional country, is regarded by many foreign investors to be far advanced in market reforms and compares favourably with other transitional countries not only in Europe but in Asia as well. Of course, its attractiveness will depend a lot on the elected government's commitment to continued economic reform and the privatisation process. Table 7.26 shows quite interesting findings. Evidence clearly suggests that there are three group of countries emerging. The first group (Poland, Hungary and the Czech Republic) which started economic reforms early, reported high scores with over 50 per cent of the survey sample naming them as preferred location sites for investment. The next group (Russia, Ukraine, Slovenia and Estonia) still in the early stages of transformation ranked in the middle as less-advanced and less-attractive investment locations with scores between 10 and 20 per cent. The last group (Belorus, Lithuania, Bulgaria, Romania, Latvia and Albania) represented the least advanced group in transition to a market economy. These countries still have major political and social problems; their institutional structures are at an early stage, and market forces are very weak. Some central planning institutions are still in force and former members of the nomenclatura are acting as a stumbling block in the transition to a market economy; the reform process is advancing slowly, and the governments are very unstable with little enthusiasm for economic

Table 7.26 *Countries' attractiveness to investors*

Rank	Country	%
1.	Poland	68.6
2.	Hungary	58.6
3.	Czech & Slovak Republic	52.0
4.	Russia	18.7
5.	Ukraine	13.1
6.	Slovenia	12.2
7.	Estonia	11.6
8.	Lithuania	10.4
9.	Belarus	8.1
10.	Latvia	7.7
11.	Bulgaria	6.0
12.	Romania	3.4
13.	Albania	2.4
14.	Moldova	1.9
15.	Mongolia	1.6
16.	Georgia	1.4
17.	Croatia	1.2
18.	Armenia	0.8

Source: Author's survey data.

reforms. One has to take into consideration the fact that many of these economies started their economic and democratic reforms much later than other countries and it will take a long time before they can be considered as potential sites for FDI.

Poland and Hungary were rated as the most attractive sites for FDI, but Poland was the most attractive site for foreign investment. Poland's high score was due mainly to the good prospects for economic growth and the size of its market. This analysis suggests that foreign investors take very seriously into consideration the progress of economic reform and the future market potential and stability of the political system in each country in their final assessments.

COMPARISON BETWEEN CHINA AND POLAND

Determinants

In the case of China, the results show that FDI is determined by the size of the host-country market. The economies of scale in marketing and production make a growing domestic market an attractive target for FDI. China's comparative advantage in the abundance of cheap labour was not considered a very important factor in influencing plant location decisions. The relative advantage that China can offer through low-cost labour has become much less important in recent years, a trend that will surely continue (Miller, 1993, p. 17). In China, the benefit of low wages has been seriously eroded due to the low productivity and efficiency of the workforce. For firms from developed countries which were domestic-market-oriented, labour costs were less important than for firms from Hong Kong, South Korea or Taiwan. For investors from NIEs, labour-cost advantages were critical for their export-oriented firms, as wage increases in their respective countries forced them to move offshore. A supply of cheap labour had become a very important factor in their location decision, since most of the firms are in labour-intensive industries.

By contrast, in Poland the size of the market was almost equally as important as the supply and cost of highly-skilled labour. Also, strategic reasons such as close proximity to Russia and the former Soviet States were important for many foreign investors. The majority of investors in Poland are large MNCs which have been pursuing both domestic and export-oriented strategies; they see Poland as the test market for further expansion to the East. Still, the potential growth of the Polish market and the purchasing power of its population have been one of the major factors influencing firms' decisions on location. However, the clear importance of market size in the survey signals a long-term disadvantage for the relatively small economies of Eastern Europe, including Poland.

In both China and Poland the importance of access to natural resources was less evident as an attractive factor influencing location decisions. The survey shows that factors such as widening sales possibilities, the economic atmosphere, technical development and high-skilled labour attracted foreign investors more than cheap labour or raw materials.

Business Environment

China's investment environment has undergone major changes in terms of policies and their implementation. Wide-ranging economic reforms, steady economic growth and political stability have generated greater investor confidence in the prospects for growth and the creditworthiness of the Chinese economy. Many government regulations have been abolished or modified, administrative procedures have been shortened and transparency and consistency better enforced. Laws, regulations and foreign investment policies have also been much improved, and tariffs and trade barriers have been reduced. Import taxes and foreign exchange regulations have been further relaxed, and services and infrastructure have to some extent been improved. On the other hand, strong concerns are expressed by foreign investors in regard to the Chinese investment environment – corruption, red tape, government inefficiency, a lack of transparency and consistency with regard to laws, policies and government regulations present strong constraints on foreign firms' operations. Many of these constraints were related purely to government policies. Import-substitution policies imposed by the Chinese government, for example, discriminated between domestic-market-oriented firms and export-oriented firms, especially against large projects from developed countries aimed at the domestic market.

By contrast, in Poland the major part of the economy has been liberalised and privatised in accordance with EU accession requirements, and the government has shown strong leadership and direction in the process of transformation to a free-market economy. Trade restrictions, imports quotas and duties have been lifted; laws, regulations and import taxes have been liberalised. Government administration has become more streamlined and institutions have been reformed in line with the OECD structure. Efficiency and productivity have also been encouraged among state and private enterprises and new incentives for production have been introduced based on international standards. The monopoly power of the state has been broken and competition introduced in the state sector. In addition, banks and financial institutions have been reformed according to the guidelines of the IMF and the World Bank. In general, Poland has liberalised and privatised its economy much further than China, and the reform process covers a larger spectrum of industry than in China. The investment environment has become more friendly and attentive for firms with large projects and high capital intensities.

CONCLUSION

Knowledge of the determinants of FDI is necessary for the assessment of the effectiveness of alternative host country policies towards FDI. The findings in this study have shown that the sectoral concentration of FDI inflow into Chinese manufacturing is strongly correlated with the growth rate of the domestic market and import-substitution incentives. FDI seems to be heavily concentrated in protected sectors due to import-substitution policies. Between 1979 and 1995 about two-thirds of formal FDI in Chinese industry was oriented towards the domestic market, particularly from Japan, the USA, Germany, Holland, France, Australia and Sweden. Abundance of cheap labour was not the major motive for these investors, although it was for Asian investors, mainly from Taiwan, Korea, Hong Kong and Singapore, who saw opportunities for their small, mostly labour-intensive, projects.

Most firms in China have problems achieving profits, and part of this problem is related to the Chinese business environment. Government policy has not always been conducive to foreign investment; heavy regulations, administrative inefficiency, high taxes and import duties, lack of transparency or consistency in the legal system as well as inappropriate enforcement of law and red tape create many constraints for the smooth running of operations in China. In short, all the above issues might lead in varying degrees to short-term uncertainty, speculation and fluctuation in business confidence. However, in the long run, despite this obstacle, the majority of foreign investors regarded China as one of the most attractive markets in Asia, with huge potential opportunities in the future. Thus it is likely that the present trend of high inflow of FDI into China will continue.

In the case of Poland, the domestic market potential and the supply of skilled labour was of equal importance to foreign investors. For many foreign investors Poland was seen in the context of its strategic position as a bridge between Russia and the newly-independent Soviet states. Investors from Italy, France, Switzerland, Holland and South Korea were mostly motivated by the potential of the domestic market, as opposed to investors from the USA, the UK, Germany and Canada who were motivated by strategic reasons as their firms were more export-oriented. One of the important factors which strongly influenced location decisions of foreign firms was a favourable business environment. Most foreign investment policies, regulations and laws have been liberalised in anticipation of Poland's OECD membership, and further investment and trade regulations will be liberalised in the process of future accession to the European Union. Most foreign investors had a positive view about the Polish business environment and believed that the process of economic reform and privatisation would continue, and that the prospects for future economic growth looked promising. Part of this optimistic view was reflected in the fact that the majority of foreign investors regarded Poland as the most attractive host country in Central and Eastern Europe. To sum up, the strong fundamental factors, including Poland's strong commitment to economic reforms and privatisation, especially by the recently-elected government at the time of our survey, continued high economic growth and a potential for development, remain unaltered. It is likely that the present trend of investment in Poland will not only continue but will increase in the near future.

8 Performance of Foreign Investment Projects

This chapter explores the performance of enterprises with foreign investment in China and Poland. In order to assess the performance of enterprises with foreign investment, the profitability, plans and strategies of the firms are analysed. The chapter also analyses whether foreign investment policies favouring advanced technology and import substitution discourage foreign investors' interest in exports.

CHINA: PROFITABILITY

Profitability is a fundamental determinant of investment, including FDI. The relevant period of profitability may be very short, but is often long-term. Surveys conducted by many authors (Hughes and You, 1969; Reuber, 1973; Dunning, 1979) have indicated that investors are influenced more by long-term prospects than by immediate short-term profits. FDI aimed at the domestic market is sensitive to local demand prospects, while export-oriented FDI is sensitive to local cost trends. Low labour costs in developing countries provide the basis for high rates of return on export-oriented projects (Reuber, 1973).

As Table 8.1 shows, 52 of the firms (55 per cent) did not achieve profits in China even though their sales increased compared with previous years. At the same time, 41 firms (44 per cent) achieved profits and had no problem with their remittance. Among the 94 respondents, an overwhelming 72.4 per cent had problems with sales in the domestic market; these problems included government restrictions, high tax rates, tariffs and other surcharges. Other problems included insufficient market information and wholesale/retail outlets, insufficient promotional channels, the lengthy application period and procedure especially for wholly-foreign-owned enterprises and indirect investment such as outward-processing. All of the respondents agreed that China's trade liberalisation measures in recent years would help to boost domestic sales. On average, they expected that

Table 8.1   *China: profitability of firms with foreign investment*

	Agriculture		Car manufacture		Dairy		Paper & cement		Total	
	No. of firms	%	No. of Firms	%	No. of firms	%	No. of firms	%	No. of firms	%
No profit/no remittance	9	36	8	36	18	72	17	77	52	55
Remittance of profit	16	64	14	64	7	28	4	18	41	44
Problems with remittance	–	–	–	–	–	–	1	5	1	1
Total	25	100	22	100	25	100	22	100	94	100

Source: Author's survey data.

such measures would raise the volume of their domestic sales in China by 35 per cent in three years (from 1996, the survey year).

Apart from these problems, the increase of bad debts had aroused more and more concerns among investors with domestic sales in China. Due to the cash-flow problems suffered by SOEs and the tightening of credit controls by banks, some investors found it increasingly difficult to collect payments. Faced with so many problems in the Chinese market, the surveyed industries expected an average growth of 8.7 per cent in sales in 1997 over 1996, the lowest forecast among all Chinese industries and far lower than the overall average growth of 17.7 per cent. At the industry level, Table 8.1 shows that the most profitable sectors were agriculture and car manufacturing with 16 firms (64 per cent) and 14 firms (64 per cent) respectively. The lowest profitability was recorded in the paper and cement sector with only four firms showing some profits.

As Table 8.2 shows, out of 100 firms, 55 who achieved profits reinvested more than 60 per cent of those profits in expansion of their operations. Another 11 firms reinvested more than 40 per cent of their profits in expansion of production. Only five firms decided not to reinvest in operations. Firms which mostly reinvested their profits came from the USA, Sweden, France, Germany and Switzerland, but 41 firms (44 per cent) remitted their profits to their home country. Ninety-three firms (95 per cent) indicated that they had chosen long-term strategies and long-term commitments to their operations (Table 8.3). Only five firms indicated short-term plans regarding their operations. These figures are illustrative of the fact that the majority of firms surveyed believed that the Chinese

Table 8.2 *China: percentage of profits reinvested by foreign firms*

Percentage range	No. of firms	% of total
None	19	19
40%	1	1
50%	2	2
>50%	2	2
70%	1	1
>70%	1	1
90%	4	4
100%	55	55
Varies	3	3
No response	12	12
Total	100	100

Source: Author's survey data.

Table 8.3 Strategic reasons for investment in China

Period of investment	No. of firms	% of total
Long term	93	95
Short term	5	5
Total	98	100

Source: Author's survey data.

government is committed to its economic reform, the creation of market-based institutions and political stability.

PRODUCTION AND INVESTMENT PLANS

The majority of foreign investors were positive about future production plans in China, and 84 of the 100 firms which responded to the survey indicated that they intended to expand operations (Table 8.4). Eighteen of those 84 firms indicated they would also diversify production in the course of production expansion (Table 8.5). The remaining firms were mostly keeping a consolidated focus on their existing product ranges; four relatively new firms (two from the paper and cement industry and two from the food-processing industry) demonstrated a particularly keen interest in expanding their businesses in China.

Table 8.4   *China: production plans*

Firms' plans	No. of firms	% of total
Expand	80	80
Keep at current level	14	14
Limit activities	6	6
Total	100	100

Source: Author's survey data.

Table 8.5   *China: diversification plans*

Firms' plans	No. of firms	% of total
No diversification	29	29
Not necessary	2	2
Not yet	2	2
No, consolidated focus	29	29
No, extend own range	3	3
No, no other knowledge	9	9
No funds	6	6
Avoid overcentralised investment	1	1
Yes	18	18
Total	99	100

Source: Author's survey data.

Of the 16 firms which had no plans to expand production, 10 would maintain production at current levels and the other six intended to reduce current production levels. These six expressed strong complaints about high import taxes, import duties and rigid industry regulations; all had a high percentage of imported inputs in their production. These findings show that the import-substitution policy has had very negative effects on the efficient development of operations. Most of these firms come from the paper and cement industries, industries which are very heavily regulated by the government. The firms which intended only to maintain production levels over the next three years saw strong constraints on their expansion in the government interference in everyday operations, poor infrastructure, high cost of finance and disincentives in the level of taxation and import duties.

Two firms also indicated that they planned to close their operations in the near future; one firm represented the car industry, the other came from the agriculture sector. Both firms cited major problems with high import duties and levies, heavy regulation of industry, quotas on the import of inputs, unclear legislation concerning tertiary-sector investment, and an inadequate transport service. Importantly, there was a view that the current government policies of import substitution and subsidised export promotion did not help their production.

Overall, the constraints most frequently considered to be the strongest against expansion of operations were import duties and levies, import quotas, cost of finance, heavy regulation, land regulations, transport service and the lack of qualified managers. These constraints were not, however, sufficient to stop foreign firms from expanding their production over the next three years following our survey. The majority of foreign firms were positive about improvements in government regulations and administration, as well as about the general climate of investment in the near future. Investors who had a positive view about improvements in the Chinese investment climate were those from Hong Kong, Singapore, Thailand, Germany and France.

TECHNOLOGY TRANSFER

One of the major expectations of the Chinese government for FDI was the transfer of the most advanced technology and managerial knowhow to upgrade local industries. It was expected that foreign firms would provide not only needed capital but high-tech, managerial and marketing skills.

As Table 8.6 shows, 85 firms (96 per cent) of the sample had transferred technology; but most of the technology transferred was either second-hand or updated. Out of 90 firms which responded to the relevant question, 31 indicated that they had transferred second-hand

Table 8.6 *China: technology transferred*

Percentage range	No. of firms	% of total
No	3	3
Not yet	1	1
Yes	85	96
Total	89	100

Source: Author's survey data.

Table 8.7   *China: level of technology transfer*

Level of technology:	No. of firms	% of total
Middle level	1	1
Out of date	7	8
Second-hand	30	33
Updated	52	58
Total	90	100

Source: Author's survey data.

technology compared with their home country standards (Table 8.7). Fifty-two firms (62 per cent) had received updated technology, but it is interesting to note that not even one firm had received the most advanced or state-of-the-art technology.

Intangible assets, including technology or patents, are very important for most foreign firms (Markusen, 1995). Due to the lack of strict enforcement of patent and trademark laws in China, transfers of most types of advanced technology become a big concern for foreign firms. Also, many US firms have become reluctant to transfer advanced technology partly because of political restrictions, partly due to a lack of confidence in the Chinese legal system, or even because of competition from local firms due to the copycat phenomenon which has been well-observed and documented in other Asian countries.

Analysis of the type of technology transferred shows some interesting findings; most went to food-processing (19 firms received transfers of technology) and agriculture (12 firms received technology transfers). In the food-processing sector, nine firms (21 per cent) out of 43 received processing technology; six firms (14 per cent) received format technology for assembly operations; and four firms received technology for production. Interesting results were also found from the source-country perspective. The most updated technology was transferred by firms from Switzerland, France, Germany, Holland and Thailand; the most second-hand technology was transferred to local firms by investors from Taiwan, South Korea, Hong Kong, Malaysia and Japan. This supports the findings from previous chapters that investors from NICs are more labour-cost motivated than investors from developed countries, and more interested in China's cheap labour than in market or other factors. They are mostly export-oriented, and are often small to medium-sized firms with low technology intensity.

FDI AND EXPORT ACTIVITIES

Foreign firms involved in operations in the surveyed industries are basically oriented towards the domestic market; they want to take advantage of the huge market and its growing potential. As Table 8.8 shows, most of their production goes to the local market with a small proportion destined for export. With a few exceptions in the car parts, paper and cement sectors, the majority of foreign-funded enterprises in the four surveyed industrial sectors devote their products to the local market.

As Table 8.8 indicates, only four firms out of the 99 exported over 50 per cent of their production; these four were are located in Guandong province and come from the agriculture, paper and cement sectors. There is some indication of export restrictions and import quotas for some inputs, even though government policies were clearly designed to encourage export through special investment incentives and the creation of economic zones.

Table 8.9 shows that over 20 firms have some administrative and regulative problems which prevent them from taking full advantage

Table 8.8   *China: export activities of foreign-based firms*

Export range (%)	No. of firms	Percentage of total
0	71	71
1–24	18	18
25–49	6	6
50–74	3	3
75–100	1	1
No response	1	1
Total	100	100

Source: Author's survey data.

Table 8.9   *China: export restrictions*

Export restriction	No. of firms	% of total
No export	8	8
No freedom, some problems	13	13
Yes, but restrictions	7	7
Yes	72	72
Total	100	100

Source: Author's survey data.

Table 8.10   *China: import restrictions for inputs*

Total sample	No. of firms	% of total
No import	5	5
None	51	54
Approval procedures	13	14
High tariffs	12	13
Quotas	5	5
High price	3	3
Import licence	2	2
Quarantine problems	2	2
Customs office difficulties	I	I
Policy restrictions	I	I
Total	95	100

Source: Author's survey data.

of their export capacity. There are strong indications that the Chinese government needs to make improvements if the government wishes to take advantage of the full export potential of the firms by encouraging an export-oriented strategy among foreign-owned enterprises. Import restrictions can also be an obstacle to export expansion. As Table 8.10 shows, approximately 50 per cent of the firms surveyed had some problems with the import of inputs for production. The most common complaint mentioned by 14 firms were high tariffs, quotas and the approval procedures. Car manufacturing was the most concentrated sector for complaints, which clearly indicates that the auto industry needs a much more liberal industrial policy and less government regulation.

FDI AND EMPLOYMENT

The emphasis on the abundance of cheap labour in China compared to other Asian countries was related to the expectation of significant benefits by the Chinese government in employment generation and the absorption of the influx of labour from rural areas. Employment creation has been a very important issue under China's state policy, especially when a labour surplus of over 120 million persons could otherwise create social problems.

Despite the rapid growth in the number of projects and increased inflows of foreign capital, the employment opportunities generated by FDI projects show only a moderate increase (Table 8.11). According

Table 8.11 *China: number of employees by firm size*

Total employees	Number of firms	% of total
Small firms		
1–50	5	5
51–100	6	6
Medium-sized firms		
101–500	48	49
501–750	8	8
Large firms		
751–1250	15	15
1251–2500	8	8
Very large firms		
>2,500	8	8
Total	98	100

Source: Author's survey data.

to the survey data, employment increased from about 25 000 in 1980 to about 75 000 in 1990 and then to 90 000 in 1996, a three-fold increase compared to 1980. If we compare the moderate increase in the growth of sales (Table 8.12) and the strong increase in the total number of FDI projects, it seems clear that the reality did not meet the expectations of the Chinese government.

Only car manufacturing indicated some concentration of very large firms employing over 2500 employees. There was also some indication of a concentration of larger firms in agriculture (six firms) and the paper and cement sector (seven firms). Smaller firms with 100 employees per firm can be seen in the food-processing sector (five firms).

Table 8.11 provides data on the number of employees by different size of employment. The majority (50 per cent) of foreign-funded

Table 8.12 *China: change in sales, 1996**

	No. of firms	% of total firms
Decrease	10	15
No change	13	20
Increase	42	65
No response	35	35
Total	100	100

* Compared with previous year.
Source: Author's survey data.

firms are medium-sized with around 500 employees on average. Large or very large firms accounted for only 23 per cent. The findings suggest that in these four industrial sectors the foreign-funded projects have been more capital and human-capital factor driven rather than labour factor driven, and have a much higher average capital–labour ratio. The above findings have revealed that production technology and the factor intensity do differ, not only between foreign enterprises and China's domestic enterprises, but also between different sectors of industry. It is very clear that foreign enterprises account for a very small proportion of China's total industrial employment.

*   *   *

POLAND: PROFITABILITY

The survey shows that in 1996, 42 of the 72 firms (58 per cent) achieved more than 10 per cent profits (Table 8.13). At the same time, around 30 firms (42 per cent) did not response to the question or, one can assume, did not achieve any noticeable profits. At the industry level, the table shows that the most profitable sector was food processing with 17 firms (24 per cent), followed by paper and cement with 13 firms (18 per cent). The lowest profitability was noted in the car sector with only six firms, and agriculture with only seven firms showing more than 10 per cent profit. The most profitable firms were Austrian, Dutch, Swedish, British and Canadian.

An analysis of firms which achieved profits shows that almost three-quarters (71.5 per cent) reinvested their profits in company

Table 8.13   *Poland: profitability of firms with foreign investment*

Sector	10 % profit		No response		Sectoral total	
	No. of firms	%	No. of firms	%	No. of firms	%
Agriculture	7	9	8	14	15	21
Food processing	17	24	7	11	24	34
Paper & cement	13	18	7	11	20	28
Car manufacture	5	8	8	12	13	18
Total sample	42	58	30	42	72	100

Source: Author's survey data.

activities or increased their firm's capital assets, while only one-third of the firms (27.5 per cent) did not reinvest at all. Most of the firms which reinvested their profits came from Germany, Britain, Holland, Norway and France. Only 14.7 per cent of firms surveyed transferred their profits overseas. This analysis clearly indicates that strategies of foreign firms changed over the period 1994–6. They no longer think about the 'quick buck' strategy (as was the case in the early 1990s) and the repatriation of all profits back home; instead they are choosing a long-term perspective and commitment to the Polish market. Also, foreign investors, through their longer commitments, indicated their belief in the progress of economic reform and the future prospects for economic growth.

From Table 8.14 we can observe that there was a continual decline in the profitability of sales and the rate of return on equity, exactly parallel to the growth in sales, again with the sharpest decrease in the rate of return occurring in 1990–91 (from about 80 per cent to less than 30 per cent). Thus, the conditions favouring a cost-efficiency-seeking strategy seem to have ceased to hold precisely as the market-seeking strategy became more attractive. Note, however, that the net profits and profit rates of sales after 1993 pick up and show an increasing trend.

The export share of sales by enterprises with foreign participation was above average for the four sectors throughout the period. Also, despite the sharp decline in profitability and returns to more moderate levels over time, the profitability on turnover of FDI-based enterprises remained much higher than the average for the economy as a whole. Thus, the share of the FDI-based sector in the economy's total gross profits increased steadily from 1.4 per cent in 1990 to more than

Table 8.14   *Poland: rates of return and profits of foreign firms*

	1990	1991	1992	1993	1994	1995	1996
Net profits (trillion zloty)	0.79	2.96	3.45	3.20	3.80	5.78	6.85
Profits as % of total gross profits	1.4	1.8	4.2	4.0	5.9	8.7	12.4
Net profits (economy-wide)[1]	28.9	50.2	−16.7	−27.8	10.4	24.6	32.3
Gross profits (economy-wide)[2]	46.6	124.6	54.3	23.7	48.9	59.4	98.7
Profit rates on sales in %	30.1	14.3	6.3	3.8	7.8	15.7	32.2
Economywide average rate (%)	22.3	10.6	−1.3	−1.6	4.7	8.8	12.1
Return on equity (%)*	98.7	65.4	24.7	16.5	24.9	65.2	89.7

*   per annum. [1,2] – in trillion zloty
Source: Author's survey data.

12.4 per cent in 1996, while its share in total exports increased from 1.4 per cent to 9.3 per cent, as indicated in Chapter 6. This confirms the competitive advantage of the foreign firms in relation to home enterprises, and this may be partly the result of ownership advantages in terms of the technologies made available for adaptation, in addition to the internalisation advantage (Dunning, 1993; Buckley et al 1992; Casson, 1992).

One important factor has to be noted about the generally low profitability of FDI-based firms. There are few explanations for this trend; the majority of foreign firms use transfer prices in their trade activities. Taking into consideration the high Polish tax on goods and services, foreign firms lower prices for their exported products but increase the prices for imports of products used in production by their subsidiaries, which decreases the profits in Poland so they can realise profits overseas. This again indicates the growing problems relating to the Polish tax system and sends out an emergency call for its reform.

PRODUCTION AND INVESTMENT PLANS

Despite progress in the transition to a market economy, there are still many problems facing the government in developing the right environment for foreign investment. The market is still undeveloped, the people's purchasing power is small, and financial institutions have a low capacity to support investment. Regardless of the problems, however, most firms indicated that they would expand their operations in the future.

Production and investment plans of foreign firms in Poland over the next two–three years following the survey are very positive. Seventy-nine firms (over 80 per cent) of the 97 indicated that they believed in the future progress of economic reform and the development of a better business environment in Poland (Table 8.15). Only five firms out of the total were thinking of limiting their business operations.

Table 8.15 *Poland: investment plans*

Statement	Number of firms	% of total
Expand operation	79	81
Keep at current level	13	13
Limit firm's activities	5	5
Total	97	100

Source: Author's survey data.

Table 8.16   *Poland: other constraints*

Statements	No. of firms	% of total
Changing legal regulations	7	8
Import duties/quotas	5	6
Social and political instability	5	6
Unfair competition from Polish firms	3	3
Increase of taxes	2	2
Sales of goods	2	2
Fiscal demand of labour union	1	1
Fiscal demand of government	1	1

Note: The figures refer to a total sample size of 89 firms.
Source: Author's survey data.

From a source-country perspective, French (83.3 per cent), American (82.8 per cent), Dutch (81.45 per cent), Swedish (79.42 per cent) and German (77.0 per cent) firms foresaw an expansion of their activities in the coming years. A limitation of their foreign activities was indicated by Austrian (4.0 per cent) firms. At the sectoral level, most firms involved in the construction and textile sectors indicated a decrease in their foreign operations. Overall, the constraints most frequently considered to be the strongest against expansion of operations were as shown in Table 8–16.

These constraints were not, however, sufficiently strong to prevent the majority of foreign firms from intending to expand their production over the coming years. Political instability and a non-transparent legal system are undoubtedly having adverse implications for long-term business investment, and regulations regarding imports also have to be taken into consideration in the long run. A well-developed import policy would definitely improve not only the firms' inputs but the general investment climate as well. This is a clear indication for a government policy change if more FDI is to be attracted in the future.

TECHNOLOGY TRANSFER

One of the great expectations of local firms is to acquire the most advanced technology through FDI-based firms; FDI can be an important vehicle for technology and new management techniques (Dunning, 1993). As the survey suggests, around 36 per cent of large firms reinvested their profits in technology, and around 68.4 per cent of firms

Table 8.17 *Poland: technology transfer*

Technology	No. of firms	% of total
No transfer	14	16
1 year old	36	40
2 years old	25	28
3 years old	11	12
Older than 3 years	3	3
Total	89	100
Reinvested profit in technology	32	36
Not reinvested	18	20

Source: Author's survey data.

based their operations on the latest technology (2 years old or less) (Table 8.17). Compared with 1993, the percentage of firms using technology and equipment not more than 1 year old had increased from 18 per cent to 40 per cent.

FDI AND EXPORT ACTIVITIES

Over the period 1994–96, foreign firms increased the value of their exports; 70 per cent indicated an increase in sales of more than $US800 000. Total exports of firms with foreign participation were around $US3765.3 mn, which was around 25.6 per cent of total exports. The share in total exports increased from 1.6 per cent to 11.6 per cent. This confirms the competitive advantage of the FDI-based firms in relation to home enterprises – and this may be partly the result of ownership advantages in terms of the technologies made available for adoption, in addition to internalisation advantages embedded in marketing, organisational, managerial and financial capabilities. It would be expected that relative growth in the FDI-based sector (such as food-processing or paper and cement), with its clear-cut ownership advantages, would have a significant impact on the pattern of structural adjustment and specialisation in the economy. The strength of this impact in these particular sectors would be a function of FDI in those sectors.

The share of FDI-based firms in total sales rose significantly between 1990–96, and the ratio of exports to sales showed an upwards trend with a strong jump in 1995/96, reinforcing the argument about the changing strategies and motives of FDI-based firms. This can be interpreted in terms of an export-oriented market strategy, with foreigninvestor firms concentrating more and more on supply to the international market. This strategy, in turn, clearly implies greenfield as the most suitable mode for technology transfer, and that the general level of technology transfer corresponds to foreign demand.

The sector exporting most in terms of value was food-processing ($US978 mn, or around 48.4 per cent of total exports of the surveyed industries). Only one-third of firms surveyed did not export their products; but on the other hand, one-third of the firms surveyed exported more than 50 per cent of their products. Some firms even exported more than 75 per cent – 6 of the total respondents. Over 50 per cent exported their products from the food-processing industry and around 25 per cent from the paper and cement and agriculture sectors.

A total of 30 firms (33 per cent) indicated that they were not involved in any export activity (Table 8.18). The remaining 62 companies (67 per cent) that were involved in export activity were relatively balanced across each of the percentage ranges with the only real concentration appearing in the 1–25 per cent category with 27 acknowledgments (29 per cent), and in the category 25–50 per cent with 20 acknowledgments (22 per cent). The 62 firms with some degree of export activity were also asked to provide information on the regional distribution of their exports.

The data indicate that most export activity was directed at serving the markets of CECs and/or FSU (Table 8.19). There was also an indication of a modest amount of export activity aimed at the markets of Western Europe (EU and/or EFTA). The slow increase in export activities to EU markets can be partly explained by the existence of

Table 8.18 *Poland: export activities of the FDI-based firms*

Percentage of production/ sales destined for export	No. of firms	% of total
0	30	33
1–25	27	29
25–50	20	22
50–75	9	10
75–100	6	7
Total	92	100

Source: Author's survey data.

Table 8.19   *Poland: regional distribution of the FDI-based firms*

Export by regions (%)	No. of firms	% of total
Western Europe (EU and/or EFTA countries)		
0	25	40
1–25	13	21
25–50	9	15
50–75	8	13
75–100	3	5
Central Eastern countries (CEC) and/or the former Soviet Union (FSU)		
0	7	13
1–25	21	33
25–50	10	16
50–75	7	11
75–100	13	21
Other regions and/or countries		
0	36	58
1–25	12	19
25–50	7	11
50–75	3	5
75–100	–	–
No response	4	6
Total of Sample	62	100

Source: Author's survey data.

tariffs and trade barriers on Polish exports. In particular, access to EU markets for Poland's agricultural and food-processing products has only partly been liberalised, average import tariffs remain much higher partly due to the conversion of non-tariffs into tariffs. Also, a number of non-tariff provisions and market-access quotas apply under the rules of the trade Common Market. For Polish exports, this kind of trade arrangement creates a stumbling block for further export expansion, especially for the food-processing and agricultural sectors where revealed comparative advantages are clearly taking place. Under the Uruguay Round agreement, agricultural tariff ceilings are to be reduced by 36 per cent in six annual instalments from 1995, but given that for most items the ceilings are not binding, actual tariff rates may not fall that much. However, in exports to other regions and countries there was very little activity.

In analysing exports by country of destination, a changing trend emerges over the period 1992–96. Germany emerges as Poland's main export partner (Table 8.20); its close historical and cultural ties, immigration and close proximity to the Polish market having created a special environment for close cooperation. Another interesting feature is the increasing importance of Russia, especially after the collapse of the CMEA block. Russia, by 1996, has moved from sixth to second position, supporting the claim that foreign firms see Poland as a springboard for expansion into Eastern European markets.

Some managers indicated that they would be able to increase exports if the trade barriers and border duties to the European Union and the newly-independent states became more liberalised. However, one-sixth of the firms surveyed indicated that they had problems collecting payments from the newly-independent states. The evidence clearly indicates that the exports of firms with foreign participation are characterised by geographical and product concentrations. Over 70 per cent of exports go to the EU and especially to FDI source countries. Most of the goods which were exported were food-processing products (around 46.6 per cent), paper and cement (29.8 per cent) and agriculture (15.3 per cent of total exports).

Imports also indicate a similar pattern to those of exports; only in terms of products were there some differences. The import of consumption goods was higher than the global average (23.4 per cent as compared to 15.6 per cent); the import of investments was similar to the import of investment goods and was around 13.5 per cent. From 1994 an increase was also noted in the import of inputs for foreign firms. By 1996, 30.4 per cent of firms did not import; and about one-fifth imported more than $US1 mn. Imports mostly came from the USA and Western Europe. Regarding imports by country, Germany,

Table 8.20 *Poland: exports by main countries (%, at current prices)*

Partner	1992		1993		1994		1995		1996	
lst	G	31.4	G	36.3	G	35.7	G	38.3	G	39.2
2nd	NL	16.8	NL	16.9	NL	17.2	NL	17.4	RU	18.8
3rd	IT	12.6	IT	12.0	RU	12.4	RU	12.8	NL	13.6
4th	RU	10.2	RU	10.5	IT	11.3	IT	11.5	IT	11.9
5th	GB	9.3	GB	9.5	GB	10.3	GB	10.6	GB	10.8
Others		29.9		14.8		13.1		9.4		5.7

Note: G = Germany; NL = Netherlands; IT = Italy; RU = Russia; GB = Great Britain.
Source: Author's survey data.

Italy, Holland and France were the major countries of supply. There is evidence of a decline in imports from the USA.

FDI AND EMPLOYMENT

Despite the rapid increase in FDI inflow and the value of committed investment, the average level of employment in enterprises with foreign participation remained stable or rose only slightly over the period under study. Enterprises with foreign participation absorbed about 1.4 per cent of total employment (an average of around 26 000) in 1990–92, and no significant increase in employment was noted until 1995 when it suddenly increased by 67 000. It then increased marginally to 70 000 in 1996, a 2.5–fold increase compared to 1990. Average employment per firm was around 50 people and was much lower than the national average (76 people) Bluszkowski and Garlicki (1996). At the industry level, most employment occurred in food-processing (12.5 per cent) and car manufacturing (11.8 per cent).

If we contrast this moderate upward trend with the rapid growth in sales by the same firms, it seems clear that exploitation of cheap labour has not been the main motive for foreign investors. The data point towards industries identified as scale- or capital- or human capital-intensive being the leading targets for FDI in Poland, rather than the traditional labour-intensive industries. This suggests that Polish unskilled labour is rather expensive in relation to other possible host countries as measured by its relative productivity, and, by contrast, skilled labour reveals some comparative advantage as expressed in terms of its relative price. This further supports the argument that Poland is moving more towards human-capital-intensive sectors, and its economic adjustment towards a more Schumpeterian mode, driven by the creativity of human capital. Further analysis of average-sized firms' employment support this kind of argument.

The level of employment was examined further by grouping the number of employees in local firms into a series of bands. The bands themselves were grouped together to represent the different sizes of the FDI-based firms. The data on employment indicate a strong concentration within the three bands encompassing the 100–500-employees level, which accounted for 26 firms (30 per cent) as shown in Table 8.21. There was also a strong showing in the 500–750 band with 15 firms (17 per cent). Furthermore, the sample

Table 8.21   *Poland: employment levels of foreign firms*

No. of employees	Number of firms	% of total
Small firrns:		
1–50	12	13
50–100	9	10
Medium firms:		
100–500	26	30
500–750	15	17
Large firms:		
750–1 250	13	15
1250–2500	2	2
Very large firms:		
>2500	7	8
No response	5	6
Total	89	100

Source: Author's survey data.

indicated that the majority of local firms with foreign participation are medium-sized, with on average 500 employees per firm.

COMPARISON BETWEEN CHINA AND POLAND

Profitability

The majority of foreign firms in China did not achieve any profits, even though their sales show an increasing trend. Most firms that are oriented towards the domestic market encountered problems in sales due to import-substitution policy measures. High import tariffs and quotas have negative effects on foreign firms' operations, especially in regard to the import of inputs for production. Strong government restrictions reduce the diversity and quality of final products for domestic as well as overseas markets. By contrast, in Poland the majority of foreign firms achieved profits of at least 10 per cent, and over three-quarters of the firms which achieved profits reinvested in further company expansion or increased their capital assets. The majority of foreign firms in Poland show better performance than in China in terms of profits and their distribution after tax. The share of FDI-based sectors shows an increasing trend in the economy's total gross profit earnings. However, there were some constraints which had a negative impact on the performance of foreign firms, especially in relation to the tax system and its transparency and operation.

Production and Investment Plans

The majority of foreign firms in both countries indicated that they would expand their operations, and some would also diversify their production. Only a small percentage had decided to keep production at current levels and only one or two had decided to close their operations in the future. This trend supports the findings that the majority of foreign firms involved in both countries had chosen long-term strategies and had made a commitment to the longer term. There were some complaints in the case of China from foreign investors about the government's constant interference in the running of everyday operations.

Technology Transfer

In both countries foreign firms transfer technology, but differences occur in quality and the advanced level of technology transfers. In the case of China most technology transfers were second-hand; firms from NIEs, in particular, transfer older technologies, in contrast to firms from developed countries which usually transfer more advanced and up-dated technology. The majority of this technology was transferred in the form of format or processing technology; little was transferred for production lines or production technology. In Poland over two-thirds of the firms surveyed transferred advanced technology not older than 1–2 years and some have been state-of-the-art technology. Most of the technology transferred was in the form of equipment for production, processing technology and high-tech by well-known large MNCs which took advantage of Poland's highly-skilled labour and at the same time created spillover effects on the competitiveness of local firms.

Export Performance

The great majority of foreign firms in China in the four sectors surveyed are oriented towards the domestic market, especially those from developed countries. The percentage of exports in their total sales is negligible. Most of them try to sell in the local market even though they encounter some restrictions and difficulties imposed by the government. Goods for export, mainly by (NEFs) Newly Industrialised Economics firms, come from low-end value-added labour-intensive goods; they were of low quality and standards. In the case of Poland, the majority of foreign firms were involved in the export of their goods, and some even exported more than 50 per cent of their production. Most of the exports were aimed at Russia and the former Soviet independent states. There was also an increase in exports to Western Europe and other developed countries. An increased number of exported goods were capital or human-capital-intensive and high value-added products.

Employment Effects

In both countries foreign firms generated only moderate employment opportunities. The level in China was a little higher than in Poland, but in relation to the total employment figures of China the number of employment opportunities created by foreign firms was negligible. Most firms are small or medium-sized, employing approximately 50 people per firm in both countries. However, there were some differences in the composition of occupational categories between China and Poland. In China the majority of jobs offered were of the assembly-line type requiring no major skills. The predominance of females in the workforce is observable, and female workers are clustered in lower-skilled (lower-paid) jobs than men. A high reliance on expatriate managerial and technical staff is also a common pattern observable across all firms regardless of the nature of their production process. The Chinese government has imposed some labour policies forcing foreign firms to employ Chinese managerial staff and to train more technical staff on the job.

In the case of Poland, foreign firms rely overwhelmingly on the domestic labour market for skilled labour requirements in all occupational categories, especially those in the age range 20–45 who have often been working and trained in foreign countries. A low reliance on expatriate managers or technical staff can also be observed across all foreign firms. Managerial policies of foreign companies often organise training for local technical and managerial staff on the job, or send them to special training programmes at their headquarters. This policy has been facilitated by the availability of qualified and easily trainable labour in Poland.

CONCLUSION

In conclusion, the performance of FDI projects in China over recent years has brought some changes in the economic structure, but its spillover effects in terms of technology transfer or export or employment creation have not been so spectacular. Technical changes in some import-substitution industries have been low. On the other hand, the capital-intensive technology transferred in some industries may not be appropriate to China, particularly in regard to employment creation and as a stimulus to exports. This chapter has found little evidence of a high export performance of enterprises with foreign investment in the four surveyed industrial sectors. The domestic-market orientation of joint ventures or foreign firms may be attributed to capital intensity, which results from Chinese policies. Most of these firms have problems in achieving profits and produce uncompetitive products using capital-intensive processes.

In the case of Poland, there is some evidence of changes in her trade structure induced by foreign firms. The spillover effects in regard to the technology transferred and employment creation have been of some significance. Especially in relation to the technology transferred there are clear indications of transfers of advanced technology and its effects on the quality of final products. Most goods produced are of a high standard and are competitive in domestic and foreign markets. The majority of foreign firms achieved profits and planned to expand and diversify their operations in the near future.

9 Conclusions

Some of the empirical conclusions of this work are specific to the patterns and determinants of FDI already studied in detail. Whilst these FDI flows have some significance in themselves, there is a more general relevance in that the conclusions are especially important for the analysis of FDI benefits in the context of the economic and investment policies of transitional economies. This chapter summarises the major findings, underlines conclusions that are of general significance, discusses the limitations of the study, outlines the economic policy implications and recommends further research areas.

FINDINGS

The identification of patterns and determinants of FDI in this work are comprehensive and can be applied to any other country in transition. Although the classification is of universal application, patterns and determinants of FDI are affected by factors that vary considerably in different countries. Much of the variation in these factors was encompassed by the theoretical analysis of determinants that was introduced in Chapters 1 and 2. Most importantly, the subsequent cross-country analysis clearly identified the major variations occurring in the study.

Some conclusions of general importance can be drawn about the patterns and determinants of FDI. There is a significant diversification in terms of the total number of source countries as well as a great concentration of source-country investments. There are also differences between developed and developing countries in terms of the size, strategy and form of their investments. The analysis in Chapter 6 revealed the differences at the country level and the different emerging trends. The most common forms of investment in both countries initially were joint ventures with an increasing shareholding by foreign partners. The projects were mostly medium-sized in terms of employment and capitalisation, and some received advanced technology for production. However, there are indications of newly-emerging trends. The rapid increase in inward investment since the mid-1990s has taken on an altogether new form, and recent

243

investment has been undertaken by foreign firms with full control of their assets and production. The wholly foreign-owned enterprises are becoming the main driving force of investment, certainly in Poland and to a lesser extent in China. They indicate a much higher propensity for exports than local firms and they are taking advantage of intangible assets like marketing skills or a brand name. The size and capitalisation of the projects invested in by these enterprises has increased significantly and the transfer of technology has become more updated.

In regard to the determinants of FDI, the survey data clearly indicated that selected market factors are the primary catalyst behind the decisions of major foreign firms to engage in FDI in the host countries. To be more specific, market factors that are oriented solely towards the local host country market, namely 'to access and supply the local market and the growth potential of the local market' are the primary motivational and locational forces for FDI within the two countries surveyed.

While local market factors were clearly the primary catalyst for FDI in these countries, both labour factors (primarily the abundance of cheap labour and the supply of skilled labour) and investment climate factors (primarily the overall stability of the host country) played very important roles in the investment decision-making process. Investment incentives like tax concessions, tax holidays or other financial incentives were not as important as the general investment climate and economic growth in the host countries. The economic domestic policy reforms, infrastructure, legal and financial systems and country characteristics including resource endowments and entrepreneurial skills are important determinants of the patterns of foreign involvement by domestic market-oriented firms. Policy stability and clear strong government leadership in the direction of a country's policy development were found to be a strong incentive for foreign firms' expansion of their operations and further diversification of their production and export bases.

In relation to the patterns and determinants of FDI, there were a number of variations between the countries surveyed. In China, the primary source countries of FDI were mainly Hong Kong and Taiwan. There was a clear indication of the importance of overseas Chinese investors in the total inflow of foreign capital into China. The developed countries, by comparison, invested very small amounts in China both in terms of their share in China's total FDI inflows and in terms of their total worldwide investments.

There were also notable differences between the developing-country investors and developed-country investors with respect to their investment strategies. The former tended to be more concerned with cost-efficient export-oriented strategies, while the developed-country investors tended to be more market-oriented, although they tended to have stronger incentives to secure control over their businesses than the developing-country investors. This is reflected by the high propensity of developed-country investors to hold the majority shares in joint ventures and to set up wholly foreign-owned enterprises. It was also noted that developing-country investors in China tended to adopt more labour-intensive technologies than developed-country investors, with lower capital-to-labour ratios and much smaller sized projects in general than the firms from developed countries.

Finally, the firms from developing countries have a higher export propensity than those from developed countries as a whole, which tended more towards import-substitution manufacturing for the domestic market. There was also an indication of tariff-jumping investment as a consequence of government import-substitution policies. This comparison is consistent with the investment patterns of the source countries.

By contrast, Poland's major source countries are much more diversified, both by their origins and by their investment strategies. The majority of the firms are mainly from Western industrialised countries, such as the USA, Holland and Germany, employing mixed strategies of domestic market and export orientation. It should also be pointed out that these market-seeking firms indicated that the opportunity to establish local firms in Poland as a base for exports to Russia and the former Commonwealth of Independent States (CIS) proved to be a significant element in both the motivation to invest and the location choice of the investment site. Most of the foreign firms which invest in Poland are large MNCs with high capitalisation ratios and advanced technology. The majority of firms are more oriented towards capital or human-capital industries. As predicted by observed trends in the survey, the main form of investment has become the wholly foreign-owned enterprise, indicating the improvements in the business environment generally and Poland's membership of the OECD and its coming full integration into the EU more particularly.

In general, whilst some variation in the patterns and determinants of FDI between the firms surveyed does exist, some consistent general patterns and determinants of FDI emerge which are of significant importance to policy and strategy development.

The framework used for analysis of the motivations of MNCs in their location decisions has a wide-ranging relevance, although the motivation of MNCs varies considerably across different industries and countries. The framework developed in Chapter 2 takes explicit account of these differences in terms of factor endowments and comparative advantages of the countries. This removes serious shortcomings in other analyses of MNCs' motivational factors affecting their final investment decisions.

The present analysis of motivations and trends of FDI reveals the need for caution in generalising about determinants of FDI. Quite a number of specific differences in the motivational decisions of MNCs was observed. Even amongst firms from the same industry or country employing the same investment strategy several differences existed, but the existence of general trends can be observed between firms' motivation or forms of investment. A hypothesis relating to market factors may prove to be more fruitful in explaining differences in investors' decisions in regard to investment in particular host countries. The confirmation of the importance of the business environment and the level of country development associated with foreign firms' decisions in regard to determinants of FDI over country incentives is of considerable importance for the theory of FDI. Factors associated with the two issues mentioned above exacerbate the argument regarding government investment incentives in general and country growth potential in particular as strong motives for foreign firms to invest in a host country.

The present study confirms the strong importance of some of the variables incorporated in the theoretical investment model and provides economic explanations of the observed trends and motivations of foreign firms. The small variations in the determinants of FDI with regard to the two transitional countries have a marginal effect on the overall trends. In general, the results support the view that recent trends and determinants of FDI cannot be explained by conventional theories. The major weakness is the lack of explanation for recently changing phenomena such as globalisation, the division of labour, information technology, the changing behaviour of firms and the attitudes of host countries towards FDI. Although the OLI framework, for example, is useful in determining conditions necessary for a firm to locate production overseas, it has little to say about the investment choices such as forming a joint venture or acquiring assets in an existing company. Generally speaking, technology-dependent or market-oriented firms are less likely to engage in joint ventures. However, firms may want to engage in joint ventures when the economic environment of the host country is risky or unfamiliar. This appears to be the case in China, where a number of MNCs have chosen, at least initially, to form joint ventures with local firms.

To sum up, the key findings from this study offer support, contradiction, clarification as well as new dimensions in regard to the available literature. However, it should be clearly stipulated that comparing and contrasting the findings from this particular study to other works in this field is subject to some limitations, as outlined in the following section. While many of the general findings can be useful to policy-makers and investors in other transitional countries, it must be remembered that certain specific country variables can produce a case of apples and oranges, common fruits but with considerable differences in shape, smell, taste or colour. To be more specific, this study has concentrated solely on FDI from a certain category of investors in two individual host countries within a set period of time. A major change in any one of these key variables may have an impact on the results. Therefore, while there may be specific variations between each country, the general findings concerning the patterns and determinants of FDI will have strong implications for other countries in transition.

LIMITATIONS OF THE STUDY

It is appropriate to comment briefly on some of the limitations of the analysis which should receive due consideration in assessing the policy relevance of the results. There are a few limitations to this particular study, most of which result from different statistical reporting methods and the general reliability and definition of FDI. Figures on FDI in China provided by different sources show a great variance in accuracy. This can lead to serious difficulties if Chinese data is to be compared either simultaneously with those of other countries, or over time, as (Wolf) 1991 notes. In order to avoid erroneous assumptions, statistics on FDI in China must be treated with care. As Pomfret (1991) stated, in China there is no strong tradition of reporting economic statistics and the collection and reporting of statistical data describing the pattern of investment is fragmented, with the resultant data not always consistent. Both the definition and calculation of FDI in China vary from source to source. For instance, equity from the Chinese side is often included in the total value of projects or JVs in some cases, which exaggerate the size of the actual inflow of foreign capital. It has not yet been clarified how much of the invested capital is 'round-trip' investment, that is investment which has been invested in foreign enterprises by Chinese companies and is now being reimported to China by the foreign company in order to make use of the preferential treatment of FDI, as Pomfret notes.

A natural time lag exists between the signing of a contract and the actual operation of the business. Woodward and Liu (1994) suggest as a possible reason for this delay the complex bureaucratic procedures which have to be followed when investments are set in motion. In a considerable number of cases, foreign-funded enterprises received the contracted investment only after being in operation for two years or more. In addition, many foreign investors, after agreeing to invest, take time to assess the investment climate and production conditions before placing their investment. Recently, China started checking how much capital investors are actually bringing into the country. In one case, equipment provided by the foreign partner in a printing joint venture was found to have a true value of only $US500 000, though it was supposedly worth more than $US2.6 million.

On the language issue there were some problems with translation of economic terms which could possibly create a small degree of bias. The OECD data was thought to be more reliable, and its consistent use avoided a distortion of cross-sectional comparisons deriving from different bases used in the reporting of FDI by different government agencies. Some different statistical sources were used for calculation of country FDI in selected industries, on which some of the analysis rests. The same figures for total FDI in individual industries were employed as were used in the aggregate calculations. In some sectors such as agriculture, where reporting was not as consistent and reliable as those of other sectors, the survey data was supplemented by data from OECD publications in order to obtain an overall picture of FDI intensity in this sector.

A second key limitation of the study relates to the actual sample size. While the researcher was fairly satisfied with the response rates obtained, that was not entirely true with respect to the actual number of local firms with foreign participation which responded positively to the survey. To be more specific, one could feel that the number of local firms with foreign participation in the sample may not be sufficiently representative of FDI in that particular host country. However, it should be stipulated that the researcher was only able to properly identify some 100 population elements for the sample. This situation was primarily the result of a serious lack of available business information on the host country. Therefore, despite the huge efforts to exercise full and due diligence in the process of determining the population stratum, only around 100 cases of FDI could be properly identified. One could also complain that the survey ignores firms from labour-intensive sectors such as toys or clothing. The choice of the four industries was based on the emerging comparative advantage of the host country in these sectors, as well as its potential and representative nature for the whole country. The representation of these chosen industries can be explained by their differential structure and nature of operation. For example in food-processing or car manufacturing, there are capital and human-capital activities as well as labour-intensive processes, giving a diverse picture at the industry level about the structure and role of FDI.

A third limitation of this study came from the specific set of characteristics. To reiterate, the first stage of the investigation focused solely on a population which comprised all the major foreign investors that have actively engaged in FDI in China and Poland. Therefore, the results from this study are relevant for these countries, but a comparison of the same results with other host countries in other regions and/or to other population types may or may not be completely valid. Overall, given the costs involved, the funds that were available, the size of the countries covered and their diverse economic, political, geographical and cultural structure, the implementation of the survey via the use of questionnaire-based interviews was considered to be the best possible choice of data-collection modes.

In conclusion, it should be stated that before the start of the study the researcher carefully reviewed the bulk of previous studies which were pertinent to this area of exploration. In doing so, one became keenly aware of pitfalls associated with doing research in the environments of China and Poland. Armed with this knowledge, the researcher did his utmost to design a research strategy that would be robust and flexible enough to allow for a meaningful and thorough investigation of the subject matter. The result of this hard work should be evident in the preceding pages. However, while no research endeavour can really ever claim to be free from defects (and this researcher certainly makes no such claim with this study), every effort has been exercised to minimise the potential for problems for the overall benefit of both academics and practitioner audiences.

POLICY IMPLICATIONS

This final section briefly considers the policy implications of the findings of the study, some of which have immediate implications. The importance of government policies in creating a favourable business environment is indicated in Chapter 4. In the globalising economy of the 1990s, national governments have to re-examine their domestic economic policies and strategies in the light of the fact that they are increasingly competing for competition-enhancing assets, which are much more footloose than they used to be. Macro-organisational policies which at one time only affected the domestic allocation and use of resources are now as likely to affect trade, FDI and cross-border alliances as much as any tariff, exchange rate or interest rate hike. The world economy of the 1990s is obliging governments to realign their domestic economic policies more closely to the needs of the international marketplace.

Governments which are successful in reducing or helping to reduce the transaction and coordination costs of economic activity, and which best enable firms to surmount the obstacles of structural change, are likely to be the most successful not only in attracting the right kind of FDI but in doing so at the least real cost. Part of the transaction or coordinating cost lies in the inefficient administration of law or government regulations (Chapters 6 and 7). Transparency and consistency of regulations and foreign investment policies are very important for the smooth operations of foreign firms. Red tape, delays in licensing approvals, and complicated application procedures only increase the costs of operation and discourage further foreign investment. The decreasing investment from developed countries in China (Chapter 5) is related to the high transaction and coordinating costs. China and Poland seem to have the capacity and ability to reduce these costs (Chapter 2), given that both countries have addressed this limitation as a top priority and in a short time span.

To take full advantage of FDI and foster efficient industrial development of a country, governments must not discriminate between import-substitution and exports and should follow outward-oriented strategies. Only then will they attract foreign firms wishing to take advantage of their resources and/or factor endowments. The distribution of FDI is thus more likely to be aligned with a country's comparative advantage and to use its domestic resources in an efficient way. Unfortunately, the present study indicates that there are many distortions in regulations across industries. Distortions raising labour costs and lowering capital costs were found in financial, labour and FDI policies. Distorted prices of goods and a scarcity of skilled labour also affected production choices. Heavy regulations and high import taxes, quotas or levies limited the potential not only of foreign firms but also of the industries themselves. So did the effects of protection, high-technology policies and investment allowances which frequently created incentives for the use of capital-intensive techniques. Inappropriate technology made production less competitive internationally.

The repressed financial system, characterised by low and even negative real interest rates, gave local and foreign investors access to subsidised interest rates; tax incentives were tied to capital investment rather than to employment; and duties on capital goods imports were usually reduced. These three measures made capital artificially cheap in relation to labour, and labour costs were rising at the same time. Measures raising costs included recruiting, insurance and other charges imposed by local governments, the turnover of workers who were not permitted to move permanently to urban areas by domicile laws, and low labour productivity arising from the inability of management to hire and fire. All of these issues are strongconstraints on the operations of foreign firms with regard to the rising cost of production and further expansion plans. They also reflect a lack of consistent, transparent investment policies. These kinds of policies pursued by governments create further limitations in the full utilisation of capital and resources, but also reduce the opportunities for further horizontal or vertical linkages between industries.

As the present study indicates (Chapter 6), FDI in Chinese manufacture was basically induced by import-substitution in the four surveyed industries. The FDI inflows into manufacturing for the domestic markets were strongly correlated with protection in the case of China (Chapter 7). Labour costs do not appear to affect FDI inflows. The low level of export-oriented FDI in manufacturing seems to be largely related to the impact of protective policies which export-oriented investors have to follow. The ratios of output exported by enterprises with foreign investment in the four industries were much lower than expected, and a domestic market orientation was dominant. Joint ventures capable of exporting were granted many concessions (Chapter 7), but foreign investors designated as import-substituting, or technology-advanced, had access to similar concessions while producing for the domestic market. Incentives for import substitution and advanced technology have discouraged decisions to export, lowering the export propensity of enterprises with foreign investment. As the present study also indicates, China's experience confirms that excessively protective import-substitution policies are likely to give foreign investors access to high monopoly rents in domestic markets. Thus, import-substitution policies linked with incentives to encourage advanced technology have had the effect of stimulating inappropriate industries and inefficient technology. As the import-substitution process continued from the easy first stage of replacing non-durable goods, it entailed production that was increasingly high-cost. It is widely accepted that when protection is granted to foreign investors under import-substitution policies, enterprises with foreign investment tend to concentrate on import substitution.

Export schemes and programmes, even if they become fully successful, do not provide a long-term solution to the low level of exports by foreign firms. These schemes are merely interim measures aimed at facilitating appropriate action. The long-term solution must be found in the overall development policies in individual countries. The economic impact of FDI inflow to specific industries, its size and location is not necessarily commensurate with the range of investment incentives offered. It is mainly the rigidity of the economic structure and heavy regulations which have adverse effects on foreign firms' export intensity. In China, the growth in the rate of formal FDI inflow and the effects of MNCs on manufactured exports have not yet met the expectations of the Chinese government on FDI into export sectors, technology transfer or the export orientation of enterprises with foreign investment. Informal foreign investment has been successful in exporting labour intensive products. The inability of formal FDI in manufacturing to play the desired role in economic development, however, results from China's policies, not from the nature of FDI.

Economic reforms in the last few decades have created an increasingly favourable environment with relatively better price signals for China's exports. Foreign exchange retention, exchange rate devaluations, tariff exemptions and rebates for exports have been among the policy instruments used to expand exports. However, fundamental problems remain: a highly regulated system, unstable macroeconomic policies, an overvalued exchange rate and severe price distortions in both commodity and factor markets are among the principal difficulties. The case for changes in domestic economic policies, combined with specific FDI policies which prevent China from turning its inherent comparative advantage into a real comparative advantage, receives strong support from our analysis. If sustained export growth with high economic efficiency is to be achieved, further reforms will be necessary, especially those which have been outlined in the present study. Incentives for undue capital intensity and excessive technological intensity are particularly harmful. With appropriate economic and investment policies, China would be well-positioned to increase its exports. Nonetheless, the material presented in this study provides a sound background to argue that to achieve satisfactory export performance by firms with foreign investment, not only are favourable investment incentives or export schemes needed, but also sound economic and foreign investment policies.

One of the major factors which is related to the general investment climate and determines the full benefits of FDI is the creation of a strong private sector to stimulate competition among local industries. Privatisation in both countries, especially in China, should be one of the major priorities of economic policy for restructuring the economy. To take full advantage of the benefits of FDI and direct it into the right sector a well-developed and efficient private sector is needed. So far the privatisation process in China is at a very early stage. Most of the medium-sized and large SOEs are still run by the state, putting strong pressures on budget deficits and creating big problems for the banks. Banks have to subsidise loss-making enterprises, putting pressure on the availability and cost of local credit. In turn, the shortage and high cost of local credit creates constraints on foreign firms in terms of the expansion of their operations and production costs. Strong government commitment to the development of a privatisation policy is needed. If the government wants to fulfil its high expectation of FDI, it must develop clear property-rights laws, trade and patent laws while privatising SOEs in order to lay down strong foundations for the private sector.

The importance of these policy options in creating an attractive business environment while achieving sustained and efficient economic development using FDI have been recognised by the Chinese and Polish governments. What is lacking is a vision by the governments of a well-structured, coordinated and unified development strategy in which all these aspects raised by the present study receive full attention.

SCOPE FOR FURTHER RESEARCH

As has been stated, this study does not discuss all aspects of the trends and determinants of FDI; it represents only the first in a series of proposed research projects designed to further study FDI. Four important aspects which call for future research attention are:

1. To extend this kind of analysis to other countries in transition to see if any different patterns or trends emerge, and if so to examine what are the main differences or similarities.
2. To expand the study into other sectors of industry which involve a strong concentration in capital–skilled or labour-intensive sectors'.
3. To broaden the coverage of the investigation to cover firms which invest less than $US1 million, with no time limit for selection so that the recent entry of new firms could be analysed.
4. To examine the low level of exports by foreign enterprises, especially in relation to the intensity of exports by wholly foreign-owned enterprises compared to their joint-venture counterparts.

Appendices

Chapter 3

A3.1

Table A3.1(a) *Poland: Output of major products*

	1990	1991	1992	1993	1994	1995
Coal (mn tonnes)	148	140	132	130	134	137
Brown coal (mn tonnes)	67.6	69.4	66.9	68.1	66.8	63.5
Coke of hard coal (mn tonnes)	13.7	11.4	11.1	10.3	11.5	11.6
Natural gas (bn m')	3 867	4 132	4 019	4 949	4 635	4 803
Electricity (bn Kwh)	136	135	133	134	135	139
Fuel oils ('000 tonnes)	2 883	2 655	2 578	2 728	2 746	2 776
Refined oil (mn tonnes)	12.9	11.7	12.6	13.4	13.4	13.4
Caustic soda ('000 tonnes)	404	324	326	296	297	327
Crude steel (mn tonnes)	13.6	10.4	9.9	9.9	11.1	11.9
Rolled steel (mn tonnes)	9.8	8.0	7.5	7.6	8.6	9.0
Electrolytic copper ('000 tonnes)	346	378	387	404	405	407
Aluminium ('000 tonnes)	46.0	45.8	43.6	46.9	49.5	55.7
Sulphur ('000 tonnes)	4 660	3 935	2 917	1 894	2 163	2 427
Phosphatic fertiliser ('000 tonnes)	467	253	329	282	415	523
Nitrogenous fertiliser ('000 tonnes)	1 303	1 148	1 167	1 224	1 386	1 619
Pesticides ('000 tonnes)	19.7	17.0	21.8	22.3	20.7	24.2
Synthetic fibres ('000 tonnes)	150	106	111	114	138	137
Synthetic rubber and latex ('000 tonnes)	103.1	79.5	88.9	75.1	83.4	104.7
Tyres ('000)	5 896	5 189	6 547	7 521	8 929	10 880
Plastics ('000 tonnes)	627	596	650	671	651	735
Paints ('000 tonnes)	202	191	209	216	233	248
Metal cuttings machines (tonnes)	27 033	15 539	8 685	7 003	6 171	7 421
Washing powders ('000 tonnes)	243	224	194	211	241	227
Agricultural tractors ('000)	35.4	17.5	8.0	11.5	15.3	21.5
Cars ('000)	266	167	219	334	338	366
Heavy vehicles ('000)	39.0	20.1	17.7	18.8	21.4	30.7
Buses (units)	3 856	1 938	1 273	1 000	1 048	1 419
Freight cars (units)	4 154	2 301	678	362	249	835
Bicycles ('000)	1 339	971	814	745	973	1 090
Shipping over 100 dwt ('000 dwt)	227	329	464	613	538	551

Table A3.1(a) *Contd.*

	1990	1991	1992	1993	1994	1995
Sewing machines ('000)	343	245	127	169	181	179
Refrigerators and freezers ('000)	604	553	500	588	605	585
Washing machines and dryers ('000)	482	336	363	402	449	419
Vacuum cleaners ('000)	913	857	961	1 001	1 143	1 156
Colour televisions ('000)	338	304	619	841	881	1 136
Radio sets ('000)	1 433	589	334	329	309	225
Taperecorders ('000)	299	108	58.9	22.2	14.3	12.1
Rechargeable cells ('000)	1 792	1 824	1 678	2 117	2 230	2 301
Light bulbs (mn)	213	209	201	216	246	277
Telephones ('000)	1 589	992	349	297	428	409
Cement (mn tonnes)	12.5	12.0	11.9	12.2	13.8	13.9
Paper ('000 tonnes)	924	949	1 031	1 070	1 199	1 335
Sawn wood (dam')	3 995	3 378	3 381	3 460	3 424	3 476
Fibre boards (mn m^2)	93	89	96	100	110	104
Cardboard ('000 tonnes)	141	111	116	114	127	142
Cotton fabric ('000 km)	428	286	239	229	256	205
Wollen fabric ('000 km)	64.7	44.3	32.9	31.8	33.4	32.6
Footwear (mn pairs)	105	71.1	58.6	50.7	56.3	62.8
Knitwear (mn)	183	114	83	85	111	127
Meat ('000 tonnes)	1 628	1 394	1 255	1 093	1 090	1 145
Cured meat products ('000 tonnes)	714	676	669	676	718	756
Sea fish ('000 tonnes)	430	410	448	360	414	–
Butter ('000 tonnes)	272	192	155	146	120	122
Milk (mn hl)	20.4	14.0	12.3	11.8	12.6	12.6
Cottage cheese ('000 tonnes)	186	164	165	168	186	197
Sugar ('000 tonnes)	1 971	1 636	1 468	1 982	1 383	1 595
Concentrated fruit juices ('000 tonnes)	80	69	105	144	113	85
Edible plant fats ('000 tonnes)	279	289	355	423	468	550
Spirits ('000 hl)	1 510	1 457	1 357	1 495	1 566	1 539
Cigarettes (bn)	91.5	90.4	86.6	90.7	98.4	100.6

Source: Centre for Eastern Europe, *Poland – Economic Surveys*, OECD, Paris, 1997, p. 172.

A3.2

Table A3.1(b) *Poland: State budget (millions of zlotys)*

		1992	1993	1994	1995	1996
Revenue		**31 277.6**	**45 901.0**	**63 125.3**	**83 721.7**	**100 171.2**
1.	Tax revenue	24 615.6	36 962.3	51 568.5	68 975.2	84 596.9
1.1	Indirect taxes	10 309.9	17 749.5	26 884.2	36 314.7	46 690.6
	Turnover tax	10 309.9	9 409.5	129.5	41.7	0.0
	Value added tax	–	5 129.1	15 013.9	20 673.4	25 698.6
	Excise tax	–	3 120.3	9 001.7	12 139.9	18 087.0
	Import surcharge	–	–	2 577.8	3 266.1	2 580.0
	Poll tax	–	90.6	161.3	192.1	325.0
	Tax on sale of securities	–	–	–	1.5	0.0
1.2	Income tax of legal entities	5 062.1	6 257.2	6 827.7	8 837.1	9 960.0
	Enterprises	3 967.3	4 837.2	5 681.8	7 911.0	8 500.0
	Financial institutions	1 094.8	1 420.0	1 145.9	926.1	1 460.0
1.3	Personal income tax	7 226.1	11 942.4	17 375.6	23 511.8	27 866.3
1.4	Tax on wage increases	1 698.8	998.7	469.3	166.9	0.0
1.5	Abolished taxes	318.7	14.5	11.7	144.7	80.0
2.	Non-tax revenue	6 161.6	8 152.5	9 937.3	12 064.8	12 979.3
2.1	Dividends	848.2	691.4	599.5	805.8	1 461.0
	Enterprises	823.2	495.2	492.6	610.3	1 311.0
	Financial institutions	25.0	196.2	106.9	195.5	150.0
2.2	Transfers from the central bank	1 211.3	1 418.2	2 355.1	2 980.0	1 850.0
2.3	Custom duties	2 677.4	4 383.2	4 888.8	5 774.5	6 460.0
2.4	Revenue of budgetary units	1 139.4	1 308.2	1 535.9	1 970.0	2 613.0
2.5	Other non-tax revenue	285.3	351.5	383.8	510.0	530.0
2.6	Foreign grants	–	–	143.5	0.0	0.0
2.7	Import levies	–	–	30.7	24.4	0.0
2.8	Revenues from local governments	–	–	–	–	65.3
3.	Privatisation receipts	484.4	780.4	1 594.9	2 641.6	2 565.0
3.1	Enterprises	480.5	726.4	1 169.7	2 120.3	2 165.0
3.2	Banks	3.9	54.0	425.2	521.3	400.0
4.	Foreign revenue	16.0	5.8	24.6	40.1	30.0
Expenditure		**38 189.1**	**50 242.8**	**68 865.0**	**91 169.6**	**109 671.2**
1.	Subsidies	1 984.0	1 956.5	2 458.5	2 994.2	3 134.5
2.	Foreign debt service	1 176.4	1 211.1	1 832.1	3 262.6	4 725.0
3.	Domestic debt service	2 438.3	4 749.9	7 400.9	11 097.1	13 214.0
4.	Social insurance	7 345.3	10 420.7	14 273.4	15 309.7	17 303.6
5.	Current expenditures	20 758.6	26 911.7	36 993.3	51 522.3	55 487.2
6.	Settlements with banks	1 778.4	1 411.0	2 225.6	2 112.5	2 604.3
7.	Capital expenditure	1 950.2	2 477.7	3 129.5	4 127.0	5 371.4
8.	Subsidies to local authorities	757.9	1 104.2	551.7	744.2	7 725.3
9.	Reserve of the Council of Ministers	–	–	–	–	105.9
Balance		**−6 911.5**	**−4 341.8**	**−5 739.7**	**−7 448.0**	**−9 500.0**

Table A3.1(b) *Contd.*

	1992	1993	1994	1995	1996
Financing					
1. Domestic	7 194.4	4 928.4	6 979.4	6 512.8	11 493.8
1.1 Banking	6 618.8	3 753.9	4 926.0	1 250.5	7 981.9
1.2 Non-banking	575.6	1 174.5	2 053.4	5 262.3	3 511.9
2. Foreign financing	−282.9	−586.6	−1 239.7	928.5	−1 993.8
Memorandum item: GDP	114 944.2	155 780.0	210 407.3	286 025.6	344 600.0

Source: As for Table A3.1.

Chapter 4

A4.1   Specific Policies towards FDI in China, 1979–95

General Measures

01.06.79   The Law of the People's Republic of China on Joint Ventures using Chinese and Foreign Investment.

30.01.82   Regulations of the People's Republic of China on the Exploitation of Offshore Petroleum Resources in Cooperation with Foreign Enterprises.

20.09.83   Regulations for the Implementation of the Law of the People's Republic of China on Joint Ventures using Chinese and Foreign Investment.

01.07.85   Foreign Economic Contract Law.

30.09.85   Provisional Regulations concerning Preferential Treatment for Port and Wharf Construction Projects Financed with Sino–Foreign Joint Equity.

26.01.86   Provisional Regulations for the Control of Financial Trust and Investment Institutions.

11.10.86   Provisions of the State Council of the People's Republic of China for the Encouragement of Foreign Investment.

12.04.86   Law of the People's Republic of China on Wholly-Foreign-Owned Enterprises.

01.07.86   Provisional Regulations on Chinese-Foreign Cooperative Designing of Engineering Projects.

17.12.87   Notice of the Ministry of Foreign Economic Relations and Trade on the Relevant Legal Problems in the Case of Establishing Chinese–Foreign Equity Joint Ventures

13.04.88   Law of the People's Republic of China on Sino–Foreign Cooperative Enterprises.

3.7.88   State Council Provisions for Encouraging Investment by Taiwan's Compatriots.

4.4.90   National People's Congress, Decision to Revise the 'People's Republic of China, Sino – Foreign Equity Joint Venture Law'.

Taxation Measures

14.12.80 Detailed Rules and Regulations for the Implementation of the Income Tax Law of the People's Republic of China Concerning Joint Ventures with Chinese Foreign Investment.

09.12.80 Stipulation Concerning the Levy of Individual Income Tax on Chinese Personnel who Work for Joint Venture Enterprises.

10.09.80 The Income Tax Law of the People's Republic of China Concerning Joint Ventures with Chinese and Foreign Investment.

10.09.80 Announcement of the State Council on Taxation of Joint Ventures and Cooperative Operations with Chinese–Foreign Investment.

10.09.80 Individual Income Tax Law of the People's Republic of China.

13.12.81 The Income Tax Law of the People's Republic of China concerning Foreign Enterprises.

08.06.81 Circular of the Ministry of Finance Concerning some Questions about the Income Tax of Joint Ventures Comprising Chinese and Foreign Investment.

08.06.81 Explanation Concerning the Levy of Profit Tax Remitted from China.

08.06.81 Stipulation Concerning Tax Exemption for Remitting from China the Tax Refund of Profit Reinvestment.

08.06.81 Stipulation Concerning the Tax Reduction and Exemption Period for Newly-Established Joint Business Enterprises.

01.01.82 Income Tax Law of the People's Republic of China Concerning Foreign Enterprises.

21.02.82 Rules for the Implementation of the Income Tax Law of the People's Republic of China Concerning Joint Ventures with Chinese and Foreign Investment.

17.03.82 Issues Concerning the Computation of Tax Payment in Renminbi Converted from Income in Foreign Currency.

15.04.82 Provisional Regulations of the General Taxation Bureau/Ministry of Finance of the People's Republic of China Concerning Tax Registration by Foreign Enterprises for the Commencement and Termination of Operations.

08.04.82 Decision Regarding Tax Cuts for Joint Ventures.

21.09.82 Announcement of the State Council on the Taxation of Joint Ventures and Cooperative Operations with Chinese–Foreign Investment.

01.01.83 Interim Provisions of the Ministry of Finance of the People's Republic of China Regarding the Reduction of, or Exemption from, Income Tax on Royalties for the Use of Proprietary Technology.

01.01.83 Interim Provisions of the Ministry of Finance of the People's Republic of China Concerning the Reduction of, or Exemption from, Income Tax to Interest Derived from China by Foreign Businesses.

05.06.83 Provisional Regulations of the Ministry of Finance Concerning the Imposition of the Consolidated Industrial and Commercial Tax and the Enterprise Income Tax on Foreign Commercial Contract Operations and the Provision of Labour Services.

02.09.83   Decision of the Standing Committee of the National People's Congress Concerning Amendment of the Income Tax Law of the People's Republic of China, Concerning Chinese–Foreign Joint Ventures.

01.12.84   Interim Provisions of the State Council of the People's Republic of China Concerning the Reduction of, and Exemption from, Enterprise Income Tax and Consolidated Industrial and Commercial Tax in the Special Economic Zones and 14 Coastal Port Cities.

21.04.86   Notice of the General Taxation Bureau/Ministry of Finance Concerning several Regulations Relating to the Levying of Income tax on Sino–Foreign Joint and Wholly-Foreign Owned Enterprises.

30.08.86   Notice on the Question of Income and Payment of Income Tax by Sino–Foreign Joint Equity Ventures, Contractual Joint Ventures, Cooperative Production Enterprises and Enterprises with only Foreign Investment.

30.01.87   Measures of the Ministry of Finance of the People's Republic of China Regarding the Implementation of Preferential Tax Treatment in Provisions of the State Council of the People's Republic of China for the Encouragement of Foreign Investment.

31.01.87   Implementation Measures of the Ministry of Finance for Putting into Effect the Preferential Terms on Taxation Provided in Provisions of the State Council on the Encouragement of Foreign Investment.

02.02.87   Ministry of Finance, General Administration of Taxation, Several Policy and Professional Questions Concerning the Levying of Income Tax From Enterprises with Foreign Investment.

08.08.87   Provisional Regulations of the State Council Concerning the Reduction of Individual Income Tax on Wages and Salaries of Foreign Nationals Working in China.

01.10.88   People's Republic of China, Stamp Duty Provisional Regulations Implementation Rules.

05.12.88   People's Republic of China, Enterprise with Foreign Investment Income Tax Laws (Draft).

15.06.88   Provisional Regulations of the Ministry of Finance of the People's Republic of China Concerning the Reduction of, and Exemption from, Enterprise Income Tax and Consolidated Industrial and Commercial Tax for the Encouragement of Foreign Investment in Coastal Open Economic Zones.

15.06.88   Measures of the Ministry of Finance of the People's Republic of China, Concerning the Reduction of, and Exemption from, Enterprise Tax and Consolidated Industrial and Commercial Tax for the Encouragement of Foreign Investment in Coastal Open Economic Zones, Tentative Provisions.

18.11.89   Levying and Exempting Stamp Duty on Enterprises with Foreign Investment and on Foreign Companies, Enterprises and Other Economic Organisations and their Business Establishments and Premises, Circular.

Credit Measures

30.08.80 Regulations for Providing Short-Term Loans in Foreign Currency by the Bank of China.

13.03.81 Provisional Regulations for Providing Loans to Joint Ventures of Chinese and Foreign Ownership by the Bank of China.

26.11.86 People's Bank of China, Tentative Procedure for Enterprises with Foreign Investment Pledging Foreign Exchange for Renminbi Loans.

12.12.86 The People's Bank of China, Provisional Measures of the People's Republic of China on Foreign-Exchange-Mortgaged Renminbi Loans for Foreign Investment Enterprises.

05.01.87 The People's Bank of China, Measures of the People's Republic of China on Foreign-Exchange-Mortgaged Renminbi Loans.

20.02.87 Provisional Measures for the Control of the Issue of Foreign Exchange Guarantees by Organisations within Chinese Territory.

24.04.87 Regulations of the Bank of China on Providing Loans to Joint Ventures Using Chinese and Foreign Investment.

24.04.87 Measures of the Bank of China on Loans for Foreign Investment Enterprises.

23.03.88 China's Construction Bank, Provisional Measures of Short-term Foreign Exchange Loans (Trial).

23.03.88 China's Construction Bank, Provisional Measures of Foreign Exchange Savings (Trial).

11.04.88 China's Industrial and Commercial Bank, Provisional Measures of Foreign Exchange Loans.

Foreign Exchange Measures

01.03.80 Provisional Regulations on Foreign Exchange Control of the People's Republic of China.

19.03.80 Provisional Regulations of the Bank of China on the Control of Foreign Exchange Certificates.

31.12.81 Rules for the Implementation of the Examination and Approval of Applications by Individuals for Foreign Exchange.

01.03.81 Provisional Regulations for Foreign Exchange Control of the People's Republic of China.

10.08.81 Rules for the Implementation of Foreign Exchange Control Relating to Foreign Institutions in China and their personnel.

10.08.81 Rules Governing the Carrying of Foreign Exchange, Precious Metals and Payment Instruments in Convertible Currency Into or Out of China.

01.01.82 Detailed Rules Concerning Foreign Exchange Control Relating to Individuals.

01.01.82 Detailed Rules for Approval of Applications by Individuals for Possessing Foreign Exchange.

01.01.83 Regulations of the Bank of China on Foreign Currency Deposits.

01.01.83 Regulations on Special Foreign Renminbi Deposits.

24.02.83 Administrative Regulations Governing the Use of Foreign Currency by Foreign Investment Enterprises when Computing Prices and Settling Accounts within China.

24.02.83 Regulations for the Use of Currency in Contributing Tax to the State and in the Settlement of Accounts with Enterprises or Individuals Residing in China by Joint Ventures with Chinese and Foreign Investment.

01.08.83 Rules for the Implementation of Exchange Control Regulations Relating to Enterprises with Overseas Chinese Capital, Enterprises with Foreign Capital and Chinese and Foreign Joint Ventures.

01.11.84 Interim Procedures Concerning the Trial Implementation of Foreign Exchange and Renminbi Comprehensive Compensation.

25.03.85 Detailed Rules and Regulations for the Implementation of Penalties for Violation of Exchange Control Regulations.

15.01.86 Regulations of the State Council Concerning the Balance of Foreign Exchange Revenue and Expenditure by Joint Equity Ventures.

01.02.86 Regulations on Joint Ventures' Balance of Foreign Exchange Revenue and Expenditure.

20.01.87 Measures of the Ministry of Foreign Economic Relations and Trade on the Purchase of Domestic Products for Export by Enterprises with Foreign Investment to Balance Foreign Exchange Revenue and Expenditure.

01.10.87 Foreign Exchange Control Measures for Non-Banking Financial Institutions.

17.07.87 Provisional Regulations on the Monitoring of External Debt.

05.03.88 Administrative Regulations on Spot and Forward Foreign Exchange Transactions by Financial Institutions on Behalf of Clients.

Trade Measures

01.04.82 Provisions of the Customs Administration and the Ministry of Finance of the People's Republic of China Concerning the Levying of, and Exemption from, Customs Duties and the Levying of a Consolidated Industrial and Commercial Tax on Imports and Exports of Goods by Joint Chinese – Foreign Ventures (Cooperative Exploitation of Off-shore Petroleum) for Exploiting Off-shore Petroleum.

10.01.84 Interim Regulations of People's Republic of China Concerning the System of Licensing Import Goods.

01.02.84 Provisions of the General Administration of Customs, the Ministry of Finance and the Ministry of Foreign Economic Relations and Trade Concerning the Supervision of, and the Imposition of, or Exemption from, Tax on Imports and Exports by Chinese–Foreign Cooperative Enterprises.

01.02.84 Regulations on the Generalised System of Preference Certificates for Export Products of Businesses which Undertake Processing and Assembling for Foreigners, and of Compensation Trade, Sino–Foreign Joint Equity and Cooperative Joint Ventures and Enterprises with Only Foreign Equity (for Trial Implementation).

01.05.84 Provisions of the General Administration of Customs, the Ministry of Finance and the Ministry of Foreign Economic Relations and Trade Concerning the Supervision of, the Imposition of, or Exemption from Tax on Imports and Exports by Chinese–Foreign Joint Ventures.

01.05.84 Provisions of the General Administration of Customs of the People's Republic of China for the Administration of the Import and Export of Articles by the Resident Offices and Resident Personnel of Foreign Enterprises, News Agencies and Other Entities.

15.05.84 Rules for the Implementation of Interim Regulations of the People's Republic of China Concerning the System of Licensing Import Goods.

01.06.84 Rules for the Implementation of Interim Regulations of the People's Republic of China on the Inspection of Import and Export Commodities.

10.03.85 Regulations of the People's Republic of China on Import and Export Duty and Procedures.

24.11.86 Measures of the Customs of the People's Republic of China for the Control of the Import of Materials and Parts Required by Foreign Investment Enterprises for the Fulfilment of Export Contracts.

01.12.86 Procedures of the Customs of the People's Republic of China for the Administration of Materials and Parts that Enterprises with Foreign Investment Need to Import in Order to Fulfil Product Export Contracts.

01.12.86 People's Republic of China Customs, Administration of Imported Materials and Components Required by Enterprises with Foreign Investment in Order to Fulfil Product Export Contracts, Procedures.

12.09.87 People's Republic of China, Import and Export Duty Regulations.

20.01.87 Implementing Measures of the Ministry of Foreign Economic Relations and Trade on Confirmation and Examination of Products Exporting Enterprises and Technologically Advanced Enterprises with Foreign Investment.

22.01.87 People's Republic of China, Customs Law.

24.01.87 Implementing Measures of the Ministry of Foreign Economic Relations and Trade on Applications of Foreign Investment Enterprises for Import and Export Licences.

24.01.87 Implementing Measures of the Ministry of Foreign Economic Relations and Trade on Enterprises With Foreign Investment Applying for Import and Export Licences.

19.10.87 Measures Relating to Import Substitution by Products Manufactured by Chinese–Foreign Equity Joint Ventures and Contractual Joint Ventures.

31.10.87 Procedures for the Control Over Import Substitution of Mechanical and Electrical Products Manufactured by Chinese–Foreign Equity Joint Ventures and Contractual Joint Ventures.

31.10.87 Measures on the Control of Import Substitute Mechanical and Electrical Products by Chinese–Foreign Equity Joint Ventures and Contractual Joint Ventures.

01.05.88 Administration of Bonded Factories Engaged in the Processing Trade Procedure.

01.05.88 Administration of Bonded Warehouse and Stored Goods Procedures.

15.05.88 Administrative Regulations of the Customs Law of the People's Republic of China on the Import and Export of Goods into and out of Economic and Technological Development Zones.

01.07.88 Administration of Imported Materials for Processing and Exported Goods Procedures.

01.04.89 Administrative Regulations of the Customs Law of the People's Republic of China on the Import and Export of Goods into and out of Coastal Open Zones.

Labour Measures

19.01.84 Provisions for the Implementation of Regulations on Labour Management in Joint Ventures using Chinese and Foreign Investment.

11.08.87 Provisional Regulations on the Provision of Political Ideological Education for Employees in Joint Equity and Sino–Foreign Cooperative Enterprises.

26.06.80 Regulations of the People's Republic of China on Labour Management in Joint Ventures using Chinese and Foreign Investment.

28.11.86 Regulations on the Autonomous Right of Enterprises with Foreign Investment to Employ Personnel, the Wages and Salaries, and the Expenses for Insurance and Welfare Benefits for Staff Members and Workers.

21.12.87 Notice of the State Council Concerning the Amendment of Paragraph 3 of Article 86 of Regulations for the Implementation of the Law of the People's Republic of China on Joint ventures using Chinese and Foreign Investment.

18.05.88 Opinion of Ministry of Labour and Personnel on Further Implementation of Employment Matters Concerning Enterprises with Foreign Investment.

Administration

01.03.82 Provisional Regulations of the General Administration of Industry and Commerce of the People's Republic of China on the Payment of Registration Fees by Joint Ventures using Chinese and Foreign Investment.

15.03.83 Procedures for the Registration and Administration of Resident Offices of Foreign Enterprises in China.

04.03.85 The Accounting Regulations of the People's Republic of China for Joint Ventures using Chinese and Foreign Investment.

20.01.87 Supplementary Regulations Concerning the Regulations on the Financial Control of Chinese–Foreign Equity Joint Ventures.

17.12.87 Notice of the MOFERT on the Relevant Legal Problems in the Case of Establishing Chinese–Foreign Equity Joint Ventures.

01.03.87 Provisional Regulations for the Proportion of Registered Capital to Total Amount of Investment of Chinese–Foreign Equity Joint Ventures.
01.03.88 Regulations on Investment Contributed by Each Party to a Chinese–Foreign Equity Joint Venture.
12.08.88 Delegation of Authority for the Approval of Wholly-Foreign-Owned Enterprises to Local Governments of Provinces, Autonomous Regions, Centrally Governed Municipalities, Special Economic Zones and Municipalities with Independent Development Plans, Circular.
01.07.89 Provisional Regulations on Control of Foreign Associations of Commerce.

Other Measures

26.6.80 Regulations of the People's Republic of China on the Registration of Joint Ventures using Chinese and Foreign Investment.
01.06.81 Additional Regulations Concerning the Registration of Resident Offices of Foreign Enterprises.
02.06.82 Provisional Advertising Control Regulations.
01.07.82 Economic Contract Law of the People's Republic of China.
01.02.83 Provisional Regulations for the Establishment of Representative Offices in China by Overseas Chinese and Foreign Financial Institutions.
01.02.83 Procedures of the People's Bank of China for Controls Relating to Establishing Representative Offices in China by Overseas Chinese and Foreign Banking Institutions.
01.03.83 Trademark Law of the People's Republic of China.
01.03.83 Detailed Implementation Rules for the Trademark Law.
30.10.89 Interim Regulations of the People's Republic of China Concerning the Control of Resident Offices of Foreign Enterprises.
01.04.85 The Patent Law of the People's Republic of China.

Special Economic Zones

26.06.80 Regulations of the People's Republic of China on the Special Economic Zones in Guandong Province.
24.12.81 Provisional Regulations on Registration of Enterprises in Special Economic Zones of Guandong Province.
24.12.82 Provisional Provisions on Land Management in Shengzhen Special Economic Zone.
24.12.82 Provisional Entry/Exit Rules for Special Economic Zones in Guandong Province.
24.12.82 Provisional Provisions on Wages in the Enterprises in Special Economic Zones in Guandong Province.
01.08.82 Interim Provisions of the Special Economic Zones in Guandong Province for the Control of Personnel Entering and Leaving China.
05.05.87 Measures of the Shengzhen Municipal People's Government to Implement the Policy of Preferential Taxation Treatment in the

Provisions of the State Council on the Encouragement of Foreign Investment.

18.5.87   Implementation Procedures for Examination and Confirmation of Exporting Enterprises and Technologically Advanced Enterprises with Foreign Investment in the Shengzhen Special Economic Zone.

01.08.87 Provisional Regulations of the Shengzhen Special Economic Zone on Labour Management for Enterprises with Foreign Investment.

03.09.87 Provisional Regulations of Shengzhen Special Economic Zone on Further Promoting its Economic Association with Inland Areas of the Country.

03.01.88 Regulations of Shengzhen Special Economic Zone for Land Management.

A4.2   Taxation in China

An initial tax holiday together with a low ongoing tax rate are typical tax incentives; but in practice, foreign-funded firms pay higher taxes than local enterprises. Before 1981, the enterprise income tax rate on equity joint venture and contractual venture income was 20 per cent. A local income tax of 10 per cent of the assessed income was levied on the renminbi currency earnings. A withholding tax of 10 per cent was levied on remitted profits. From late 1981, the enterprise income tax on contractual joint ventures, foreign wholly-owned enterprises and cooperative developments was set at a rate increasing with taxable income (Table A4.2(a)).

Before 1988, staff and workers of a joint venture were required to pay individual income tax in accordance with the Individual Income Tax Law of the PRC. Chinese nationals and foreigners received the same treatment – Table A4.2.(b). On 8 August, however, the personal income tax liability of foreign investors in China was reduced by one-half in accordance with the Individual Income Tax Law 1980.

Foreign investors who reinvest their profits for a period of not less than five years are refunded the total amount of enterprise income tax already paid on the reinvested portion. A joint venture in China that reinvests its share of

Table A4.2(a)   *Foreign enterprise income tax*

Range of annual income (RMB, million)	(%)
Up to 250 000	30
250 000 to 500 000	32.5
500 001 to 750 0000	35
750 001 to 1 million	37.5
over 1 million	40

Sources: MOFERT, *Economic Report*, Beijing, Jan. 1982; Wei Jia, *Chinese Foreign Investment Law and Policies*, 1994.

Table A4.2(b) *Individual income tax rates (renminbi yuan)*

Total monthly income	Percentage
800 or less	exempt
801–1500	5
1501–3000	10
3001–6000	20
6001–9000	30
9001–12 000	40
Over 12 000	45

Source: Chinese government, *Rules for the Implementation of the Individual Tax Law of PRC*, Beijing, 14/12/80.

profits for not less than five years is refunded 40 per cent of the income tax already paid on the reinvested portion. Between 1986 and 1988, enterprises which exported more than 70 per cent of their output (reduced to 50 per cent after 1988 in some coastal areas) could obtain a two-year tax exemption and a concessional income tax rate of 15 per cent after the first two years of no tax payment. After the expiration of the concessional period of enterprise income tax, export enterprises were to pay 50 per cent of enterprise income tax for an indefinite period. The full rate of enterprise income tax is only 10–15 per cent in special economic zones, in economic and technology development zones and most coastal open economic zones – Table A4.2.(c).

Table A4.2(c) *Tax rates in special economic zones, economic and technology development zones and coastal open economic zones, 1979–89*

Tax payer	Any foreign enterprise
Enterprise income tax	15 per cent
Export enterprise income tax	10 per cent
Local tax	May be exempted or reduced
Withholding tax	None
Depreciation	From 5 to 20 years with 10 per cent scrap value
Tax holidays	First 2 years
and tax reduction	50 per cent for next 3 years
Loss carryover	5 years
Tax rebate (reinvested profit)	40 per cent of taxes paid refunded (less than 5 years); 100 per cent of taxes paid refunded (equal to or more than 5 years)

Source: Based on China's laws and regulations since 1979, see Appendix A4.1.

Table A4.2(d) *Major tax incentives for foreign-invested enterprises in China's special investment zones*

	Nationwide	Special Economic Zones (SEZs) (5 areas)	Economic and Technological Development Zones (ETDZs) (30 areas)	Pudong New Development Area of Shanghai
'Manufacturing' Enterprise' Income Tax Rates	30%	15%	15%	15%
Except for those in the petroleum, natural gas & rare metals sectors, manufacturing enterprises with terms of at least 10 years qualify for tax exemptions for the first 2 profit-making years, followed by a 50% reduction for the next 5 years	Same	Same as nationwide. Infrastructure and agricultural FIEs with 15-year terms in Hainan receive additional benefits	Same as nationwide	Same, but enterprises with 15-year terms engaged in energy or transportation construction are exempt each profit-making year for 5 years and receive a 50% reduction for the next 5 years
Non-manufacturing 'Service Industry' Enterprise Tax Rates	30%	15%	15%	15%
Service industry enterprises investing over $5 million with terms of at least 10 years qualify for tax exemption for the first profit-making year, followed by a 50% reduction for the next 2 years	No nationwide exemptions	Tax exemption the first profit-making year, followed by a 50% reduction for the next 2 years (7.5% tax rate). Additional incentives also may be provided	Tax exemption the first profit-making year, followed by a 50% reduction for the next 2 years (7.5% tax rate)	Same as ETDZs
Foreign Joint-Venture Banks or Branches (investing of least $10 million for at least 10 years)	30%	15%, but tax exemption for the first profit-making year, followed by 50% reduction for the next 2 years	30% for bank representative offices; 15% for bank branches approved by the State Council	15%
Income Tax Rates for Enterprises Certified as Export-Oriented or Technologically Advanced	15% in any year they export more than 70% of their output	10% upon the expiry of income tax exemptions if an export-oriented	Same as ETDZs	Same as ETDZs

Table A4.2(d) *Contd.*

	Nationwide	Special Economic Zones (SEZs) (5 areas)	Economic and Technological Development Zones (ETDZs) (30 areas)	Pudong New Development Area of Shanghai
		enterprise; technologically advanced FIEs qualify for 50% reduction for 3 years after expiry of exemption (7.5% rate)		
Income Tax Refunds For FIEs with Reinvested Profits	40% tax refund paid on profits reinvested or used to establish other enter-prises for at least 5 years	Same	Same	Same
Local Income Tax Rates	generally 3% (10% of national tax rate), but often waived by the locality	0%, but subject to locality	0%, but subject to locality	0%, but subject to locality
Withholding Tax Rates On dividends, interest, and other non-earned income; on repatriation of profits	10% for US companies; 10%	10% exempt	Same as SEZs	Same as SEZs

Sources: MOFERT, *Tax Incentives*, Beijing, 1995; US–China Business Council, *Investment in China*, Washington DC, 1995.

These provisions were extended by the State Council in the Act on the Reduction of, and Exemption from, Enterprise Income Tax and Consolidated Industrial and Commercial Tax in Special Economic Zones and 14 Coastal Cities in 1987. To facilitate the expansion of economic and technological exchange in coastal open economic zones (Liaodong Peninsula, the Shandong Peninsula, the Changjiang and Pearl River Deltas and the Southern Fujian, Xiamen and Quanzhou Delta Area), similar concessions were extended to the

Table A4.2(e) *Capital depreciation rates of enterprises with foreign participation, 1982–90*

Types of fixed assets	Rate of depreciation (per cent per year)	Service life
House and buildings	0.05	20 years
Railways rolling stock. machinery and other equipment	0.10	10 years
Electronic equipment, means of transport other than railing stock and boats and ships	0.20	5 years

Source: State Statistical Bureau, *Tax Incentives*, Ministry of Foreign Economic Relation and Trade (MOFERT), Beijing, 21 February 1982.

coastal open economic zones in 1988. Consolidated industrial and commercial tax, as on products produced and sold within special economic zones, are levied at half the tax rate.

Depreciation was not considered in the regulations until 1982. In the depreciation of fixed assets, a 'scrap value' (communist concept – no accounting equivalent) was first estimated and then deducted from the original cost; scrap value was in principle 10 per cent of the original cost. A very considerable body of research had concluded that tax concessions were not effective in attracting foreign investment. Survey studies of foreign investors' motives usually rate tax incentives as less important than key non-tax factors governing pre-tax rates of return (Caves, 1982). Studies suggest that, at best, they are of modest importance in influencing investment decisions in comparison to market considerations (Lim, 1983). For example, for US firms these tax incentives in the form of exemptions, reductions or refunds have no effect whatsoever upon their investment decision (Wei Jia, 1994).

A4.3 Differences between Legal Firms in Poland

Table A4.3(a) *Poland: basic differences between limited liability (Sp.z. o.o.) and joint-stock (S.A.) companies*

	Sp.z.o.o.	S.A.
No. of founders Polish and foreign	At least 1 person	At least 3 persons
Minimum initial capital	4000 Zl	100 000 Zl
Capital to be paid in prior to registration	100%	25%
Capitalisation of pre-operational period costs	Not allowed	Max. 5-years write off
Increase of capital requires	66.7% votes	75% votes
General Assembly approval minimum no. of members of		

Table A4.3(a) *Contd.*

	Sp.z.o.o.	*S.A.*
board	1	1
Supervisory board and/or auditing comittee	Either or both may exist, minimum 3 members	At least one must exist, minimum 5 members
Obligatory reserve out of after-tax earnings	No	8%
Obligatory audit	Yes if: paying a dividend abroad; or certain size criteria are met	Always
General assembly convenes if company bears loss	If loss exceeds reserve capital and 50% of share capital	If loss exceeds reserve and 33.3% of share capital
Earliest time after liquidation announced for distribution of assets	6 months	12 months
Notarial reports of General Assembly required	If company articles are altered	Always

Source: PAIZ, *Foreign Investment Guide to Poland*, PAIZ, Warsaw, May 1996, p. 57

A4.4 Taxation in Poland

The main taxes of Poland are:

- Personal income tax: effective January 1992, and levied on all personal incomes (except some agricultural income). Withheld at the source for wage income at a rate of 21 per cent (for incomes over Zl12 120 Zl), 33 per cent (for incomes over Zl90,800.Zl), 45 per cent (for incomes over Zl 181 600 Zl). Tax rates were raised in 1994 from 20, 30 and 40 per cent. Some deductions are allowed, and joint returns are possible.
- Corporate income tax: effective January 1990, levied on all legal entities (whether state-owned, cooperative or private). Rate 40 per cent which is one of the highest corporate profit tax rates in Europe, having negative implications for the Polish economy and foreign investors. According to The New Economic Strategy 'Poland 2000', corporate tax should slowly be reduced and modified.
- Value added tax (VAT): introduced 5 July 1993 to replace turnover tax. Rates 22 per cent (general rate), 7 per cent (energy products, construction, some consumption goods), 0 per cent (exports and associated services). Further changes are expected in the sales of goods and services which

attract 0 per cent tax: these are pharmaceuticals, books and press, means of production for agriculture, farm tractors, farm machinery and facilities, fertilisers, feeds and pesticides.

- Small taxpayer turnover presumption: presumptive tax assessed as a proportion of sales if the previous year's turnover is less than Zl1.2 billion (2.5 per cent for trade, 7.5 per cent for services and 0.5 per cent for production).
- Excises: introduced with the VAT and applicable to several luxury goods and to petroleum products.
- Customs duties: the tariff code ranges from 0 to 40 per cent and there are exemptions and tariff quotes. Import tax was reduced from 6 per cent in 1992 to 3 per cent in 1996, and will be abolished from 1997. The tariff on industrial goods should be gradually reduced starting from 1 January 1995, annually by 20 per cent and totally abolished by 1 January 1999, except on the import of cars where tariffs will be abolished by the year 2000.
- State enterprise-based taxes and duties: dividend tax compulsory from state enterprises based on the re-evaluated value of 'founding organ' contribution to enterprise capital. Rates vary by class and age of assets. Tax on excessive wage increase (*popiwek*) abolished by 1 April 1994.
- Main local tax: real estate tax, levied on urban and rural property at a rate established yearly by the Ministry of Finance (but does not exceed 0.1 per cent for housing and 2 per cent for commercial buildings) on assessed value.

A4.5 Tax Agreements with Poland

Table A4.5(a) *Poland: country withholding tax rates for double tax treaty relief*

	Dividends		Interest		
	Preferential	*Normal*	*Licence Fees*	*Copyright*	*Other*
Austria		10	0	10	10
Australia		15	10	10	10
Belarus	30/10	15	10	10	10
Belgium		10	10	10	10
Bulgaria		10	10	5	5
Canada		15	15	0	10
China		10	10	10	7
Cyprus		10	10	5	5
Czech Rep.	20/5	10	10	5	5
Denmark	25/5	15	0	10	10
Estonia	25/5	15	10	10	10
Finland	25/5	15	0	20	10
France	10/5	15	0	0	10
Germany	25/5	15	0	0	0
Greece		20	10	10	10
India		15	15	22.5	22.5
Indonesia	20/10	15	10	15	15

Table A4.5(a) *Contd.*

	Dividentds		Interest	
	Preferential	*Normal*	*Licence Fees*	*Copyright*	*Other*
Italy		10	10	10	10
Israel	15/5	10	5	10	10/5
Japan		10	10	0	10
Korea	10/5	10	10	10	10
Latvia	25/5	15	10	10	10
Lithuania	25/5	15	10	10	10
Malaysia		0	15	15	15
Malta	20/5	15	10	10	10
Morocco	25/7	15	10	10	10
Netherlands	25/0	15	0	0	10
Norway	25/5	15	0	0	10
Pakistan	33/15	20	20	20	20
Romania	25/5	15	10	10	10
Russia		0	0	0	0
Singapore		10	10	10	10
Slovak Republic	20/5	15	10	5	5
South Korea	10/5	10	10	10	10
Spain	25/0	15	0	0	10
Sri Lanka		15	10	0	10
Switzerland	25/5	15	10	10	10
Sweden	25/5	15	0	10	10
Thailand	25/20		10	5	15
Tunisia	5	10	12	12	12
Turkey	25/10	15	10	10	10
Ukraine	25/5	15	10	10	10
United Arab Emirates		5	5	5	5
UK	10/5	15	0	10	10
US	10/5	15	0	10	10
Uruguay		15	15	15	15/10
Vietnam	25/10	10	10	10	10
Yugoslavia	25/5	15	10	10	10
Zimbabwe		10	10	10	10

Source: PAIZ, *Foreign Investment Guide to Poland*, PAIZ, Warsaw, 1996, p. 57.

A4.6 Methods of Privatisation in Poland

Table A4.6(a) *Poland: the six steps of privatisation through liquidation ('Recasting')*

Step 1   *Initiation*
Enterprises or Founding Body decides to initiate the process, often with a consulting firm.

Step 2   *SOE Decision*
Workers' council presents opinion on whether to privatise. SOE chooses its preferred method (i.e. buy-out, assets sale, contribution into company). Business plan is drafted and Ministry of Privatisation questionnaire regarding financial and legal data is completed. Documents are given to Founding Body (local government or branch ministry).

Step 3   *Founding Body's Decision*
Founding Body appoints Preparatory Team to examine documents and renders an opinion on the application. If not satisfied with valuation, can hire a different consulting firm.
Preparatory Team discusses its opinion with SOE. Can choose a privatisation method other than that preferred by SOE.
Founding Body examines results of documentation submitted by Preparatory Team and renders an opinion and drafts a decree on privatisation of SOE.
Documentation and decree is submitted to Ministry of Privatisation.

Step 4   *Ministerial Decision*
Ministry of Privatisation reviews documents and evaluates the financial and legal status; approves or disapproves of privatisation plan.

Step 5   *Implementation*
Founding Body administers liquidation process, or resolves any problems in cooperation with Founding Body.

Step 6   *Methods*
Assets sale.
Contribution into company. A new company is created between Treasury and domestic or foreign investors.
Management/Employee Buy-out. Requires 20 per cent down payment, the rest on instalment.

Source: Department of Privatisation, *Privatisation Report*, Ministry of Privatisation, Warsaw, 1996.

Table A4.6(b) *Poland: nine steps of privatisation through transformation*

Step 1   *Initiation*
The enterprises approaches the government and expresses an interest. In some cases, the Prime Minister can order privatisation on proposal from Ministry of privatisation.

Step 2 *Feasibility Study*
Usually done by a consulting firm.

Step 3 *Decision*
To go ahead with process.

Step 4 *Complete Documentation*
Formal application from either management or worker's council.
Opinions from workers delegation, founding body (e.g. Ministry of Industry).
Proposal by worker's council on employee share ownership (up to a maximum of 20 percent of total shares).
Draft of company statues and proposed capitalisation.
Decision of anti-monopoly office.

Step 5 *Additional Appointments (as required)*
Advisers (chosen by tender to work on: auditing, legal analysis, business plan and valuation, privatisation option.

Step 6 *Ministerial Decisions*
Minister decides on:
Transformation with or without conditions.
Company statues.
Selection of 2/3 of supervisory board (1/3 chosen by employees).
Capital structure.

Step 7 *Transformation*
SOE becomes a state-owned corporation governed by commercial code. Notary and court registration of company.

Step 8 *Decision of privatisation strategy. Options*:
Trade sale, to one or more parties.
Public offer for sale of shares.
Management/employees buy-out.
Some combination of above.

Step 9 *Implementation*
Advisers assist in such matters as: sales documents, auctions, selections of short-list of bidders, contract negotiations, prospectus, public relations, share distribution and marketing.

Source: As for Table A4.6(a).

Table A4.6(c) *Poland: mass privatisation programme (MPP) in brief, circa 1993–94*

- The programme gives all adult citizens the opportunity to obtain an equal stake in the privatised enterprises through the acquisition of share certificates (SCs) in National Investment Funds (NIFs).
- NIFs will take the form of closed-end funds registered as joint-stock companies. Up to 20 NIFs will be created. Each of these will be managed by a firm or consortium selected through competitive bidding from among the most reputable investment banks, funds and management organisations from many countries.

Table A4.6(c) *Contd.*

- NIFs will have supervisory boards representing the interests of their owners. These owners will be Polish citizens who acquire SCs, and the State Treasury, which will initially retain 15 per cent shares for use as part of compensation packages for fund managers.
- MPP includes about 600 (now 450) large and medium-sized Polish enterprises, primarily manufacturing plants.
- The commercialised joint-stock companies formed from the original state enterprises will have the following shareholding structure: 33 per cent by a 'lead' NIF; 25 per cent distributed evenly among all NIFs; 30 per cent retained by the state treasury; and 19 per cent distributed free of charge to enterprise employees.
- The 'lead' NIF in each company will be chosen through a draft line process by the 20 NIFs; each NIF will have in its portfolio a 'lead' shareholding in 30 companies.
- The fund management companies managing the NIFs will have a management and performance contract which provides strong financial incentives to manage these funds in such a way as to maximise the long-term value of the NIF in the interests of the shareholders through restructuring, modernisation and refinancing. It is expected that NIFs will exist for 10 years.
- After one year of operation and preparation of prospectuses, the NIFs will be listed on the Warsaw Stock Exchange (WSE). Soon after that, Polish citizens will be able to obtain SCs in bearer form at a nominal fee of approximately $US25 (10 per cent of an average monthly salary). These SCs give Polish citizens the right for at least four years to trade within and outside the official market for one share in each NIF listed on the exchange. The trading procedure for NIFs will be the same as for all WSE stocks.

Source: As for Table A4.6(a)

Table A4.6(d)   *Poland: the sectoral approach to privatisation, in brief, circa 1993–94*

Step 1   *Choosing a Sector*
Government identifies sector to be privatised. Selection criteria are positive potential of sector; investors interest, eagerness of firms to privatise; and national economic importance of sector.

Step 2   *Choosing an Adviser*
Sector assigned to project manager by Ministry;
Project manager drafts terms-of-reference outlining goals and questions to be addressed;
Competitive bid is organised targeting investment banks and consulting firm, often forming consortia and joint ventures;
Firms submit proposal; talks held to clarify proposal;
Ministry chooses sector adviser from among competing firms;

Ministry decides on financing, which may come from Ministry budget or foreign aid (e.g. PHARE, USAID or World Bank).

Step 3 *Phase I: Analysis*
Sector adviser prepares a comprehensive analysis of sector, including a study of the individual companies, based partly on on-site visits.

Step 4 *Phase II: Strategy Development*
Based on previous analysis, sector adviser develops a restructuring/privatisation policy for sector;
He also works out concrete strategies and action plans for individual companies, choosing between trade sales, IPOs, auction, and management/employees buy-outs;
Sector adviser contacts potential investors to ascertain the extent of their interest in this sector and helps them understand the privatisation process;
He reports to the Ministry.

Step 5 *Phase III: Implementation*
Adviser conducts privatisation of major companies in sector;
He assists smaller companies in liquidation;
He works with government agencies to develop ideas for restructuring other companies;
He makes available his knowledge to interested parties and funding organisations.

Source: As for Table A4.6(a)

Chapter 5

A5.1 China: Source Countries

Table A5.1(a) *China: FDI inflows by source country and economy 1983–94 ($US mn at current prices)*

Source country	1983–86	1987	1988	1989	1990	1991	1992	1993	1994
NIEs	883	1610	2095	2121	2153	2961	8799	21277	24959
Hong Kong	876	1588	2068	2037	1880	2437	7507	17275	19665
Taiwan	0	0	0	0	222	466	1051	3139	3391
Singapore	7	22	28	84	50	58	122	490	1180
South Korea	0	0	0	0	0	0	119	374	723
ASEAN	8	15	11	16	10	30	144	513	692
Thailand	6	11	6	13	7	20	83	233	235
Philippines	2	4	4	2	2	6	16	123	140
Malaysia	0.31	0.13	1.3	0.4	0.64	1.96	24.67	91.42	201
Indonesia	0.14	0	0.32	1.37	1.00	2.18	20.17	65.75	115.7
Japan	247	220	515	356	503	533	710	1324	2075
USA	256	263	236	284	456	323	511	2063	2491
West Europe	151	55	195	218	151	264	277	714	1634
UK	54	5	34	28	13	35	38	221	689
Germany	19	3	15	81	64	161	89	56	259
France	33	16	23	5	21	10	45	141	192
Italy	20	16	30	31	4	28	21	100	206
Netherlands	0.66	0.21	20.62	17.73	15.98	6.67	28.41	84	111
Switzerland	0.79	0	6.15	8.72	1.48	12.31	29.14	41.02	70.54
Norway	0	1.5	32.01	18.66	2.23	6.05	5.06	1.43	24.18
Belgium	8.82	7.54	3.89	0	8	0.1	4.46	25.74	31.83

Table A5.1(a) Cont.

Source country	1983–86	1987	1988	1989	1990	1991	1992	1993	1994
Denmark	2.91	2.42	19.8	8.31	10.39	0	11.79	4.15	1.65
Austria	5.44	0.9	0.35	0.69	1.38	0.04	0.29	10.8	10.1
Sweden	4.41	1.81	0	3.25	0.11	0.77	1.99	14.96	24.18
Finland	1.48	0	10.34	11.26	1.5	0	0.16	0.51	1.18
Spain	1.31	0.25	0	1.62	7.25	0.94	1.65	9.7	10.18
Other DCs	29.15	20.25	10.31	61.37	41.79	26.47	96.09	256	413
Australia	24.77	4.96	4.16	44.42	24.87	14.91	35.03	110	118
Canada	3.92	10.22	6.06	16.95	8.04	10.76	58.24	137	216
New Zealand	0.46	5.07	0.13	0	8.88	0.8	2.82	9.12	9.07
Other Asia	0.26	10.37	30.03	41.45	58.18	50.41	229	718	627
Macau	0	10.27	27.6	40.69	33.42	50	202	587	509
East Europe	1.41	21.3	0.5	0	0	1.16	20.68	53.74	48.62
Latin America	2.67	2.05	0	1.39	6.82	3.56	23.93	58.88	165
Africa	0	0.18	3.37	0	0.28	0	3.06	38.43	13.56
Others	55	98	96	293	107	174	193	499	648
All developing countries	950	1756	2237	2473	2335	3220	9413	23158	27153
All developed countries	684	558	957	920	1152	1145	1595	4357	6614
Total	1634	2314	3194	3393	3487	4366	11008	27515	33767

Sources: State Statistical Bureau, *China Foreign Economic Statistics*, China Statistical Information and Consultancy Service Centre, Beijing, various issues; State Statistical Bureau, *Almanac of China's Foreign Economic Relations and Trade*, China Statistical Publishing House, Beijing, various issues.

A5.2 Poland: Source Countries

Table A5.1(b) *Poland: FDI countries of origin (December 1996)*

Country	Equity & loans $US mn	Commitments $US mn	No. of companies
USA	2 965.6	2 669.9	77
Germany	1 524.4	756.4	113
International Corps.	1 493.0	188.4	15
Italy	1 223.8	1 199.8	29
Holland	951.7	309.1	32
France	899.9	537.3	42
UK	509.0	363.9	21
Sweden	361.3	82.6	30
Switzerland	357.7	13.6	8
Australia	328.1	67.0	3
Austria	315.3	19.3	30
Denmark	328.2	22.9	16
South Korea	184.5	1 225.0	3
Ireland	105.7	11.4	3
Spain	94.3	103.5	2
Canada	94.1	23.0	19
Finland	92.9	62.9	9
Norway	80.1	12.0	5
Belgium	46.5	54.3	14
Japan	32.5	13.0	7
South Africa	25.0	40.0	1
China	25.0	25.0	1
Turkey	23.0	60.0	2
Russia	20.0	–	1
Singapore	13.0	60.0	1
Liechtenstein	12.3	10.0	4
Slovenia	4.9	–	1
Greece	3.6	3.0	2
Luxembourg	2.3	–	1
Total	12 027.7	7 933.3	492

Source: PAIZ, *List of Major Foreign Investors in Poland*, PAIZ, Warsaw, 1997.

Chapter 6

A6.1 Sample Questionnaire used with Surveyed firms

1. Year company was formed?
2. Legal Status
     sole proprietor
     partnership
     private limited ownership
     public ownership

3. How many people are employed now in your firm?
     (a) full-time
          part-time
     (b) short contract
          long contract

4. How many people did your firm employ three years ago?
5. What are the areas of your firm's main activity?
6. In which industry is your firm's investment located?
7. What is the total value of the company's assets?
8. Why did your company invest in this country?
9. For what strategic reasons does your firm invest in the chosen country?
     (a) short-term
     (b) long-term

10. What determines your firm's investment in the host country?
11. Why does your company invest in that particular industry?
12. What are the major obstacles and advantages in doing business in the chosen host country?
13. What are your major complaints about the host-country's foreign investment climate?
14. What percentage of your firm's profit do you reinvest in the host country?
15. What percentage of your firm's product is sold:
     (a) on the domestic market
     (b) exported?

16. What percentage of you firm's inputs are:
     (a) imported
     (b) sourced domestically?

17. What restrictions if any are involved in the import of inputs?
18. What was the value of your firm's sales in the last few years?
19. What was the change in sales compared with the previous fiscal year?
20. How do you compare the quality of your firm's products with other foreign competitors'?
21. How do you compare quality of labour with your home country and other countries of your investment?
22. Does the state own part of your company? If yes, what percentage?
23. What are your firm's production plans over the next three years?

(a) keep production at current level
(b) expand production
(c) reduce production?

24. What kind of technology does your firm transfer to local firms:
    (a) type
    (b) year of amortisation?

A6.2   Sample of Letter Sent to Survey Firms, Prior to Interview

Contemporary China Centre
Research School of Pacific &
Asian Studies
Australian National University

Dear Sir,

Based on the recommendation of the Ministry of Privatisation and the Polish Agency for Foreign Investment which have supplied me a list of major foreign investors in Poland, I have chosen prospective firms for participation in my study relating to foreign direct investment. With great pleasure I inform you that your company has been one of those chosen for interview.

I will be in Poland for a period of five months commencing on 28 April 1996. During this time I would very much like to discuss the issues relating to foreign investment and the general business environment in Poland with the manager or director of your firm who would be able to help me in this matter. I will ring your office upon my arrival in Poland and, if you are agreeable, make an appointment to see the appropriate person.

As I am interested in motivational issues of firms that have invested in Poland, I am interested in talking to the manager or director of the company who is responsible for the major investment decisions.

I enclose a questionnaire which will indicate the nature of my interests. I do not expect all firms to have access to information on all the questions included. I would rather see the questionnaire as a framework for a more general discussion.

All information will be treated as strictly confidential. Any publications based on your replies will contain the aggregate of replies from a large number of Polish firms.

I would be most grateful for your cooperation and help in this matter.

Yours faithfully,

Michael Du Pont
(Research Scholar)

Bibliography

Access China (1997) 'New Foreign Exchange System of China', Asia-Pacific Research Institute, Graduate School of Management Macquarie University, Sydney, no. 25, pp. 28–30.

Agarwal, J.P. (1985) 'Emerging Third World Multinational: A Case Study of the Foreign Operations of Singapore Firms', *Contemporary Southeast Asia*, vol. 7, no. 3, pp. 193–208.

Agarwal, J.P., Gubitz, A. and Nunnenkamp, P. (1991) 'Foreign Direct Investment in Developing Countries, the Case of Germany', *Kieler Studien*, no. 238, Tübingen.

Agarwal, J.P. and Langhammer, R.J. (1995) 'Export Expansion and Diversification in Central and Eastern Europe: What can be Learnt from East and Southeast Asia?', *Kiel Discussion Papers* no. 261, Kiel Institute for World Economics, Kiel.

Aghion, P. and Messerlin, P. (1992) 'Towards the Establishment of a Continental European Customs Union', in J. Fleming, and J.M. Rollo, (eds), *Trade, Payments and Adjustment in Central and Eastern Europe*, London.

Agmon, T. and Lessard, D.R. (1977) 'Investor Recognition of Corporate International Diversification, *Journal of Finance*, vol. 32, September, pp. 1049–55.

Ahmad, E., Gao Qiang and Tanzi, V. (1995) *Reforming China's Public Finance* (Washington, D.C.: IMF).

Aiello, P. (1991) 'Building a Joint Venture in China: The case of the Beijing Jeep Corporation', *Journal of General Management,* vol. 1, no. 17, pp. 47–64.

Aldcroft, D.H. and Morewood, S. (1995) *Economic Change in Eastern Europe since 1918* (Aldershot, UK: Edward Elgar).

Aliber, R.Z. (1970) 'A Theory of Foreign Direct Investment', in C.P. Kindleberger (ed.), *The International Corporation* (Cambridge, Mass. The MIT Press).

Aliber, R.Z. (1971) 'The Multinational Enterprises in a Multiple Currency World', in J.H. Dunning (ed.), *The Multinational Enterprises* (London: Allen & Unwin).

Aliber, R.Z. (1993) *The Multinational Paradigm* (Cambridge, Mass.: The MIT Press).

Amsden, A.H. (1994) 'Beyond Shock Therapy: The Path to East European Recovery', *Global Issues in Transition*, no. 7.

Anderson, E. (1990) 'Two Firms, One Frontier: On Assessing Joint Venture Performance', *Solon Management Review*, vol. 31, no. 1, pp. 19–30.

Anderson, K. (1990) *Changing Comparative Advantages in China* (Paris: Development Centre Studies, OECD).

Ash, R.F. and Kueh, Y.Y. (1996) *The Chinese Economy under Deng Xiaoping* (Oxford: Clarendon Press).

Asian Business (1994) 'Strategies of Japaenese Foreign Investment', April, p. 20.

Athukorala, P. (1989) 'Export-Oriented Foreign investment in New Exporting Countries: Patterns and Determinants with Evidence from Sri Lanka', *World Competition*, vol. 13, no. 1, pp. 63–81.

Athukorala, P. (1996) 'Foreign Direct Investment and Manufacturing for Export in a New Exporting Country: The Case of Sri Lanka', *The World Economy*, vol. 18, no. 4, pp. 543–64.

Athukorala, P., and Huynh, F.C.H. (1987) *Export Instability and Growth: Problem and Prospect for the Developing Countries*, Croom Helm, London.

Athukorala, P., Jayasuriya, S.K., and Oczkowski, E. (1994) 'Developed and Developing Country Multinationals and Export Performance in Developing Countries: Some Analytical Issues with New Empirical Evidence', *Journal of Development Economics* (forthcoming).

Athukorala, P., and Menon, J. (1995) 'Korean Foreign Direct Investment-Trends, Determinants and Prospects', *World Competition*, vol. 18, no. 4, pp. 55–65.

Athukorala, P., and Menon, J. (1997) 'AFTA and the Investment–Trade Nexus in ASEAN', *The World Economy*, vol. 20. no. 2, pp. 159–73.

Audretsh D.B. (1995) 'Industrial and Trade Policies for the Emerging Market Economies', In: L.A Winters Editor.

Auster, E.R. (1987) 'International Corporate Linkages: Dynamic Forms in Changing Environments', *Colombia Journal of Business*, vol. 22, no. 2, pp. 3–6.

Bachmann, D., and Yang, D.I. (1991) *Yan Jiaqi and China's Struggle for Democracy*, M.E. Sharpe, New York.

Baird, I.S., Lyles, M.A., and Wharton, R. (1990) 'Attitudinal differences between American and Chinese managers regarding joint venture management', *Management International Review*, vol. 30, no. 4, pp. 53–68

Baka, M., and Kulawczuka, P. (1996) *Analiza wplywu investycji zagranichnych na polska gospodarke*, Institute Badan and Demokracja Przedsiebiorstw Prywatnych, PAIZ, Warsaw.

Balcerowicz, L. (1995) *Socialism, Capitalism, Transformation*, Central European University Press, Budapest.

Baldwin, R.E., Francoi, J.F., and Porters, R. (1997) 'The Costs and Benefits of Eastern Enlargement: the impact on the EU and Central Europe', *Economic Policy*, April.

Balicka, M. (1997) 'Export–Import, Doczekac zniw', *Politika*, no. 45, November, Warsaw.

Barme, G., and Jaivin, L. (1992) *New Ghosts, Old Dreams*, Times Books, New York.

Barnett, A.D. (1981) *China's Economy in Global Perspective*, The Brooking Institution, Washington D.C.

Barnett, A.D. (1985) *The Making of Foreign Policy in China*, Westview Press, Boulder.

Barnett, A.D. (1992) 'Will China follow the USRR?' *China Business Review*, vol. 19, no. 2, pp. 32–65.

Barnowe, J.T. (1990) 'Paradox Resolution in Chinese Attempts to Reform Organisational Cultures', in J. Child, and M. Lockett, (eds), *Reform Policy and the Chinese Enterprises*, Advance in Chinese Industrial Studies 1A, Greenwich, CN, JAI Press.

Barnowe, J.T., Yager, W.F., and Wu Nengquan. (1992) *Leaping Forward: Management Experiences of Firms with Foreign Investment in Southern Guangdong, China Paper* given to the Conference on Current Developments in Joint Ventures in the PRC, Hong Kong, June.

Bass, H.H., and Wohlmuth, K. (1996) *China in der Weltwirtschaft*, Mitteilungn Des Instituts Fur Asienkunde, No. 271, Hamburg.

Bauer, E. (1986) China Takes Off – *Technology Transfer and Modernisation*, University of Washington Press, Seattle.

Beamish, P., and Banks, J.C. (1987) Equity Joint Ventures and The Theory of The Multinational Enterprise', *Journal of International Business Studies*, vol. 17, no. 1, pp. 1–16.

Beijing Review (1986) Provisions of the State Council Encouraging Foreign Investment: State Council Official Answers Questions. vol. 29, no. 43, pp. 26–8.

Beijing Review (1991) 'First Indefinite Time Limit Joint Venture', vol. 34, no. 40, p. 30.

Beijing Review (1992a) Speed up Reform, Open the Doors Wider. 35/10, 9–15 March, p. 4.

Beijing Review. (1992b) More Autonomy Given to State Enterprises. vol. 35, no. 32, p. 4.

Beijing Review (1992c) 66 Enterprises Go Bankrupt. vol. 35, no. 33, p. 28.

Beijing Review (1993) Foreign Trade Volume of JVs Rises. vol. 36, no. 34, p. 28.

Beijing Review (1996) 'Report on the outline of the Ninth Five-Year Plan for national economic and social development and the long-range objectives to the year 2000', 3–16 April.

Bell, J., and Rostowski, J. (1995) 'A Note on the Confirmation of Podkaminer's Hypothesis in Post-liberalisation Poland', *Europe–Asia Studies*, vol. 47, no. 3, pp. 527–530.

Belka, M. (1993) 'Industry Case Study: Poland-Glass Industry', *Eastern European Economics*, pp. 79–97.

Belka, M. (1993) 'Industry Case Study: Food-Processing Industry-Chocolate and Confectionery', *Eastern European Economics,* pp. 63–78.

Belka, M., Krajewska, A., Krajewski, S., and Santos, A. (1993) 'Country Overview Study-Poland'. Eastern European Economics.

Bemish, P.W. (1989) 'Investing in China via Joint Ventures,' '*Management International Review*', vol. 1, no. 29, p. 32.

Berruet. G. (1994) *The Chinese Economy and the Relations with the European Union*, Club de Bruxelles, Commission of EU, Brussels.

Bhagwati, J. (1982) *Import Competition and Response*, Chicago University Press, Chicago.

Bhagwati, J. (1985) *Investing Abroad,* Esmee Fairbairn Lecture, University of Lancaster.

Bhagwati, J., and Brecher, R.A. (1980) 'National Welfare in an open Economy in the Presence of Foreign-Owned Factors of Production', *Journal of International Economics*, no. 10, pp. 103–115.

Bhagwati, J., and Eckaus, R.S. (1972) *Development and Planning*, George Allen & Unwin Ltd, Oxford.

Bhagwati, J., Jones, R.W. and Mundel, R.A. (1971) *Trade balance of payments and growth*, North-Holland Publishing Company, Amsterdam.

Bhagwati, J., and Tironi, E. (1980) 'Tariff change, Foreign Capital and Immiserization', *Journal of Development Economics*, no. 7, pp. 71–83.

Blecher, M. (1991) 'Developmental State, Entrepreneurial State: the Political Economy of Socialism Reform in Xinji Municipality and Guanghan county', in White, G.W. (ed.), *The Chinese state in the era of Economic Reform*, Macmillan, London, pp. 265–94.

Blejer, M.I. *et al.* (1991) 'The Evolving Role of Fiscal Policy in centrally Planned Economies under reform: the case of China'', IMF Working Paper, Asian and Fiscal Affairs Department, IMF, Washington D.C.

Bloodworth, D. (1995) *The Risk and Rewards of Investing in China*, Times Academic Press, Singapore.

Blomstrom, M., and Kokko, A. (1996) *Foreign Direct Investment and Politics: The Swedish Model*, Discussion Paper no. 1266, CEPR, London.

Blumberg, G. (1989) 'Investment in Manufacturing', *Business International*, January 23, p. 22.

Bluszkowski, J. and Garlicki, J. (1993) Social Conditions of Foreign Investor Operations in Poland (Warsaw: Friedrich Ebert Stiftung and PAIZ).

Bluszkowski. J. and Garlicki. J. (1996) Companies with Foreign Participation in their Local Environment PAIZ, Warsaw.

Boeker W. (1989) 'Strategic change: The effects of founding and history', *Academy of Management Journal*, vol. 32, no. 2, pp. 489–515.

Boisot, M.H. (1992) 'The Nature of Managerial Work in the Chinese Enterprise Reforms', A Study of Six Directors, *Organisation Studies*, no. 13, pp. 168–184.

Boisot, M.H. and Xiang Guao Liang. (1991) 'The nature of Managerial Work in China', in N., Campbell, S.R.F. Plasschaert, and D.H. Brown, (eds), *The Changing Nature of Management in China*, Advances in Chinese Industrial Studies, 2. Greenwich, CN, JAI Press.

Bond, H.M. (1991) *Beyond Chinese Face,* Oxford University Press, Oxford.

Bosworth, B.P., and Gur Ofer. (1995) *Reforming Planned Economies in an Integrating World Economy*, The Brooking Institution, Washington, D.C.

Bracker, J., and Pearson, J.N. (1986) 'Planning and Financial Performance of Small, Mature Firms', *Strategic Management Journal*, vol. 12, no. 7, pp. 503–522.

Brada, J.C., and Slay, B. (1995) 'The Role of International Financial Institutions in Central and Eastern Europe', *Journal of Comparative Economics*, vol. 20, no. 3, pp. 49–56.

Branson, W.H., and de Macedo, J.B. (1995) 'Macroeconomic Policy in Central Europe', *Discussion Paper* no. 1195, CEPR, London.

Bratkowski, A.S., and Dabrowski, M. (1995) *Fiscal Policy in Poland under Transition*, Center for Social & Economic Research, Warsaw.

Broadman, H.G., and Xiaolun Sun. (1997) 'The distribution of Foreign Direct Investment in China', *The World Economy*, vol. 20, no. 3, pp. 339–353.

Brown, L. (1995) *Stage of the World: 1995* (New York: W.W. Norton).

Browning, G. (1989) *If Everybody Bought One Shoe* (New York: Hill & Wang).

Bryant, C.G., and Mokrzycki, E. (1994) *The new great transformation?, Change and continuity in East-Central Europe*, Routledge, London.

Buckley, P.J and M.C. Casson (1976) *The Future of Multinational Enterprise.* London: Macmillan.

Buckley, P.J and Casson M.C (1985), *The Economic Theory of the Multinational Enterprise*, Macmillan, London.

Buckley, P.J. 1987. *The Theory of the Multinational Enterprise*, Macmillan, London.

Buckley, P.J. (1990) *International Investment*, Edward Elgar Publishing Ltd, Vermont, US.

Buckley, P.J. *et al.* (1992) *Servicing International Markets: Competitive Strategy of Firms*, Oxford, UK.

Buckley, P.J., Pass, C.L. and Prescott, K. (1992) *Servicing International Markets: Competitive Strategies of Firms*, (The Cambridge Mass. Cambridge Center, US).

Bucknall, K. (1989) *China and the open Door Policy*, Allen & Unwin, London.

Buiter, W.H., and Stern, N. (1996) 'Promoting an Effective Market Economy in a Changing World', Discussion Paper No. 1468, Centre for Economic Policy Research (CEPR), London.

Business Times (1994) Japanese Firms, 18 May, p. 4.

Business Tokyo (1992) Japanese engagement abroad, July, pp. 10–15.

Byrd, William, A. (1992) *Chinese Industrial Firm under Reform*, Oxford University Press, Oxford.

Cable, V., and Persaud, B. (1987) *Developing with Foreign Investment*, Croom Helm, London.

Campbell, N. (1986) *China Strategies-The Inside Story*, University of Hong Kong, Hong Kong.

Campbell, N. (1989) *A Strategic Guide to Equity Joint Ventures in China*, Pergaman Press, Oxford.

Campbell, N., and Cheng Yee. (1991) ' Relationship Management in Equity Joint Ventures in China: A Preliminary Exploration, in N. Campbell, S.R.F. Plasschaert and D.H. Brown (eds), *The Changing Nature of Management in China*, Advances in Chinese Industrial Studies, 2. Greenwich, CN, JAI Press.

Campbell, N., Plasschaert, S.R.F., and D.H. Brown (eds), 1991. *The Changing Nature of Management in China*, Advances in Chinese Industrial Studies, 2. Greenwich, CN, JAI Press.

Cannon, T. (1988) 'Opening up to the Outside World', in R. Benewick and P. Wingrove (eds), *Reforming the Revolution: China in transition*, Macmillan, London.

Carter, C.A., and Fang Cai (1996) *China's ongoing Agricultural Reform*, The 1990 Institute, San Francisko, US.

Carter, N.M. (1990) 'Small Firm Adaptation: Responses of Physicians Organisation to Regulatory and Competitive Uncertainty', *Academy of Management Journal*, vol. 33, no. 2, pp. 307–333.

Casson, M.C. (1982) 'The Theory of Foreign Direct Investment', in J. Black and J.H. Dunning (eds), *International Capital Movements,* Macmillan, London.

Casson, M.C. (1986) 'Introduction and Summary', Casson, M.C. (ed.), *Multinationals and World Trade: Vertical integration and the Division of Labour in World Industries*, Allan & Unwin, London.

Casson, M.C. (1987) *The firm and the market: study on multinational enterprises and the scope of the firm*, Cambridge, The MIT Press, MAS, US.

Casson, M.C. (1992) 'Internalisation Theory and Beyond', in Buckley, P.J. (ed.), *New Directions in International Business*, Edward Elgar, Aldershot, Hants.

Caves, R.E. (1974) 'Multinational Firms, Competition and Productivity in Host-Country Industry', *Economica*, vol. 41, May, pp. 176–193.

Caves, R.E. (1982) *Multinational Enterprises and Economic Analysis*, Cambridge University Press, Cambridge.

Central Daily, The (1994) 'China Trade', July.

Centre for Co-Operation with the Economies in Transition. (1995) *Review of Agriculture in Poland*, OECD, Paris.

Centrum Badan Marketingowych Indicator (1996) *Companies with Foreign Participation in their Local Environment*, Survey by Indicator, Friedrich Ebert Foundation, Warsaw.

Chai, J.C.H. (1994) 'Transition to market economy: the Chinese Experience', *Communist Economies & Economic Transformation*, vol. 6, no. 2.

Chamberlain, H.B. (1987) 'Party-management relations in Chinese industries: some political dimensions of economic reform', *China Quarterly*, no. 112

Chan, S. (1995) *FDI in a Changing Global Political Economy*, Oxford University Press, Oxford.

Chan, T., Chen, E.K.Y., and Chin, S. (1986) 'China's special economic zones: ideology, policy and practice' in Y.C. Jao and C.K. Leung (eds), *China's SEZs: Policies, problems and prospects,* Oxford University Press, Oxford.

Chen Bo-chih (1995) 'Mainland China's Monetary and Financial Policies: Operational Changes', *Issues & Studies*, vol. 3, no. 5, pp. 23–32.

Chen Chunlai (1996) *Recent Developments in Foreign Direct Investment in China*, Chinese Economy Research Unit, The University of Adelaide.

Chen, E.K.Y. (1990) 'Foreign Direct Investment in Asia: Developing Country Versus Developed Country Firms', in K.Y. Edward Chen (eds), *Foreign Investment in Asia*, Tokyo: Asian Productivity Organisation.

Chen, E.K.Y. and Drysdale P. (1995) *Corporate Links and Foreign Direct Investment in Asia and the Pacific*, Harper Educational Publishers, Pymble, NSW, Australia.

Chen Fuhong (1990) [Yige Zhongxing, Yige Renwu]. 'One Target, One Task', *China Enterprise Daily*, 22 January, p. 4.

Chen Jingcheng (1985) 'Problems in technology absorption', *Fujian Luntan*, 5 July 1985, pp. 13–16 (in Chinese).

Chen Nai-Ruenn (1986) Foreign Investment in China: Current trends, *US Dept. of Commerce*, Washington D.C., March.

Chen Wenhoug and Wei Jia (1993) 'Foreign direct investment in China and its relationship with overseas chinese capital from Hong Kong, Taiwan and ASEAN Countries', Mimeograph.

Cheng Gang. (1992) 'Chinese Employees in Foreign-Funded Ventures', *Beijing Review*, vol. 35, no. 46, pp. 21–23.

Child, J. (1990) *The Management of Equity Joint Ventures in China*, Beijing, China-European Community Management Institute.

Child, J., Crozier, R., and Mayntz, R. (1993) Societal Change between Market and Organisation, Aldershot, Avebury.

Child, J., and Lockett, M. (1990) *Reform Policy and the Chinese Enterprise*, Advances in Chinese Industrial Studies, 1A, Greenwich, CN, JAI Press.

Child, J., and Markoczy, L. (1993) 'Host-Country Managerial Behaviour and Learning in Chinese and Hungarian Joint Ventures', *Journal of Management Studies,* vol. 30, no. 5, pp. 611–631.

Child, J., Markoczy, L., and Cheung, T. (1994) 'Managerial Adaptation in Chinese and Hungarian Strategic Alliances with Culturally Distinct Foreign Partners', in Stewart, S. (ed.), *Joint Ventures in the People's Republic of China,* Advances in Chinese Industrial Studies, no. 4, Greenwich, CN, JAI Press.

Child, J., and Lu Yuan. (1992) 'Institutional Constraints on Economic Reform: The Case of Investment Decisions in China', *Research Paper in Management Studies,* no. 8, University of Cambridge, Cambridge.

Chilosi, A., Krajewska, A., and Kwiatkowski, E. (1995) 'Poland: From traditional to New Forms of Financial Participation', *Labour Management Relations Services,* no. 80, ILO, Geneva.

China Business Review, The (1995) 'China Data', May–June, pp. 56–8.

China Business Review, The 1996. 'China Data', May–June, pp. 40–1.

China Daily, The (1997) 'High-grade production of cement in the works', 17 March.

China Daily, The (1997) "Small firms must reform to survive', 5 April.

China Daily The (1997) 'YMC turns limstone into gold', 6 April.

China Enterprise Daily. (1989) Weihu Changzhang Zhongxing Diwei Jiajiang Qiye Deng De Jiashe (Protect the Central Position of the Factory Director and Strengthen the Construction of the Party Organisation in the Enterprise). 11 September, no. 1.

China Enterprise Daily. (1990) Fahui Qiye Dang Zuzhi Zuoyong De Bianzheng Sikao [Dialectical Study of the Party Organisation's Role in Enterprises]. 8 February, no. 3.

China–European Community Management Institute (1990) The Management of Equity Joint Ventures in China, Brussels.

China News Analysis (1996) 'Fighting Regional Disparities', 1 September, pp. 2–9.

China News Analysis (1996) 'Will the reform of state enterprises succeed?', 1 October, pp. 2–10.

China Statistical Yearbook (1992) State Statistical Bureau, Beijing.

China Trade Report (1996) 'More bread, less butter', January, Beijing.

——(1996) "Creating a culture', March, Beijing.

——(1997) 'Car trouble?, May, Beijing.

——(1997) 'Uphill battle', August, Beijing.

Choksi, A.M., and Papageorgiou, D.M. (1991) *Liberalising Foreign Trade,* vol. 1, Blackwall, Oxford.

Chu, Baotai. (1986) *Foreign Investment in China: Questions and answers,* Foreign Language Press, Beijing.

Chu, Derong. (1985) 'The Trends and Patterns of Foreign Direct Investment in China' *Working Paper,* no. 2, Centre for Contemporary Asian Studies, University of Hong Kong, October.

Chyungly Lee (1997) 'Foreign Direct Investment in China: Do State Policies Matter?', *Issues & Studies,* vol. 33, no. 7, pp. 40–61.

Cieslik, A. (1996) Foreign Direct Investment in Central Europe's Transition: Early Results, *Economic Discussion Papers* No. 28, University of Warsaw, Warsaw.

Clegg, S.R. (1990) *Modern Organisation; Organisation Studies in Post modern World*, Sage, London.

Clegg, S.R. (1990) *Capitalism in contrasting cultures*, Walter de Gruyter, New York.

Coady, D., Qiao Gang. and Hussain, A. (1990) 'The Production, Marketing and Pricing of Vegetables in China's Cities', *Research Program on the Chinese Economy Paper* no. 6, London School of Economics.

Cohen, J.A. (1988) 'An American perspective on China's legislative problems', *China Business Review,* March/April, pp. 6–8.

Contractor, F.J., and Lorange, P.L., (eds) (1988) *Cooperative Strategies in International Business*, Lexington Books, New York.

Corden, W.M. (1974) 'The Theory of International Trade', Dunning, J.H. (ed.), *Economic Analysis and the Multinationals Enterprise*, Allan & Unwin, London.

Corne, P.H. (1997) *Foreign Investment in China-The Administrative Legal System*. Hong Kong University Press, Hong Kong.

Cornell, K.F. (1995) 'The Transforming Economies of Central and Eastern Europe', *World Policy Journal*.

Cow, I.H. (1992) 'Chinese Managerial Work', *Journal of General Management*, vol. 17, no. 7, pp. 53–67.

CPC. (Communist Party of China) (1984) *China's Economic Structure Reform: Decision of the CPC Central Committee*, Beijing, Foreign Language Press.

CPC. (1988) Document on the Implementation of the Enterprise Law, issued by the Central Committee of the CPC, 28 April, Beijing.

CPC. (1989) Discussion Meeting of Older Cadres in the Organisation Department of the CPC on Enhancing Party-building, *People's Daily* (overseas edition), 18 July, no. 1.

Crane, G. (1990) *The Political Economy of China's SEZs*, Sharpe, M.N, New York.

Csaba, L. (1996) 'The Political Economy of the Reform Strategy: China and Eastern Europe Compared', *Communist Economies and Economic Transformation*, vol. 8, no. 1, pp. 53–65.

Culem, C. (1988) 'The Locational Determinants of Direct Investment among Industrialised Countries', *European Economic Review*, vol. 32, pp. 885–904.

Cushman, D.O. (1985) 'Real Exchange Rate Risk, Expectations and the Level of Direct Investment', *Review of Economics and Statistics*, May, pp. 297–308.

Cyr, D.J., and Frost, P.J. (1991) 'Human Resource Management Practice in China'-A Future Perspective, *Human Resource Management*, vol, 30, no. 6, pp. 199–216.

Dabrowski, J.M. (1995) *Investment Risk in Poland-IV Ranking of Countries, Regions and Branches*, The Gdansk Institute for Market Economies, Polish Development Bank Publications, Warsaw.

Dabrowski, J.M. (1995) *Different Strategies of Transition to a Market Economy: How do They Work in Practice?*, Polish Academy of Science Institute of Economics, Paper presented at the seminar of the Polish Academy, October, Warsaw.

Dabrowski, M. and Stanislawczyk, J. 1997 'Pulp and paper industry', *Encyclopaedia* of *Polish Industry*, Sterling Publishing Group, London.

Daniels, J.D., Krug, J., and Nigh, D. (1985) 'US joint ventures in China: Motivation and Management of Political Risk', *California Management Review*, vol. 27, no. 4, pp. 46–58.

Davidson, W.H. (1980) 'The Location of Foreign Direct Investment Activity: Country Characteristic and Experience Effects', *Journal of International Business Studies*.

De Bruijn, E.J., and Jia Zinanfeng. (1992) 'Transferring Technology to China via Joint Ventures: Product Selection Perspective', Paper given to the Conference on Current Developments in Joint Ventures in the PRC, Hong Kong, June.

Dehejia, V.D. (1997) *Will Gradualism Work when Shock Therapy Doesn't?*, Discussion Paper no. 1552, CEPR, London.

De Mente, B. (1989) *Chinese Etiquette and Ethics in Business*, NTC Business Books, Illinios, US.

Deng Xiaoping. (1987) ' On Reform of Political Structure', *Beijing Review*, 18 May, pp. 14–17.

Denny, D.L. (1987) 'Provincial trade patterns' in *China Business Review*, Sept/Oct, pp. 18–22.

DiMaggio, P.J. (1988) ' Interest and Agency in Institutional Theory', in L.G. Zucker, (ed.), *Institutional Patterns and Organisation*, (Cambridge, Mass.: Ballinger).

DiMaggio, P.J., and Powell, W.W. (1991) 'Introduction', in W.W. Powell and P.J. DiMaggio (eds), *The New Institutionalism in Organisational Analysis*, University of Chicago Press, Chicago.

Dittmer, L. (1990) 'Patterns of elite strife and succession in Chinese politics', *China Quarterly*, no. 123, pp. 405–30.

Doner, G. (1991) 'Japanese takeovers – automobil industry', *Business Taiwan*, 12 February.

Drabek, Z., and Smith, A. (1995) *Trade Performance and Trade Policy in Central and Eastern Europe*, Discussion Paper no. 1182, CEPR, London.

Drysdale, P. (1988) *International Economic Pluralism*, Allen & Unwin, North Sydney.

Dunning, J.H. (1977) 'Trade, location of economic activity and the MNC' a search for the eclectic approach, B. Ohlin, P.O. Hesselborn and P.M. Wijkman (eds), *The International Allocation of Economic Activity*, Macmillan, London.

Duning, J.H. 1979. 'Trade, location of economic activity, and the multinational enterprise: some empirical effects', *Journal of International Business Studies* no. 11, Spring-summer, pp. 9–13

Dunning, J.H. (1980) 'Towards an eclectic theory of international production: some empirical effects', *Journal of International Business*, vol. 11, Spring/Summer, pp. 9–31.

Dunning, J.H. (1984) 'Non equity forms of foreign economic involvement and the theory of international productions in R.W., Moxon, T.W. Roehl and J.F. Truitt (eds), *International Business Strategies in the Asia-Pacific Region*, JAI Press, Greenwich, CA, US.

Dunning, J.H. (1985) *Multinational Enterprises, Economic Structure and International Competitiveness*, John Wiley & Sons, Chichester, UK.

Dunning, J.H. (1988) 'The eclectic paradigm of international production: update and some possible extensions, *Journal of International Business Studies*, vol. 19, no. 2, pp. 1–31.

Dunning, J.H. (1991) 'Governments and multinational enterprises: from confrontation to cooperation', *Millenium Journal of International Studies*, vol. 20, pp. 223–244.

Dunning, J.H. (1992) *Multinational Enterprises and the Global Economy*, Addison-Wesley, Wokingham.

Dunning J.H. (1993) *Multinational Enterprises and the Global Economy*, Workingham, Berkshire, Addison Wesley.

Dunning J.H. (1994) *Globalisation: The Challenge for National Economic Regimes*, Dublin: The Economic and Social Research Council.

Dunning, J.H. (1995a) 'Reevaluating the Benefits of Foreign Direct Investment', *Discussion Paper* no. 188, Department of Economics, University of Reading.

Dunning, J.H. (1995b) 'Globalisation, Technological Change and the Spatial Organisation of Economic Activity', *Discussion Papers* no. 211, vol. 8, series B, Department of Economics, University of Reading, Reading, UK.

Dutkiewicz, J., and Sowinska, M. (1996) *Fine-Tuning the Market Economy, Poland Consolidates its Progress*, The Warsaw Voice, Warsaw pp. 57–65.

Dyker, D.A. (1997) *The Technology of Transition*, Central European University Press, Budapest.

Economic Information Daily, 1995. 'State Reform', May.

Economist, The (1992) 'China Goes for Broke', 25 July.

—— (1992) 'A Survey of China: When China Wakes', 28 November.

—— 1993. 'The Future Surveyed', 11 September, pp. 70–72.

—— 1995. 'Trade and investment in China', 18 March.

—— (1996) 'Tigers or tortoises?', 26 October.

Eisenhardt, K.M. (1989) 'Agency Theory: An Assessment and Review;, *Academy of Management Review*, vol. 14, no. 3, pp. 57–74.

Electronic Business Asia. (1993) 'Investment in semiconductor', July, pp. 32–47.

Elteto, A., Pal Gaspar. and Sass, M. (1995) *Foreign Direct Investment in East-Central Europe in Comparative Analysis with Spain and Portugal*, *Working Paper* no. 51, Committee on Science Policy, ACE Project, Hungary.

Ernst, M., Alexeev, M., and Marer, P. (1996) *Transforming the Core-Restructuring Industrial Enterprises in Russia and Central Europe*, Westview Press, Boulder, Colorado.

European Bank for Reconstruction and Development (EBRD) (1994) 'Country in Transition Report', London: EBRD.

European Communities Commission. (ECC) (1997) *Commission Opinion on Poland's Application for Membership of the European Union*, European Communities Publications, Luxembourg.

Faini, R., and Porters, R. (1997) *European Union Trade with Eastern Europe-Adjustment and Opportunities*, CEPR, London.

Falkenheim, V. (1986) 'Fujian's open door experiment', *China Business Review*, Jan/Jun, pp. 38–42.

Fan, Q. and Nolan, P., (eds) (1994) *China's Economic Reforms*, Macmillan, London.

Far Eastern Economic Review (1996) 'Wake-up call for China's state sector', 12 September, p. 62.

Ferreira, M.P. (1995) 'The Liberalisation of East-West Trade: An Assessment of its Impact on Exports from Central and Eastern Europe', *Europe-Asia Studies*, University of Glasgow, vol. 47, no. 7, pp. 1205–1223.

Federation of Hong Kong Industries, Industry and Research Division, (1990–95), *Investment in China*, Survey of Members of Federation of Hong Kong Industries, Hong Kong.

Financial Review (1996) 'Cheap labour loses its allure for investors', 19 July, London.

Financial Times (1996) 'Survey: World motor industry', 5 March, London

—— (1997) 'Polish banking sales advance on two fronts', May 22, London.

Fiol, C.M., and Lyles, M.A. (1985) 'Organisational Learning', *Academy of Management Review*, vol. 10, no. 3, pp. 803–813.

Fitzgerald, E.V.K. (1985) 'The problem of balance in the peripheral socialist economy: a conceptual note', *World Development*, vol. 13, no. 1.

Flamm, K. and Grunwald, J. (1985) *The Global Factory: Foreign Assembly in International Trade*, Brooking Institution, Washington D.C.

Foreign Trade Research Institute (FTRI) (1995) *Poland Country Report*, FTRI, Warsaw.

Freeman, N.J. (1994) 'Vietnam and China: Foreign Direct Investment Parallels', *Communist Economics and Economic Transformation,* vol. 6, no. 1.

Froot. Kenneth A. (1991) 'Japanese Direct Foreign Investment', *NBER Working Paper* no. 3737, June.

Froot, Kenneth A. (1993) Foreign Direct Investment, The University of Chicago Press, Chicago.

Frost, K.A. and Stein, J.C. (1989) Exchange rates and foreign direct investment: an imperfect capital market approach', Working Paper Series no. 2914, National Bureau of Economic Research, New York.

Fukosaku K. and Solignac–Lecomte.H.B, (1995) 'Economic Transition and Trade Policy Reform: Lessons from China', *XLIV'eme Congres annuel de science economique*, Paris, September.

Gabrisch, H. (1993) 'Difficulties in Establishing Joint Ventures in Eastern Europe', *Eastern European Economics*, Summer.

Garland, J., and Farmer, R.N. (1986) *International Dimensions of Business Policy and Strategy*, Kent International Business Series, London

Garnaut, R. (1988) *China: one country, two systems*, Australian National University, Canberra.

Garnaut, R. (1991) *China's growth in Northeast Asian Perspective*, Research School of Pacific Studies, ANU, Canberra.

Garnaut, R. (1992) *Economic Reform and Internationalisation: China and the Pacific Region*, Allen & Unwin, North Sydney.

Garnaut, R. (1994) *Asian Market Economies: Challenges of a Changing International Environment*, Institute of Southeast Asian Studies, Singapore.

Garnaut, R., and Drysdale, P. (1989) *A Pacific free trade area?*, Australian National University, Canberra.

Garnaut, R. and Drysdale, P. (1994) *Asia Pacific Regionalism: Readings in international economic relations*, Harper Educational Publishers, Pymble, NSW.

Garnaut, R., and Liu Guoguang (1992). *Economic Reform and Internalisation*, Allen & Unwin, St. Leonards NSW.

Garnaut, R. and Liu Guoguang (1992), *Economic Reform and Internalisation*, Allen & Unwin, St. Leonards NSW, Australia.

Gatling, R. (1993) *Foreign Investment in Eastern Europe*, The Economist Intelligence Unit, London.

Geringer, J.M. (1991) 'Measuring Performance of International Joint Ventures', *Journal of International Business Studies*, no. 22, pp. 249–60.

Geringer, J.M. (1991) 'Strategic Determinants of Partner Selection Criteria in International Joint Ventures, *Journal of International Business Studies*, vol. 22, no. 5, pp. 42–62.

Geringer, J.M., and Hebert, L. (1989) 'Control and Performance of International Joint Ventures', *Journal of International Business Studies*, vol. 20, no. 4, pp. 235–254.

Gibson, J., and Cielecka, A. (1995) 'Economic Influences on the Political Support for Market Reform in Post-communist Transitions: Some Evidence from the 1993 Polish Parliamentary Elections', *Europe-Asia Studies*, vol. 47, no. 5, pp. 765–785.

Gnat Z. (1996) 'Opportunities in Polish Construction Business', PAIZ, Warsaw.

Goldenberg, S. (1988) Hands across the Ocean: Managing JVs with spotlight on China and Japan, *Harvard Business School Press, Cambridge, Mass.*

Gomez-Casseres, B., and Yoffie, David, B. (1993) *The International Political Economy of Direct Foreign Investment*, vol: I and II, Edward Elgar, Vermont, US.

Gomulka, S. (1994) *Lessons from Economic Transformation and the Road Forward*, Studies & Analysis, CASE, Warsaw.

Gora, M. (1994) *Rynek Pracy w Polsce*, Centre for Social and Economic Research (CASE), Warsaw.

Gorbachev, M. (1987) *Perestroika*, London, Collins.

Gordon, M. (1990) Sino-Western Manufacturing Joint Ventures: The Automotive Experience, Paper given to the Canada-China International Management Conference, Xian, August.

Gordon, R.H., and Li, D. (1997) 'Taxes and Government Incentives: Eastern Europe Versus China', *Discussion Paper* no. 1657, CEPR, London.

Grabowski, M., and Smith, S. (1996) *The Taxation of Entrepreneurial Income in a Transition Economy: Issues Raised by Experience in Poland*, Discussion Paper no. 1166, CEPR, London.

Granick, D. (1990) *Chinese State Enterprises: A Regional Property Rights Analysis*, University of Chicago Press, Chicago.

Graza Letto-Cillies (1992) *International Production*, Polity Press, Cambridge.

Gray, H.P. (1996) 'The eclectic paradigm: the next generation', *Transnational Corporations*, vol. 5, no. 2, pp. 51–65.

Greenaway, D., and Winters, L.A. (1987) Surveys in International Trade, Blackwell, Oxford.

Grubel, H.G. (1974) 'Taxation and the rate of return from some US asset holdings abroad 1960–69', *Journal of Political Economy*, vol. 82, May-June, pp. 469–488.

Grunwald J., and Flamm. K. (1985) *The Global Factory*, The Brooking Institution, Washington D.C.

Guisinger, S.E. (1985) *Investment Incentives and Performance Requirements*, Praeger Publishers, New York.

Glowny Urzad Statystyczny (GUS), 1996. *Finansowe Podmiotow Gospodarczych z Udzialem Kapitalu Zagranicznego w 1995*, Department of Companies, GUS, Warsaw.

Hakam, A.N., and Chan, Kok Yong. (1990) 'Negotiations between Singaporeans and Local Firms in China', in N. Campbell and J.S. Henley (eds), *Joint Ventures and Industrial Change in China*, Advances in Chinese Industrial Studies, 1B. Greenwich, CN, JAI Press.

Hamel, G. (1991) 'Competition for Competence and Inter-Partner Learning within International Strategic Alliances,' *Strategic Management Journal*, vol. 12, no. 3, pp. 83–103.

Hamilton, Gary G., and Waters, T. (1994) 'Economic Organisation and Chinese Business Networks in Thailand', paper presented at 21st Pacific Trade and Development Conference: "Corporate Links and Direct Foreign Investment in Asia and the Pacific", Centre of Asian Studies, The University of Hong Kong, 1–3 June.

Harding, H. (1992) *A Fragile Relationship: The United States and China since 1972*, Brookings Institution, Washington.

Hardy, J., and Rainnie, A. (1994) 'Transforming Poland?', *Labour Focus on Eastern Europe*, no. 47, pp. 43–57.

Harringan, K.R. (1986) *Managing for joint Venture Success*, Lexington Books, New York.

Heap, A., and Campbell, N. (1990) Winning Large International Projects in China: A Network Approach, Paper given to the Conference on Management and Economics in China Today; Similarities with Eastern Europe?, Maastricht, November.

Helleiner, G.K. (1973) 'Manufactured Exports from Less-Developed Countries and Multinational Firms', *The Economic Journal*, vol. 83, no. 1, pp. 21–47.

Helleiner, G.H. (1976) *A World Divided – The Less Developed Countries in the International Economy* (Cambridge: Cambridge University Press).

Helleiner, G.K. (1978) 'Manufactured for Export, Multinational Firms, and Economic Development', in V. Cable, and B. Persaud (eds), *Developing with Foreign Investment* (London: Croom Helm).

Helleiner, G.K. (1988) 'Direct Foreign Investment and Manufacturing for Export in Developing Countries: A Review of the Issues', in S. Dell (ed.), *Policy for Development* (London: Macmillan).

Helliwel J.F., (1995) 'Asian Economic Growth', in Dobson W. and Flatters F. (ed.), *Pacific Trade and Investments: Options for the 90s*.

Henderson, A. (1995) 'The Politics of Foreign Investment in Eastern Europe: Lessons from the Polish and Hungarian Experience', *Problems of Post-Communism*, May/June, pp. 51–56.

Hendryx, S.R. (1986) 'Implementation of a technology transfer in the People's Republic of China: a management perspective', *Colombia Journal of World Business*, vol. 3, no. 2, pp. 57–66.

Henley, J., and Nyaw, M.K. (1988) 'The system of management and performance of joint ventures in China: some evidence from Shenzhen special economic zone', *Working Paper Series, 88/15*, University of Edinburgh, Edinburgh.

He Wei and Wei Jie. (1992) *Zhongguo Jingji De Fei Juheng Fa Zhang* [The Uneven Development of the Chinese Economy], People's University Press, Beijing.

Hildebrandt, H.W., and Liu Jinyun. (1988) 'Career and Education Patterns of Chinese Managers', *The Chinese Business Review*, Nov-Dec, pp. 36–8.

Hill, H. (1987) *Foreign Investment and Industrialisation in Indonesia*, Singapore, Oxford University Press.

Hill, H. (1990) 'Foreign Investment and East-Asian Development', *Asian-Pacific Economic Literature*, vol. 4, no. 2, pp. 21–58.

Hirsh, S. (1967) *Location of Industry and International Competitiveness*, Oxford University Press, Oxford.

Hirsh, S. (1976) *An international trade and investment theory of the firm*, Oxford University Press, Oxford.

Hoekman, B., and Djankov, S. (1996) *Intra-industry Trade, Foreign Direct Investment and the Reorientation of East European Exports*, Discussion Paper no. 1377, CEPR, London.

Hong Kong Times, The (1997) 'Programme to promote homes for next century', 17 March.

Hou, C.M. (1965) '*Foreign investment and Economic Development in China: 1840–1937*', *Harvard University Press*, Cambridge, US, vol.6. no. 3, pp. 23–45.

Houben, L.G., and Nee, O.D., Jr. *The form of Foreign Investment in China with Case Studies*, unpublished (Hong Kong: Coudert Bros).

Howell, J. (1990) 'The impact of China's open policy on labour', *Labour, Capital and Society*, November, pp. 288–324.

Howell, J. (1991) 'The impact of the open door policy on the Chinese state' in White, G.W. (ed.), *The Chinese State in the Era of Economic Reform.*, Macmillian, London.

Howell, J. (1992) 'The myth of autonomy: the foreign enterprise in China' ch. 7 in Smith, C. and Thompson, P. (ed.), *Labour in Transition: the labour process in Eastern Europe and China*, Routledge, London.

Howell, J. (1993) *China Opens Its Doors*, Lynne Rienner Publishers, Colorado, US.

Huang Fangyi. (1987) 'China's introduction of foreign technology and external trade', *Asian Survey*, vol. 27, no. 5, pp. 577–594.

Huang Yasheng. (1996) *Inflation and investment controls in China*, Cambridge University Press, Cambridge, US.

Hughes, H. and You, P.S. (1969) *Foreign investment and industralisation in Singapore*, ANU Press, Canberra.

Hunya Gabor (1996) '*Foreign Direct Investment in Transition Countries in 1995*', Monthly Report no. 1, The Vienna Institute for Transition Countries, Vienna.

Hussein, A. (1983) 'Economic reforms in Eastern Europe and their relevance to China' in S. Feuchtwang and A. Hussein (eds), *The Chinese Economic Reforms*, Croom Helm, London, pp. 91–120.

Hussain, A. (1992) The Chinese Economic Reforms in Retrospect and Prospect, *Research on the Chinese Economy, Paper* no. 24, August, London School of Economics, London.

Hymer, S. (1960) *The International Operations of National Firms: A Study of Direct Investment*, PhD dissertation (MIT Press, 1976).

Hymer, S. (1976) *The International Operations of National Firms: a study of direct investment*, MIT Press, Cambridge, Mass.

ILO (International Labour Organisation), (1996) 'Economic performance, labour surplus and enterprise response', Labour Market Paper no. 13, Department of Employment, ILO, Geneva.

ILO (International Labour Organisation) (1995–97) Yearbook of Labor Statistics', Geneva.

Imai, K. (1985) Network Organisation and Incremental Innovation in Japan, Institute of Business Research, Hitotsubashi Discussion Paper no. 122.

IMF (International Monetary Fund) (1977) *Balance of Payments Manual*, 4th Edition, IMF, Washington D.C.

IMF (1994) *Poland–The Path to a Market Economy*, Occasional Paper no. 113, IMF, Washington D.C.

IMF (1996) *China Report*, Occasional Paper no. 107, IMF, Washington D.C.

Institute of Developing Economies (IDE) (1995) *Investment Risk in Post-Deng China*, IDE Spot Survey, March, Tokyo.

Itaki, M. (1991) 'A critical assessment of the eclectic theory of the multi-national enterprises', *Journal of International Business Studies*, vol. 22, pp. 445–460.

Jackson, S. (1992) *Chinese Enterprise management Reforms in Economic Perspective*, De Gruyter, Berlin.

Jarosz, M. (1996) *Kapital Zagraniczny w Prywatyzacji*, Political Study Institute, Polish Academy of Science, Warsaw.

Jermakowicz, W.W. (1994) 'Privatization and Foreign Investment in Poland 1990–1993. Methods and Result', Iliana Zloch-Christy ed. *Foreign Investument in Eastern and Central Europe*, Praeger, New York.

Jermakowicz, W.W., Bochniarz, Z. and Toft, D. (1994) *Foreign Privatization in Poland*, Centre for Social and Economic Research (CASE), Warsaw.

Jermakowicz, W. W. and Bochniarz, Z. (1991) 'Direct Foreign Investment in Poland', *Development and International Cooperation*, vol. 7, no. 12, June.

Jiang Zemin. (1992) 'Accelerating the Reform, the Opening to the Outside World and the Drive to Modernisation, so as to Achieve Greater Success in Building Socialism with Chinese Characteristics'. Report to the 14th National Congress of the Communist Party of China, Printed in full in *Beijing Review*, vol. 35, no. 43, pp. 9–23.

Jia Wei. (1994) *Chinese Foreign Investment Laws and Policies*, Quorum Books, Westport. US.

Jones, R.S., and Klein, M. (1993) 'Economic Integration between Hong Kong, Taiwan and the Coastal provinces of China', *OECD Economic Studies*, no. 20, OECD, Paris.

Journal of Asian Business (1996) 'Conference Report–The Automotive Industry in Asia', vol. 12, no. 2, p. 71.

Kabaj, M. (1995) '*Active Labour Market Policy and the Role of Employment Councils in Poland in Counteracting Unemployment*', paper presented at the 5th European ILO Conference, Ministry of Labour and Social Policy, September.

Kamm, J. (1989) 'Reforming Foreign Trade' in Vogel, E.F. (ed.), *One Step Ahead in China: Guangdong under reform*, Harvard University Press, Cambridge, US.

Kao, J. (1993) 'The Worldwide Web of Chinese Business, *Harvard Business Review,* March-April, pp. 24–36.

Katseli, Louka T. (1992) 'Foreign Direct Investment and Trade Interlinkages in the 1990s: Experience and Prospects of Developing Countries', *Discussion Paper No. 687.* London, Centre for Economic Policy Research.

Kearney, A. (1988) *Manufacturing Equity Joint Ventures in China*, Unpublished Report, Beijing.

Kennedy, R. (1997) 'A Tale of Two Economies: Economic Restructuring in Post-Socialist Poland', *World Development*, vol. 25, no. 6, pp. 841–865.

Khan, K. (1987) *Multinationals of the South* (London: Pinter).

Khan, Z.S. (1991) Patterns of Foreign Direct Investment in China, *World Bank Discussion Papers*, No. 130, World Bank, Washington, D.C., September.

Kidyba, A., and Wrobel A. (1994) *Public Administration in Poland-Its Structure and Powers*, Economic and Social Policy Series no. 34, Friedrich Ebert Foundation, Warsaw.

Kindleberger, Charles, P. (1969) *American Business Abroad: Six Lectures on Direct Investment*, Yale University Press, Yale.

Kindleberger, C. (1970) *The International Corporation-A Symposium*, The MIT Press, Cambridge, US.

Klavens, J., and Zamparutti, A. (1995) *Foreign Direct Investment and Environment in Central and Eastern Europe. A Survey*, A Report for the Environmental Action Programme, The European Bank for Reconstruction and Development, (EBRD) London.

Kleinberg, R. (1990) *China's opening to the Outside World: Experiment in foreign capital*, Westview Press, Boulder.

Klein, M.W. and Rosengren, E.S. (1990a) *Determinants of Foreign Direct Investment in the United States*, Worcester, Bostob, mimeo.

Klein, M.W. and Rosengren, E.S. (1990b) *Foreign direct investment outflow from the United States: an empirical assessment*, Worcester, Boston, mimeo.

Knickerbocker F.T. (1973) *Oligopoliestic Reaction and the Multinational Enterprise Cambridge, MA, Haward University Press.*

Knirsch, P. (1994) Foreign Direct Investment and the Reconstruction of the Economies of Central Europe, *Acta Oeconomica*, vol. 46, no. 3–4, pp. 371–380.

Kogut, B. (1988) 'Joint ventures: Theoretical Empirical Perspective', *Strategic Management Journal*, vol. 8, no. 4, pp. 319–332.

Kogut, J. (1992) 'Chinese Fight for Jobs as Capitalism Creeps', *Sunday Times*, 2 August.

Kojima, K. (1973) 'Reorganisation of North-South Trade: Japan's Foreign Economic Policy for the 1970's', *Hitotsubashi Journal of Economics*, vol. 13, February, pp. 1–28.

Kojima, K. (1977) 'Transfer of Technology to Developing Countries-Japanese Type Versus American type', *Hitotsubashi Journal of Economics*, vol. 23, no. 1.

Kojima, K. (1978) *Direct Foreign Investment", a Japanese Model of Multinational Business Operations* (London: Croom Helm).

Kojima, K. (1982) 'Macroeconomic Versus International Business Approach to Direct Foreign Investment', *Hitotsubashi Journal of Economics*, vol. 23, no. 1.

Kojima, K. (1990) *Japanese Direct Investment Abroad*, International Christian University, Social Science Research Institute, Tokyo, monograph series 1.

—— 1990 The Road to a Free Economy, London, Norton.

Kojima, K. and Ozawa T. (1984) 'Micro and Macro Economic Models of Foreign Direct Investment: Towards a Synthesis', *Hitotsubashi Journal of Economics*, vol. 25, no. 2, pp. 1–20.

Kokubun, R. (1986) 'The Politics of Foreign Economic Policy-making in China: The Case of Plant Cancellations With Japan', *China Quarterly*, no. 105, pp. 155–69.

Kolodko, G.W. (1996) *Poland-2000, The New Economic Strategy*, Poltext Publishers, Warsaw.

Kolodko, G.W. (1996) *Strategy for Poland*, PAIZ, Warsaw.

Komiya, R., Wakasugi, R. (1990) 'Japanese Foreign Direct Investment', *MITI/RI Discussion Paper* no. 90, Tokyo, May.

Kopint-Datorg Institute, 1992 'Economic Trends in Eastern Europe', Economic Developments in the Eastern European Region, no. 1. Kopint–Datong Institute, Budapest.

Kornai, J. (1980) *The Economics of Shortage*, Amsterdam, North-Holland

—— (1986), The Hungarian Reform Process, *Journal of Economic Literature*, no. 24, pp. 1687–1737.

—— (1990) *The Road to a Free Economy*, London, Norton.

KPMG Poland (1995) *Investment in Poland*, PAIZ, Warsaw.

Kramer, M. (1995) 'Polish Workers and the Post-communist Transition, 1989–93', *Europe-Asia Studies*, vol. 47, no. 4, pp. 669–712.

Kraus, W. (1985) 'Joint venture–Erfahrunggen in und mit der VR China', *Asian*, no. 16 pp. 5–31.

Kraus, W. (1991) *Private Business in China*, University of Hawaii Press, Honolulu.

Kravis T.B and Lipsey. R.E. (1982) 'US–owned affiliates and Host–Country exports.' *NBER Working Paper* no. 1037, Cambridge, Mass: National Bureau of Economic Research.

Krugman, P. R. (1986) *Strategic Trade Policy and the New International Economics*, The MIT Press, Cambridge, US.

Krugman, P. R. (1995) 'Growing World Trade: Causes and Consequences', *Brooking Papers on Economic Activity*, MIT Press.

Kubielas, S. (1996) *Technology Transfer and the Restructuring of New Market Economies: The Case of Poland*, STEEP Discussion Paper no. 32, Science Policy Research Unit, University of Sussex.

La Croix, S.J., Plummer, M. and Lee, K. (1995) *Emerging Patterns of East Asian Investment in China from Korea, Taiwan and Hong Kong*, An East Gate Book, New York.

Lall, S, and Siddharthau, S. (1982) 'The Monopolistic Advantage of Multinationals: Lesson from Foreign Investment in the US', *Economic Journal*, vol. 92, pp. 668–83.

Lall, S. (1983) *The New Multinationals*: The Spread of Third World Enterprises. John Wiley, New York and Chichester.

Lall, S. (1993) 'Foreign Direct Investment in South Asia', *Asian Development Review,* vol. 11, no. 1, pp. 102–119.

Lall, S., and Wignaraja, G. (1992) 'Foreign Involvement by European Firms and Garment Exports by Developing Countries', Development Studies Working papers No. 54, International Development Centre, Queen Elizabeth House, Oxford University. Oxford.

Laksonen, O. (1988) *Management in China During and After Mao*, Walter de Gruyter, New York.

Langlois, A. (1997) 'Car trouble', China Trade Report, May–August, 1997.

Lardy, N.R. (1983) *Agriculture in China's Modern Economic Development*, Cambridge University Press, Cambridge.

Lardy, N.R. (1992) *Foreign Trade and Economic Reform 1978–1990*, Cambridge University Press, Cambridge.

Lardy, N.R. (1994) *China in the World Economy*, Institute for International Economics, Washington D.C.

Lardy, N.R. (1995) The Role of Foreign Trade and Investment in China's Economic Transformation, *The China Quarterly.*

Lee-in Chen Chiu and Chin Chung (1993) 'An Assessment of Taiwan's Indirect Investment Toward Mainland China', *Asian Economics Journal*, vol. 7, no. 1, pp. 41–70.

Lemoine, F. (1994) *CEEC Exports to the EC (1988 1993) Country Differentiation and Commodity Diversification*, Centre D'Etude Prospectives Et D'Informations Internationales, December, Paris.

Lemoine, F. (1996) *Trade Policy and Trade Patterns During Transition: A Comparison Between China and the CEECs*, Centre D'Etudes Prospectives Et D'Informations Internationales, February, Paris.

Lessard, D.R. (1976) World, Country and Industry Relations in Equity Returns: Implications for Risk Reduction Through International Diversification, *Financial Analysts Journal*, vol. 32, pp. 32–38.

Lessard, D.R. (1982) 'Multinational diversification and Direct Foreign Investment', in D.K. Eiteman and A. Stonehill (eds), *Multinational Business Finance*, Addison-Wesley, Reading, MA.

Leung, H.M., and Thoburn, J.T. (1991) 'Contractual Relations, Foreign Direct Investment and Technology Transfer: The Case of China', *Journal of International Development*, vol. 3, no. 3, pp. 277–291.

Leung, J. (1989) 'Return of "Big Brother" Irks China's Investors', *Asian Wall Street Journal*, 28 December.

Levy, H. and Sarnat, M. (1970) 'International Diversification of Investment portfolios', *American Economic Review*, vol. 60, pp. 668–675.

Liberthal, K. and Oksenberg, M. (1987) *Policy Making in China: Leaders, Structures and Processes*, Princeton, NJ. Princeton University Press.

Liberthal, K. (1992) *Bureaucracy, Politics and Decision Making in Post-Mao China*, University of California Press, Berkeley. US.

Li Kui-Wei. (1997) *Financing China Trade and Investment*, Praeger Publishers, Westport, US.

Lim, D. (1983) 'Fiscal Incentives and Direct Foreign Investment in Less Developed Countries,' *The Journal of Development Studies*, vol. 19, pp. 207–12.

Lim, L. and Fong, P.E. (1991) *Foreign direct investment and industralisation in Malaysia, Singapore, Taiwan and Thailand*, OECD Development Centre, Paris.

Lin, Y.J. (1994) 'China's Economic Reforms: Pointers for Other Economies in Transition?', Policy Research Working Paper no. 1310, China Centre for Economic Research, Peking University, June.

Lin, Y.J. (1995) 'Dynamics of Change and Productivity Effects of Agricultural Liberalisation on China's Agriculture', Staff paper, China Centre for Economic Research, Peking University.

Li Rongxia. (1993) 'Landmark of China's Economic Growth', *Beijing Review*, vol 36, no. 1, pp. 15–19.

Liu Guoguang. (1992) 'Several Problems Concerning Development Strategy of China's SEZs', *Chinese Economic Studies*, vol. 25, no. 3, pp. 12–32.

Liu, W.H. (1986) 'Construction of A Post-Mao Macroeconomic Model and Foreign Trade', *Issues and Studies*, vol. 22, no. 1–2.

Liu, X.D. and Woodward, I. (1994) *Guide to Chinese Foreign Economic and Trade Policies*, Beijing, Economic Management.

Lockett, M. (1985) 'Cultural Revolution and Industrial Organisation in a Chinese Enterprises, the Beijing General Knitwear Mill 1966–81', *Management Research Paper 85/7*, Templeton College, Oxford.

Long, M. and Rutkowska, I. (1995) 'The Role of Commercial Banks in Enterprise Restructuring in Central and Eastern Europe', *Policy Research Working Paper no. 1423*, The World Bank, Washington D.C.

Long, S. (1992) China to 2000: Reform's Last Chance?, *The Economist Intelligence Unit*, London.

Lu Yuan and Heard, R. (1995) 'Socialised Economic Action: A Comparison of Strategic Investment Decisions in China and Britain', *Organisation Studies*, no. 16.

Lucas, R.E.B. (1993) 'On the Determinants of Direct Foreign Investment: Evidence from East and Southeast Asia', *World Development*, March, vol. 21, no. 3, pp. 391–406.

Lyles, M.A. (1987) 'Common Mistakes of JV Experienced Firms', *Colombia Journal of World Business*, vol. 22, no. 2, pp. 79–85.

Lyles, M.A. and Baird, I.S. (1994) 'Performance of International Joint Ventures in Two Eastern European Countries: The Case of Poland and Hungary', *Management International Review*, vol. 34, no. 4, pp. 313–29.

Lyles, M. A. and Byers, K.M. (1994) 'An Examination of a Health Care International Joint Venture in Poland', *International Studies of Management*, vol. 24, no. 4, pp. 31–47.

MacDougall, G.D.A. (1960) 'The Benefits and Costs of Private Investment from Abroad: A Theoretical Approach'', *Economic Record*, vol. 36, March, pp. 13–35.

Makowski, P. (1997) 'Maluch mialby Szanse,' *Politika*, No. 29, 17 July. Warsaw.

Mann, J. (1989) *Beijing Jeep*, Simon and Shuster, New York.

Markoczy, L. (1993) 'Managerial and Organisational Learning in Hungarian-Western Mixed Management Organisation', *International Journal of Human Resource Management*, no. 4, pp. 277–304.

Markowski, S. and Jackson, S. (1994) 'The Attractiveness of Poland to Direct Foreign Investors', *Communist Economies and Economic Transformation*, vol. 6, no. 4, pp. 513–533.

Markusen, J.R. (1995) 'The Boundaries of Multinational Enterprises and the Theory of International Trade', *Journal of Economic Perspective*, vol. 9, no. 2, pp. 169–89.

Martin, C. and Velazquez, F.J. (1996) *The Determining Factors of Foreign Direct Investment in Spain and the Rest of the OECD: Lessons for the CEECS*, Discussion Paper no. 1637, CEPR, London.

Mason, M. (1994) 'The Paucity of Direct Foreign Investment in Japan: Causes, Consequences and Proposed Remedies', Paper presented at 21st Pacific Trade and Development Conference: 'Corporate Links and Direct Foreign Investment in Asia and the Pacific', Centre of Asian Studies, the University of Hong Kong.

Mason, R.H. (1980) 'A Comment On Professor Kojima's Japanese Type Versus American Type of Technology Transfer', *Hitotsubashi Journal of Economics*, February.

McCulloch, R. (1988) 'International Competition in Services', in M. Feldstein (ed.), *The United States in the world economy*, University of Chicago Press, Chicago.

McCulloch, R. (1993) 'New Perspective on Foreign Direct Investment', in K.A. Froot (ed.), *Foreign Direct Investment*, The University of Chicago, Chicago.

Mesnil, De G. (1995) 'Trade Policies in Transition Economics: A Comparison of European and Asian Experiences,' Delta, May.

Messerlin, P. (1993) 'The Association Agreements between the EC and Central Europe: Trade Liberalisation vs Constitutional Failure?', in J. Fleming & J.M. Rollo (eds), *Trade, Payments and Adjustment in Central and Eastern Europe*, Royal Institute of International Affairs, EBRD, London.

Messerlin, P. (1993) 'The EC and Central Europe: The Missed Rendez-Vous of 1992?', *Economics of Transition*, vol. 1, no. 1, pp. 23–43.

Michalet, C.A. (1994) 'Transnational Corporations and the Changing International Economic System', *Transnational Corporations*, vol. 3, no. 1, p.12.

Mickiewicz, T. (1994) Structural Responses to Economic Transformation, *Communist Economies and Economic Transformation*, vol. 6, no. 2, pp. 24–35.

Miller, R.F. (1992) Economic and Political Reform in Poland: Privatisation and the Emergence of Civil Society, unpublished conference paper.

Miller, R.F. (1993) *Transformation of the Former Soviet-type Economies: Implications for Foreign Trade*, Paper presented at ABARE's National Agricultural and Resources Outlook Conference, 2–3 February, Canberra.

Miller, R.F. (1995) 'The Lessons of Economic and Political Reform in Eastern Europe', unpublished conference paper.

Miller, R. F. (1997) 'Agriculture and Economic Reform in Eastern Europe: The Special Case of Poland', unpublished conference paper.

Ministry of Foreign Economic Relations of Poland (1996) *Polish Foreign Trade, PFT Monthly,* March, Warsaw.

Ministry of Foreign Economic Relation and Trade of China (MFERTC). (1983) *Guide to China's Foreign Economic Relations and Trade,* Beijing.

Minister of Foreign Trade of Poland (1995). *Poland Country Report*. Foreign Trade Research Institute, Warsaw.

Moser, M.J. (1985) 'Law and Investment in the Guangdong SEZs' in M.J. Moser (ed.), *Foreign Trade, Investment and the Law in the P.R. China*, Oxford University Press, Oxford, pp. 143–178.

National Council for US–China Trade (NCUSCT) (1987) *US Joint Ventures in China: A Progress Report* (Washington, D.C.: NCUSCT).

Naughton, B. (1995) Growing Out of the Plan: Chinese Economic Reform 1978–1993, CUP.

Newsweek (1991) 'Trade and Reforms', May.

Nolan, P. and Fureng, D. (1990) *Market Forces in China*, Zed Books Ltd, New Jersey, US.

Nee, V. (1992) 'Organisational Dynamics of Market Transition: Hybrid Forms, Property Rights, and Mixed Economy in China, *Administrative Science Quarterly*, no. 37, pp. 1–27.

Nyaw, M.K. (1991) 'The Significance and Managerial Roles of Trade Unions in Joint Ventures with China', in O. Shenkar (ed.), *Organisation and Management in China 1979–1990*, M.E. Sharpe, Armonk, New York.

Oke, S. (1986) 'China's Relations with the World Economy: Trade, Investment and Contemporary Developments', *Journal of Contemporary Asia*, vol. 16, no. 2, pp. 237–46.

Oman, C. (1984) *New Forms of Investment in Developing Countries*, OECD, Paris.

Oman, C. (1996) The Policy Challenges of Globalisation and Regionalisation, Policy Paper No. 11, OECD, Paris.

Organization for Economic Cooperation and Development (OECD) (1983) *Detailed Benchmark Definition of Direct Foreign Investment*, OECD, Paris.

—— OECD (1995) *OECD Review of Agricultural Policies: Poland*, Centre for Co-operation with the Economies in Transition, Paris.

—— OECD (1997) *OECD Economic Survey – Poland*, Paris.

Orr, A. (1990) 'Evolution of External Trade and Payments of China, Mongolia and Viet Nam', *Journal of Development Planning*, Special Issue, vol. 20.

Ozawa, T. (1995) 'Japan: the Macro-IDP, Meso-IDPs and the Technology Development Path' in J.H. Dunning and Rajneesh Narula (ed.), *Foreign Direct Investment and Government: Catalyst for Economic Restructuring*, Routledge, London.

Polish Agency for Foreign Investment (PAIZ) (1996) *Poland-The Soaring Eagle of Europe*, PAIZ, Warsaw.

—— PAIZ (1997) 'Polish Food-processing Industry', PAIZ Data Sheet Series, S.1.a, August, Warsaw.

—— PAIZ (1997) *Opportunities in Polish Construction Business*, PAIZ Construction Updated, April, Warsaw.

—— PAIZ and Ministry of Physical Planning and Construction (1997) *Polish Construction Industry: regulations and procedures overview*, pp. 3–12, Warsaw.

—— PAIZ (1997) *Automotive Sector in Poland*, Bulletin, Warsaw.

—— PAIZ Industry Updated (1997b) *Paper Industry in Poland*, PAIZ Data Sheet Series, S.2.b, Warsaw.

—— PAIZ (1997a) *Encyclopaedia of Polish Industry*, (London: Sterling).

—— PAIZ (1997) *Monitoring of the Inflow of FDI and Joint Ventures with Foreign Participation in Czech Republic, Hungary, Ireland, Spain and Thailand*, Report by PAIZ, Warsaw.

—— PAIZ (1990–97) *The List of Major Foreign Investors in Poland*, PAIZ, Warsaw.

Papageorgiou, D., Michaely, M. and Choksi, A.M. (1991) *Liberalising Foreign Trade*, vol. 1, Blackwell, Oxford.

Pearson, M. (1991) *Joint Ventures in the PRC: control of FDI under socialism*, Princeton University Press, Princeton, NY, US.

Pearson, M. (1997) *China's New Business Elite: The Political Consequences of Economic Reform* (Berkeley: University of California Press).

People's Daily (1990) 'Trade Statistics', August.

Perrow, C. (1986) 'Economic Theories of Organisation', *Theory and Society*, no. 15, pp. 11–14.

Petri, P.A. (1994) 'Trade and Investment Interdependence in the Pacific', paper prepared for 21st Pacific Trade and Development Conference, 'Corporate Links and Direct Foreign Investment in Asia and the Pacific', Centre of Asian Studies, The University of Hong Kong.

Petrochilos, G.A. (1989) *Foreign Direct Investment and the Development Process*, Avebury Gover Publishing Company Ltd, Aldershot.

Phillips, D.R. (1986) 'SEZ in China's Modernisation: Changing Policies and Changing Fortunes', *National Westminster Bank Quarterly Review*, February, pp. 37–50.

Pilarczyk, J.J. (1996) 'Food Industry-Current Situation, Trends of Development', *Polish Food*, vol. 4, pp. 7–9.

Podkaminer, L. *et al.* (1997) *Year–end 1996: Mixed results in the Transition countries*, The Vienna Institute for Comparative Economic Studies, No.223, February, Vienna.

Podkaminer, L. *et al.* (1997) *China as an Emerging Economic Power*, The Vienna Institute for Comparative Economic Studies, March, Vienna.

Polish Food (1996) 'Food Industry', Warsaw, Autumn, pp. 7–21.

Polish Food (1997) 'Polish Agro-food Products', Warsaw, Autumn, p. 12.

Pomfret, R. (1991) *Investing in China: Ten Years of the 'Open Door' Policy*. Harvester Wheatsheaf, London.

Ponte Ferreira, M. (1995) 'The Liberalisation of East-West Trade: An Assessment of its Impact on Exports from Central and Eastern Europe', *Europe-Asia Studies*, vol. 47, no. 7, pp. 1205–23.

Porter, M.E. (1985) *Competitive Advantage: Creating and Sustaining Superior Performance*, The Free Press, New York.

Porter M.E. (1990a) *The Competitive Advantage of Nations*, New York, Free Press.

Porter M.E. (1990b) 'Centralisation De-Centralisation and Development in China: The Automobile Industry', in N. Campbell and J. Henley (ed.) *Joint Ventures and Industrial Change in China*, Greenwich, Conn. and London: JAI Press.

Portugal, Luis (1995) 'Restructuring Polish Agriculture', *OECD Observer*, no. 192, February/March.

Powell, B.H. (1984) *Fourth Business Leader Symposium*, Beijing.

Pye, L. (1986) 'The China Trade, Making the Deal', *Harvard Business Review*, July-Aug, pp. 74–80.

Pyrgies, J. (1995) *Ownership Transformation in Polish Agriculture*, Centre for Social and Economic Research (CASE), Warsaw.

Qian Yingyi and Xu Chenggang (1993) Why China's Economic Reforms Differ: The M-Forum Hierarchy and Entry/Expansion of the Non-State Sector. Research Program on the Chinese Economy, Paper no. 25, July, London School of Economics.

Quaisser, W., Woodward, R. and Blaszczyk, B. (1995) Privatization in Poland and East Germany: A Comparison, Working Papers no. 180–81, vol. I and II, Osteuropa-Institut Munchen, Munchen.

Raiser, M. (1995) 'Lessons for Whom, from Whom? The Transition from Socialism in China and Central Eastern Europe Compared', *Communist Economies and Economic Transformation*, vol. 7, no. 2, pp. 12–24.

Rana, Pradumna, B. (1995) Reform Strategies in Transitional Economies: Lessons from Asia, *World Development*, vol, 23, no. 7, pp. 1157–1169.

Rana, Pradumna, B. and Dowling, J.M. (1994) 'Big-Bang's Bust – An Asian Alternative', *Global Issues in Transition*, No. 7, March.

Redding, S.G. (1990) *The Spirit of Chinese Capitalism*, De Gruyter, Berlin.

Remer, C.F. (1968) *Foreign Investment in China*, Howard Fertig, New York.

Reuber, G.L. et al. (1973) *Private Foreign Investment in Development*, Clarendon Press, Oxford.

Richet, X. (1993) 'Transition Towards the Market in Eastern Europe: Privatisation, Industrial Restructuring and Entrepreneurship', *Eastern European Economics and Economic Transformation*, vol. 5. no. 2, pp. 23–56.

Riskin, C. (1987) *China's Political Economy The Quest for Development since 1949*, Oxford University Press, Oxford.

Robinson, R.D. (1987) *Foreign Capital and Technology in China*, Praeger Publishers, New York.

Rodrik, D. (1995) Trade Strategy, Investment and Exports: Another Look at East Asia, Discussion Paper no. 1305, CEPR, London.

Rojec, M. and Svetlicic, M. (1994) 'Foreign Direct Investment and transformation of Central European Economies', *Management International Review*, vol. 34, no. 4, pp. 293–312.

Rollo, J.M. (1992) *Association Agreements between the EC and the CSFR, Hungary and Poland: a Half Empty Glass?*, The Royal Institute of International Affairs, London.

Rollo, J.M. and Smith, A. (1993) 'The Political Economy of Eastern European Trade with the EC: Why so Sensitive?', *Economic Policy*, no. 16, April.

Roney, J. (1997) 'Cultural Implications of Implementing TQM in Poland', *Journal of World Business*, vol. 32, no. 2, pp. 152–166.

Rowley, C. and Lewis, M. (1996) *Greater China-Political Economy, Inward Investment and Business Culture*, Frank Cass and Company, London.

Rugman, Alan M. (1975) 'Motives for Foreign Investment: The Market Imperfections and Risk Diversification Hypothesis', *Journal of World Trade Law*, vol. 9, September–October, pp. 567–73.

Rugman, Alan M. (1979) *International Diversification and the Multinational Enterprises*, Lexington Books, Lexington, MA.

Rugman, Alan M. (1980) 'Internalisation as A General Theory of Foreign Direct Investment, A Reappraisal of the Literature', *Weltwirtschaftliches Archiv*, vol. 116, no. 2, pp. 365–79.

Rugman, Alan M. (1982) *New Theories of the Multinational Enterprise*, Croom Helm, London.

Rugman, Alan M. and Verbeke, A. (1990) *Global Corporate Strategy and Trade Policy*, Routledge, New York.

Rutkowski, M. (1995) Workers in Transition, World Development Report Working Paper, The World Bank, Washington D.C..

Sachs, J. (1995) *Reforms in Eastern Europe and the Former Soviet Union in Light of the East Asian Experiences*, CASE Research Foundation, Warsaw.

Sachs, J. (1996) 'Notes of the Life of State-led Industrialisation', *Japan and the World Economy*, vol. 8, pp. 153–174.

Sachs, J. and Wing Thye Woo (1996) *'China's Transition Experience, Reexamined Policy Research Department'*, *The World Bank*, vol. 7, no. 3–4, pp. 1–5.

Sachs, J. and Warner, A.M. (1996) 'Achieving Rapid Growth in the Transition Economies of Central Europe', *Studies and Analysis*, no. 73, CASE Foundation, Warsaw.

Saich, T. (1991) 'Much Do About Nothing: Party Reform in the 1980s', in G.W. White (ed), *The Chinese State in the Era of Economic Reform,* Macmillan , London, pp. 149–174.

Sander, B. (1995) *Siemens-A Multinational's Strategy to Invest in the Central-East European Transformation Countries*, Kiel Working Paper no. 709, The Kiel Institute of World Economics, Kiel, Germany.

Schaan, J.L. (1988) 'How to Control a Joint Venture Even as a Minority Partner', *Journal of General Management*, vol, 14, pp. 4–16.

Schmidt, K.D. (1994) *Foreign Direct Investment in Central and Eastern European Countries: State of Affairs, Prospects and Policy Implications*, Kiel Working Paper No. 633, The Kiel Institute of World Economics, Germany, Kiel.

Scott, J. (1985) *Corporations, Classes and Capitalism*, Hutchinson, 2nd eds, London.

Segal, G. (1990) *Chinese Politics and Foreign Policy Reform*, Kegan Paul International, London.

Seligman, S.D. (1990) *Dealing with the Chinese: A Practical Guide to Business Etiquette*, Mercury Books, London.

Shaffer, B.B. (1981) *'To recapture Public Policy for Politics'*, Institute of Development Studies, University of Sussex, Falmer, October.

Shama, A. (1995) 'Entry Strategies of US Firms to the Newly Independent States, Baltic States, and Eastern European Countries', *California Management Review*, vol. 37, no. 3, pp. 34–45.

Shahul Hameed, P.M. (1995) China's Special Economic Zones, Unpublished Conference Paper.

Shenkar, O. (1990) *Organisation and Management in China*, M.E. Sharpe Inc, New York.

Shi Qinglin (1985) 'The Function of Foreign Exchange Balance in the Overall Balance of the SEZ, *Xiamen Tequ Diaoyan* (in Chinese), no. 4, December, pp. 20–2.

Shore, L. M., Eagle, B.W. and Jedel, M.J. (1993) 'China–United States Joint Ventures: A Typological Model of Goal Congruence and Cultural Understanding and their Importance for Effective Human Resource Management', *International Journal of Human Resource Management*, vol. 4, pp. 67–83.

Schultz, S. (1997) 'Foreign Direct Investment in Transition Countries', *Economic Bulletin*, vol. 34, no. 1, pp. 3–10.

Sikora, J. (1993) 'Investycje zagraniczne-Klopoty duze i male', *Gazeta Wyborcza*, no. 27, July, Warsaw.

Sikora, J. (1993) 'Portret Investora', *Gazeta Wyborcha*, no. 49, December, Warsaw.

Sinn, H.W. and Weichenrieder, A.J. (1997) 'Foreign direct investment, political resentment and the privatization process in Eastern Europe', *Economic Policy*, April.

Sklair, L. (1985) 'Shenzhen: a Chinese "development zone" in global perspective', *Development Change*, vol. 16, no. 6, pp. 571–602.

Smolarek, R. (1996) 'Polish Agri-food Products,' *Polish Food*, vol. 4, pp. 9–11.

Solinger, D.J. (1989) 'Urban Reform and Relational Contracting in post-Mao China. An Interpretation of the Transition from Plan to Market', *Studies in Comparative Communism*, vol. 23, no. 3, pp. 171–85.

South China Morning Post (1995) Investors Happy with China Move, 27 April.

South China Morning Post (1996) 'FDI in China', 13 February.

Staar, R.F. (1993) *Transition to Democracy in Poland* (New York: St Martin's Press).

State Council Research Office (1989) 'The Last Decade: Bridging the Economic Gap', *Beijing Review*, vol. 35, no. 5, pp. 16–23.

State Statistical Bureau (1988) 'A Decade of Reform: Facts and Figures', A series of ten articles in *Beijing Review,* vol. 31, no. 3, pp. 39–47.

State Bureau of Statistics, (1982–9, 1990). *Statistical Year book for Asia and Pacific*. China Statistical Publishing House, Beijing.

Stehn, J. (1992) 'Auslanddische Direktinvestitionen in Industrielandern, Theoretissche Erklarungsansatze und Empirische Evidenz', Kieler Studien no. 245, Tübingen.

Stewart, S. (1992) 'China's Managers', *The International Executives*, no. 34, pp. 165–79.

Stewart, S. and Yeung, D. (1992) 'The Latest Asian Newly Industrialised Economy Emerges: The South China Economic Community', *Colombia Journal of World Business*, vol. 27, no. 2, pp. 56–63.

Stewart, S. and Yeung Yun Choi. (1990) 'Chinese Decision-making: A Case Study of How the Hexian Paper Pulp Project was Accepted for Possible Inclusion in China's Seventh Five Year Plan', *Public Administration and Development*, no. 10, pp. 41–51.

Stiglitz, J. (1989) *The Economic Role of the State*, Oxford, Basil Blackwell.

Sung Yun-Wing. (1991) *The China–Hong Kong Connection: The key to China's open door policy*, Cambridge University Press, Cambridge.

Sung Yun-Wing. (1994) 'Subregional Economic Integration: Hong Kong, Taiwan, South China and Beyond', *Paper prepared for The 21st Pacific*

Trade and Development Conference: Centre of Asian Studies, The University of Hong Kong, Hong Kong, 1–3 June.

Tain-Jy Chen, Yin-Hwa Ku and Meng-Chun Liu (1994) Direct Foreign Investment in High-Wage Countries vs. Low-Wage Countries: The Case of Taiwan, Paper presented at 21st Pacific Trade and Development Conference:" Corporate Links and Direct Foreign Investment in Asia and the Pacific", Centre of Asian Studies, The University of Hong Kong, 1–3 June.

Tam, O.K. (1991) 'Prospects for Reforming China's Financial System', Economics and Management Working Paper No. 4, Department of Economics and Management, University of New South Wales.

Teagarden, M.B. and Von Glinow, M.A. (1991) 'Sino-Foreign Strategic Alliance Types and Related Operating Characteristic', in O. Shenkar (ed.), *Organisation and Management in China 1979–1990*, Sharpe M.E, Armonk, New York.

Totten, G. and Shulian, Z. (1992) *China's Economic Reform*, Westview Press, San Francisco.

Tung, R.L. (1989) 'A Longitudinal Study of US–China Business Negotiations', *China Economic Review*, vol. 1, no 1, pp. 34–42.

Tung, R.L. (1991) 'Motivation in Chinese Industrial Enterprise', in R.M. Steers and L.W. Porter (eds), *Innovations and Work Behaviour*, 5th Ed, McGraw-Hill, New York, pp. 56–87.

UNCTAD (1996) *World Investment Report: Investment Trade and International Policy Arrangements*, United Nation Publication, New York.

UNCTC (1988) *Foreign Direct Investment in People's Republic of China*, New York.

UNCTC, World Investment Report (1992–1996) *Investment, Trade and International Policy Arrangement*, New York.

UNCTC, *World Investment Directory (1992) Asia and Pacific*, vol. 1, New York.

United Nations Economic Commission for Europe (UNCE) (1994) *Economic Survey of Europe in 1993–1994*. Secretariat of the Economic Commission for Europe, United Nations Publications, Geneva.

United Nations Industrial Development Organisation (UNIDO) (1996) '*Foreign Investors Guide to Poland*', PRIMOOFFSET, Lublin, Poland.

United Nations Transnational Corporations and Management Division, *World Investment Directory (1992) Central and Eastern Europe*, vol. 2, New York.

Urban, W. (1996) 'China's FDI Policy Reconsidered', *The Vienna Institute Monthly Report* No. 1. The Vienna Institute for Transition Economics, Vienna.

Urban, W. (1996) *Structural Change in China and in the Central and East European Countries in Transition*, The Vienna Institute for Comparative Economic Studies, Vienna.

US–China Business Council (USCBC) (1990) *US Investment in China* (Washington, D.C.: China Business Forum).

US Department of Agriculture (1997) *Spotlight on Foreign Direct Investment-Newly Independent States & Baltic Update*, Economic Research Service, 20 October.

US Department of Commerce (1976) *Direct Foreign Investment in the US,* Washington D.C., vol. 1, p. 5.

Vernon, R. (1966) 'International Investment and International Trade in the Product Cycle', *Quarterly Journal of Economics,* no. 80, pp. 190–207.

Vernon, R. (1971) *Sovereignty at Bay: The Multinational Spread of US. Enterprises,* Basic Books, New York.

Vernon, R. (1977) Storm over the Multinationals: *The Real Issues,* London.

Vernon, R. (1979) 'The Product Cycle Hypothesis in a New International Environment', *Oxford Bulletin of Economics and Statistics,* vol. 41, no. 5, pp. 255–67.

Vienna Institute Report, The (1997) 'China as an Emerging Regional Economic Power', Vienna, March, pp. 37–48.

Vienna Institute Report, The (1997) 'China: Growth of GDP Distorted by Inventory Gult', Vienna, May-September.

Vogel, E.F. (1989) *One Step Ahead in China: Guangdong Under Reform,* Cambridge. US.

Vukmanic, F. (1985) Multinationals as Mutual Invaders, Oxford University Press, Oxford.

Walder, A. (1987) 'Wage Reform and the Web of Factory Interests', *China Quarterly,* no. 109, pp. 22–41.

Walder, A.G. (1986) *Communist Neo-traditionalism: Work and authority in Chinese industry,* University of California Press, Berkeley, US.

Walder, A.G. (1989) 'Factory and Manager in an Era of Reform', *The China Quarterly* , no 118, pp. 242–64.

Wallis, J.J. and North, D.C. (1986) 'Measuring the Transaction Section in the American Economy 1870–1970', in S.L. Eugerman and R.E. Gallman (ed.) *Long Term Factors in American Economic Growth,* Chicago, Univeristy of Chicago Press.

Walters, H.J. (1997) *China's Economic Development Strategies for the 21st Century,* Quorum Books, Westport, US.

Wang, N.T. (1984) *China's Modernisation and Transnational Corporations,* Lexington Books, MA, US.

Wang, Z.Q. and Swain, N. (1995) *The Determinants of Foreign Direct Investment in Transforming Economies: Empirical Evidence for Hungary and China,* Weltwirtschaftliches Archiv, Kiel Institute of World Economics, University of Kiel, Germany.

Wang Jingzhong (1986) *Speeches on the Director Responsibility System,* Enterprise Management Publishing House, Beijing.

Wang Ya-ke (1994) 'A Study of Mainland China's Foreign Exchange Policies and Systems', Paper presented at the First Cross-Straits Forum on Finance and Banking, Chung-Hua Institution for Economic Research, 18–19 May.

Warner, M. (1992) *How Chinese Managers Learn: Management and Industrial Training in China,* Macmillan, London.

Warner, M. (1993) 'Human Resource Management with Chinese Characteristic', *International Journal of Human Resource Management,* no. 4, pp. 45–65.

Warner, M. (1994) 'Japanese Culture, Western Management: The Impact of Taylorism on Human Resource in Japan', *Organisation Studies,* no. 15.

Wells, L.T. (1979) 'Developing Country Investors in Indonesia', *Bulletin of Indonesian Economic Studies,* vol. 15, no. 1, pp. 69–84.

Wells, L.T. (1983) *Third World Multinationals*, MIT Press, Cambridge, MA, US.

Wells, L.T. (1986) 'Investment Incentives: an Un-necessary Debate', *CTC Reporter*, Autumn, pp. 58–60.

Wells, L.T. (1993) 'Mobile Exporters: New Foreign Investors in East Asia' in K.A. Froot (ed.), Foreign Direct Investment, The University of Chicago Press, Chicago.

Wheeler, D. and Mody A. (1992) 'International Investment Location Decisions: The Case of US Firms', *Journal of International Economics*, vol. 33, pp. 57–76.

White, G.W. (1987) 'The Politics of Economic Reform in Chinese Industry: the introduction of labour contract system', *China Quarterly*, September, pp. 365–89.

White, G.W. (1987) 'The Changing Role of the Chinese State in the Labour Allocation: Towards the Market?', *Journal of Communist Studies*, vol. 3, no. 2, pp. 129–53.

White, G.W., Howell, J., Zhe Xiaoye, Wang Ying and Sun Baoyang (1991) 'Rise of civil society in China', *UNRISD Research Report*, pp. 1–168.

Whitley, R.D. (1994) 'Varieties of Effective Forms of Economic Organisation: Firms and Markets in Comparative Perspective, *Organisation Studies*, no. 15.

Williamson, O.E. (1975) *Markets and Hierarchies*, Free Press, New York.

Williamson, O.E. (1985) *The Economic Institution of Capitalism*, Free Press, New York.

Williamson, O.E. (1986) *Economic Organisation*, Wheatsheaf, Brighton.

Williamson, P. and Qionghua Hu (1994) *Managing the Global Frontier-Strategies for Developing Markets*, Pitman Publishing, London.

Wing Thye Woo (1995) 'Chinese Economic Growth: Sources and Prospects', Conference Paper presented at Australian National University, Canberra.

Winters, L.A. (1994) Who Should Run Trade Policy in Eastern Europe and How?, Discussion Paper no. 1043, CEPR, London.

Woetzel, J.R. (1989) *China's Economic Opening to the Outside World-The politics of Empowerment*, Praeger Publisher, New York.

Wolf, T. (1991) 'The Lessons of Limited Market-Oriented Reform' *Journal of Economic Perspectives*, vol. 5, (Fall 1991), pp. 45–58.

Wong, C.P., Heady, C. and Woo, Wing T. (1995) *Fiscal Management and Economic Reform in the People's Republic of China*, Oxford University Press, Oxford.

Woo, W.T. (1994) 'The Art of Reforming Centrally Planned Economies: Comparing China, Poland, and Russia', *Journal of Comparative Economics*, vol. 18, pp. 276–308.

Wood, E.M. (1991) 'The Use and Abuses of Civil Society', in R. Miliband, L. Panitch and Saville (eds), *Socialist Register 1990: The retreat of the intellectuals*, Merlin Press, London, pp. 60–84.

Woodward, I. and Liu, W.H. (1994) *Guide to Chinese Foreign Economic and Trade Policies*, Economic Management, Beijing.

World Bank, Country Economic Report (1985) China long-term Development Issues and Options, The Johns Hopkins University Press, Baltimore, US.

World Bank, The. (1988) *China: External Trade and Capital*, The World Bank, Washington D.C..

——, The (1990) *Report on China*, The World Bank, Washington D.C..

——, The (1994) *Poland – Policies for Growth with Equity*, The World Bank, Washington D.C..

——, The (1996) *World Development Report – From Plan to Market*, Oxford University Press, New York.

World Economic Herald (1987) 'China's reforms', July.

World Economy Research Institute (1996) *Poland-International Economic Report 1995/96*, Warsaw School of Economics, Warsaw.

Wu F.W. (1982) 'The political risk of FDI in post-Mao China: a preliminary assessment', *Management International Review*, vol. 22, pp. 13–23.

Wu Shuqing (1990) 'Can China Practise Market Economy?', *China Daily*, 25 January, p. 4.

Xiamen Municipal People's Government Industrial Research Office and Xiamen SEZ Research Institute (ed.) (1987) Xiamen SEZ, Research into Foreign Investment, Minjiang Publishing House, Xiamen (in Chinese).

Yang, M.M.H. (1989) 'Between State and Society: The Construction of Corporateness in a Chinese Socialist Factory', *The Australian Journal of Chinese Affair*, no. 22, pp. 31–60.

Yang Xiaobing (1988) 'Enterprise Law: A Milestone for Reform', *Beijing Review*, vol. 31, no. 18, pp. 20–2.

Yang Xiaogong. (1992) 'Foreign-Funded Enterprises in China', *Beijing Review*, vol. 35, no. 5–6, pp. 20–2.

Yao, Yilin (1989) Report on the Draft 1989 Plan for National Economic and Social Development delivered to the 2nd Session of the 7th National People's Congress, 21 March 1989, *Beijing Review*, vol. 32, pp. 1–7 May, centrefold.

Yoffie, D.B. (1993) 'Foreign Direct Investment in Semiconductors', in K.A. Froot (ed), *Foreign Direct Investment*, The University of Chicago Press, Chicago.

Yongwoong, J. and Simon, D.S. (1994) Technological Changes and its Impact on the Foreign Investment Behaviour of Firms in Asia and the Pacific: the Evolving Role and Strategic Posture of Japanese Corporations, Paper presented at 21st Pacific Trade and Development Conference: 'Corporate Links and Direct Foreign Investment in Asia and the Pacific', Centre of Asian Studies, The University of Hong Kong, Hong Kong, 1–3 June.

Zamet, J.M. and Bovarnick, M.E. (1986) 'Employee relations for multinational companies in China', *Colombia Journal of World Business*, vol. 21, no. 1, pp. 13–9.

Zheng Tuobin (1987) 'The Problem of Reforming China's Foreign Trade System', *Chinese Economic Studies*, vol. 21, no. 1, pp. 27–49.

Zhu Nai Xiao (1994) 'Research on the New Economic Integration in Pacific Rim', Paper presented at 21st Pacific Trade and Development Conference: 'Corporate Links and Direct Foreign Investment in Asia and the Pacific', Centre of Asian Studies, The University of Hong Kong, Hong Kong, 1–3 June.

Zou Erkang (1986) 'Special Economic Zones Typifies Open Policy', *Chinese Economic Studies*, vol. 19, no. 2, pp. 56–76.

Zou Siyi. (1983) 'The Problem of Export Strategy', *Chinese Economic Studies*, vol. 16, no. 3, pp. 23–34.

Zweig, D. (1994) 'Internationalising China's Countryside: Political Economy of Exports from Rural Industry', *China Quarterly*, no. 128, December, pp. 716–41.

Index

Note: **bold** indicates tabular/illustrative material.